Lusosex

Lusosex

Gender and Sexuality in the
Portuguese-Speaking World

Susan Canty Quinlan and Fernando Arenas, Editors

University of Minnesota Press

Minneapolis

London

An earlier version of chapter 8 appeared as "Gender and Postcolonial Difference in the Fiction of Orlanda Amarílis," *ellipsis: Journal of the American Portuguese Studies Association* 1 (1999). Reprinted by permission of *ellipsis*.

Published by the University of Minnesota Press
111 Third Avenue South, Suite 290
Minneapolis, MN 55401-2520
http://www.upress.umn.edu

Library of Congress Cataloging-in-Publication Data

Lusosex : gender and sexuality in the Portuguese-speaking world / Susan Canty Quinlan and Fernando Arenas, editors.
     p.   cm.
   Includes bibliographical references and index.
   ISBN 0-8166-3920-5 (hc : alk. paper) — ISBN 0-8166-3921-3 (pbk. :
alk. paper)
    1. Brazilian literature—History and criticism. 2. Portuguese
literature—History and criticism. 3. African literature (Portuguese)—
History and criticism. 4. Sex in literature. 5. Sex in popular culture—
Portuguese-speaking countries. 6. Sex custom—Portuguese-speaking
countries. I. Quinlan, Susan Canty, 1948–   II. Arenas, Fernando, 1963–
PQ9522.S48 L86 2002
869.09'3538—dc21   2002005414

Printed in the United States of America on acid-free paper

The University of Minnesota is an equal-opportunity educator and employer.

12 11 10 09 08 07 06 05 04 03 02   10 9 8 7 6 5 4 3 2 1

Ao Francisco Caetano Lopes Jr.
Com Saudades, Sempre

To Flora Mary Quinlan Laird
The Sweetest Memory

Contents

Acknowledgments

The labor involved in putting together this book is the result not only of the passion that we share for the Portuguese language and the rich and fascinating cultures that speak it, but also of an intellectual and political commitment to the issues contemplated throughout this anthology. We hope that our work will decisively contribute to a more open and intellectually fruitful discussion on matters related to sexuality throughout the Portuguese-speaking world and across the globe.

There are a number of key individuals to whom we wish to express our deepest gratitude for their intellectual, emotional, and moral support throughout the various phases of this project: Greg Mullins, Bill Fitt and Nate Jess, Kate Quinlan, Oliver Laird, Henry Feargal Quinlan Laird, Alberto "Tico" Arenas, Martine Fernandes, Beatriz Muñoz, Juan Pablo Arenas, Izetta Irwin, Lauro Belchior Mendes, Maria João Pombo Lopes, Neil Fischer, Ed Burke, James N. Green, Louise Mirrer, Carol Klee, Constance Sullivan, Joanna O'Connell, Amy Kaminsky, Ofelia Ferrán, and Alberto Egea.

John Gledson's vast experience, intellectual caliber, and personal grace were vital to our project. His editing and translation skills were most welcome. And, of course, we warmly thank all of our collaborators for their creativity, enthusiasm, and patience with this project. We are very grateful to Rebecca Ulland for her excellent indexing skills.

The support by colleagues and students in our respective universities is gratefully acknowledged, especially the Office of the Vice President for Research and the Department of Romance Languages at the University of Georgia and the Department of Spanish and Portuguese Studies at the University of Minnesota.

Finally, we would like to thank Richard Morrison, who brought his support and expertise to this project from the very start, and Josiah Blackmore, together with our anonymous readers, who provided valuable insights, comments, corrections, and suggestions, including lively debates about the title. Afinal, queriamos só chamar a atenção.

Athens, Key Largo, and Minneapolis

Introduction

Fernando Arenas and Susan Canty Quinlan

Frameworks and Boundaries

Since the 1980s in the English-speaking world, particularly in the United States, there has been an explosion of studies in the humanities, most notably in the fields of literary and cultural studies, that place sexuality at the center of their analyses of human subjectivity in ancient and modern societies, as well as within national cultures. This explosion has led to the formation of the academic discipline known as gay and lesbian studies. The rapid expansion and consolidation of this discipline, as well as its political and conceptual evolution, have led to the rise of queer theory, signaling an institutional transformation of gay and lesbian studies. The analyses of sexuality under the purview of gay and lesbian studies and queer theory have shown much originality, intellectual acumen, and political urgency, to the point of transforming the humanities, and, to a certain degree, the social sciences. Geopolitically speaking, however, only recently have studies of sexuality devoted their attention to cultures considered peripheral in relationship to the world economic, political, or cultural centers of the late twentieth and early twenty-first centuries. With *Lusosex* we wish to fill a gap with regard to the place occupied by sexuality—as a field of cultural inquiry—in Portuguese-speaking societies.

Lusosex focuses on representations of sexuality throughout the Lusophone (Portuguese-speaking) world in the fields of literature, history, popular culture, and modern dance. The term *Lusophone* includes those nation-states and communities, spanning several continents, where Portuguese is currently spoken, and where Portuguese-speaking cultures have played a major role.[1] The essays included in this collection investigate the myriad ways in which sexuality intersects with nationhood and gender identities within Portuguese-speaking cultures in the Americas (Brazil), Europe (Portugal), and Africa (Angola and Cape Verde).[2] The pan-Lusophone character of this volume brings a particularly unique, rich, and diverse spectrum of insights given the cultural specificities as well as heterogeneity of each of the nations it encompasses. Simultaneously, it addresses the historical and cultural similarities that these nations reveal among each other as a result of the experience of colonialism. At the same time, there are important productive differences between them owing to contrasting historical, political, and socioeconomic circumstances, as well as varying geopolitical locations in today's globalized world. With regard to sexuality, Portugal, Brazil, and Lusophone Africa (specifically Cape Verde and Angola) do share, in differing degrees, a Western Judeo-Christian cultural matrix that has historically informed attitudes and beliefs about practices of sex and sexuality. In spite of the hegemony historically exerted by this European matrix, there are also key influences stemming from Amerindian, Bantu, and Sudanese cultures in the case of Brazil, West African cultures in Cape Verde, and a wide spectrum of Central and Southern African ethnicities in the case of Angola.[3]

Until now, minimal attention has been devoted to the study of sexuality in the realm of Lusophone cultures, with the exception of Brazil.[4] Sexuality as a central category for literary and cultural inquiry has been amply addressed in the study of English-speaking societies, and to a certain degree in French and Francophone studies. More recently, this has been the case in the field of Hispanic studies (devoted to Spain and Spanish-speaking America).[5] With regard to Brazil, discussions of sexuality have taken place primarily in anthropological, historical, or cultural studies by authors such as Marilena Chaui, Jurandir Freire Costa, Roberto Da Matta, Gilberto Freyre, Peter Fry, James Green, David Higgs, Heloísa Buarque de Hollanda, Don Kulick, Ruth Landes, Lia Zanotta Machado, Luiz Mott, Richard Parker, Margareth Rago, Nancy Scheper-Hughes, and João Silvério Trevisan, among others.[6]

The essays contained in this volume deal with various sexualities: hetero-, bi-, and homosexuality (although the emphasis clearly lies on the latter). Some essays are informed by the insights of queer theory; others are shaped by the authors' own personal, academic, political stances and experiences, displaying clear points of identification with queer theory, whether or not the issues discussed are explicitly theorized. Some of the essays deal with authors or literary and cultural materials that reveal a "gay" or "queer" sensibility; others do not.[7] Where most essays do converge is in their questioning of the "naturalization" of sexuality and gender, a gesture that lies at the heart of queer theory, according to Annamarie Jagose.[8] At the same time, all essays in this collection posit sexuality, in its various expressions, as a traditionally marginalized cultural site that nevertheless challenges and redefines the boundaries of nationhood at various historical moments. Some essays work from within or through the theoretical frameworks of Lacanian psychoanalysis, New Historicism, deconstruction, feminism, and/or postcolonial theory, but others keep a certain distance from the methods and conceptual repertoire of contemporary canonical academic theory. In some essays, the disciplinary protocols of literary and cultural criticism are imbued with a self-conscious lyrical/poetic vein, thus pointing to an even wider and richer spectrum of critical practices available today in academia. Despite their plurality of approaches, all essays contained in *Lusosex* are engaged to one degree or another in opening new spaces of articulation, challenging or subverting traditionally dominant cultural paradigms, and expanding the meaning of citizenship or the definition of the nation-family.

The insights of queer theory seldom have been incorporated into academic research in the various Lusophone fields, and when they have, it has taken place mainly in the North American academic milieu. This volume is no different in that most essays were produced by scholars residing in the United States, a number of them informed by queer theory. In spite of a wide call for contributors, we received only a few essays produced in Brazil, one essay in Portugal, and none in Lusophone Africa. This can be explained by the continued conservatism associated with the subject matter and the reluctance of most academic institutions—reflecting societal prejudices—to open spaces for new and controversial fields of inquiry in Brazil, Portugal, or Lusophone Africa. However, in the Brazilian academic world, there are signs of increased openness toward work conducted in the field of gay and lesbian studies and queer theory.

Queer theory has proven to be extremely useful and productive as it privileges sexuality as a key construct for the study of culture, much as feminism has successfully done with gender. But only recently has academic feminism even started to make inroads in Portuguese universities, with nascent programs at Coimbra and the Universidade Nova de Lisboa, for example. In Brazil, on the other hand, it can be argued that social activism around gender and sexuality issues is much more prevalent than academic theorization. However, women's studies centers and programs are found at most federal and private universities. There are also two scholarly presses dedicated solely to gender issues (Editora Mulher, in Florianópolis, and Editora Rosa dos Tempos, in Rio de Janeiro). In 1998, a publishing house specializing in gay and lesbian topics (Edições GLS) opened in São Paulo, and the prestigious Brazilian publishing house Editora Record has started a special gay and lesbian collection, *Contraluz.* There is also a gay, lesbian, bisexual, transgender (GLBT) bookstore in São Paulo: Futuro Infinito. The first academic conference on literature and homoeroticism took place in 1999 at the Universidade Federal Fluminense in Niterói (near Rio de Janeiro) with most papers focusing on Brazilian and Portuguese literature. In Lisbon, a transgendered-owned bookstore—Esquina Cor de Rosa—opened in 1999, catering to a gay, lesbian, bisexual, and especially transgendered clientele.

In Portuguese-speaking Africa (mainly in Angola, Mozambique, and Cape Verde), more women are writing fiction and poetry than ever before. There is also a significant presence of academic women as students, professors, and researchers in both Mozambique and Angola (as well as African women academics working in Portugal). At the same time, little evidence has been seen in these countries thus far of feminist academic structures per se. However, in Mozambique and Angola, women's organizations were created during the independence movements in the 1970s and were closely linked to the parties in power in postindependence years (FRELIMO [Front for the Liberation of Mozambique] and the MPLA [Popular Movement for the Liberation of Angola]).[9] Also, a great debate took place as to the degree of emancipation experienced by women in Marxist-dominated one-party systems. With the shift to market economies and multiparty systems in the 1990s, women's continued socioeconomic progress has yet to be fully concretized.[10] With regard to sexuality in the two African countries featured in this volume—Angola and Cape Verde—discussions of (hetero)sexuality or erotic desire in general are a recent phenomenon.[11] There is little evidence in Portuguese-speaking Africa of any communities or movements that openly assume the identity categories of "gay," "lesbian," or "bisexual," and the topic of alternative sexualities remains strictly taboo.[12] Given the urgency of addressing certain basic needs such as peacekeeping and infrastructural rebuilding—in Angola, after more than two decades of civil war, peace continues to be elusive, and in Cape Verde a severe shortage of natural resources poses particularly daunting developmental problems—(hetero)sexuality, as a public object of discussion or political debate is a rare occurrence. In both countries, nonmaterial politics have played a secondary and limited role in public debates to this date.

Cultural Trends

Some of the greatest achievements of the lesbian and gay movements in various parts of the world are to have posited the question of human rights for sexual minorities as an integral part of the struggles for social justice. By the same token, the intellectual work conducted within the contemporary field of gay and lesbian studies and queer theory, primarily in English-speaking societies, has brought into the open the issue of sexuality as a key component for the study and understanding of human culture, much the same way feminism has done with the issue of gender. Nevertheless, just as contemporary feminisms have recognized the nonessential and nonuniversal character of the construct "women," we too recognize the perils of applying sexual identity categories that have been developed mainly, though not exclusively, in highly industrialized English-speaking societies, which may or may not be suitable for the diverse cultures being addressed in *Lusosex*.

Most essays in this collection argue that sexuality and sexual identity are key to the understanding of nationhood and national identity.[13] Some essays thematize implicitly or explicitly the tendency toward the globalization of certain identity categories, such as "gay." This particular dynamic points, on the one hand, to the limits of monolithic conceptions of the nation and national identity that tend to exclude or absorb differences—in this case, differences based on sexual orientation—but, on the other hand, it also highlights the fact that some identity categories have become transnational, especially among the middle and upper-middle classes in various parts of the world.[14] Furthermore, we acknowledge the paradox of adopting identity categories from the hegemonic language of globalization (i.e., English) as an instrument of liberation for sexual minorities. This is illustrated not only by the increased use of the term *gay*, but also of the terms *transgender, drag queen,* or even *gay pride,* a phenomenon that is not limited to Brazil or Portugal. Moreover, this development illustrates a class dynamic in a deeply stratified country such as Brazil where sexual identity categories, as illustrated by Richard Parker (1991: 86–87), are migrating from the bourgeoisie of the larger urban areas to the rest of the population. This dynamic is largely owing to the hegemony exerted by the middle and upper classes in the media, and the generalized exposure to the media and popular culture of the United States and its increased thematization and coverage of gay and lesbian issues. This dynamic is applicable to Portugal, as well as to other countries throughout Europe, Latin America, and beyond. We see the contemporary transnationalization of certain identity categories related to sexuality and gender that predominate in highly industrialized English-speaking cultures (though not exclusively) as an inevitable epiphenomenon of globalization that has had healthy emancipatory effects across the globe.

Historical Contexts and Political Movements

In Brazil and Portugal, there have been remarkable improvements in the cultural environment for lesbians, gays, and bisexuals. Both countries have benefited from greater political democratization than ever before. After one of the longest dictatorships on the European continent (1933–74), and after a bloodless left-wing revolution in 1974 that also led to the collapse of one of the oldest colonial empires, Portugal has been rapidly transforming into a modern nation. Postrevolutionary and postcolonial Portugal has also seen a process of cultural liberalization that has had positive effects on the lives of women, and, more recently, of sexual minorities. Today there are several visible and well-structured gay, lesbian, and bisexual organizations, among them ILGA (International Lesbian and Gay Association/Portugal) and ABRAÇO (which focuses on AIDS education and prevention). However, Portugal does not have a long history of community activism based on identity politics (Gameiro 1997), and, in fact, gay or queer activism in the 1990s started as an offshoot of AIDS activism. The substantial improvement in the standard of living, largely a result of Portugal's entry into the European Union in 1986, has resulted in a significant expansion of the urban middle class. This, in turn, allowed for a certain economic independence for gays, lesbians, and bisexuals vis-à-vis their families, which by extension leads to the possibility of overtly assuming their sexual orientation. Prior to the late 1980s, there already was, particularly in Lisbon, a growing commercial gay culture in the form of bars, clubs, restaurants, and bathhouses, typical of many urban areas in the Western world. However, there remained a gap between the availability of commercial venues catering to lesbians, gays, and bisexuals and the absence of sociopolitical structures advocating the rights for sexual minorities. This scenario has been rapidly changing since the 1990s with the organization of "gay pride" festivals and parades, AIDS marches, lesbian and gay film festivals, and so on. These events have brought widespread media attention to the political agenda of sexual minorities, as well as to their cultural presence within Portuguese society. There are also specifically gay magazines as well as Web sites catering to GLBT interests. Successful lobbying efforts have taken place in favor of the inclusion of "sexual orientation" in the nondiscrimination clause in the Portuguese constitution, as well as for the legalization of "domestic partnerships."[15]

Like Portugal, Brazil too experienced a long dictatorship, between 1964 and 1984. The authoritarian agenda of rapid modernization and economic expansion produced a hypernationalistic discourse alongside repressive measures against the political and cultural opposition. After 1978 came the *abertura,* a period that lasted until 1985 during which censorship and other repressive mechanisms were progressively lifted. This transitional period from dictatorship to democracy saw massive citizen mobilization, as well as the formation of grassroots organizations (of women, Indians, landless peasants, and others). Lesbian and gay organizations in Brazil came to life during this period. The first was the group Somos, in 1979. Soon after, other groups were formed: Grupo Gay da Bahia (which now houses the largest archive of newspapers, magazines, and other printed material on the history of homosexuality in Latin America) and the Grupo Lésbico-Feminista, which later became Grupo Ação Lésbica Feminista, signaling the important intersection between women's issues and lesbian issues. Today, there are more than seventy GLBT and AIDS service organizations throughout the country.[16] Several gay magazines and Web sites cater to GLBT interests. In addition, sexual minorities in Brazil have gained a great deal of media exposure through hugely popular *telenovelas,* gay pride celebrations and parades, and carnival shows, as well as AIDS marches, and important film festivals (named MIX Brasil) in both Rio de Janeiro and São Paulo.[17] The visibility of openly gay cultural and intellectual figures, and the inclusion of gay and lesbian rights in the platform of the Partido dos Trabalhadores (Worker's Party, one of the largest political parties in Brazil), are examples of other important developments.[18] There have also been concerted legislative efforts to legalize a limited version of "gay marriage." Despite the substantial progress made by sexual minorities in Brazil, however, there is still a great degree of poverty, corruption, violence, and impunity in the society at large. The most marginalized sectors among gays and lesbians (transvestites, sex workers, and working-class gays in general) are routinely harassed and sometimes killed. Throughout the 1980s and 1990s, there were numerous reports of human rights violations against lesbians and gays in Brazil (as elsewhere in Latin America, for example, in Colombia and Mexico).[19]

Meanwhile, in the United States the academic field of lesbian and gay studies or queer studies has been stimulated by the phenomenal growth of queer political movements since the massive marches in Washington in 1979, 1987, and 1993, which were themselves the result of years of grassroots activism centered on gay and lesbian rights in the 1970s, and, in the 1980s, the strong and urgent response to the AIDS crisis. Bill Clinton's presidency was an important factor in allowing a more favorable cultural and political climate toward lesbian and gay issues, in spite of his hesitation regarding gays in the military or opposition to gay marriage. It must also be pointed out that the greater visibility acquired by gays and lesbians in the United States has had a profound impact abroad, particularly as societies across the planet are more globally interconnected through the English language, under the hegemony of U.S. pop, consumer, and media culture. Moreover, the increased political power of lesbians and gays in the United States serves—in a paradoxical way—as a catalyst to empower "queer peoples" around the world and to promote a greater openness toward sexual difference transnationally and cross-culturally.

Today, the development of lesbian and gay or queer studies in academia, focusing on the Portuguese- and Spanish-speaking worlds, is taking place mostly within the relatively safe confines of North American universities. However, there are signs of change in the Brazilian academy with the ongoing symposia on homoeroticism and culture at the Universidade Federal Fluminense near Rio de Janeiro in 1999, 2000, and

2001; subsequent events are promised. It is from the vantage point of a more favorable political and cultural climate throughout North America, parts of Western Europe, and Latin America (at least Brazil) that scholars are dealing openly with sexuality issues or working on a variety of bisexual, lesbian, or gay authors. They are also rethinking the concept of nation from a queer perspective—in general—reshaping the academic fields of Luso-Brazilian or Lusophone studies, Hispanism or Latin American studies. We hope that this volume will prove to be a valuable contribution to this dynamic.

Nations, Sex, and Sexualities

What are the contours of the title *Lusosex* and what are its definitions? "Luso," or "Lusus," was the son of Bacchus, the mythical founder of the Roman province of Lusitania at the westernmost end of the Iberian Peninsula, where Portugal is located today. The term *luso* now designates "things" Portuguese or related to the Portuguese language or to Portuguese-speaking cultures (e.g., Luso-Brazilian, Lusophone). We are aware of its possible neocolonial connotations in that it is being used as an umbrella term incorporating former colonizing and colonized nations. From a pragmatic standpoint, however, we believe that no other term is as succinct as *lusophone* to designate the multiplicity of cultures that we are working with. There are unavoidable paradoxes in working simultaneously with former colonizing powers and the nations that are the result of colonial processes. Ultimately, we wish to stress the productive tension that derives from the usage of the term *luso*, as we add to it the charged signifier *sex*. We consider the juxtaposition of these two cultural constructs as an appropriating, as well as a subversive, gesture by which we are reevaluating the historical weight and ideological implications of the term *luso*, and at the same time we are evaluating the place of sexuality in Portuguese-speaking societies. Numerous essays in this volume argue that right-wing or left-wing puritanical regimes in Portugal, Brazil, and Portuguese-speaking Africa did not successfully "repress" sexual desire, but rather that discourses around sex and sexual desire multiplied under them. For instance, during the puritanical and ultranationalistic dictatorial regime of António Oliveira Salazar in Portugal (1933–74), the "sacred" Portuguese or "Luso" family was to be safeguarded by containing sexuality. As Ana Paula Ferreira points out in her essay, in spite of the attempts of the Salazar regime to interdict desire, there was in fact a proliferation of female voices in the Portuguese literature that discreetly defied the mandate to restrain their sexual desire, or to refuse male or female seduction.

Histories of Desire

The cultural and literary references to homoerotic desire and/or same-sex acts throughout Portuguese and Brazilian history have been manifold. One of the richest sources of information on the subject is the accounts of the Portuguese Inquisition, as it realized its goal to observe, record, contain, interdict, and castigate sexual activity outside of prescribed norms and customs as dictated by Catholic church dogma in the Portuguese metropole, as well as in its overseas colonial possessions. In fact, the archives of the Portuguese Inquisition are today the most extensive in Europe and are housed at the Torre do Tombo National Archives in Lisbon (Higgs 1999). These accounts have been widely researched by Brazilian anthropologist Luiz Mott.[20] The Inquisition archives are one of very few sources of information regarding same-sex practices in early modern Portugal and colonial Brazil. The European chronicles of discovery, conquest, and settlement of Brazil in the sixteenth century also provide invaluable information regarding sexual practices among Amerindians. In his essay published here for the first time in English, João Silvério Trevisan discusses sexual practices and identity among Brazilian Indian males as witnessed through travel literature and ethnographic accounts from the sixteenth century until today.[21]

In late-nineteenth-century Brazilian literature, several novels of interest address sexuality and gender questions with a degree of openness unseen in previous centuries.[22] Raul Pompéia's *O ateneu*, published in 1888, reveals a homoerotic subtext that transpires through the sociocultural structure of the boarding school of the same name. In this novel, gender ideology serves as the prism for viewing sexuality, which results in the feminization (and concomitant devalorization) of male homosexuality within patriarchal society. Adolfo Caminha's *Bom-crioulo,* published in 1895, is considered a landmark text in the history of modern literary representations of same-sex desire for its overt thematic treatment of homosexuality in the context of a cross-racial and cross-generational relationship. In this novel, the narrator wavers between a frank and almost sympathetic portrayal of the relationship between the two male lovers and a pathologization of homosexuality, as well as of "the black race."[23] The representation of lesbianism as another "instance" of human pathology is a subtheme in Aluísio Azevedo's novel *O cortiço* (1890) *(The Slum: A Novel)*—a scathing naturalist portrait of nineteenth-century monarchical Brazilian society.

In Portuguese literature, one of the earliest novels in which the plot revolves around the explicit homosexuality of the main character was published in 1891: Abel Botelho's naturalist work, *O Barão de Lavos*. This novel belongs to Botelho's cycle titled *Patologia social*. *O Barão de Lavos* sets out to describe minutely and with deep fascination—through the medical and scientific prism of the time period—the homosexual underworld of late-nineteenth-century Lisbon.[24] By the early twentieth century in Portugal, Modernist poète maudit António Botto's *Canções* (1921) represented one of the most overtly (homo)sexual bodies of work in the history of Portuguese literature, creating much controversy and scandal. However, his literary merits were greatly overshadowed by his exuberantly "out" public persona, as well as by the weight of his much better known fellow Modernists Mário de Sá-Carneiro and Fernando Pessoa. Critical readings of Sá-Carneiro and Pessoa, on the other hand, have invariably downplayed or ignored questions of sexuality that we believe to be key in order to understand their existential malaise. The ontological crisis at the heart of their artistic production is, to a large extent, connected to a sense of unrealized (homo)erotic desire. It can be argued that homosexual desire or the anguish derived from its impossibility is a key driving force within Portuguese Modernism, one of Europe's most fascinating avant-garde movements. In this volume we include the first essay ever to explore the possibility of a "gay heteronym" created by Fernando Pessoa (Richard Zenith's "Fernando Pessoa's Gay Heteronym" features a previously unpublished poem in which Pessoa deals most overtly and unambiguously with homoerotic desire). Same-sex desire has continued to play an important role in the production of numerous male poets in Portugal beyond the Modernists (Mário Cesariny, Eugénio de Andrade, Al Berto, Joaquim Manuel Magalhães, João Miguel Fernandes Jorge, Helder Moura Pereira, Luís Miguel Nava, Gastão Cruz, Paulo Teixeira, and Eduardo Pitta, among others). In fact, critic Eduardo Prado Coelho points out that homosexuality has been one of the richest and most recurrent themes in contemporary Portuguese poetry.[25]

In the early twentieth century, Brazilian Modernism[26] provides one of its most complex and paradigmatic texts: Mário de Andrade's *Macunaíma*. In this novel (or "rhapsody," as the author defines it), Brazilian national identity is posited as liminal—located in a space between races, cultures, and even sexualities. Sexuality in *Macunaíma* appears multiple, ambivalent, and fluid—all in all, "polymorphously perverse." Modernist women writers also explored sexuality issues by thematizing sexual liberation, prostitution, and same-sex desire: Laura Villars *(Vertigem),* Ercília Nogueira Cobra *(Virgindade inútil, Virgindade anti-higiênica),* Patrícia Galvão or "Pagú" *(Parque Industrial), [Industrial Park],* and the poetry of Gilka Machado.[27] Since the 1960s, ambiguous sexualities and gender identities—which are most epitomized by the annual ritual of carnival—have become a staple of Brazilian popular culture as reflected in music, pulp fiction, and television. For instance, throughout the 1980s and early 1990s, male-to-female transsexual Roberta Close was popularly considered the most beautiful woman in Brazil. MPB, or Brazilian Popular Music, has revealed itself as one of the richest sites for sexual ambiguity and fluid identities through many of its representative artists, such as Caetano Veloso, Ney Matogrosso, Gal Costa, Gilberto Gil, Maria Bethânia, Simone, Marina Lima, Zizi Possi, and Milton Nascimento. In contrast to Portugal, where the contemporary thematization of same-sex desire has taken place almost exclusively within the realm of poetry written by men, in Brazil such thematization has taken place in both poetry and prose fiction produced by women writers such as Lygia Fagundes Telles, Márcia Denser, Lya Luft, Ana Cristina César, Leila Míccolis, and Miriam Alves, among others, and by numerous male writers, including Caio Fernando Abreu, Silviano Santiago, Bernardo Carvalho, João Silvério Trevisan, Herbert Daniel, and Valdo Motta.[28]

In the context of contemporary Portuguese-speaking African cultures—more specifically, in postindependence Angolan and Cape Verdean literature—the thematization of sexuality is a recent development. During the struggles for independence in the 1960s and early 1970s, questions regarding the body or erotic desire were almost completely absent from literary production, to say nothing of official political discourse, given the puritanical Marxist dogma that dominated the respective independence movements and political parties that would eventually govern postindependence Angola, Mozambique, Cape Verde, Guinea-Bissau, and São Tomé and Príncipe.[29] Furthermore, the protracted civil wars in Angola and Mozambique, with well-known tragic consequences for both nations, were not conducive for the thematization, let alone the problematization, of nonmaterial concerns. Yet, a handful of fiction writers and poets have been exploring issues related to erotic desire and (hetero)sexuality, as they question the boundaries of national culture, political discourse, and literary production, mostly, though not exclusively, from the perspective of women: Angolan women poets Ana Paula Tavares, Ana de Santana, and Maria Alexandre Dáskalos, alongside fiction writers Pepetela, João Melo, and Rosária da Silva, in addition to poets José Craveirinha and Vera Duarte, from Mozambique and Cape Verde, respectively.

Lusosex is divided into four sections. Part I, "Early Stories of Desire," suggests a chronological framework whereby all essays featured focus primarily on texts, authors, or historical periods prior to the Stonewall riots in New York City in 1969. These riots marked the beginning of the contemporary gay and lesbian movement in the United States as well as throughout the world. The essays here deal mostly with various modalities of male same-sex desire that are expressed in cultural and historical contexts in spite of suffering the fate of near invisibility, taboo, and/or illegitimacy.

In his essay "Tivira, the Man with the Broken Butt: Same-Sex Practices among Brazilian Indians," João Silvério Trevisan points to the continued cultural gap between sexual systems prevalent among indigenous Brazilians and the sexual paradigms of Westernized "white" Brazilians, an ideological gap that takes root at the moment of the Portuguese arrival in the New World in 1500.[30]

In "Machado de Assis and Graciliano Ramos: Speculations on Sex and Sexuality," John Gledson focuses on two of the greatest Brazilian novelists who wrote prior to 1960: Machado de Assis (considered the most original Latin American writer of the nineteenth century) and Graciliano Ramos (the famed regionalist and social realist who wrote between the 1930s and 1950s). Gledson argues that both Machado and Graciliano, in differing ways, offer lucid insights into the complex interaction between power and sexuality. He suggests that—well ahead of their times and contrary to prevalent ideologies of their respective historical moments—both authors present subtle (and inevitably understated) points of view regarding the underpinnings of sexual desire and sexual identity, including a certain philosophical openness toward homosexuality.

Richard Zenith's "Fernando Pessoa's Gay Heteronym?" includes a translated version as well as a textual analysis of a previously unpublished and untitled poem by Pessoa written in 1919 in which homoerotic desire is most unabashedly expressed. This essay makes the case for (homo)sexuality as being central to the understanding of the poetic universe of the greatest Portuguese literary and cultural figure of the twentieth century, as well as one of the major modern poets of Europe. Zenith studies different configurations of sexuality apparent throughout the poetic works of Pessoa's heteronyms or "literary personalities," who embodied multiple and contradictory facets of their creator. These various expressions of sexuality shed greater light on this elusive poet who most dramatically emblematizes the notion of the modern subject's "shattered ego."

In the next essay, "Brazilian Homoerotics: Cultural Subjectivity and Representation in the Fiction of Gilberto Freyre," Jossianna Arroyo examines the fictional work of world-renowned Brazilian sociologist Gilberto Freyre. Arroyo reads Freyre's proposals on national culture and nationality as liminal texts in which homoeroticism intermingles with complex arguments about race, gender, and class. Freyre's homoeroticism is crossed by a socioanthropological discourse about culture that problematizes ethnocentric and fixed definitions of race, sexuality, and gender.

In "Fictions of the Impossible: Clarice Lispector, Lúcio Cardoso, and 'Impossibilidade,'" Severino João Albuquerque explores the dynamics of concealed identities and thwarted erotic desire in a society such as Brazil—subaltern and dependent, carnivalizing and cannibalistic. Using pertinent ideas put forth by Eve Kosofsky Sedgwick and Judith Butler, the author examines the complex relationship between Clarice Lispector and Lúcio Cardoso—two prominent twentieth-century writers—as it informed their identities and, to an extent, even their literary production.

Most essays in Part II, "On Subjects, on Sex," deal with reconfigurations of female subjectivity and erotic desire (either hetero- or homosexual) in response to authoritarian regimes of power or national mythologies from which both have been either suppressed or excluded. In "Loving in the Lands of Portugal: Sex in Women's Fiction and the Nationalist Order," Ana Paula Ferreira studies the representations of female relationships in the state-controlled "women's novels" of the 1930s and 1940s in Salazar's Portugal. In these novels it is possible to detect subversive ideological intentions that seek to undermine the hegemonic concepts of nationhood propagated by the Portuguese fascist state. Ferreira's essay examines how "women's novels," and in particular the lesbian relationships depicted within these novels, reconstruct female identity.

Regarding African fiction writers in Portuguese, Russell G. Hamilton's essay, "Not Just for Love, Pleasure, or Procreation: Eroto-Racial, Sociopolitical, and Mystic-Mythical Discourses of Sexuality in Pepetela's *A geração da utopia,*" discusses how gender and sexuality finally are being incorporated into the cultural debates around national identity in the once fledgling Marxist-Leninist state of Angola. In "Border Writing, Postcoloniality, and Critical Difference in the Works of Orlanda Amarílis," Phyllis Peres focuses on Cape Verdean short-story writer Orlanda Amarílis through the lenses of postcolonial theory, third-world feminism, Diaspora writing, and border writing, to discern the multiple layers of subjectivity encountered in Amarílis' female characters. Peres provides an in-depth background to the history of Cape Verdean letters, as well as an incisive analysis of questions pertaining to Cape Verdean emigration, alterity, female subjectivity, and sexuality.

In the final essay in Part II, "'I Was Evita,' or *Ecce Femina:* Lídia Jorge's *The Murmuring Coast,*" Ronald W. Sousa analyzes the contemporary Portuguese novel *A costa dos murmúrios.* Sousa observes how female characters are obliged to face not only their own capacity to maneuver within a heterosexual relationship (in this case, in colonial Mozambique in the 1960s), but also how they are forced to cope with hidden aspects of the self, demonstrated by their ambivalent erotic desire toward other women. Looking at prerevolutionary and colonialist Portuguese national identity, Sousa's essay examines how sexuality reformulates or reconfigures political space.

The two essays in Part III, "Brazilian Performativities," analyze the performative aspects of identity—a staple in some currents of feminist and gender theory, as well as queer theory, for some time now, particularly as a result of the influence of the early work of Judith Butler. Thus, through the attention paid to the performative aspects of being, one witnesses the "denaturalization" of gender and sexuality. The essays included here—one focusing on popular music and the other on contemporary literature—explore what happens to the ideas of nationhood (in this case, Brazilian nationhood) when confronted with the instability of gender and sexual identities.

MPB (Brazilian Popular Music) has proven to be a rich site for the exploration of gender and sexual ambiguity and fluid identities among its most representative artists such as Caetano Veloso or Chico Buarque, among many others. In "Supermen and Chiquita Bacana's Daughters: Transgendered Voices in Brazilian Popular Music," César Braga-Pinto explores notions of gender and sexual identity, as well as performance in one of the world's most dynamic popular music scenes. As identity reveals itself as performance, the repetition of the performance may also redefine the performer's identity. The result is not simply a conceal-ment of sexual identities behind ambiguous representations. Rather, the performance of a displaced sexual identity enables new interpretations or the reappropriation of hegemonic identity categories within Brazil-ian culture.

In "Cross-dressing: Silviano Santiago's Fictional Performances," Susan Canty Quinlan explores Silviano Santiago's works *Stella Manhattan* and *Keith Jarrett no Blue Note.* Quinlan discusses Santiago's subversion of gender and sexual identity binaries, as well as his critique of the cultural stereotypes that these binaries perpetuate. Furthermore, she observes how the performative aspects of gender and sexuality point to the prob-lematic associated with creating national and aesthetic identities in the prose work of the renowned cultural critic.

The final section of this book, "Queer Nations in Portuguese," partly evokes the U.S.-based activist organization Queer Nation, a group that emerged in 1990 as an offshoot of the radical AIDS group Act-Up, which staged a series of political "happenings" during the 1990s. Queer Nation forced mainstream society to confront the overt expression of alterna-tive sexualities and/or gender identities, at the same time as it posited a cross-cultural and transnational "queer identity." Among other things, the essays in Part IV appropriate and translate the notion of "queer" and wonder to what extent it may or may not speak for the cultural specificities of Brazil and Portugal.

In "Small Epiphanies in the Night of the World: The Writing of Caio Fernando Abreu," Fernando Arenas examines the writings of one of the first Brazilian intellectuals to thematize AIDS and one of the most out-spoken cultural figures affected by the disease. Arenas's essay reflects on the limits encountered by the subject and the nation in Abreu's fiction when confronted by the cultural markers of (bi- and homo)sexualities, as well as by AIDS. Not only does Caio Fernando Abreu problematize essential and static notions of individual and collective subjectivities, but he also reconfigures and renegotiates Brazil's cultural and geopolitical location in the late twentieth century.

André Torres Lepecki offers a queer reading of contemporary Portuguese dance choreography in "The Impossible Body: Queering the Nation in Modern Portuguese Dance," focusing on the work of artist Francisco Camacho. Lepecki argues that Camacho's choreography radically disrupts normative and pedagogical discourses on gender, sexuality, nation, and history, forcing the dance spectator (perhaps for the first time) into a critical, sensorial, and semantic rethinking of the culture and self-image of Portugal as a colonial power.

Mário César Lugarinho, "Al Berto, In Memoriam: The Luso Queer Principle," on the other hand, offers a genealogy of representations of same-sex desire among modern and contemporary Portuguese gay male poets, privileging the poetry of Al Berto as its most fertile expression. Through a theoretically "cannibalistic" gesture, Lugarinho attempts to culturally consume, translate, and assimilate the construct of "queer" for Portuguese-speaking cultures, bearing in mind the geopolitical complexities of such a move, but also its promise.

Lusosex represents only a beginning for new scholarship on the Portuguese-speaking world in the fields of literary and cultural studies focusing on sexuality—in all of its manifestations—as a crucial element for the understanding of culture, both nationally and transnationally. Several essays argue persuasively for the impossibility of disassociating sexuality from gender identities as they inform individual and collective subjectivities. In addition, the intrinsic heterogeneity of the cultures that are the object of study here becomes most evident when witnessing the distinct phases in which discussions on sexuality find themselves today as one moves from Brazil to Portugal or to Lusophone Africa. As *Lusosex* was coming into shape, we began to notice signs of the emergence in Brazil of gay and lesbian studies and queer theory as areas of academic inquiry focusing on Brazilian and Portuguese national realities. This is a welcome development from which we anticipate significant scholarly contributions in the near future. Still, there is more to be done in areas such as film, poetry, theater, popular music, visual and performance arts, digital culture, biography, and history, to name some of the most obvious. There also continues to be a relative scarcity of academic research focusing on lesbian or bisexual desire, or on transgendered identities in the Lusophone world, as opposed to the increasing amounts of work focusing on gay male desire. We hope that *Lusosex* will instigate new research and open up spaces for greater dialogue inside and outside of academia on some of the more controversial and exciting topics of our times as they bear upon the Portuguese-speaking world and as they become increasingly shaped by the interaction of local, national, and global forces.

Notes

1. Here we refer to Portuguese-speaking nation-states as well as communities. The term *communities* refers, on the one hand, to those places such as Goa or Macao that are not independent nations but where the Portuguese language continues to have a limited presence. On the other hand, there are also many Portuguese, Brazilian, and Cape Verdean immigrant communities around the world where Portuguese still constitutes a primary language. Our use of the term *Lusophone* is primarily cultural and linguistic (i.e., to refer to cultures that share the Portuguese language) and it is being used here in an analogous fashion to the terms *Francophone* and *Anglophone*. *Lusophone* is now widely accepted and used in Portugal and Portuguese-speaking Africa, whereas at a popular level in Brazil there is a certain ambiguity as to whether the term pertains to it as well. Among Brazilian academic and intellectual circles, however, as well as in the printed media, the term is increasingly recognized as pertaining to Brazil and to the larger Portuguese-speaking universe.

2. The essays in this volume do not address the African nation-states of Mozambique, Guinea-Bissau, and São Tomé and Príncipe, newly independent East Timor, or other Lusophone communities in Asia, such as Goa and Macao. This is primarily owing to the lack of entries focusing on these particular national/cultural realities.

3. The most obvious example of the cultural syncretism alluded to here is reflected in Afro-Brazilian religions practiced widely throughout Brazil, but most particularly in the state of Bahia. Various scholars have pointed out the greater fluidity in terms of sexuality and gender identities within Afro-Brazilian religious practices, in contrast to Catholicism. For more information, see Landes (1940, 1947), Fry (1982), and Wafer (1991).

4. Renowned Brazilian anthropologist Luiz Mott (1988a, 1988b) has done extensive archival research on homosexuality in Brazil as well as in Portugal, particularly during the Inquisition. David Higgs (1999) has also conducted important historical research on "gay" urban spaces in early Lisbon and Rio de Janeiro. See also Churchill (1967).

5. Several essay collections to date focus mostly or exclusively on the representations of sexualities in Spanish-speaking literature and cultures: Bergmann and

Smith, *¿Entiendes?* (1995); Foster and Reis, *Bodies and Biases* (1996); Melhuus and Stolen, *Machos, Mistresses, Madonnas* (1996); Balderston and Guy, *Sex and Sexuality in Latin America* (1997); Foster, *Sexual Textualities* (1997); Molloy and Irwin, *Hispanisms and Homosexualities* (1999); Blackmore and Hutcheson, *Queer Iberia* (1999); Chávez-Silverman and Hernández, *Reading and Writing the Ambiente* (2000). Martin Duberman's *Queer Representations* (1997) includes several essays dedicated to Spanish-American literature.

6. Among the critical works referenced in note 6, only *Bodies and Biases* and *Sex and Sexuality in Latin America* include essays focusing on Brazilian literature and culture, and even then, only a very limited number; *Queer Iberia* includes two essays on medieval Portugal. See Marilena Chaui, *Repressão sexual: essa nossa (des)conhecida* (1984); Jurandir Freire Costa, *A inocência e o vício: estudos sobre o homoerotismo* (1992); Roberto Da Matta, *Carnivals, Rogues and Heroes: An Interpretation of the Brazilian Dilemma* (1991); Gilberto Freyre, *The Masters and the Slaves* (1964); Fry (1982); James N. Green, *Beyond Carnival: Homosexuality in Twentieth-Century Brazil* (1999); Higgs, (1999; this volume includes a chapter on the urban gay history of Rio de Janeiro as well as Lisbon); Heloísa Buarque de Hollanda, *Tendências e impasses: o feminismo como crítica da cultura* (1994); Don Kulick, *Travesti: Sex, Gender, and Culture among Brazilian Transgendered Prostitutes* (1998); Landes (1947, 1994); Lia Zanotta Machado, "Estudos de gênero: para além do jogo entre intelectuais e feministas" (1997); Luiz Mott, *O lesbianismo no Brasil* (1987); Richard Parker, *Bodies, Pleasures and Passions* (1991), *Beneath the Equator* (1999); Margareth Rago, *Os prazeres da noite* (1991); Nancy Scheper-Hughes, *Death without Weeping: The Violence of Everyday Life in Brazil* (1992); João Silvério Trevisan, *Perverts in Paradise* (1986). This is by no means an exhaustive list. (To aid the English-language reader, we cite the English translations whenever available.)

7. "Gay sensibility" entails various cultural expressions, as well as ways of seeing (or being in) the world, or types of awareness or consciousness that are specific to the experience of male homosexuality. "Queer sensibility," meanwhile, goes beyond the parameters of gender and sexuality presupposed by the category "gay," to include other countercultural modalities of sex, gender, and sexuality that defy the conventions and expectations of bourgeois and/or patriarchal heterosexuality.

8. According to Jagose (1996), queer theory focuses on the instabilities encountered within sex, gender, sexuality, and desire. Institutionally, queer theory is the result of the expansion of lesbian and gay studies since the early 1990s in order to include studies on bisexuality, transvestism, and transgendered identities—all in all, subjectivities that cannot be easily accommodated into binaries such as male/female or heterosexual/homosexual.

9. In Mozambique, the Organização da Mulher Moçambicana (OMM; Organization of Mozambican Women), and in Angola the Organização das Mulheres de Angola (OMA; Organization of Angolan Women).

10. The continued progress and emancipation of women is profoundly linked to the degree of political and socioeconomic democratization in years to come. In societies such as Angola and Mozambique that have undergone massive historical traumas in recent decades, including protracted wars for independence and subsequent civil wars, with their devastating human and material consequences, the political climate remains unstable (especially in Angola). In Mozambique, continued peace, political stability, and economic growth since the civil war ended in 1992 are

xxxii Fernando Arenas and Susan Canty Quinlan

reasons to be hopeful for the future. For more information on the history of women in Angola and Mozambique, see Scott (1994) and Sheldon (1994), respectively.

11. One of the most sexually explicit films in Africa dealing overtly and sympathetically with male homosexuality was released in Guinea/Conakry by director Mohamed Câmera (*Dakan* [1997]). The documentary *Woubi, Chéri* by directors Philip Brooks and Laurent Bocahut, which was released in 1998, focuses on gay life in Abidjan (Ivory Coast). These are two very rare films dealing with gay male subject matter to emerge from Africa. Meanwhile, *Forbidden Fruit*, a groundbreaking video focusing on sexual identity and lesbian desire in rural Zimbabwe, was released in 2000 by directors S. Bruce, B. Kurath, and Y. Zückmantel.

12. There are, however, communities and political movements of self-identified black gay, lesbian, and transgendered Africans in South Africa, Namibia, and Zimbabwe, as well as open political discussion of sexuality issues in other southern African (Anglophone) states. Yet, throughout most of the African continent, any sexuality outside of heterosexuality is still considered taboo and rarely an object of public discussion. (We wish to thank Greg Mullins and the "Africa Project" of the International Gay and Lesbian Human Rights Commission in San Francisco for this information.)

13. David Halperin defines sexuality as a "constitutive feature of human personality" that constructs, organizes, and interprets facts such as sexual acts, desires, and pleasures. Sexuality, according to Halperin, would generate sexual identity—a personal essence defined in sexual terms (Halperin 1993: 417). On the other hand, Michel Foucault—one of the "founding figures" of gay and lesbian studies and queer theory—argues that in concurrence with the rise of the modern state in the eighteenth century emerged a series of techniques and mechanisms of power utilized by legal, social, pedagogical, and, eventually, medical institutions that were able to "produce sexuality" as a site of knowledge or science, rather than simply suppress it. At this historical juncture (the eighteenth and nineteenth centuries), according to Foucault (1978: 18), a multiplication of discourses around sex in the field of power itself took place that are the result of the institutional excitement to speak about sex. There is a desire on the part of agencies of power to hear about sex and to cause it to speak explicitly with an endless accumulation of detail.

14. In "Global Gaze/Global Gays" (1997), Dennis Altman argues that in spite of some obvious differences between gay worlds transnationally, as well as within or between "developing" and "developed" countries, there are important similarities that derive from a greater urbanization as well as modernization of cultures, accompanied by the global explosion of mass media and consumer societies. See also Altman's *Global Sex* (2001).

15. In March 2001, the Portuguese National Assembly voted in favor of recognizing domestic partnerships. This political victory will have a significant legal, economic, and cultural impact on the lives of Portuguese gays, lesbians, bisexuals, and transgenders.

16. For an exhaustive list of GLBT and AIDS service organizations in Brazil, see Parker (1999: 239–47).

17. The largest GLBT pride parade in Latin America took place in São Paulo in June 2002, bringing together more than four hundred thousand people. The São Paulo parade has mushroomed in the last few years. Meanwhile, as of 2001, major

political advances had been made in Brazil at the local and regional levels regarding antidiscrimination laws protecting the rights of sexual minorities (the most ambitious laws are in the state of Rio de Janeiro).

18. In September 1997, CAEHUSP (Centro Acadêmico de Estudos Homoeróticos [Academic center for homoerotic studies] of the University of São Paulo organized a month-long "Ciclo de Conferências sobre os Direitos Humanos dos Homossexuais" (Lecture series on the human rights of homosexuals) as part of a larger series of debates titled "Direitos Humanos no Limiar do Século XXI" (Human rights at the dawn of the twenty-first century). The development of a student-based organization with official legal status at the nation's largest university reflects a deeper process of an expanding gay, lesbian, bisexual, and transgender movement in Brazil. The political movement that emerged in the late 1970s during the political liberalization that marked the demise of the military's grip on the government faltered in the early 1980s. The 1990s saw the resurgence of activism, which culminated in 1995 in the formation of the Brazilian Association of Gays, Lesbians, and Transvestites with some forty affiliate groups throughout the country (James N. Green, E-mail, November 26, 1997).

19. For more information, see Mott (1996).

20. See for example, Mott's *O sexo proibido: virgens, gays e escravos nas garras da Inquisição* (1988a). For a study that focuses specifically on lesbians and the Inquisition, see Bellini (1987). For a discussion in English on the Inquisition in Brazil and homosexuality, see Trevisan (1986b).

21. A much earlier version of the essay included in *Lusosex* appears in *Devassos no paraíso: a homosexualidade no Brasil da colônia à atualidade* (1986a) and in its English translation, *Perverts in Paradise* (1986b). *Devassos no paraíso* was reedited and brought up to date in 2000 and published by Editora Record with 257 new pages.

22. In the late eighteenth century, however, the first novel about a woman crossdresser was published in Portugal, written by Brazilian writer Teresa Margarida da Silva e Orta (1993: 56–196).

23. For a more detailed analysis of Bom-crioulo, see Foster's "Adolfo Caminha's Bom-crioulo: A Founding Text of Brazilian Gay Literature" in *Gay and Lesbian Themes in Latin American Writing* (1991).

24. For possible connections between Brazilian novel *Bom-crioulo* and Portuguese novel *O Barão de Lavos*, see Robert Howe's preface to the English translation of *Bom-crioulo* (1982).

25. See Eduardo Prado Coelho's *A noite do mundo* (1988), 113–32.

26. Not to be confused with Spanish-American Modernism of the preceding century.

27. For a completely modernized and annotated version of Nogueira Cobra's novel and essay, see Quinlan (1997). For *Industrial Park*, see Galvão (1993). Other early literary representations of male homoerotic desire in Brazilian and Portuguese literatures include works by Fialho d'Almeida (the short story "O funâmbulo de mármore," from the collection *Contos* [1881]); Machado de Assis (the short story "Pílades e Orestes," originally published in *Relíquias de Casa Velha* [1906]); Antônio Patrício (the short story "O homem das fontes" from the collection *Serão Inquieto* [1910]); João Guimarães Rosa (*Grande sertão: Veredas*, [1958; *The Devil to Pay in the*

Backlands]); and Lúcio Cardoso (*Crônica da Casa Assassinada* [1959]). For an excellent critical overview of these and other texts as they pertain to the treatment of homoerotic desire, see Barcellos (1998).

28. Very few contemporary Portuguese prose writers have explored the theme of male homoerotic desire. See Rui Nunes (*Grito* [1997], *Cães* [1999]), Eduardo Pitta (*Persona* [2001]), Alexandre Pinheiro Torres (*Amor, só amor, tudo amor* [1999]), Guilherme de Melo (*A sombra dos dias* [1981], *O que houver de morrer* [1989]), and Inês Pedrosa (*Nas tuas mãos* [1997]).

For more information on selected writers who have thematized same-sex desire throughout the history of Brazilian literature, see David William Foster, *Gay and Lesbian Themes in Latin American Writing* (1991) and *Latin American Writers on Gay and Lesbian Themes: A Bio-Critical Sourcebook* (1994). For a critical literary study of three women writers, see Susan C. Quinlan, *The Female Voice in Contemporary Brazilian Narrative* (1991). For an exhaustive study of Brazilian women poets of the 1980s, including those who thematize lesbian desire, see Kátia Bezerra, "Poetas brasileiras nos anos oitenta: a heterogeneidade como locus de resistência e construção" (1999).

29. In the former Portuguese colonies in Africa, independence took place mostly in 1975 (Guinea-Bissau declared its independence in 1973). Three of the former colonies (Angola, Mozambique, and Guinea-Bissau) gained their independence through protracted wars that started in the early 1960s. All five former colonies, including Cape Verde and São Tomé and Príncipe, saw the implementation of Marxist-oriented single-party regimes at independence. At the same time, Angola, and shortly thereafter, Mozambique, became submerged in civil war, which in the case of Mozambique lasted until 1992, when a peace agreement was signed. Since then, Mozambique has experienced a remarkable period of peace, democratization, reconstruction, political stability, and economic growth. In the case of Angola, in spite of the fact that both warring parties signed the Lusaka Protocol or peace accord in 1994, peace and stability continue to be elusive. Both warring parties remained in the battlefields throughout this rich yet tragic country until 2002 when UNITA (Union for the Total Independence of Angola) leader Jonas Savimbi was killed by government troups. Peace in Angola now seems a distinct possibility. By 1994, multiparty elections had already been held in all Lusophone African states, as well as in most of sub-Saharan Africa. At the same time, those countries that were once governed by Marxist-oriented single-party regimes have been undergoing substantial economic reforms, making a rapid transition toward market economies.

30. Renowned novelist and cultural critic João Silvério Trevisan published one of the first studies that trace the history of homosexuality in Brazilian culture since colonial times (*Devassos no paraíso* [1986, 2000]).

Works Cited

Altman, Dennis. 1997. "Global Gaze/Global Gays." *GLQ* 3: 417–36.
———. 2001. *Global Sex*. Chicago: University of Chicago Press.
Assis, Machado de. 1952. *Relíquias de casa velha*. Rio de Janeiro: W. M. Jackson.

Azevedo, Aluísio. 1984. *O cortiço.* São Paulo: Editora Ática.

———. 2000. *The Slum: A Novel.* Trans. David H. Rosenthal. Oxford and New York: Oxford University Press.

Balderston, Daniel, and Donna J. Guy, eds. 1997. *Sex and Sexuality in Latin America.* New York and London: New York University Press.

Barcellos, José Carlos. 1998. "Identidades problemáticas: configurações do homo-erotismo masculino em narrativas portuguesas e brasileiras (1881–1959)." *Boletim do Centro de Estudos Portugueses da Faculdade de Letras da UFMG* 18: 7–42.

Bellini, Lígia. 1987. "A coisa obscura: mulher, sodomia e inquisição no Brasil colonial." Diss., Universidade Federal da Bahia.

Bergmann, Emilie L., and Paul Julian Smith, eds. 1995. *¿Entiendes?.* Durham, N.C.: Duke University Press.

Bezerra, Kátia. 1999. "Poetas brasileiras nos anos oitenta: a heterogeneidade como locus de resistência e construção." Diss., University of Minnesota.

Blackmore, Josiah, and Gregory S. Hutcheson. 1999. *Queer Iberia.* Durham, N.C.: Duke University Press.

Botelho, Abel. 1982. *O Barão de Lavos.* Porto: Lello.

Botto, António. 1921. *Canções.* Lisbon: Libânio da Silva.

Caminha, Adolfo. 1982. *Bom-Crioulo: The Black Man and the Cabin Boy.* Trans. E. A. Lacey. San Francisco: Gay Sunshine Press.

Cardoso, Lúcio. 1959. *Crônica da casa assassinada.* Rio de Janeiro: Ediouro.

Chaui, Marilena. 1984. *Repressão sexual: essa nossa (des)conhecida.* São Paulo: Brasiliense.

Chávez-Silverman, Susana, and Librada Hernández. 2000. *Reading and Writing the Ambiente: Queer Sexualities in Latino, Latin American, and Spanish Literature.* Madison: University of Wisconsin Press.

Churchill, Wainwright. 1967. *Homosexual Behavior among Males: A Cross-Cultural and Cross-Species Investigation.* New York: Hawthorn Books.

Coelho, Eduardo Prado. 1988. *A noite do mundo.* Lisbon: Imprensa Nacional-Casa da Moeda.

Costa, Jurandir Freire. 1992. *A inocência e o vício: estudos sobre o homoerotismo.* Rio de Janeiro: Relume Dumará.

D'Almeida, Fialho. 1972. *Contos.* Lisbon: Clássica.

Da Matta, Roberto. 1991. *Carnivals, Rogues and Heroes: An Interpretation of the Brazilian Dilemma.* Trans. John Drury. Notre Dame, Ind.: University of Notre Dame Press.

Duberman, Martin, ed. 1997. *Queer Representations.* New York and London: New York University Press.

Foster, David William. 1991. *Gay and Lesbian Themes in Latin American Writing.* Austin: University of Texas Press.

———. 1997. *Sexual Textualities: Essays on Queer/ing Latin American Writing.* Austin: University of Texas Press.

———, ed. 1994. *Latin American Writers on Gay and Lesbian Themes: A Bio-Critical Sourcebook.* Westport, Conn.: Greenwood Press.

Foster, David William, and Roberto Reis, eds. 1996. *Bodies and Biases: Sexualities in Hispanic Cultures and Literatures.* Hispanic Issues 13. Minneapolis: University of Minnesota Press.

Foucault, Michel. 1978. *The History of Sexuality.* Vol. 1, *An Introduction.* Trans. Robert Hurley. New York: Random House.

Freyre, Gilberto. 1964. *The Masters and the Slaves.* Trans. Samuel Putnam. New York: Knopf.

Fry, Peter. 1982. *Para inglês ver: identidade e política na cultura brasileira.* Rio de Janeiro: Zahar Editores.

Galvão, Patrícia. 1993. *Industrial Park.* Trans. K. David and Elizabeth Jackson. Lincoln: University of Nebraska Press.

———. *Parque industrial.* 1994. Porto Alegre: Mercado Aberto; São Carlos: Editora da Universidade Federal de São Carlos.

Gameiro, Octávio. 1997. "Aspectos sociais e políticos da população homo e bissexual em Portugal." *ILGA Portugal,* November 15; <http://www.ilga-portugal.org>.

Green, James N. 1999. *Beyond Carnival: Homosexuality in Twentieth Century Brazil.* Chicago: Chicago University Press.

Halperin, David M. 1993. "Is There a History of Sexuality?" *Lesbian and Gay Studies Reader.* New York and London: Routledge.

Higgs, David. 1999. *Queer Sites.* London and New York: Routledge.

Hollanda, Heloísa Buarque de. 1994. "Introdução—Feminismo em tempos pós-modernos." In *Tendências e impasses: o feminismo como crítica da cultura.* Rio de Janeiro: Rocco.

Jagose, Annamarie. 1996. *Queer Theory: An Introduction.* New York: New York University Press.

Kulick, Don. 1998. *Travesti: Sex, Gender, and Culture among Brazilian Transgendered Prostitutes.* Chicago: University of Chicago Press.

Landes, Ruth. 1940. "A Cult Matriarchate and Male Homosexuality." *Journal of Abnormal and Social Psychology* 35: 386–97.

———. 1947. *City of Women.* New York: Macmillan.

———. 1994. *The City of Women.* Albuquerque: University of New Mexico Press.

Machado, Lia Zanotta. 1997. "Estudos de gênero: para além do jogo entre intelectuais e feministas." In *Gênero sem fronteiras,* ed. Mônica Raisa Schpun. Florianópolis: Editora Mulheres. 93–139.

Melhuus, Marit, and Kristi Anne Stolen. 1996. *Machos, Mistresses, Madonnas: Contesting the Power of Latin American Gender Imagery.* London and New York: Verso.

Melo, Guilherme de. 1981. *A sombra dos dias.* Lisbon: Livraria Bertrand.

———. 1989. *O que houver de morrer.* Lisbon: Editorial Notícias.

Molloy, Sylvia, and Robert McKee Irwin. 1999. *Hispanisms and Homosexualities.* Durham, N.C.: Duke University Press.

Mott, Luiz. 1988a. *O sexo proibido: escravos, gays e virgens nas garras da Inquisição.* Campinas, Brazil: Papirus Editora.

———. 1988b. "Pagode português: a subcultura gay em Portugal nos tempos inquisitoriais." *Ciência e Cultura* 40.

———. 1996. *Epidemic of Hate: Violations of the Human Rights of Gay Men, Lesbians and Transvestites in Brazil.* San Francisco: International Gay and Lesbian Human Rights Commission.

———. 1987. *O lesbianismo no Brasil.* Porto Alegre: Mercado Aberto.

Nunes, Rui. 1997. *Grito.* Lisbon: Relógio D'Agua Editores.

———. 1999. *Cães.* Lisbon: Relógio D'Agua Editores.

Parker, Richard. 1991. *Bodies, Pleasures and Passions.* Boston: Beacon Press.

————. 1999. *Beneath the Equator.* New York and London: Routledge.

Patrício, António. 1979. *Serão inquieto.* Lisbon: Assírio & Alvim.

Pedrosa, Inês. 1997. *Nas tuas mãos.* Lisbon: D. Quixote.

Pitta, Eduardo. 2001. *Persona: ficções.* Lisbon: Angelus Novus.

Pompéia, Raul. 1963. *O ateneu.* Rio de Janeiro: Edições Melhoramento.

Quinlan, Susan Canty. 1991. *The Female Voice in Contemporary Brazilian Narrative.* New York: Peter Lang.

————, ed. 1997. *Visões do passado, previsões do futuro: duas modernistas esquecidas, Ercília Nogueira Cobra e Adalzira Bittencourt.* With Peggy Sharpe. Rio de Janeiro: Tempo Brasileiro; Goiânia: Universidade Federal de Goiás.

Rago, Margareth. 1991. *Os prazeres da noite.* Rio de Janeiro: Paz e Terra.

Rosa, João Guimarães. 1984. *Grande sertão: Veredas.* Rio de Janeiro: Editora Nova Fronteira.

Scheper-Hughes, Nancy. 1992. *Death without Weeping: The Violence of Everyday Life in Brazil.* Berkeley: University of California Press.

Scott, Catherine V. 1994. "'Men in Our Country Behave Like Chiefs': Women and the Angolan Revolution." In *Women and Revolution in Africa, Asia, and the New World,* ed. Mary Ann Tétreault. Columbia: University of South Carolina Press. 89–108.

Sheldon, Kathleen. 1994. "Women and Revolution in Mozambique: A Luta Continua." In *Women and Revolution in Africa, Asia, and the New World,* ed. Mary Ann Tétreault. Columbia: University of South Carolina Press. 33–61.

Silva e Orta, Teresa Margarida da. 1993. *Teresa Margarida da Silva e Orta: Obra Reunida.* Introduction, bibliography, and notes by Ceila Montez. Rio de Janeiro: Gráphia Editorial.

Torres, Alexandre Pinheiro. 1999. *Amor, só amor, tudo amor.* Lisbon: Caminho.

Trevisan, João Silvério. 1986a. *Devassos no paraíso: a homossexualidade no Brasil da colônia à atualidade.* São Paulo: Editora Max Limonad.

————. 1986b. *Perverts in Paradise.* Trans. Martin Foreman. London: Gay Men's Press.

————. 2000. *Devassos no paraíso.* 2d ed. Rio de Janeiro: Editora Record.

Wafer, Jim. 1991. *The Taste of Blood: Spirit Possession in Brazilian Candomblé.* Philadelphia: University of Pennsylvania Press.

Part I
Early Stories of Desire

CHAPTER ONE

Tivira, the Man with the Broken Butt

Same-Sex Practices among Brazilian Indians

João Silvério Trevisan
Translated by Susan Canty Quinlan and Izetta Irwin

When Brazil's discoverer, Pedro Álvares Cabral, and his Portuguese squadron made port in Brazil in 1500, its members were awed before the beauty of the country and fertility of its lands, but also aghast at the nudity and laxity of its native inhabitants' sexual practices. Indeed, the natives' sexual codes shared nothing with the era's Western Puritanism. For example, they gave little importance to virginity and condemned celibacy; in this vein, in 1556, the French clergyman and chronicler André Thévet observed that the Indians offered their daughters to the foreigners in exchange for trifles. In the same period, the German traveler Hans Staden related that, among the aborigines, the conquered enemy had the right to sleep with his captor's wife and daughter, before being killed.[1] Several foreign chroniclers also refer to the fact that the Indians liked to recount their sexual deeds in public, without modesty and, more than likely, making up the better part of their stories. With the same exhibitionistic motive, they habitually increased the size of their virile members (which some European voyagers considered too small for the natives' tall stature). To achieve this, according to the tale of the scandalized Portuguese Gabriel Soares de Sousa (1987: 305–8) in the sixteenth century, the Indians customarily wrapped the penis with the hide of a venomous beast in order to increase its dimensions by swelling.

Of all the wanton customs of the inhabitants of this tropical paradise, however, nothing was more shocking to the Christians of the time than the practice of the "pecado nefando" [nefarious sin], "sodomia" (sodomy) or "sujidade" [filthiness], the names given to sexual acts between males that, according to the chaste historian Abelardo Romero, "grassava há séculos entre os brasis, como uma doença contagiosa" (1967: 149) [had raged for centuries among the Brazilian aborigines, like a contagious disease].[2] Such horror is understandable: for the Europeans— Catholic or reformed—sodomy was one of the four *clamantia peccata* (sins that cry out to the heavens) as reported in medieval theology. In 1587, Gabriel Soares de Sousa already noticed that:

> os selvagens . . . são mui afeiçoados ao pecado nefando, entre os quais não se têm por afronta; e o que serve de macho se tem por valente, e contam esta bestialidade por proeza; e nas suas aldeias pelo sertão há alguns que têm tenda pública a quantos os querem como mulheres públicas. (Quoted in Freyre 1963: 177)

> [the savages . . . are very attached to this nefarious sin, which, among them, is not considered an affront; and he who serves as male is considered valiant, and they speak of this bestiality as prowess; and in their villages in the wilderness there are some who set up a public tent for all those who desire them, like female prostitutes.]

In other words, there then existed something like today's male prostitution. In 1576, another Portuguese—Pêro de Magalhães Gândavo—also observed that the Indians "se entregam ao vício (da sodomia) como se neles não houvera razão de homens" (quoted in Romero 1967: 149) [give themselves over to the vice (sodomy) as though they had not human reason in them]. In 1578, the Frenchman Jean de Léry related that, when they argued among themselves, the Brazilian Indians used the epithet *tivira,* synonym of "viado" ["queer" in Brazilian Portuguese] in the Tupi language—which literally meant "homem do traseiro roto" [man with a broken butt].[3] Centuries later, in 1859, the German researcher Robert Avé-Lallement noted, among the Botocudo Indians, not just men and women, but men-women and women-men.[4] Their physical constitution did not vary much from one sex to the other, as it does in the Western patriarchal system, responsible for the standard of muscularity for men and fragility for women. Voyaging through central Brazil, in 1894, the German Karl von den Steinen bore witness that, inside the *baito* (or house of men, where entrance was allowed only to males, after severe initiation ordeals), the youths of the Bororó tribe had sexual relations among themselves, completely naturally, besides dedicating themselves to extremely delicate tasks, in the words of Steinen:

Quão elegante e nitidamente os homens trabalhavam, notava-se
principalmente no arranjo das flechas. Havia aí muitas habilidadezinhas
que parecia mais natural devessem ser confiadas às delicadas mãos
femininas. Por exemplo, o adorno feito de miúdas e variegadas penugens,
que eram postas uma a uma no chão e meticulosamente arranjadas.
E mesmo numa roda de fiandeiras não se podia tagarelar e rir mais do
que aí no baito! . . . Certamente, era pouco feminino quando de repente,
para variar, levantavam-se dois dos trabalhadores e ofereciam o espetáculo
de uma luta corporal que os demais acompanhavam com o maior
interesse. Erguiam-se, lutavam, derrubavam-se e depois continuavam
seu trabalho, ou deitavam-se para o *dolce far niente*. Muitas vezes
encontravam-se pares enamorados que se divertiam debaixo de um
mesmo cobertor vermelho. (Quoted in Freyre 1977: 96, 141)

[The men worked with an elegance and precision principally notable in
the fashioning of the arrows. There were many little touches that would
have seemed more naturally entrusted to delicate feminine hands. For
example, an ornament made of tiny and variegated feathers, which were
laid out one by one on the ground and meticulously arranged. And even
in a circle of women spinning there would not be such chattering and
laughter as there in the *baito!* Certainly, it was less than feminine when
suddenly, for variety's sake, two workers got up and presented the spectacle of a physical contest that the others watched with the greatest
interest. They arose, fought, knocked each other down, and afterwards
continued with their work, or lay down together for the *dolce far niente*
(pleasing inactivity). Enamored couples were often found enjoying
themselves under the same red blanket.]

One can imagine the Christians' alarm upon ascertaining that indigenous medicine itself was frequently practiced by means of sexual
relations between the *pajé* [shaman] and his patients, including anal intercourse, or that the *pajé* should transmit his knowledge of medicine
to his students through a sexual act. Voyaging through Brazil between
1817 and 1820, the German naturalist Karl Friedrich von Martius once
inquired of an old *pajé,* Gregório of the Coeruna tribe, about the manner in which he cured his patients; in response, the old man stuck out
his tongue, used his hands to make "um movimento indecente, indicando
os órgãos genitais, e sorriu com expressão de maliciosa astúcia" (Martius 1979: 128–30) [an indecent gesture, indicating the genital organs,
and smiled with an expression of malicious cunning].

Von Martius reported, quite incensed, that the oldest *pajé* customarily transmitted the knowledge of remedies to his youngest students "à custa da prostituição" [by dint of prostitution], in which "o sedutor, no ato da cópula carnal, simula, em vez de gozar, comunicar em recompensa disso uma força desconhecida" [the seducer, in the act of carnal copulation, pretends he is, rather than taking pleasure, a hidden force in recompense]. He further observed that, among the Brazilian Indians, the old *pajé* selected a youth with whom he spent some time in a solitary spot. For the tribe, this absence signified an initiation into the secrets of sorcery, but for von Martius it served "apenas para entregar, sexualmente, o aluno ao seu mestre" (128) [only to sexually deliver the pupil to his master]. The youth so initiated generally received some object—for example, a root, a piece of burned wood or bone, an animal's claw, a tooth—as a kind of wedding ring, which he always carried as an amulet and immediate source of help in case of sickness. Von Martius also verified that everything expelled by the human organism, especially semen, was considered impure and subject to utilization in the diabolic arts. But the *pajé*'s saliva and urine were curative substances, this last being administered internally as a stimulant and an emetic.

In the face of what the Europeans considered "frouxidão de costumes" [looseness of customs] and evidently attributed to paganism, it is no wonder that the Portuguese of the era called the Indians "bugres" [buggers] or "gentios" [heathen]. The first term (already known in the Middle Ages) and the second (used since biblical times) were applied indiscriminately to the heretic and the practitioner of sodomy; this because the "pecado nefando" [nefarious sin] was almost always associated with the sin of disbelief or heresy. But, if the Europeans manifested horror at pagan licentiousness, it is also true that they became fascinated by it, inasmuch as it signified liberation from their sins. The colonists who came from Europe were plagued by doctrinal disputes and firmly watched over by the Inquisition. In the words of Brazilian historian Paulo Prado:

> o ardor dos temperamentos, a amoralidade dos costumes e toda a contínua tumescência da natureza virgem era um convite à vida solta e infrene em que tudo era permitido. (1972: 159)

> [the ardor of the temperaments, the amorality of the customs, and all the continual tumescence of virgin nature were an invitation to a free and unrestrained life in which everything was permitted.]

For the Portuguese chronicler Simão de Vasconcelos, the colonists of the seventeenth century were no different from the Indians, "porque sendo cristãos viviam a modo dos gentios" (Romero 1967: 183) [because being Christians they lived like heathens]. Pierre Moreau, a French traveler who was also in Brazil in the seventeenth century, relates that during the brief period of Dutch colonization in Pernambuco, "todos levavam vida escandalosa: judeus, cristãos, tapuias, mulatos, mamelucos e crioulos" [everyone carried on a scandalous life: Jews, Christians, non-Tupi natives, mulattos, *mamelucos* (offspring of white and Indians— *Trans.*) and blacks]. To the foreigners who arrived in Brazil, it was "infra equinoxialem nihil peccari" (below the Equator, there is no sinner), as a proverb of the period said (quoted in ibid.).

In addition to the testimony of the voyagers of old, prestigious contemporary anthropologists and researchers confirm the incidence of same-sex relations as a natural component of many indigenous cultures in Brazil: Darcy Ribeiro noted them among the Cadiuéu, Thomas Gregor among the Mehinaku, Lévi-Strauss among the Nhambiquara, Florestan Fernandes and Alfred Métraux among the Tupinambá.

Lévi-Strauss tells how the privileged polygamy of the Nhambiquara chief causes some disequilibrium among the numbers of marriageable young men and women, so that there end up being more single men than women. One of the methods the tribe found to resolve the problem, according to Lévi-Strauss, was to structure male-male relations, which the Nhambiquara poetically refer to as "tamindige kihandige," or "amor mentira" [lying love]. Such relations are common among youths and take place more publicly than opposite-sex relations: to make love, the male pairs do not go to the forest, as do adults of opposite sex, but place themselves next to a campfire. In front of them, the neighbors laugh and amuse themselves with generally unobtrusive jokes, for such acts are considered infantile, not provoking any greater attention. Lévi-Strauss was unable to say whether such encounters always include sexual acts or if they are restricted to sentimental effusions and erotic games characteristic of conjugal relations in the tribe. But it is certain that there exist publicly admitted sexual relations among young boys who are "primos cruzados," that is, when one is destined to marry the sister of the other—as if the brother served the brother-in-law as a substitute for the future wife. Even in adulthood, the brothers-in-law continue to show great emotional freedom toward each other, it not being rare to find two or three of these men, already married and paterfamilias, going for an evening walk tenderly entwined (310–11).

Among the Kaingang, anthropologist Jules Henry noted the pleasure that the young men, married or not, have in sleeping together: they lie with faces pressed together and bodies intertwined as would actual lovers. Although Henry believed that such moments never led to actual sexual relations, he noted that he never saw this sort of intimacy between heterosexual couples (cited in Cardin 1984: 109–10).

Ethnographer Alfred Métraux pointed out the existence among the Mbayá or Guaicuru (who belong to the same line as the Caduveo) of many berdaches, that is, males living and speaking as women, claiming to menstruate, and performing feminine activities. They were considered the village prostitutes (ibid.).[5]

Among the Yanomami, anthropologist Jacques Lizot informs us that children and young boys took passive pleasure in anal intercourse, it being commonplace to see youths of all ages simulating it in public. The participants are brothers-in-law, in general united by reciprocal and lasting affection, but it is not uncommon for sexual relations to occur between brothers and "primos-irmãos" [first cousins]. Although it is disgraceful to "comer a vagina" [eat the vagina] (an expression used by the Indians) of one's sister, no one raises a scandal over the act of "comer o ânus" [eating the anus] of one's brother. But the sexual relation between brothers-in-law differs, according to the anthropologist, from that between brothers. In the first case, there is a mutual feeling of friendship between two boys, who swap women and material goods and treat each other as equals. In the case of brothers and cousins, the relation is more circumstantial, not involving emotions and occurring between unequal partners: the older males "eat the anus" of the younger males, a clear sign of exercise of authority (35).

Anthropologist Charles Wagley tells of the existence of a curious myth among the Tapirapé Indians, a small Brazilian tribe of the Tupi group, now almost extinct. A puma wanted to "eat the anus" of a turtle, who was willing to comply if permitted, first, to do the same with the puma. Because the turtle was so small, the puma agreed. But, to his surprise, the *jabuti* [turtle] had a very large penis, so that upon being penetrated in the anus the puma screamed with pain and dashed headlong into the heart of the forest. Among the Tapirapé, Wagley heard of married Indians who at night gave themselves to other men, in the "house of men." There were also those men who even adopted a feminine name and did all the work of a woman—such as preparing manioc flour, cooking, carrying water, and weaving cotton ornaments and hammocks. One such man painted his body with the genipap fruit, like a woman, and was married to one of the leaders of the community; according to the Indians, his death had been caused by pregancy: in the absence of a uterus, his stomach had become overblown. Wagley recounts the existence of Indians who were taken on long hunts, merely for the sexual use of the other men, who treated them as favorites (158–59). This custom seems to have been known by the Xavante, who are in the habit of preparing a boy, from childhood, to assume the sexual and social functions of a woman, especially during warlike and hunting expeditions, where a feminine presence is not allowed. Because of his importance, this *tivira* enjoyed great prestige in the tribe.

This information was related to me in 1983, by a student, Sérgio Domingues, who lived for many years in central Brazil, among the Kraô Indians, a tribe of delicate and polite customs, where it is common to see two young men holding hands. Also, the single men sleep together, in the males' space (called *kó*) in the night air, in the village's central open space, where the women do not enter—just as the men may not enter the females' space (the house, called *ikré*) until after marriage. In their meetings, the men rest on each other, heads propped now on the chest, now on the shoulder of the other; also it is common to see two young men sitting, one behind the other, arms around each other's waists; they like to comb each other's hair and, quite often, they caress each others' genital organs in public. According to my interviewee (who does not define himself as homosexual), the single youths fifteen to twenty years old often have sex with each other, in such cases preferring to go to the forest. Moreover, in this tribe he came to be acquainted with a transvestite Indian, who carried out feminine functions and dressed as a woman, with absolutely no molestation from the others. Sérgio became friends with a handsome fifteen-year-old Kraô who repeatedly invited him to "make *cunin*": "Eu ponho na sua bunda, depois você põe na minha" [I'll put it up your butt, then you put it up mine]. He went as far as to propose this invitation in public, penis already erect, while laughing happily. Used to the physical contact so important in his tribe, once this young Indian casually hugged a white driver from the Fundação

Nacional do Índio (FUNAI) [National Indian Foundation], who pushed him away, saying, "Não gosto de macho estar me abraçando" [I don't like a man to be hugging me].

This, in my view, is a perfect example of how radical differences between the two cultures still are: just as in the time of the discovery of America, the civilized whites are still unable to call things by their true name.

Notes

1. For references to André Thévet and Hans Staden regarding sexual culture among Amerindians in Brazil during the sixteenth century, see Abelardo Romero's *Origem da imoralidade no Brasil*, 146–48.

2. Sodomy, as it is used here in the sense of "pecado nefando," is clearly defined in the first Portuguese penal code of 1446: "Although not restricted to homosexuals, the crime of sodomy was generally associated with love between individuals of the same sex, as indicated in the so-called *Ordinances of the Kingdom of Portugal,* in whose books all Portuguese laws, from the Constitution to the civil and penal codes, were compiled from the time of the Renaissance. . . . The oldest of these various compilations was the *Afonsine Ordinances,* proclaimed in the reign of Afonso V and published in 1446." (Trevisan 1986: 57–59). It already listed (book 5, section 17) the penalty of burning for sodomy—"of all sins the most vile, unclean and foul" and the cause whereby "God set the Flood upon the earth." The *Manueline Ordinances* (published in 1521 in the reign of Dom Manuel) and the *Philipine Ordinances* (petitioned by Philip I but only published in 1603 in the subsequent reign) were based on the *Afonsine Ordinances,* but reformulated and brought up to date. The *Manueline Ordinances,* in force in Portugal at the time of the Discovery, were the oldest penal code applied in Brazil. They placed sodomy on the same level as lèse-majesté. As well as burning at the stake, the confiscation of the condemned man's goods and infamy on his children and descendants were added to the punishment. Unlike the earlier ordinances, in the *Philipine Ordinances* women were no longer excluded from the law (of sodomy), "for some commit the sin against nature with others in the manner with which we have spoken of men" (ibid., 66–67). The confirmation that the act of sodomy implied some sort of unnatural sexual penetration is clearly understood in light of all the debates between the moralists and the theologians of the time. For most of these scholars, if there was no penetration, the mere presence of carnal acts between women did not result in sodomy. "The consensual agreement used to characterize sexual penetration finally included the artificial instruments that women could use between themselves. We know this to be true from the many statements given by accused women to the Inquisition in Brazil about the 'pecado nefando.' In these statements, the women asked whether or not they used penetrating instruments asking them specifically about the 'pecado nefando'" (Trevisan 2000: 130).

3. See Léry 1980: 224. In note 531 on the same page, Tupinologist Plínio Ayrosa refers to Léry's French transcription "*typire*" from the Tupi term "*tebira*" or "*tebiró*," which meant sodomite or also prostitute or loose woman.

4. For reference to Avé-Lallement's observations regarding gender definitions among the Botocudo Indians, see Freyre (1977: 96).

5. See Pierette Désy, "El hombre-mujer: los 'bardajes' entre los indios de América del Norte (Primera parte)," trans. José de la Colina, *Vuelta* 4:46 (September 1980): 15–21; "El hombre-mujer (Segunda y última parte)," trans. José de la Colina. *Vuelta* 4:47 (October 1980): 26–35; and Richard Trexler, *Sex and Conquest: Gendered Violence, Political Order and the European Conquest of the Americas* (Ithaca, N.Y.: Cornell University Press, 1995).

Works Cited

Cardin, Alberto. 1984. *Guerreros, chamanés y travestis*. Barcelona: Tusquets.

Freyre, Gilberto. 1963. *Casa-grande e senzala*. Brasília: Editora da Universidade de Brasília.

———. 1977. *Sobrados e Mocambos*. Rio de Janeiro: José Olympio.

Lévi-Strauss, Claude. 1986. *Tristes trópicos*. Lisbon: Edições 70.

Léry, Jean de. 1980. *Viagem à terra do Brasil*. Belo Horizonte, Brazil: Itatiaia/Edsup.

Lizot, Jacques. 1988. *O círculo dos fogos*. São Paulo: Martins Fontes.

Prado, Paulo. 1972. *Retrato do Brasil*. Rio de Janeiro: José Olímpio.

Romero, Abelardo. 1967. *Origem da imoralidade no Brasil*. Rio de Janeiro: Conquista.

Sousa, Gabriel Soares de. 1987. *Tratado descritivo do Brasil em 1587*. 5th ed. São Paulo: Companhia Editora Nacional.

Trevisan, João Silvério. 1986. *Perverts in Paradise*. Trans. Martin Foreman. London: Gay Men's Press.

———. 2000. *Devassos no paraíso: a homosexualidade no Brasil, da colônia à atualidade*. 3d ed. Rio de Janeiro: Record.

von Martius, Karl F. P. 1979. *Natureza, doenças, medicina e remédios do índios brasileiros*. São Paulo: Companhia Editorial Nacional.

Wagley, Charles. 1988. *Lágrimas de boas-vindas*. Belo Horizonte, Brazil: Itatiaia/Edsup.

CHAPTER TWO

Machado de Assis and Graciliano Ramos

Speculations on Sex and Sexuality

John Gledson

baixemos nossos olhos aos desígnios
da natureza ambígua e reticente:
ela tece, dobrando-lhe o amargor
outra forma de amar no acerbo amor.
                    —Carlos Drummond de Andrade, "Rapto" (1967: 250)

[Let us lower our gaze before the designs
of nature, ambiguous and reticent:
she weaves, redoubling its bitterness
another form of love within sharp love.]

This essay deals with Machado de Assis and Graciliano Ramos, two writers whose (well-justified) claim to fame has, at least apparently, nothing to do with their attitude to homosexuality. There are two reasons for this: one is the extreme paucity of the kind of relatively explicit material we have become more used to since the 1960s; the other is simply that the depth, richness and, I was going to say, honesty—and can still find no better word—of both writers' works makes even their "incidental" comments worth paying attention to.

João Guimarães Rosa and Clarice Lispector, who each began to publish in the 1940s, produced a fundamental change in the possibilities open to Brazilian fiction. Their ambition, their linguistic experimentalism and daring, and their familiarity with such writers as Virginia Woolf, Katherine Mansfield, James Joyce, Thomas Mann, and others immeasurably widened the possibilities for Brazilian writers, and changed the whole literary landscape. Their work was, in a way, an introduction to international modernism, and as such was quite different from the Brazilian *modernismo* of the 1920s.

What has been less noticed, though it is an entirely natural part of this process, is the part these writers played in changing literary attitudes to sexuality. The plot of *Grande sertão: Veredas (The Devil to Pay in the Backlands)* revolves around a case of mistaken sexual identity (Diadorim/ Reinaldo), and of the turbulent emotions this causes in Riobaldo. Lispector's work, as recent critics have shown, is molded to a great degree, from the very beginning, by the fact that so many of its protagonists are women, and women whose sexuality, less or more repressed, is an intrinsic part of Lispector's portrayal of them.[1] Of course, Rosa and Lispector were not alone; Lúcio Cardoso, whose *Crônica da casa assassinada* was published in 1959, is another example of the way the wind was blowing. But it is perhaps significant that homosexuality did not come to the surface in this first "wave" of the process. Some things were still too shocking. Overtly gay writers only appear later, in the wake of the emergence of gay liberation in the United States at the end of the 1960s, and of the scandal produced at much the same time by events such as the popular singer-composer Caetano Veloso's attack on his (largely left-wing) audience's prejudices, most famously and directly at a concert in the Maracanãzinho stadium in Rio in September 1968.[2]

Homosexuality was not absent from Brazilian literature before this (still ongoing) process of change allowed it to surface. It would be truer to say that it could only be talked about in ideological contexts that made it difficult to understand or more simply distorted its reality. The strangest of all—exotic, marginal, and yet extraordinarily direct—is that of José Joaquim de Campos Leão Qorpo-Santo (1829–83), the *gaúcho* dramatist whose work was never staged in his lifetime, and in fact almost disappeared altogether, surviving in a single copy that only became known in the 1960s.[3] At the end of *A separação de dois esposos* (1866) (232–48), in a short scene lasting no more than a page, but that provides a climax to the play, two comic servants, Tamanduá and Tatu (Anteater and Armadillo), figures who should be "as mais exóticas que se pode imaginar" (as exotic as can be imagined) (245) suddenly start showing an affection whose nature cannot be misunderstood ("meu queridinho" [roughly, "my pet"]). However, when Tatu reveals that this is carnal as well as spiritual love, Tamanduá tells him that he is not a woman, cannot give birth, and that it is "o vício mais danoso que o homem pode praticar" (the worst vice a man can indulge in), which leads them to fight and tear each other's clothes to shreds: end of scene, end of play.

At the end of the nineteenth century, the religious parameters that, however tenuously, seem to circumscribe Qorpo-Santo, were replaced by "scientific" ones. Brazilian Naturalism, no less than its French model, was explicit about sex, as such scandalously famous novels as Júlio Ribeiro's *A carne* (1888) show, and the movement produced a remarkable novel about homosexuality, Adolfo Caminha's *Bom-crioulo* (1895). Caminha, who was in all likelihood not gay himself, nevertheless portrays Amaro, the black sailor-hero of the novel, with remarkable sympathy.[4] Ultimately, however, the plot, which involves a pair of lovers (one of whom becomes possessive to the point of murder while the other goes through a "phase" that leads to him being taken up by a woman), cannot be said to be free of the kind of normative bias that sees homosexuality as a deviation akin to illness or madness. As Peter Fry has argued (1982), *Bom-crioulo* is partly interesting and valuable *in spite of* the ideology that informs it.

As the (pseudo)scientific Naturalist model began to lose its attraction, a more open and culturally oriented view of human beings and their development began to operate: in Brazil, the theories and ideas of Gilberto Freyre began to grip the imagination. Freyre wrote a great deal about sex, and was himself remarkably perceptive and unshockable. His influence on other writers, particularly Northeasterners, was enormous, and he opened the way to a different treatment of sexuality (homosexuality included), which still, however, subjected it to a kind of pattern, perhaps best seen in a novel such as José Lins do Rego's *Menino de engenho,* in which the hero, Carlos de Melo, an unhappy and unstable child, goes through an initiation process that lasts for most of the novel, and that involves masturbation and sex with plants, animals, boys, and girls from the ex-slave classes, leading finally to falling in (unrequited) love with a girl of his own class. The change from the Naturalist scheme of things is, in fact, not as fundamental as it might seem: Carlos is no role model, and ideas of degeneracy which gained currency in the late nineteenth century are still operative in his case.

I hope that this quick guide to the portrayal of sexuality, and of homosexuality in particular, in Brazilian fiction before the 1950s and 1960s can be accepted, at least *grosso modo.* Were there any exceptions—in other words, any writers who had the sense, or the courage, to see beyond the ultimately constraining patterns of these dominant ideologies, to something more interesting, less stereotyped and predictable, more humane? I am aware of two cases, involving indisputably great writers, perhaps the greatest of the nineteenth and twentieth centuries, respectively: Machado de Assis and Graciliano Ramos. Both see sex and sexuality in an entirely different light to that of their contemporaries. Although they are very different, both went through a rejection, more or less explicit, of the "scientific," Naturalist model: what is perhaps less expected, but has its reasons, is that both involve scenes, historical or contemporary, of homosexual rape.[5]

I shall never forget my first reading of *Casa velha*, a short novel published by Machado de Assis in 1885–86 in a ladies' magazine, *A Estação*, and never republished in his lifetime. It counters many of the traditional expectations about this author: it is not ironic in the style of his great novels of the 1880s and 1890s, but neither is it polite and constrained like the four novels of the 1870s. It is remarkably frank in its portrayal of a patriarchal oligarchic family, and the unpleasant and ultimately self-destructive means it sometimes has to use to maintain its power and exclusiveness. The story's narrator, a priest, is evidently not happy with his own complicit role in separating Félix, the male heir to the family, from Lalau, the *agregada* (family dependent) whom he loves; nor does Machado hide the risks, in this case extending to incest, of the (deceased) patriarch's philandering: Lalau could have been his daughter, though in fact she is not. *Casa velha* constitutes a powerful argument for seeing Machado as a devastating critic of the society in which he was, personally, so successful. But what extra charge of anger or mischief led him to face the lady readers of *A Estação* with the following piece of superfluous erudition?[6] The priest is in the library of the house with Félix:

casualmente, dei com os olhos na *Storia Fiorentina*, de Varchi, edição de 1721. Confesso que nunca tinha lido esse livro, nem mesmo o li mais tarde; mas um padre italiano, que eu visitei no Hospício de Jerusalém, na antiga Rua dos Borbonos, possuía a obra e falara-me da última página, que em alguns exemplares faltava, e tratava do modo descomunalmente sacrílego e brutal com que um dos Farneses tratara o bispo de Fano.

—Será um exemplar truncado? disse eu.

—Truncado? repetiu Félix.

Vamos ver, continuei eu, correndo ao fim. Não, cá está: é o cpo. 16 do lv.
XVI. Uma coisa indigna: *in quest'anno medesimo nacque un caso*...Não
vale a pena ler: é imundo.

Pus o livro no lugar. Sem olhar para Félix, senti-o subjugado. Nem
confesso esse incidente, que me envergonha, senão porque, além da
resolução de dizer tudo, importa explicar o poder que desde logo exerci
naquela casa, e especialmente no espírito do moço.[7]

[accidentally, my eyes rested on the *Storia Fiorentina,* by Varchi, an
edition of 1721. I confess that I had never read the book, nor did I even
read it later; but an Italian priest, whom I had visited in the Jerusalem
Hospice, in the old Rua dos Barbonos, had a copy in his possession and
had spoken to me of the last page, which was missing in some copies,
and treated of the extraordinarily sacrilegious and brutal way in which
one of the Farneses had treated the bishop of Fano.

"Could it be one of the abridged copies?" I said.

"Abridged?"

Let's see, I went on, going to the end. No, here it is: it's the sixteenth
chapter of book 16. An outrageous thing: *in quest'anno medesimo nacque
un caso*...It's not worth reading: it's filthy.

I put the book in its place. Without looking at Félix, I felt him to be
subjugated. Indeed, I only confess this incident, of which I am ashamed,
because, apart from the resolve to say everything, it is important to
explain the power that from the start I exercised in that household, and
especially on the spirit of the young man.]

What is referred to here, as many readers might at least half-divine, is
the rape of the young bishop—he was twenty-four—by Pier Luigi de
Farnese, the son of Pope Paul III. The bishop died forty days later, apparently of shame. It is an incident designed to cast the Catholic church
in the worst possible light—when the event created a scandal at Rome,
Paul III, who had been inclined to overlook the event as a "leggerezza
giovanile," was moved to absolve his son via a papal bull.[8]

There is an obvious motive for referring to this shocking event:
Machado wants to suggest that the priest-narrator obtains a power over
Félix that is violent, destructive, and sexual in its intensity. There are no
prizes for guessing which book Félix will read next time he is in the library alone. In the case of Lalau, the priest admits to "loving" the girl
himself, and that this intensifies his desire to separate the young lovers.
In each case, the relationship is seen as perverted. It is perverted less, I
would suggest, by any homosexual overtones to the relationship with

the "subjugated" Félix (after all, the only actual sexual encounter takes place in the deliberately distanced Varchi text) than by the priest's real and false "neutrality"—real in that his vow of celibacy makes him in a sense "neuter," false in that he is as motivated by sexual desire, power, and jealousy as the next man.

To understand this strange moment, it is worth thinking a little further about Machado's view of sex, a subject on which not much has been written. Perhaps this is not surprising, in that it does not lie on the surface of his novels and stories. It is not, as the episode in *Casa velha* shows, a question of prudery, or even, fundamentally, of "moral" censorship, though of course there were limits to what could be said overtly. Machado, in these matters as in others, enjoyed reflecting, and playing with his readers' assumed prudery. But his well-known opposition to Naturalism is not simply an objection to its explicitness: it has to do with the ideological framework in which sex is understood. In the case of Naturalism, influenced as it was by Darwinian evolutionism, sex is above all seen in the context of heredity, of the link between one generation and the next. It is hardly surprising, then, that homosexuality, which provides no such link, and is so difficult to account for from a Darwinist perspective, should have been difficult to accommodate. Machado was ideologically opposed to Naturalism, and to much of the social Darwinism of his time, for reasons that were partly personal, though they were none the worse for that: a mulatto and an epileptic, he no doubt found some of the theories about miscegenation and hereditary illness repulsive.[9] But the necessary conclusion follows: if sex was to rear its ugly (or beautiful) head in his fiction, it would do so in a non-Naturalist way, free of the preoccupation with heredity. What follows is an attempt to see what this might mean.

One episode that has been critically discussed in terms appropriate to its complexity and power to shock is that of Brás Cubas's encounter with Eugênia (chapters 29–34 of *Memórias póstumas de Brás Cubas*), the subject of sustained analysis in Roberto Schwarz' *Um mestre na periferia do capitalismo—Machado de Assis* (1990). What Schwarz finds, inevitably and rightly, is that sex and power are a great deal enmeshed: the sexual attraction between the two is real, but no sooner does it exist than the social situations of the rich young man and the pretty "daughter of the bushes" (i.e., the product of an illicit affair) assert their prerogatives. What interests me is that in this episode Machado, though careful not to separate two aspects of the relationship, goes out of his way to show that sex, desire, and physical urges play their part.

Thus, in the sarcastically playful chapter 31, concerning the black butterfly that flutters through Brás's brain, he thinks through the possible social connections that could exist between him and Eugênia, which are quite simple: she could choose either to be his mistress or not, and if she chose the first option, she would still be at his mercy, to be rejected when he tired of her—"não teria mais segura a vida" (her life would be no safer). All this is premised on his power, and the satisfaction he gets from it (to the point of being made insecure by the possibility that she might reject him). Only in the next chapter, having reached the end of this line of reasoning, does he discover that she is lame from birth ("coxa de nascença"). Put at its bluntest, this is a turnoff; it does not stop Brás from kissing her the next day, but it does prevent any ideas of keeping her as his mistress. It also moves him, as Schwarz has shown, to exercise his wit at her expense by punning on the two meanings of *coxa*, "lame" and "thigh": his supposed "intellectual" superiority to the two "superstitious" women toward the end of chapter 31 is replaced by vicious verbal sadism.

Schwarz is quite right to say that the dominant parameters here are social: "a lógica e o desfecho do episódio fixaram-se em função de inferioridades *sociais,* e a imperfeição *natural* superveniente não afeta a marcha da situação" (88) (the logic and the conclusion of the episode have been fixed in terms of *social* inferiority, and the natural imperfection that is added to this does not affect the course of events [2001: 61]). This is true, but it is perhaps not the whole truth. What Eugênia's lameness and Brás's reaction to it give is an extra "kick" to the situation—a cynical, and predominantly sexual, violence. What follows can only be pure speculation, but I wonder if Machado might not have taken up a suggestion from an essay by Schopenhauer, which he not only read, but was strongly affected by—the famous chapter 44 of *The World as Will and Representation,* "The Metaphysics of Sexual Love," one of the most remarkable discussions of sex written in the nineteenth century.[10] Machado cites it at least twice. The first time is in a short (and discreetly feminist) article on women's education published in 1881 (around the time *Memórias póstumas de Brás Cubas* was being written).[11] The second, more famous, citing of this essay was many years later, when Machado went out of his way to attack the determinist element in Schopenhauer's theory in the famous *crônica* about the death of Abílio.[12] In this chapter Schopenhauer argues, in terms that anticipate Darwin, that physical beauty and health bring sexual attraction, and so ensure the prolongation of the species (it is this premonitory echo of Darwin that attracted Machado's anger). The reverse is also the case, of course: "Further, we feel most strongly every want of proportion in the *skeleton*: for example, a stunted, dumpy, short-legged figure, and many such; *also a limping gait, where this is not the result of an external accident*" (Schopenhauer 1966: 543; the last emphasis is mine). It is an interesting coincidence: if it is true that it is more than that, it underlines what I think the text shows—that Machado has no wish to deny what he could hardly ignore, that sex as a purely physical, "specific" urge has its own importance, giving relationships an explosive dynamism.

This, I think, is the fundamental role of sex in Machado's work, at least in structural terms: it parallels and reflects causal patterns already in existence, giving them extra power and conviction. It can easily be seen that this avoids Naturalism's preoccupation with sex as a link in a causal chain. This is not to say, of course, that sex has no dynamic of its own. As Roberto Schwarz says of the affair between Brás Cubas, and Virgília,

> o desejo corre um ciclo à parte, com estações peculiares. Inquietação e saciedade, curiosidade e tédio, atração e repugnância, com momentos de plenitude pelo meio, estes são os pólos nada cristãos entre os quais se agita a fome amorosa, em sucessão rápida, uns alimentando e espicaçando os outros. (1990: 134)

> [desire follows a separate cycle, with its own seasons. Anxiety and satiety, curiosity and boredom, attraction and repugnance, with moments of plenitude along the way—these are the poles, with nothing Christian about them, between which love's appetite moves, in rapid and recurrent succession, each feeding the others and spurring them on.] (2001: 95)

One moment in this process has, to my knowledge, never been commented on. Chapter 102, "De repouso," is one of those short, witty, and sometimes enigmatic chapters that are a feature of *Memórias póstumas*. It occurs toward the end of the affair, and immediately after Brás has felt a certain jealousy of a diplomat who turns Virgília's head, only to be called back to his country ("suponhamos que a Dalmácia" [let's suppose Dalmatia]). But, Machado says, this man who was so happy that the other had gone, this same man did something some time later. But Brás refuses to explain what this something is, apart from saying that he is ashamed, that it was a "crass, vulgar" *(grosseiro)* act, and, it is implied in the opening of the next chapter that it made him come late to a tryst with Virgília. The clear implication is that it is something sexual: has he been unfaithful to his mistress? Picked up a prostitute? As the affair draws to its natural close, "the pale, sleepy nose of satiety" (chapter 97) pokes through.

Surprisingly for a writer supposed to be prudish, we are allowed a glimpse of Palha and Sofia's bedroom in *Quincas Borba.* In the knowingly playful chapter 71 of the novel, Sofia welcomes Palha's sexual approaches (they even enjoy a little sadomasochistic touch as he grips her by the chin and she moans *[gemeu]* that he is hurting her). Unlike a previous night when she found out that they owe Rubião a lot of money, and as a result "has a headache" (chapter 50), she has danced and flirted with Carlos Maria without her husband suspecting anything untoward, and feels exhilarated. Her "availability" is a complex mixture of fantasies of adultery, conjugal reality, and the real satisfaction she feels at their social success, so that the ironic, and supposedly "false," cause of the contrast between the two reactions ("é que os morros serão doentios, e as praias saudáveis" [the hills must be unhealthy, and the beaches healthy]) has, in a double bluff entirely typical of Machado, a dose of truth to it: she does feel happier in chic Flamengo, by the now fashionable (because supposedly healthy) beach, than on the "inferior" hills of Santa Teresa.

Of course, such power games reflect the hold that institutions—class, clientelism, marriage—have over individuals, and can, indeed, reveal them in something like "naked" truth. Another case is that of Marocas in the marvelous short story "Singular ocorrência" of 1883:[13] it is plain to me that when she picks up a man—any man—in the street while her protector/lover is absent with his family, she is motivated by a need for warmth and company that is both emotional and (why not?) sexual. In all these cases, sex is simply a natural, if obviously vital, part of the complex relations between people, though of course it may be, as in the case of Andrade in "Singular ocorrência," that stereotypes and notions of honor distort their view, something naturally more likely to happen with men than with women (I think in particular of the narrator and his companion, who try in vain to understand her action according to their own preconceptions).

The two novels, *Casa velha* and *Dom Casmurro*, which have priests and celibacy at their heart, are necessarily more complex, for the denial of sex does not, naturally, mean that it does not exist, but that its course is perverted. The influence of the church is also psychologically pervasive. It produces the repressions and feelings of guilt that are so characteristic of Bentinho, who has had "orgies of Latin" but is a virgin where women are concerned.[14] A vivid example involves homosexuality again: in chapter 94, Bento is so impressed by his friend Escobar's skill at mental arithmetic that he embraces him, only to be seen by the priests:

> Era no pátio; outros seminaristas notaram a nossa efusão; um padre que estava com eles não gostou.
> A modéstia—disse-nos—não consente esses gestos excessivos; podem estimar-se com moderação.

> [It was in the courtyard; other seminarists noticed our exuberance; a priest who was with them did not approve.
> "Modesty," he said to us, "does not permit such effusive gestures; your esteem can be expressed with moderation."]

It is obvious what crosses the priest's mind here, and *modesty,* a word with a sexual coloring, makes the point clear, though nothing of the sort seems to be on the friends' minds.

Can the same be said later, in chapter 118, when, the night before Escobar is drowned, Bento feels his friend's arms, strong and used to swimming?

> Apalpei-lhe os braços, como se fossem os de Sancha. Custa-me esta confissão, mas não posso suprimi-la; era jarretar a verdade. Nem só os apalpei com essa idéia, mas ainda senti outra coisa; achei-os mais grossos e fortes que os meus, e tive-lhes inveja; acresce que sabiam nadar.

> [I felt his arms, as if they were Sancha's. This is a painful confession to make, but I cannot suppress it; that would be to avoid the truth. Not only did I feel them with that idea in mind, but I felt something else as well; I thought they were thicker and stronger than mine, and I envied them; what's more, they knew how to swim.]

I admit to finding it difficult to know what is going on here, though it seems unlikely that homosexuality, in any explicit sense, has anything to do with it. Even though there may be hints that Bento is not as "manly" as he might be—Capitu was "more of a woman than I was a man" (chapter 31)—such limited evidence should not be taken too far; after all, José Dias treats Bento with "a mother's care," and one would hardly draw too many conclusions from that. Certainly, Bento feels Escobar's arms, and feels sexual attraction, which brings on a complex of emotions including envy and guilt, but the attraction he feels is toward Sancha, not Escobar, unless one argues for some kind of unconscious and repressed feelings toward his friend, guilt over which might contribute to his posthumous "discovery" of Escobar's adultery with Capitu. The truth is that there is not enough evidence in the text, or in anything else Machado wrote (pending further research, perhaps), to be certain.

This tentative discussion of the role of sex in some of Machado's fiction perhaps allows us to understand better the extraordinary moment with which I began, the allusion to homosexual rape in *Casa velha*. It is, as far as I am aware, the only unambiguous allusion to a homosexual act or relationship in Machado's work, and even then it is—quite naturally—only alluded to.[15] Its meaning in the story, of course, is plain enough, in spite of Magalhães Júnior's mystification (see note 6): it illustrates the "subjugation" (this strong word is used in the text) of Félix to the priest, and the perverting role of celibacy in the conduct of human affairs. Yet, it could be argued, Machado could have shown this without recourse to this shocking and arcane piece of knowledge. In part, I think, the reference to a sexual act gives a real punch to Machado's point, and makes it the exact parallel to the priest's "love" for Lalau. This scene is also, however, a neat illustration of Machado's view of sex, which has a large element in it of principled opposition to exclusively materialist, Naturalist views. Sexual relationships are always seen as a reflection of others, which they parallel without themselves playing a centrally causal role. What is transmitted here from one generation to the next is not, so to speak, genetic material, but a relationship of power and oppression.[16] What is perhaps ultimately most remarkable is that Machado felt that the intensity of that repression could only be conveyed by reference to such an extraordinary event.

Machado's ideological independence was a vital factor in allowing him, so to speak, a less impeded view of human sexuality, as well as of other things. It is also one reason his influence is difficult to assess: he has been admired, imitated, and even worshiped more than understood.

Small wonder that writers of the Modernist generation, such as Mário de Andrade and Graciliano Ramos—even Carlos Drummond de Andrade in his impetuous youth—should have been impolite to his memory.[17]

The tradition that Graciliano Ramos (our second author) inherited still carried a heavy charge of the Naturalism Machado so hated. Although, in his first novels—*Caetés* (1933), *São Bernardo* (1934), and *Angústia* (1936)—matters are always complicated by the role of the various narrators, the insistent comparisons of human beings to animals, and human subjection to physical and hereditary imperatives, creating an atmosphere from which it is nearly impossible to escape. The crucial change to his later work—primarily, *Vidas secas* (1938), *Infância* (1945), and the posthumous *Memórias do cárcere* (1953)—as vitally connected to the terrible experiences recounted in the last of these works, the one and a half years spent as a political prisoner under the Vargas regime, in 1936–37.[18] *Memórias do cárcere* is not an easy book to read: the dreadful scenes unflinchingly recounted, and the aggressive tone Graciliano uses, make it an actively unpleasant and somewhat monotonous, if also fascinating, book.[19] But the humiliation suffered by the author and his fellow inmates seems to have had the paradoxical effect of giving him a more dignified view of human beings: a comparison between Luís da Silva in *Angústia* and Fabiano in *Vidas secas* is one way of making the point. When people are oppressed by the law and the police, more abstract theories of human nature can be ignored. *Memórias do cárcere* is a journey through the depths of Brazilian society, all the harder, and all the more revealing, for the fact that it was forced. One of the frequent targets of Graciliano's anger is any view of that society as characterized by racial and class harmony.[20] Though Gilberto Freyre is not mentioned by name, it is the kind of "congraçamento," sexual and other, described and advocated in *Casa-grande e senzala (The Masters and the Slaves)* that he hates, because it easily leads to the ignoring of the reality of— often physical—violence: "a brandura dos nossos costumes, a índole pacífica nacional apregoada por sujeitos de má fé ou idiotas" (the softness of our customs, our peaceful national temperament, preached about by dishonest or idiotic people) (Ramos 1965, 2:63 [part III, chapter 12]).

The chapter that mainly concerns me (chapter 19 of part II of the book) appears at a significant moment. Having suffered the fearful conditions on board the ship, the *Manaus,* bringing the prisoners from the northeast to Rio de Janeiro, Graciliano is now in prison in the capital.

After a riot about their food, they are punished, but the punishment exceeds the time limit set by the authorities. This arbitrary exercise of power irritates Graciliano profoundly. As he says, at least in the *Manaus* they were animals: "Na verdade éramos bichos." But then comes the terrible irony—the human condition is worse: "Regressávamos à condição humana, impunham-nos um castigo—e percebíamos que ele era um embuste" (We returned to the human condition, they imposed a punishment on us—and then we realized it was a trick) (Ramos 1965, 1:282 [part 2, chapter 18]).[21] This leads to a revelation of the total subjection of the average Brazilian criminal, not to the law, but to the whims of the police, symbolized by the phrase "a ordem do chefe" (284), which can be used at any moment to rearrest a person. In the end, this turns society itself into a prison, to such a degree that the unfortunate person adopts the role imposed on him, and will even commit another crime to stay in jail: Graciliano has just heard of a case of a prisoner who committed murder apparently for this purpose. Somehow, however, he doubts his own conclusions; he can admit that the crime was deliberate, but the murder must have been a mistake: "Ladrões têm horror ao sangue" (285) (Thieves have a horror of blood), he says.

Chapter 19 begins with a noise of screaming: "Uma noite ouviram gritos desesperados" (287) (One night they heard desperate cries). The truth gradually emerges, though Graciliano's words, probably reflecting his own thoughts at the time, are at first of some nameless horror: "daí conseguirmos entrar naquele subterrâneo. É sujo e infame. De supetão divisamos hábitos inimagináveis, relações estranhas, uma esquisita moral, sensibilidade muito diversa da que revelam as pessoas comuns" (ibid.) (that's how we manage to get into this underworld. It is dirty and vile. Suddenly we make out the shapes of unimaginable habits, strange relationships, a weird morality, a sensibility very different from that displayed by ordinary people). Such is his sense of shock that, once out of prison, he says, "passamos involuntariamente a raspadeira neles" (ibid.) (we involuntarily erase them from our minds), and even have to check with others to make sure we are not adorning the truth (this insistence on the literal truth of what he is saying is a frequent occurence in *Memórias do cárcere*). But, by the third paragraph, he is explicit: "Os gritos daquela noite eram de um garoto violado" (288) (The shouts of that night were those of a raped lad); the shocked writer learns that this kind of thing is part of a network of corruption, which involves the prison guards as well as the older prisoners.

The most remarkable part of the chapter follows: as happens so often in this book in which Graciliano is repeatedly faced with unimagined but real events, he again asks why. First, of course, he realizes that "num meio onde só vivem machos" (ibid.) (in a milieu where there are only males), such a thing is at the very least likely. People who come to the prison system mature may be able to keep free of the "contagion," but (and here Graciliano unobtrusively joins those looking and judging) our disgust gradually wanes, and we feel pity, and in the end even that disappears:

> achamos aqueles invertidos pessoas vulgares submetidas a condições especiais: semelhantes aos que perderam em acidente olhos ou braços. Certo são desagradáveis quando neles predomina a linha curva, afetam ademanes femininos, têm voz dulçurosa, gestos lânguidos rebolando os quadris. Nem todos são assim, de ordinário não se distinguem por nenhum sinal particular. Nada que mereça desprezo. Como se iniciaram? Os angustiosos e inúteis apelos noturnos davam a resposta. (288–89)

> [we think these inverts are common people who have been subjected to unusual conditions: like someone who has lost an eye or a hand in an accident. Certainly they are disagreeable when the curved line predominates, they affect feminine gentures, have a sickly sweet voice, and languid gestures, swinging their hips. Not all of them are like that; usually they do not stand out by any particular sign. Nothing that deserves contempt. How did they become initiated? The anguished and useless cries in the night gave the answer.]

Along with the comforting realization that not all homosexuals are screaming queens, the assumption is that they are in some way incomplete, and the suggestion that no male would do such a thing unless he was "initiated." In the next paragraph, after recounting how young men can be forced by "pederastas calejados" (289) (hardened pederasts) to submit to their will, Ramos also says that the love affairs that result from this are characterized by "um calor desconhecido nas relações heterossexuais. De fato não é ternura: é desejo absorvente, furioso, quase a encher a vida com uma única necessidade" (ibid.) (an intensity unknown in heterosexual relationships. In fact, it is not tenderness; it is an absorbing desire, furious, almost filling life with a single need). One is reminded of Amaro's consuming passion in *Bom-crioulo.* Maybe, Graciliano thinks, the crime in the previous chapter was committed by someone desperate to stay with his *companheiro:* "Pelo menos é fácil admitirmos que um sentimento obsessor, vizinho da monomania, leve alguém a lesar os seus próprios interesses" (ibid.) (At least it is easy for us to admit that an obsessive feeling, close to monomania, might make someone harm his own interests).

But the end of the chapter is the most remarkable moment, and reveals Graciliano's true stature as a writer and a human being. The entire passage is worth quoting:

> As minhas conclusões eram na verdade incompletas e movediças. Faltava-me examinar aqueles homens, buscar transpor as barreiras que me separavam deles, vencer este nojo exagerado, sondar-lhes o íntimo, achar lá dentro coisa superior às combinações frias da inteligência. Provisoriamente, segurava-me a estas. Por que desprezá-las ou condená-las? Existem—e é o suficiente para serem aceitos. Aquela explosão tumultuária é um fato. Estupidez pretender eliminar os fatos. A nossa obrigação é analisá-los, ver se são intrínsecos à natureza humana ou superfetações. Preliminarmente lançamos opróbrio àqueles indivíduos. Por quê? Porque somos diferentes deles. Seremos diferentes, ou tornamo-nos diferentes? Além de tudo ignoramos o que eles têm no interior. Divergimos nos hábitos, nas maneiras, e propendemos a valorizar isto em demasia. Não lhes percebemos as qualidades, ninguém nos diz até que ponto se distanciam ou se aproximam de nós. Quando muito, chegamos a divisá-los através de obras de arte. É pouco: seria bom vê-los de perto sem máscaras.
>
> Penso assim, tento compreendê-los—e não consigo reprimir o nojo que me inspiram, forte demais. Isto me deixa apreensivo. Será um nojo natural ou imposto? Quem sabe se ele não foi criado artificialmente, com o fim de preservar o homem social, obrigá-lo a fugir de si mesmo? (290)

[My conclusions, in truth, were incomplete and shifting. I would need to examine those men, try to cross the barriers that separated me from them, overcome this exaggerated disgust, explore their intimate selves, and find there something superior to the cold constructions of the intelligence. Provisionally, these were the ones I held on to. Why should one despise them or condemn them? They exist—that is enough for them to be accepted. That confused explosion is a fact. How stupid to want to get rid of facts. Our duty is to analyze them, to see if they are intrinsic to nature or excrescences. As a preliminary, we disapprove of these people. Why? Because we are different from them. Are we different, or have we become different? Apart from anything else, we do not know what goes on inside them. We diverge in our habits, our manners, and our propensity is to value such things too much. We cannot see their qualities, and nobody can tell us how close or how distant we are from them. At the outside, we get a glimpse of them through works of art. It is not enough: it would be good to see them close up, without masks.

I think this way, I try to understand them—and I cannot suppress the disgust they inspire in me. This makes me apprehensive. Is the disgust natural or imposed? Who knows if it was not created artificially, with the aim of preserving the social man, and to force him to flee from himself?]

The crucial move, of course, is the one that makes Graciliano look at himself, and question his own motives, his status as a social animal: might not his disgust be as much a social product as their homosexuality?

There are other scenes involving homosexuality in *Memórias do cárcere*: the punishment of the informer at the hands of the fearsome Moleque Quatro, who, having first condemned him to death, "commutes" his sentence to "trinta enrabações" (307) (thirty buggerings); and the fat, beardless mulatto, with his "olhos mansos" and "beiços flácidos" (meek eyes and flaccid lips), who tries to help Graciliano eat in chapter 20 of the third part (2: 98–101), and who first of all produces disgust, then the realization that "na torpeza nauseante havia alguma coisa muito pura" (101) (in the nauseous vileness there was something very pure). But the essential point seems to be made here: homosexuality is one of the catalysts that produced the change of heart, and resultant change of ideology, which in turn produced his later work, including, of course, the *Memórias do cárcere* themselves.

It is worth emphasizing that it is only one factor: scarcely less moving and significant is the scene in which he encounters the young Francisco Chermont, the son of a senator, who has been arbitrarily arrested and sent to the infamous Colônia Correcional on Ilha Grande where Graciliano himself goes in the third part of *Memórias do cárcere*. At the beginning of chapter 22 (1: 303–4), he simply fails to recognize him, and thinks he is "a sordid vagabond." Only when Chermont speaks does his polished language make the author realize that he is not from the favelas.

This is another vivid example of the plasticity of human nature under stress, and of the shocked inability of the author to keep track of it, which forces him to change his view of that "nature" and of his own ability to understand it and portray it in literary or any other terms. As he says at the beginning of chapter 19: "À força de repetições, chegáva-mos a admiti-las, pelo menos como possíveis à natureza humana, con-tingente e vária, capaz de tudo" (287) (by force of repetition, we came round to admitting these things as possible to a human nature that is contingent and variable, capable of everything).

At bottom, I think, this is what the change in Graciliano meant. I have used the word *catalyst*—always useful when one does not want to commit oneself about the exact causal nature of a change—nevertheless seems appropriate. It may even be that Graciliano's literary develop-ment itself had something inevitable about it: the sheer complexity of the interwoven patterns of psychological and social causation in *Angús-tia* approach the impossible, and the doubts, approaching disgust, he expresses about the book in *Memórias do cárcere* may well have causes beyond the author's obsessive self-doubt.[22] But there is no doubt in my mind that Graciliano's terrible experiences in jail—forced as he was to undergo the kind of "experiment" and research into the existences of other social groups and classes that the good Naturalist was supposed to undertake—at the very least accelerated and radicalized that process.

What conclusions can be drawn from these analyses of a few moments in the works of two great writers? The most basic one, I think, concerns their attitude to reality and to realism. First of all, they force us to make a sharp distinction between realism and Naturalism: in this context, sex turns out to be a kind of litmus test. In the social Darwinist world of Naturalism, sexual acts are part of a causal, hereditary chain, linking one generation to the next, often with disastrous results—transmitting disease, madness, alcoholism, and mixing racial traits in dangerous ways. Machado's complete, principled rejection of these theories was not, of course, a rejection of realism: it simply gave his realism greater depth and acuity. Graciliano's case is rather different, for in his earlier works, most thoroughly in *Angústia,* he takes these causal theories, extended into the unconscious mind through the use of Freudian imagery, al-most to their logical conclusion. Already dissatisfied with the result, and then forced to witness things not imagined in the Naturalist universe, he also had to change the way he wrote: not so much, again, in an anti-realist direction, but toward a different kind of realism, with something of Machado's depth and acuity. *Vidas secas* proves the point: the novel began as a short story about the death of the dog Baléia, which gradually accreted further episodes in a way that completely negates the kind of causal construction so carefully put together in *Angústia*.[23] It leads, finally, to the insistent realism of *Memórias do cárcere*, the continual assault on the reader's assumptions, and indeed on the writer's, but the insistence that this *did* happen.

If sex in general is a litmus test, homosexuality turns out to be an even more indicative one. This may well be in part because it posed a real problem for the social Darwinist, and for Darwinism in general— as, in fact, it still does—because homosexual acts take no part in the hereditary chain, whether or not they are the result of it. What do they mean, then? For many people, obviously, nothing or worse than nothing: at best, as in José Lins do Rego's *Menino de engenho*, for instance, a step on the road to normality for a young man with problems inherited from his father, who murdered his mother. In Machado, it seems to me, the "Varchi" episode in *Casa velha* places sex in an entirely different causal chain: that of the imposition of power through rape, and perhaps even the transmission of power, through the way in which Félix is forced to obey the dictates of the patriarchal family. In *Memórias do cárcere*, homosexuality again appears in the form of rape, and again power is at the heart of the matter: the prison system not only isolates the male of the species, it creates a ladder of power involving the warders, the older convicts, and the younger, which also—and this is the important point— continues into society at large. Graciliano refuses to segregate these two worlds and pretend that one has little or nothing to do with the other. In the end, the continuum involves him as well, and so affects his position as observer, changing his view of literary objectivity.

Do these investigations have anything to tell us about the course of Brazilian literary history, or, more generally, the public profile of homosexuality in Brazil? In her stimulating and influential book *Tal Brasil, qual romance?* Flora Süssekind argues against what she sees as a harmful, recurrent tradition in Brazilian fiction, one that in effect argues for a simple, often naive realism, and whose origins she identifies in Naturalism: its three most salient moments, according to her, are the Naturalist movement itself in the late nineteenth century; the realist, regionalist novel of the 1930s most frequently associated with the northeast and with such writers as José Lins do Rego and Jorge Amado; and the "romance-reportagem" of the 1970s, itself influenced by American "faction" writers such as Truman Capote.[24] Her argument has a great deal to recommend it: a kind of naive realism does characterize all these movements, which have all had considerable success with the public. It might be arguable that a kind of unholy alliance between such Naturalist ideas and journalism has recurrently infected Brazilian literature,[25] and has produced a view of reality superficially convincing, but in fact very ideologically skewed. Machado and Graciliano are great writers in part because they saw the dangers of this pact, though in rather different ways—Machado a priori, so to speak, in all probability because of his own racial origins and epilepsy, and Graciliano after painful experience, both literary and actual. It follows, given the dominance of the opposing trend—and perhaps because theirs is a difficult road—that their influence on other writers has been small or, more accurately, superficial, or so deep and diffuse as to be undetectable.

What do these writers tell us about the public profile of homosexuality in Brazil? Rather little, I suspect. Especially in Machado's case, I think it is probably impossible, from the evidence I have adduced, to tell what he thought on the subject. In Graciliano's case, do his painfully changed views, and their remarkable openness, reflect anything wider? Probably. Freyre's rather different openness is another case in point, Drummond's yet another. But the openness remains circumscribed to an intensely personal experience, in a very strange and abnormal environment. Perhaps, in a sense, this is still prehistory; what happens after the 1960s is, thankfully, a different story.

Notes

1. Perhaps the best example of this critical tendency is Marta Peixoto's *Passionate Fictions* (1994).

2. The best description I have read of Caetano's famous challenge to his student audience ("Vocês não estão entendendo nada, nada") at the third Festival Internacional da Canção is in Zuenir Ventura's *1968: o ano que não terminou*, (1988), 201–8.

3. See Qorpo-Santo (1980). For the facts of its original publication, see the introductory material by the editor, Guilhermino César. I am grateful to Robert Howes for sending me a copy of this text.

4. For this and other information on *Bom-crioulo*, I am grateful to Robert Howes, who let me see an unpublished article on the novel, the fruit of remarkable research on its ideological and journalistic background.

5. A third indisputably great writer, the poet Carlos Drummond de Andrade, also has a poem that is fundamentally about homosexuality, and centers on a (mythical) scene of homosexual rape, that of Ganymede. The poem, "Rapto," coincides with the poet's extraordinary outpouring of painful and ecstatic love poems to

a woman much younger than he, in the early 1950s: in fact, it precedes what to me is the most wonderful of these poems, "Campo de flores." Its last four lines serve as epigraph to this essay.

6. Coherent with his traditional view of the author's respectability, Raymundo Magalhães Júnior is unable to see why Machado should have added half a page to the narrative, without contributing to its development (Magalhães 1971: 82). See also Gledson (1986: 31–33).

7. Machado had a Trieste edition of Varchi, of 1858–59, in his library. See Massa (1961: 208). I consulted an edition printed in Milan (Presso l'Ufficio Generale di Commissioni ed Annunzi, nd).

8. The scene as Varchi recounts it is still shocking today, and it is small wonder that he gives it a long preamble, wondering if he should recount this "crudelíssima e ignominiosíssima" event. The bishop was held down by Farnese's men, for he himself could hardly stand up, being ill with syphilis *(malfranzese)*. The story reached the Lutherans in Germany, who said that "this was a new way of martyring the saints."

9. One can only imagine with what emotions Machado must have read the characterizations of mulattos and epileptics as degenerate and unbalanced in Euclides da Cunha's *Os sertões*. It did not stop him voting for Euclides for membership in the Academia Brasileira de Letras.

10. Schopenhauer's influence on Machado is well known, and Eugênio Gomes's discussion of it in his short essay "Schopenhauer e Machado de Assis," in *Machado de Assis* (1958: 91–98), and in some comments in *O enigma de Capitu* (1967: 140–41), is the most perceptive I have read. I have the strong impression, however, that more work remains to be done.

11. *"Cherchez la femme"* is a short item, also published in *A Estação*, on August 15, 1881, that welcomes the setting up of courses for women at the Liceu de Belas Artes. Machado says, "e se devemos aceitar a original teoria de um filósofo, ela [a mulher] é quem transmite a porção intelectual do homem" (and if we should accept the original theory of a philosopher, it is she who is the transmitter of the intellectual part of man). He is certainly citing Schopenhauer, and probably from this essay, which can be found in *The World as Will and Representation* (1966, 2: 531–72; the relevant quotation is: "But the qualities of *intellect* do have an influence here, because they are inherited from the mother" [545]).

12. The column about Abílio, a child abandoned to an awful death by negligent parents, and often known as "O autor de si mesmo" (His own progenitor), was published on June 16, 1895: see Machado (1962, 3: 655–57). Here Machado gives chapter and verse from *The World as Will and Representation*. No doubt it was the more shocking to Machado in that Schopenhauer's philosophy is not generally determinist: I suspect that that explains the virulence of his attack on a philosopher for whom he had great respect. It is curious that this chapter has an appendix (560–67) containing an interesting, and for the period remarkably sympathetic, discussion of homosexuality, which, as Bryan Magee (1983: 322–25) argues in his excellent book on the philosopher, leads one to believe that Schopenhauer knew whereof he spoke.

13. This argument is given at somewhat greater length in the introduction to my edition of Machado's short stories, *Contos—uma antologia* (1998: 47–49).

14. In *The Deceptive Realism of Machado de Assis* (Gledson 1984: 87–88), I argued that chapter 58 is a reasonably covert, but also plain, description of masturbation,

seen from the point of view of someone whose "ignorance and fear in sexual matters" is such that he hardly knows what is happening.

15. There is a possible exception, the curious late story "Pílades e Orestes," first published in 1903, and later collected in *Relíquias de casa velha* (1906), which tells of two inseparable friends, Quintanilha and Gonçalves, so close as to be called by one lady "casadinhos de fresco" (just married). But, however hard one tries to read the story as that of a gay relationship, the text seems almost deliberately constructed to prevent such a reading: they end up falling for the same girl, a cousin of Quintanilha, the richer and more emotional of the two, who is the first to fall for her, but who gives her up to his friend—Machado then summarily bumps him off with a stray bullet during the 1893 naval revolt. Although there is no doubt that it is a better and more suggestive story, "Pílades e Orestes" reminds me of some of Machado's earlier pieces dealing with the vicissitudes of male friendship, which have, as far as I can see, no hint of sexual overtones—"Almas agradecidas," for instance, published in the *Jornal das Famílias* in 1871. (It can be found in the Jackson edition of the *Obras completas*, vol. 11 *[Histórias românticas]*, 91–130.)

16. This is perhaps the appropriate moment to say that, in spite of my repeated use of the idea of power in this essay, I mean no specific reference to the work of Michel Foucault in such influential works as *The History of Sexuality*, vol. 1, *An Introduction* (1981). Stimulating and suggestive as his work is, his view of power as omnipresent and all-embracing (see, e.g., pp. 92–102) does not easily fit an analysis that attempts, however uncertainly, to fit literary works into their specific social, literary, and ideological contexts.

17. See Mário de Andrade (1967: 87–93), Graciliano Ramos (1967), and Carlos Drummond de Andrade (1925). It is fair to add that all these writers deplore Machado's influence, rather than his writings themselves. Drummond, one of his most fervent and genuine admirers in later life, was in fact thoroughly ashamed of his youthful aggressiveness, and never allowed the article to be republished.

18. The classic treatment of the development of Graciliano's art from fiction to autobiographical works is Antonio Candido, "Ficção e confissão," printed as the introduction to *Caetés* (1965).

19. In another article on Graciliano, "Os bichos do subterrâneo" Candido (1971: 115) says that it is an uneven book ("O livro é desigual"), though with magnificent passages. This is perhaps a fair assessment: it should be remembered that Graciliano did not live to see it through publication.

20. One result of Graciliano's refusal to conform to this common wisdom is the almost aggressive way he has in *Memórias do cárcere* of describing people according to their racial features (as mulattos, *caboclos*, etc.).

21. Unless otherwise stated, all subsequent quotations are from this first volume.

22. I argued this point in some detail in an article published some time ago, but whose conclusions I still agree with: "Civil servants as narrators: *O amanuense Belmiro* and *Angústia*" (1981). I argued that *Angústia* is so controlled as a causal structure, in everything from Luís da Silva's social background to his psychological formation, that his responsibility for the murder of Julião Tavares is questionable. It is a very tight determinism, which leaves very little, if anything, to chance or free will.

23. João Condé's "arquivos implacáveis," an interview in which Graciliano gave him detailed information about the construction of *Vidas secas*, are quoted in Affonso Romano de Sant'anna, *Análise estrutural de romances brasileiros* (1973: 153–79).

24. "Repete-se a estética naturalista, mas sob a forma do *caso clínico*, na virada do século: do *ciclo*, em Trinta; do *flagrante*, na década de Setenta" (The late-nineteenth-century naturalist aesthetic repeats itself under the guise of a "clinical case" from the "cycle" in the 1930s to the "flagrant" in the 1970s) (Süssekind 1984: 88).

25. This idea is the subject of a famous and stimulating interview/article by Davi Arrigucci Jr.: "Jornal, realismo, alegoria: o romance brasileiro recente" (1979).

Works Cited

Andrade, Carlos Drummond de. 1925. "Sobre a tradição em literatura." *A Revista* 1 (July): 32–33.

———. 1967. *Obra completa*. Rio de Janeiro: Aguilar.

Andrade, Mário de. 1967. "Machado de Assis (1939)." In *Aspectos da literatura brasileira*. São Paulo: Martins. 87–105.

Arrigucci, Davi, Jr. 1979. "Jornal, realismo, alegoria: o romance brasileiro recente." In *Achados e perdidos: ensaios de crítica*. São Paulo: Polis. 79–115.

Assis, Machado de. 1938. *Relíquias de casa velha*. Rio de Janeiro: W. M. Jackson.

———. 1962. *Obra completa*. Rio de Janeiro: Aguilar.

———. 1998. *Contos—uma antologia*. Ed. and introd. John Gledson. São Paulo: Companhia das Letras.

Caminha, Adolfo. 1966. *Bom-crioulo*. Introd. and notes M. Cavalcanti Proença. Rio de Janeiro: Edições de Ouro.

———. 1982. *Bom-Crioulo: The Black Man and the Cabin Boy*. Trans. E. A. Lacey. San Francisco: Gay Sunshine Press.

Candido, Antonio. 1965. Introduction. *Caetés*. São Paulo: Martins. 11–71.

———. 1971. "Os bichos do subterrâneo." In *Tese e antítese*. São Paulo: Editora Nacional. 95–118.

Cunha, Euclides da. 1985. *Os sertões*. São Paulo: Brasiliense.

Foucault, Michel. 1981. *The History of Sexuality*. Vol. 1, *An Introduction*. Trans. Robert Hurley. Harmondsworth, England: Penguin.

Freyre, Gilberto. 1985. *Casa-grande e senzala*. Caracas: Ayacucho.

Fry, Peter. 1982. "Léonie, Pombinha, Amaro e Aleixo: prostituição, homossexualidade e raças em dois romances brasileiros." In *Caminhos cruzados: linguagem, antropologia e ciências naturais*. São Paulo: Brasiliense. 35–51.

Gledson, John. 1981. "Civil servants as narrators: *O amanuense Belmiro* and *Angústia*." In *Before the Boom: Four Essays on Latin American Fiction before 1940*, ed. Steven Boldy. Liverpool: University of Liverpool Centre for Latin American Studies. 1–17.

———. 1984. *The Deceptive Realism of Machado de Assis*. Liverpool: F. Cairns.

———. 1986. *Machado de Assis: Ficção e História*. Rio de Janeiro: Paz e Terra.

Gomes, Eugênio. 1958. *Machado de Assis*. Rio de Janeiro: Livraria São José.

———. 1967. *O enigma de Capitu*. Rio de Janeiro: José Olympio.

Magalhães Júnior, Raymundo. 1971. *Vida e obra de Machado de Assis*. Rio de Janeiro: Civilização Brasileira.

Magee, Bryan. 1983. *The Philosophy of Schopenhauer*. Oxford: Clarendon Press.

Massa, Jean-Michel. 1961. "La Bibliothèque de Machado de Assis." *Revista do Livro* 21–22 (March–June): 195–238.

Peixoto, Marta. 1994. *Passionate Fictions: Gender, Narrative, and Violence in Clarice Lispector.* Minneapolis: University of Minnesota Press.

Qorpo-Santo, José Joaquim de Campos Leão. 1980. *Teatro completo.* Ed. Guilhermino César. Rio de Janeiro: Ministério de Educação e Cultura/Serviço Nacional de Teatro.

Ramos, Graciliano. 1965. *Memórias do cárcere.* São Paulo: Martins.

———. 1967. "Os amigos de Machado de Assis." In *Linhas tortas.* São Paulo: Martins. 109–11.

Sant'anna, Affonso Romano. 1973. *Análise estrutural de romances brasileiros.* Petrópolis: Vozes.

Schopenhauer, Arthur. 1966. *The World as Will and Representation.* Trans. E. F. J. Payne. New York: Dover Publications.

Schwarz, Roberto. 1990. *Um mestre na periferia do capitalismo—Machado de Assis.* Rio de Janeiro: Duas Cidades.

———. 2001. *A Master on the Periphery of Capitalism: Machado de Assis.* Trans. and introd. John Gledson. Durham, N.C.: Duke University Press.

Süssekind, Flora. 1984. *Tal Brasil, qual romance?* Rio de Janeiro: Achiamé.

Ventura, Zuenir. 1988. *1968: o que ano que não terminou.* Rio de Janeiro: Nova Fronteira.

CHAPTER THREE

Fernando Pessoa's Gay Heteronym?

Richard Zenith

The notion that Pessoa was probably a repressed homosexual and that this fact shaped his work is not new: João Gaspar Simões said as much in the biography he published in 1950.[1] But this was one of the biographer's points of view that tended to be scorned, and since then little more on the topic has been written in Portugal, or elsewhere. Robert Bréchon, in his recent biography, instead of exploring the theme further, prefers to skirt it, though he also recognizes a "latent homosexuality" as a "component of [Pessoa's] personality" (306). Homosexual and homoerotic elements permeate Pessoa's work to a far greater extent than has generally been noticed, appearing explicitly in poetry written under his own name and informing his almost obsessive use of the literary alter egos he called heteronyms. There were, among all the dozens of voices and masks, not only several bisexuals, but one that was clearly homosexual.

For readers not so familiar with Portugal's greatest Modernist writer, the notion of heteronymy needs explaining, and even those who know his work and have read Michael Hamburger's excellent discussion of it in *The Truth of Poetry* may not realize how vast a system it is. Pessoa (1888–1935) contended that the many names under which he wrote prose and poetry were not mere pseudonyms, for it was not just the names that were false.[2] They belonged to invented others, to fictional writers with points of view and literary styles that were different from Pessoa's. He dubbed them "heteronyms," and elaborated individual biographies, personalities, and physical descriptions for the most important ones.

The three main poetic heteronyms—Alberto Caeiro, Ricardo Reis, and Álvaro de Campos—came into existence around 1914, but Pessoa began to invent literary playmates in his early childhood. He spent eight and a half of his formative years in the British-governed town of Durban, South Africa, where he created Alexander Search and Charles Robert Anon, his two most important English heteronyms, who were joined several years later (c. 1907) by a French heteronym: Jean Seul. The last heteronym invented by Pessoa may have been the Baron of Teive, a suicidal alter ego that probably came into existence in 1928. Teresa Rita Lopes published a famous list of seventy-two names under which Pessoa wrote (1:167–69), but it is by no means exhaustive. There is, for example, a Dr. Florêncio Gomes, author of a fragmentary *Tratado de doenças mentais* (Treatise on mental diseases) (catalog #27^{9}E^2/6, in the Pessoa archives, National Library of Lisbon) and a Professor Jones, author of an "Essay on Poetry, Written for the Edification and Instruction of Would-be Poets" (catalog #14^6/72).

The following paragraphs survey some of the homosexual elements found in the poetry and prose signed by Pessoa himself or attributed to his heteronyms, but there is still a vast, fascinating area of research that awaits exploration: homosexuality as a motivating factor for the very origin and concept of Pessoa's heteronymy. Pessoa offers a clue on this subject when he writes, "The multiplication of the I is a frequent phenomenon in cases of masturbation" (Lopes 2:477), because masturbation—which is "sexual inversion" in the most literal sense, that is, monosexuality—is the only kind of sex that remains for repressed homosexuals, unless they take the (for them) unnatural, heterosexual route.

Fernando Pessoa's sexuality, whatever it was, was willfully, deliberately sublimated, according to his own words. In his letter of November 18, 1930, to Gaspar Simões (*Cartas*, 66), Pessoa wrote: "There is in all of us, however little we may be inclined toward obscenity, a certain element of this order, which obviously varies in degree from person to person. Since these elements, no matter how small, will in some way be a hindrance to superior mental processes, I decided to eliminate them twice, by the simple expedient of expressing them intensely."[3] In the context of his letter, the word *obscenity* refers to nothing more shocking than sexual desire, or, if we want to try to put it "obscenely," sexual lust. Pessoa's word choice is itself highly significant, as Gaspar Simões noted (448).

The two instances of "elimination" were, according to Pessoa's letter, his two longest poems in English—the heterosexual "Epithalamium" and the homosexual "Antinoüs"—which means that we have, in the author's own words to his future biographer, a forthright declaration of bisexuality, or of a bisexual drive. "Epithalamium," written in 1913 and published by Pessoa in 1921, is daringly graphic, but, far from being erotic, it almost seems that the author was striving for a comic effect.[4] We read, for example, in the fourteenth stanza:

> The bridegroom aches for the end of this and lusts
> To know those paps in sucking gusts,
> To put his first hand on that belly's hair
> And feel for the lipped lair,
> The fortress made but to be taken, for which
> He feels the battering ram grow large and itch.

"Antinoüs" is less sexually explicit but far more convincing as a poem of love and sexual desire. It portrays the emperor Hadrian grieving next to the dead body of Antinoüs, stretched out naked on a couch. At one point Hadrian recalls the sad circumstances of his young lover's death by drowning, in the Nile River, and the poem's narrator reports (vv. 85–94):

> Even as he thinks, the lust that is no more
> Than a memory of lust revives and takes
> His senses by the hand, his felt flesh wakes,
> And all becomes again what'twas before.
> The dead body on the bed starts up and lives
> And comes to lie with him, close, closer, and
> A creeping love-wise and invisible hand
> At every body-entrance to his lust
> Whispers caresses which flit off yet just
> Remain enough to bleed his last nerve's strand . . .

And the emperor proceeds to run his lips all over the cold corpse without, however, tasting death, for "it seems both are dead or living both / And love is still the presence and the mover."

In Pessoa's vast output of poetry written in English, "Antinoüs" ranks as one of his finest works, and though it did not have the technical brilliance found at certain points in the 35 Sonnets, Pessoa obviously cared for it a great deal, having published it twice, in 1918 and, with extensive revisions, in 1921.

Pessoa wrote a few other, much shorter homosexual poems in English during the 1910s, including "Le Mignon" (*Poesia Inglesa II*, 88–89), in which Hadrian addresses a still-living Antinoüs, saying, "let us love as maid and boy are said / To love."[5] Several poems wistfully recall Bathyllus, the young page to whom Anacreon (c. 570–485 B.C.) addressed some adoring odes, and these are no longer set in antiquity. The narrator (Pessoa? Some heteronym?) belongs to the twentieth century, where he does not seem happy to be:

> My heart is sad. There is no reason for
> My sadness save my life and my sense of it,
> There is a mighty opening of the door
> That parts my heart from all the things that love it.

Several stanzas later, the narrator does offer a reason for his sadness:

> Ah, to have been Anacreon and to have had
> That boy to love, nor think it ill to love him.

These verses are from a poem dated September 28, 1915 (*Poesia inglesa II*, 74–75). In a poem written five days earlier (73–74), we read:

> What have they done with thee? Where is that Greece
> That bore thy loveliness?
> . . . .
> Love, my lost love, that never wert my love
> Out of Anacreon's verse thou risest fair
> And thy sweet presence is now interwove
> With my modernity's despair.

The longings and frustrations expressed in the Bathyllus poems are rather abstract, and it is possible that the narrator is exalting pederasty in mere homage to the Greek world, understood as a more serene time and place, unafflicted by "modernity's despair." But if the theme was literary, it persisted and seemed to hit deeper, taking on a personal hue. In a fragmentary, unpublished poem from 1920, Pessoa transposes Antinoüs to the present, or rather, he imagines a present-day homosexual love transported to the more congenial world of Antinoüs:[6]

> The boy Antinoüs whom Hadrian kissed
> I would that thou hadst been, and that I were
> The imperial master [unfinished line]
> But that thou hadst the fate to there
> [unfinished line] most fair

Rather than this closed age of many minds
And close-packed pressure of opinions many,
The [breaks off here]

Antinoüs, in this fragment, is no longer a third-person historical tale but an anguished first-person dream of acceptance. The narrator, with no mask but English (an essentially literary language for Pessoa) and the fact that he is writing poetry, confesses his frustration at having to hide his homosexual love in the "closed age" he happened to be born into. Unlike any of the other poems discussed so far, these fragmentary verses are addressed to a specific, twentieth-century male with whom the narrator is clearly in love.

Pessoa wrote "Antinoüs" in 1915, the same year he produced his longest poem ever, the "Ode Marítima" (Maritime ode) of Álvaro de Campos.[7] This poem has often been cited as evidence of Pessoa's homosexual side, because of passages expressing a masochistic desire to be bodily possessed by men. We have, for example:

To be in my passive body the Everywoman
Who has been raped, killed, cut and mauled by pirates!
To be in my subjugated flesh the woman they have to have!
And to feel all this—all at once—running down my spine!

O my hairy and gruff heroes of adventure and crime!
My seafaring brutes, husbands of my imagination!
(Pessoa, *Maritime Ode*, 32)

And further on:

To always take the gloriously submissive part
In bloody deeds and interminable sensualities!
Fall on me like massive walls,
O barbarians of the ancient sea!
Rip me and wound me!
Streak my body with blood
From east to west!
Kiss with cutlasses, whips and rage
My blissful carnal fear of belonging to you,
My masochistic yearning to submit to your fury,
(37)

Of course, all this desire to be physically, sexually possessed by men may have been, and in a certain way surely was, feigned, but imagination in literature, to be effective, is usually based on something real—if not experience, which may be first- or secondhand, then at least a real feeling, or desire, however fleeting.

Whatever we may conclude about the *Maritime Ode,* the naval engineer was, according to the script Pessoa gave him, a practicing bisexual. In "Passagem das Horas" (Time's passage), Álvaro de Campos recalls not only a Mary with whom he read Robert Burns's poetry, but a "Freddie, whom I called Baby, because you were blond, fair, and I loved you" (*Fernando Pessoa & Co.,* 148). And in one of his sonnets Campos mentions a boy who afforded him "many hours of joy" (144).[8] It should be said, however, that Campos, as he grows older with his creator, does not wax nostalgic over any male lovers from his youth; he recalls, instead, several women who seem not to have been actual lovers but whom he apparently once loved, or could have loved.

Another of the three major heteronyms, Ricardo Reis, was likewise bisexual, and it was Álvaro de Campos, always a bit ahead of his time, who "outed" him. In a typed text first published by Teresa Rita Lopes (Lopes 2:475), Campos points out that the female lovers whom Ricardo Reis addresses in his odes—Chloe, Lydia, Neaera—were mere abstractions, with "only enough reality to be regarded as existing," and he goes on to prove, by observing an easily missed enclitic pronoun, the masculine *o* attached to the end of a verb, that the beloved flower extolled by Reis in an ode published in 1924 is not his ethereal Chloe or Lydia but a young man.[9] Campos accuses Reis of having used his difficult syntax as a "veil of modesty," that is, as a means to hide his sexuality, and we must wonder: Who did Reis get the idea from, if not from his creator?

Reis, by the way, did not actually need to be "outed" by his fellow heteronym, for in the second stanza of a lesser-known ode, he reveals his other side (*Fernando Pessoa & Co.,* 114):

> I was never one who in love or in friendship
> Preferred one sex over the other.[10]

And in the penultimate stanza of the same poem:

> The gods who gave us this path of love
> To which we have given the name beauty
> Did not place it only in women

Álvaro de Campos had a rather different feeling about the poems that constitute Alberto Caeiro's *O Pastor Amoroso* (The shepherd in love). They were, he wrote, "among the world's great love poems, for they are love poems by virtue of being about love and not by virtue of being poems. The poet loved because he loved, and not because love exists" (Campos 69). But Campos calls Caeiro's one and only love a "futile interlude," because it distracted him from his vocation as Nature's poet, and in another passage he expresses his disdain for the beloved in question whom he never met and never wants to meet, hoping instead that her name will always remain anonymous (95). No need to worry about that. Caeiro's beloved was even more impalpable than Reis's Lydia and Chloe, who at least had names. Caeiro's love poems describe a euphoric feeling of being in love, but nothing concrete about the woman (except for a passing mention of her blond hair) or their involvement, if there ever was any. "Love is a company," reads the first verse of one of the poems (*Obra Poética,* 229), and "love" here means only the feeling of love.

Most of the eight poems from *O Pastor Amoroso* were written in 1929–30, which is also when Pessoa, after an apparent hiatus during the 1920s, returned with a vengeance to the *Livro do desassossego (The Book of Disquiet),* whose new and prolific fictional author, Bernardo Soares, confesses that he, like the shepherd, was in love just once.[11] More accurately, he reports that "circumstances mischievously led me to suppose that I loved and to verify that the other person truly loved me" (202). This "other person" could very well refer to Ophelia Queiroz, because she truly loved Pessoa, who probably at one time thought he loved her.[12] But what is odd in this rather long passage describing Bernardo Soares's feeling of tedium during the whole nonaffair (for it quickly aborts) is that he scrupulously avoids mentioning the sex of the would-be paramour. Did Pessoa want us to wonder if his semi-heteronym, like two of the poetic heteronyms, was also sexually ambiguous?

Elsewhere in *The Book of Disquiet,* the assistant bookkeeper tells of his feeling of camaraderie with waiters, barbers, and delivery boys, and of his friendly affection for the "bons rapazes" (good guys) he sometimes talks to or takes meals with (Soares 374, for example).[13] These details would normally mean nothing, but in the landscape of a soul that had little social life and no love life they stand out. Soares often mentions women, or even addresses them, but they are all—with one exception—of the idealized, sexless variety, with the title of a passage from *Disquiet,* "In Praise of Sterile Women" ("Glorificação das Estéreis," 288), serving as a good summary of his basic attitude. In one of the book's longest and dreamiest sequences, "Our Lady of Silence" (whose title, once again, is eloquently revealing), Soares writes phrases such as the following: "Your sex is that of dreamed forms.... Your breasts are not the kind one would imagine kissing.... The substance of your flesh isn't spiritual, it's spirituality. You are the woman before the Fall.... My horror of real women endowed with sex is the road that brought me to you.... You aren't a woman. Not even within me do you evoke anything that feels feminine to me.... But you, in your vague substance, are nothing. You have no reality." It is hardly surprising that at a certain point he complains: "What a pity I must pray to you as to a woman, and cannot love you ... as one loves a man."[14] Various other passages are replete with similar sentiments.

As for the one exception, there is an amusing sequence titled "Advice to Unhappily Married Women" ("Conselhos às Mal-Casadas") (395–97), in which dissatisfied wives are taught how to cheat on their husbands by "imagining yourselves reaching orgasm with man A while copulating with man B," a practice that yields best results "in the days immediately preceding menstruation." Was Pessoa just having some good fun when he generously explained to women that "the height of sensuality, if you can achieve it, is to be the lewdest slut imaginable and yet never unfaithful to your husband"? No doubt he was having fun. And did he also amuse himself by wondering exactly what kind of lewd fantasies might fill the minds of these sensual but nonpromiscuous women?

That not one of Pessoa's dozens of heteronyms and sub-heteronyms was married or even seriously involved with a woman may not seem strange, since these "literary personalities" (Pessoa's epithet) after all embodied various aspects of their creator—of what he was or of what he dreamed of being, at least in some corner of his soul—and he was an ultraconfirmed bachelor. Fair enough. But then why an admittedly bisexual Álvaro de Campos, a bisexual or perhaps even homosexual Ricardo Reis? And why not a heteronym who has a full-fledged affair with a woman? Or even a full-fledged passion, albeit unrequited? There is one heteronymic love letter that is really rather moving, but it was written not by a man to a woman but by Maria José, Pessoa's only female heteronym, to one Senhor António, a handsome metalworker who passed by her window every day on his way to work. It begins:

Dear Senhor António,

You won't ever read this letter, and I'll probably never read over what I've written, because I'm dying of TB, but I have to write you what I feel or I'll burst.

You don't know who I am, or rather, you know but it's like you didn't know. You've seen me look at you from my window when you pass by on your way to the metalworks, because I know when you're going to pass by, and I wait for you. I doubt you've ever given a second thought to the hunchback girl who lives on the second floor of the yellow building, but I never stop thinking about you.

And Maria José goes on for several pages, talking about her miserable existence as an invalid but also about her feelings for the metalworker. And she ends the letter as follows:

Good-bye, Senhor António. My days are numbered, and I'm only writing this letter to hold it against my chest as if you'd written it to me instead of me to you. I wish you all the happiness I'm able to wish, and I hope you never find out about me so as not to laugh, for I know I can't hope for more.

I love you with all my heart and life.

There, I said it, and I'm crying.

Maria José[15]

Male writers, particularly novelists, often write from out of the heads and hearts of female characters, and this only becomes noteworthy in Pessoa (as I have already suggested) because of the dearth of actively heterosexual perspectives in his work. In other words, it is not surprising that a male writer who writes from dozens of points of view should occasionally adopt a female's perspective, but it is indeed strange when, in matters of sex and passion, he consistently assumes the female position. Pessoa's writing is, apparently, most often asexual, but when passion and desire are actually confronted, we meet unattractive Maria José hopelessly in love with a metalworker, we meet the sexually passive, quasi-female narrator of the *Maritime Ode*, we meet the assistant bookkeeper, who in one of *The Book of Disquiet*'s shorter passages writes, "O prince of better days, I was once your princess, and we loved each other with another kind of love" (326), we meet—it seems—Pessoa's heteronymic capacity and/or preference for putting himself in the place of a woman who desires a man instead of the other way around.

In the poetry signed by Pessoa's own name, there are various poems addressed to women in Portuguese and French. There is also an unsigned and previously unpublished poem, written in 1919, which is stridently homosexual, and it happens to read as if it came straight from the heart. Not that I am saying it did, for we can never say that about Pessoa, who was almost all head, but, as I have already argued, Pessoa was not able to fake all feelings with equal flair. We may, instead of calling this a gay poem by Pessoa, call it the poem of an unnamed heteronym, Pessoa's anonymous gay heteronym. Perhaps that is how he would have preferred it. And that anonymity, as we look at the poem, will become poignant.

The poem is untitled, three pages long, written in decasyllabic verses that sometimes form quatrains, with an abab rhyme scheme, but it is full of lacunas, which is probably why it has never been published. The narrator addresses a man whom he loves but, like the love letter of the hunchback girl to the metalworker, this poem will never be shown to the addressee. The narrator, alas, feels certain that the man he loves is not gay.[16]

> Sei que não és quem quero que tu sejas,
> Sei que és como outros.
> Vulgares bocas de mulheres beijas.

> [I know you're not how I wish you were.
> I know you're like other men.
> You kiss the ordinary lips of women.]

Several stanzas later, the narrator makes a confession of love like no other found in the poetry of Pessoa:

> Ah, se soubesses com que mágoa eu uso
> Este terror de amar-te, sem poder
> Nem dizer-te que te amo, de confuso
> De tão senti-lo, nem o amor perder.

> [Ah, if you knew with what pain I endure
> This horror of loving you without being able
> To tell you my love, so dazed am I by this
> Emotion, and without being able to shed it.]

The narrator, as happens to people who fall in love, longs, in spite of his fear, to declare himself, and fantasizes this happening. Not only that, he fantasizes the man accepting the declaration with "friendly surprise" and a seeming willingness to love him in return. But even were the timid narrator miraculously able to get this far, he suspects he might remain frozen, paralyzed, unable to act on the love he has confessed. "Que sei! que sei! há tanta gente em mim!" (Who knows! who knows! with so many people in me!), he exclaims in true-to-form Pessoa fashion.

On page 2 of the poem he goes back to moaning about how difficult it is for him to tell what he is dying to tell, and this difficulty is really the poem's thematic, if not technical, refrain. He recalls a conversation with his beloved friend in which the subject of "Shakespeare's vice" came up. The narrator had greatly longed for this opportunity to gently, slowly, open up his heart on the matter, but, "traidor a mim . . . com a voz sem mim só condenei" (traitor to myself . . . with my voice—without me—I condemned it). After comparing the unspoken rejection of his unspoken love to a cruel exile "onde vivo / Só da tua imagem" (where I live / Only off your image), he takes comfort in the memory of Antinoüs, Ganymede, and Bathyllus.

On the third page of the poem, the narrator tells how frustrating it is to talk to his secret beloved as a friend, since love is, after all, so different from friendship, and since he is forever fighting off his nagging compulsion to declare himself. And then, toward the end of the poem, there are three highly significant stanzas in which the narrator admits that he feels ashamed not only to confess his love out loud but even to himself, on paper, "em escrita voz," for he feels himself blush merely for "Amando-te ou dizendo-o, ou só sentindo" (Loving you or telling my love, or just feeling it).

Is it possible that all the feeling and anxiety packed into this poem was imposture? That Pessoa merely put himself in the place of a fearful, repressed homosexual? Yes, it is. With Pessoa, who made himself into nothing so that he could become everything, we can never be certain. In *The Book of Disquiet* (131–32), Pessoa wrote:

> Everything stated or expressed by man is a note in the margin of a completely erased text. From what's in the note we can extract the gist of what must have been in the text, but there's always a doubt, and the possible meanings are many.

Substituting the terms of this passage, we may see Pessoa as the erased text, the erased life, and all his writings as the marginal notes that shed light on the text, on his life, but a light so fraught with possible meanings and interpretations that we can never draw sure conclusions. But can we at least extract the gist?

Let us consider again Pessoa's words to João Gaspar Simões in that letter from 1930, in which he first affirms that everyone has "a certain element" of "obscenity" (a word he uses merely to mean sexual desire), and then goes on to write: "Since these elements, no matter how small, will in some way be a hindrance to superior mental processes, I decided to eliminate them twice, by the simple expedient of expressing them intensely." This unequivocal declaration of intent, corroborated by the evidence of Pessoa's twenty-five thousand surviving manuscript sheets, suggests that he did, in a certain way, eliminate sex from his system, otherwise how could he have had so much time and energy for writing? From this point of view, all the mentions of sex in his work can be seen as a kind of nostalgia for what he never lived. But we may also suspect that Pessoa's exercise in elimination was, after all, not so successful, or not so instantaneous. We may suspect that the erased life kept reappearing, so that it needed to be reerased over and over. That the gist and genius of Pessoa was in his repression, or rather, in its failure. That he had to keep on writing intensely, almost pathologically, so as to continuously eliminate, day after day, his instinctive sexual drive or drives that relentlessly asserted themselves.

A Fragmentary Gay Poem by Fernando Pessoa

Transcribed and Translated by Richard Zenith

The following poem, cataloged in the Pessoa archives under the number 43/50–51, has never before been published, nor was it even mentioned by any researcher until November 1999, when I quoted from it in a paper (an embryonic version of my essay in this volume) delivered at a conference on Pessoa in New York. In the transcription presented here, the spelling has been modernized (Pessoa did not heed the 1911 government mandated orthographic reform), obvious typographical errors have been corrected, and the length of the dividing lines between sections has been standardized. All spacing (including blank spaces in the middle of verses) and punctuation have been respected. The original takes up three full, typewritten pages; it is unlikely, but possible, that further pages—now lost—were produced.

5 7 1919.

Sei que desprezarias, não somente
A mim, mas ainda mais o meu amor,
Se eu ousasse, numa hora
Dizer-te quem tu és pra a minha dor.

Levo comigo, inútil confidente
Do meu próprio martírio,

———

Quantas vezes, falando com tuas falas,
Me esqueço delas de pensar em ti;
Olhas-me, estranhas, e, ofendido, calas.

E não te sei explicar por que não te ouço.
Busco desculpas
Mas a razão   não posso.

———

Sei que não és quem quero que tu sejas,
Sei que és como outros,
Vulgares bocas de mulheres beijas
E eu só o sonho vão da tua boca.

Nada de mim, salvo o amor vão, te toca
No corpo, e nem sequer não me desejas;
Pois tudo ignoras que há entre mim e a louca
Ideia que me faço de ti

———

Ah, se soubesses com que mágoa eu uso
Este terror de amar-te, sem poder
Nem dizer-te que te amo, de confuso
De tão senti-lo, nem o amor perder.
Se soubesses com que ódio a não saber
Falar-te do que quero, a mim me escuso,
Se soubesses? E se o soubesses? Quê?
Que gesto teu pra mim melhoraria
Este mal-estar de mim comigo e o amor?

———

Sei eu ao certo, se pudesse ter-te
Que quereria ter-te? Se eu ousasse
O que sinto por ti um dia dizer-te,
E a tua surpresa amiga o aceitasse,
Sei eu, sim, se não ficaria inerte

E sem que a outra ousadia me faltasse,
De, tendo a tua promessa, ir colher-te
Ao ramo que a tua   aproximasse?
Que sei! que sei! há tanta gente em mim!
Tanto ímpeto perdido e contradito
Sou a meu próprio ser tão pouco afim
Que talvez a maior tortura fosse
Aceitares-me e eu ver-me, atado e aflito,
Incapaz do último acto[1] . . . . . .

———

Ah, como invejo, se te às vezes sonho,
Os sedutores
Os que ousam, como os outros mais normais,
Dizer, propor,

Que não sou belo sei; outros também
Desses não o são mais, e ousam falar
O amor que têm, e querem que lhes tenham.

———

Um dia, num acaso da conversa
Que houve entre nós, entre a tua mente e eu todo,
Falámos, já mal sei de que   modo
Desta

Do vício de Shakespeare

E eu, que ansiava esse momento contigo,
Para um momento, levemente, aos poucos,
Dar a entender minha alma sem perigo,
Porque talvez . . . , quem sabe . . . como sei?
Ah, fui traidor a mim
E com a voz sem mim só condenei.

———

No exílio para onde, sem querer
Nem o saber, me expulsas, e onde vivo
Só da tua imagem, tenho mais sofrer
Que o verdadeiro êxul
Ele, da pátria longe,

Eu sou de ti êxul perto de ti,
Quando falo contigo amigamente,
Estamos inimigos. Se sorri
A tua boca vejo o seu sorriso
Que é para mim, mas não é meu

Antínoo, Ganimedes, Batilo, ora
Um ora outro

De ti me refugio com Antínoo
E a Ganimedes canto porque existes.
O amor é grande e fere quer procure
De homem ou mulher, mulher ou homem.

Anteros![2] Cerca a tua campa antiga

———

Não sei que intimidade ter contigo.
Só sei aquela ter que não me basta.
Falo-te em voz igual e boa de amigo—
E ah! quanto co'a amizade o amor contrasta!
Dói-me a alma cada vez que o que te digo
Do que quero dizer-te se me afasta,
E se vou a dizê-lo, como a um perigo
Fujo, e a oculta   em mim se arrasta.
Por que não fazes um gesto casual
Em tal dia, em tal hora, que eu possa
Ousar?

———

Põe, amor, sobre a fronte aquelas rosas
Que Catulo ou Horácio cantariam

———

Quê? Há-de ser só justo e natural
Cantar o amor que pra a mulher impele?
Que mal há, se é na alma há bem ou mal,[3]
Em cantar outro amor que não aquele?

Contigo nada ouso; calo, e fale
Por mim a escrita voz
Mas não tão pouco ouso que me cale
Comigo, e em escrita voz me não rebele.

Por que vício da mente hei eu vergonha
Em te cantar? Que influxo doutrem vindo
Faz com que eu core a sós quer me suponha
Amando-te ou dizendo-o, ou só sentindo?

———

Se te amo como a homem ou mulher?
Não sei; se eu o soubesse, não te amava.
O que é que de ti   minh'alma quer?
Ou quereria

Given the fragmentary character of this poem, full of incomplete verses, imperfect rhymes, and nonuniform stanzas, I have privileged clarity in the translation, without attempting to replicate the poetic devices. Lacunas are indicated by the symbol ▌, but only when the missing word or phrase causes a break in the flow of the English.

July 5, 1919

I know you would scorn me
And scorn my love even more,
If I ever dared tell you
What you mean to my sorrow.

The useless confidant of my own
Suffering, I bear inside me
▌

———

How often, when we talk, I stop hearing
Your words, thinking only of you,
And you look at me, put off, and fall silent.

And I can't tell you why I get distracted.
I look for excuses ▌
But I cannot ▌ the reason.

———

I know you're not how I wish you were.
I know you're like other men, ▌
You kiss the ordinary lips of women,
And I just the useless dream of your lips.

No real part of me—only my vain love—touches
Your body, and you don't even not desire me,
For you know nothing of what goes on
Between me and my crazy idea of you ▌

———

Ah, if you knew with what pain I endure
This horror of loving you without being able
To tell you my love, so dazed am I by this
Emotion, and without being able to shed it.
If you knew how I hate always making excuses,
Because I can't tell you what I long to tell,
▌

And if you knew, then what? Then what?
What gesture of yours would relieve the anguish
I feel in myself and in the face of this love?

———

If you could be mine, who knows if I'd really
Want to have you? Were I bold enough
To tell you one day what I feel for you,
And your friendly surprise accepted it,
Who knows if I wouldn't remain frozen,
Without that other boldness (despite
Your assurances) to go and pluck you
From the branch that your ▌ had brought near?
Who knows! who knows! with so many people in me!
With so many lost and denied urges,
I'm so far removed from my own self
That perhaps the greatest torture would be
To win your acceptance but be too anguished
And wound up to take the final step . . . . . .

———

Whenever I dream of you, ah, how I envy
Seducers ▌
Those who, more normal than me, dare
To suggest, to propose, ▌

I know I'm not handsome, but others,
No more handsome than I, dare to tell
The love they feel and seek to be loved back.

———

One day, in a conversation between us
—Between your mind and my whole being—
We somehow or other got on to the subject
Of that ▌
▌
Of Shakespeare's vice ▌

And I, who had longed for that moment with you,
For a moment when I could slowly, gently
And safely open up my heart to you,
Since perhaps . . . , who knows . . . How be sure?
Ah, I was a traitor to myself ▌
And with my voice—without me—I condemned it.

———

In the exile to where you unintentionally,
Unknowingly banish me, and where I live
Only off your image, I suffer more
Than the true exile ▌
Far from his homeland, ▌

Close to you, I'm exiled from you;
When I talk to you as a friend,
We're enemies. If your lips
Smile, I see their smile
That's for me but isn't mine
▌

Antinoüs, Ganymede, Bathyllus, now one
Now another ▌
▌

I take refuge from you in Antinoüs,
And I sing to Ganymede because you exist.
Love is great and always wounds, whether
It seeks a man or woman, a woman or man.

Anteros! Your ancient tombstone is surrounded
▌

———

I know not what intimacy I want with you,
But I know that the one we have is too little.
I talk to you with the same warm and friendly
Voice as you, but ah, how friendship differs
From love! It tortures my soul each time I fail
To tell you what I want to tell; when I'm about
To tell it, I flee from the right words as from
Danger, and the hidden ▌ drags on in me.
If some day, at some moment, you would make
The casual gesture that would embolden me
To speak! ▌

———

Place on your brow those roses, my love,
That Catullus or Horace would have sung
▌

———

What? Must it be right and natural to sing
Only of the love that goes out to women?
What's wrong (if right or wrong exists
In the soul) with singing of a different love?

Too shy to speak with you, I hush, letting
The written voice speak for me,
But I'm not so shy that I hush in myself,
And with my written voice I indeed rebel.

What mental tic makes me ashamed
To sing of you? What presence of what other
Makes me blush, all alone, if I imagine myself
Loving you or telling my love, or just feeling it?

———

Whether I love you as a man or a woman?
I don't know; if I knew, I wouldn't love you.
What does my soul ▌ want from you?
Or what would it want ▌

Notes

1. At various points, particularly in the chapters titled "Sexualidade frustrada" and "Polémica em Sodoma," Gaspar Simões implies or directly suggests that Pessoa was a repressed homosexual, relying not only on evidence in the writer's literary work but on biographical details, such as Pessoa's unusually impassioned defense of António Botto (1897–1959), a poet whose openly homosexual verses (including the collection titled *Canções*, published in 1921 and republished the next year by Olisipo Editora, Pessoa's short-lived enterprise that also brought out several chapbooks of his own poetry in English) aroused considerable controversy in the Portuguese press in the early 1920s. Gaspar Simões explains Pessoa's probable but in any case "merely platonic" (6th ed., 452) homosexuality by following a beeline to his alleged Oedipal complex, because the impossibility of finding a woman who lives up to the perfect image of one's overidealized mother is "the origin of most cases of homosexuality" (ibid.).

2. In the chapter "Multiple Personalities" (138–47), after discussing Pound, Eliot, and Gottfried Benn, Hamburger turns to Pessoa, "the most extreme case of multiple personality and self-division in modern poetry" (138). For a thorough treatment of Pessoa's poetry, or poetries, the first major study to be published perhaps still ranks as the best: Jacinto do Prado Coelho's *Diversidade e unidade em Fernando Pessoa*.

3. All translations in this essay are by Richard Zenith.

4. The poem, published by Pessoa's own Olisipo Editora, carries the date "Lisbon, 1913." Although there is no manuscript evidence to corroborate that date (and Pessoa was fond of inventing fictitious dates of composition for his works), Pessoa, in a letter from 1915 to an Englishman, mentions some "longer poems written in English" that would offend English "public morality," and he is no doubt referring to "Epithalamium" and "Antinoüs" (*Correspondência*, 175).

5. The original manuscript, which is typed, contains a handwritten and hard-to-decipher sequel (unpublished) in which the narrator is not Hadrian but a man who likens himself to the Roman emperor and to Jupiter, and his boy lover to Antinoüs

and to Ganymede. The Pessoa Archive contains various other handwritten homo-sexual poems—in Portuguese, English, and French—that are still waiting to be transcribed and published.

6. Catalog #58A/21a. The verses take up the bottom part of a sheet with two other fragmentary poems written in English, apparently all at the same sitting. The date October 8, 1920, appears at the top.

7. The date affixed to the published version, "Lisbon, 1915," is amply confirmed by the manuscript evidence.

8. Written probably in 1915, the sonnet was published by Pessoa in 1922 as "Um Soneto Já Antigo" (An already old sonnet).

9. The twelfth Reis ode ("A flor que és, não a que dás, eu quero") in a group of twenty published by Pessoa in *Athena,* October 1924. Published in various book editions, including *Obra poética,* 275–76, and *Poemas de Ricardo Reis,* 69–70.

10. The original begins "Eu nunca fui dos que a um sexo o outro" (*Poemas de Ricardo Reis,* 184).

11. *The Book of Disquiet* was a sprawling and chaotic prose work, left as more than five hundred passages written between 1913 and 1935 and never organized by Pessoa into a book; its title, therefore, is marvelously self-descriptive. Pessoa pub-lished just twelve passages of the work in magazines, and nearly all the rest had to wait until 1982, when the bulk of the passages (scattered among the reams of manu-script sheets left by Pessoa) had been located, transcribed, assembled into book form, and published. Pessoa initially attributed the work to himself, then to a cer-tain Vicente Guedes, and at last to Bernardo Soares, whom he called a semi-het-eronym, "because his personality, although not my own, doesn't differ from my own but is a mere mutilation of it" (in a letter to Adolfo Casais Monteiro, dated Jan-uary 13, 1935). Four English translations of the work were published in 1991. My own, titled *The Book of Disquietude* (Manchester: Carcanet Press), was the only unabridged version. The translated passages that follow, however, were not taken from that volume but from a new version, titled *The Book of Disquiet* (Penguin, 2001).

12. Pessoa met Ophelia Queiroz in late 1919, when she applied—and was hired—for a job as a secretary in one of the firms where Pessoa worked as a freelance, writ-ing business letters in English and French. Pessoa courted Ophelia with a certain show of passion, and although she soon switched jobs, they wrote and saw each other regularly for close to a year before Pessoa, in a letter, broke off the relation-ship. It started up again nine years later, in the fall of 1929, but this second phase did not last long or seem serious for Pessoa. Ophelia, however, kept writing unanswered letters for another year and a half.

13. Soares, according to his "biography," was an assistant bookkeeper who worked in downtown Lisbon (the "Baixa") and lived in a fifth-floor rented room.

14. "Nossa Senhora do Silêncio" (Soares 458–64). The phrases are culled from various paragraphs, and the ellipses all represent skipped text save the last one, where a blank space occurs in the original. The cited English version is from *The Book of Disquiet,* 436–42.

15. The "Carta da Corcunda para o Serralheiro" (Letter from a hunchback girl to a metalworker) was the only text attributed to Maria José. The letter (first published in Lopes 2:256–58) was typed on three and a half pages, but Pessoa-Maria signed her name next to the title. One of the remarkable features of the letter is the language,

for Pessoa succeeds in rendering the simple but long-winded diction characteristic of Maria José's economically disadvantaged social class. The cited English version is from *The Selected Prose of Fernando Pessoa* (2001), 314–18.

16. The entire poem, in the original and with a (rather literal) translation, is published at the end of this essay.

Notes to a Fragmentary Gay Poem

1. Alternate version: "Incapaz do gesto último."
2. Eros's brother, the avenger of unrequited love.
3. *(sic):* The sense of the phrase seems to be "se é que na alma."

Works Cited

Portuguese authors, in accord with the most frequent editorial practice in Portugal, are listed by the very last of their names, rather than by their full surname (which sometimes, but not always, includes the metronymic).

Bréchon, Robert. *Étrange étranger: une biographie de Fernando Pessoa.* Paris: Christian Bourgois, 1996.

Campos, Álvaro de (Fernando Pessoa). *Notas para a recordação do meu Mestre Caeiro.* Ed. Teresa Rita Lopes. Lisbon: Editorial Estampa, 1997.

Coelho, Jacinto do Prado. *Diversidade e unidade em Fernando Pessoa.* Lisbon: Revista Ocidente, 1949; Lisbon: Editorial Verbo, 1991 (10th ed.).

Hamburger, Michael. *The Truth of Poetry.* New York: Harcourt, Brace and World, 1969.

Lopes, Teresa Rita. *Pessoa por conhecer.* 2 vols. Lisbon: Estampa, 1990.

Pessoa, Fernando. *Antinoüs.* Lisbon: Monteiro & Co., 1918.

———. *The Book of Disquiet.* Ed. and trans. Richard Zenith. London: Penguin, 2001.

———. *Cartas de Fernando Pessoa a João Gaspar Simões.* Introduction and notes by João Gaspar Simões. Lisbon: Publicações Europa-América, 1957.

———. *Correspondência 1905–1922.* Ed. Manuela Parreira da Silva. Lisbon: Assírio & Alvim, 1999.

———. *English Poems I-II.* Includes "Inscriptions" and a revised version of "Antinoüs." Lisbon: Olisipo Editora, 1921.

———. *English Poems III.* Contains only the long poem "Epithalamium." Lisbon: Olisipo Editora, 1921.

———. *Fernando Pessoa & Co.—Selected Poems.* Ed. and trans. Richard Zenith. New York: Grove Press, 1998.

———. *Maritime Ode.* Trans. Richard Zenith. Lisbon: Assírio & Alvim, 1997.

———. *Obra poética.* 7th ed. Ed. Maria Aliete Galhoz. Rio de Janeiro: Editora Nova Aguilar, 1977.

———. *Poemas de Ricardo Reis.* Ed. Luiz Fagundes Duarte. Lisbon: Imprensa Nacional—Casa da Moeda, 1994.

———. *Poesia inglesa II.* Ed. Luísa Freire. Lisbon: Assírio & Alvim, 2000.

———. *The Selected Prose of Fernando Pessoa.* Ed. and trans. Richard Zenith. New York: Grove Press, 2001.

————. *35 Sonnets*. Lisbon: Monteiro & Co., 1918.

Simões, João Gaspar. *Vida e obra de Fernando Pessoa*. Lisbon: Livraria Bertrand, 1950; Lisbon: Publicações Dom Quixote, 1991 (6th ed.).

Soares, Bernardo (Fernando Pessoa). *Livro do desassossego*. Ed. Richard Zenith. Lisbon: Assírio & Alvim, 1998.

CHAPTER FOUR

Brazilian Homoerotics

Cultural Subjectivity and Representation in the Fiction of Gilberto Freyre

Jossianna Arroyo

Desire, Representation, and Culture

> A expressão literária é, em varios casos, purgação; e sempre, revelação. Acentue-se mais uma vez: a literatura brasileira é como outras literaturas nacionais, uma literatura impura.
> —Gilberto Freyre, "Heróis e vilões no romance brasileiro"

> [Literature acts in many ways, sometimes as a purgative and always as a revelation. We must repeat it again: Brazilian literature is as impure as any other national literature][1]

National literatures have had a long and intense commitment to desire. From patriotic desire we have seen ideal descriptions of cultural nationalism written in pages of essays, fiction, sociology, and so forth (Sommer). In the specific case of writing national discourses, we can confirm that these two main components—fiction and national desire—coexist depending on each other in a narcissistic way. Cultural identities, as the main components of national discourses, are also a fiction constructed with imaginary borderlines: between selfhood and otherness. Cultural subjectivity derives from this paradox of risking *one's own self* to build one's identity in relation to the other. Therefore, national culture is an imaginary that is never completed and has to rely entirely on the displaced desire for the other. A writer is consequently split into two; acting both as a constructed self and as a sociocultural entity risking her or his subjectivity into the other.

Latin American and Caribbean writers provide what I consider the best example of this complex self/other relationship in their construction of national cultures. Identified by Western European discourses as "impure," "hybrid," and "chaotic," these nation-building projects have been written to solve the heterogeneous character of their countries. As Partha Chatterjee has suggested, the production of a unified national front, with a particular cultural subjectivity, became the answer to these countries' social conflicts, particularly those related to race, gender, and sexualities (8–10). In Brazil, the solution to these social conflicts is exemplified by Gilberto Freyre's theory of "racial democracy."

Described by Carlos Guilherme Mota as the strongest cultural ideology of Brazilian nationality, the theoretical concept of "racial democracy" was developed in Freyre's canonical 1933 essay *Casa-grande e senzala*— translated into English as *Masters and Slaves* (1945) (53–74). Originally written as a dissertation in the department of anthropology at Columbia University, the essay criticized social structures of slavery and patriarchal power in the Brazilian *casa grande* or master house, and its dominant power in the *senzalas* or slave quarters. This conflictive model simultaneously created a special relationship between the two systems that subsequently came together harmoniously to create a Brazilian national culture (Arroyo 32). According to this model, Brazilian national culture emerged from racial contact and miscegenation where the black slave became an agent of culture, civilization, and education for the white master. Influenced by Hegelian dialectics, Freudian psychoanalysis, and the Boasian school of cultural relativism, Freyre presented a complicated picture for Brazilian intellectual circles. His ethnographic discourse about Brazilian national culture was described as "too close to literature" and "sexually graphic" (Arinos de Melo Franco 81–88). Like other modern writers of his time, Freyre believed that words were physical and sensual because they materialized the writer's desires (*Alhos e bugalhos,* 178). His "Proustian" style was nevertheless criticized by some sociologists. As an author, Freyre understood that the graphic nature of his sexual metaphors and, most of all, their allusions to sexual contact between blacks and whites constituted the best way to present the modern subject as a desiring subject.

The two chapters titled "The Negro Slave in the Sexual and Family Life of the Brazilian" clearly show "racial democracy" as a power relationship between whites and their Others (black men and women). Black boys, *mulatas,* and, particularly, *mães pretas* or black nannies played the most important role in the "Brazilianization" of culture.[2] In Freyre's words, these black men and women, who had been "sexualized" and "contaminated" by slavery, also had the mission of creating a new cultural subjectivity, by "corrupting" their masters as they helped to create Brazilian culture. Consequently, miscegenation is presented as a productive source because it not only destroyed slavery through "love" and sexual contact, but also created a new patriarchal order (Arroyo 40–41). Although Freyre's "racial democracy" erases class conflicts, the juxtaposition of race, gender, and sexuality reorganizes social and power structures. For example, the *mãe preta* is the symbolic mother of the Brazilian nation, as well as a border figure that makes miscegenation possible (Ramos; Stoler). At the same time, a problematic fraternal bonding is established between white and black men with the main purpose of building a new patriarchal order. Both of these models present contradictory views in terms of their uses of race, gender, and sexuality as well as of the kind of cultural subjectivity portrayed.

In this essay I will examine these contradictions through two fictional works by Gilberto Freyre: *Dona Sinhá e o filho padre* (1964) (*Mother and Son* [1967]) and *O outro amor do Dr. Paulo* (1977).[3] Defined as "seminovelas" (semi-novelettes), these texts, like most of his ethnographic and sociological works, focused on representing national culture through race, gender, and sexuality. Nevertheless, they possess a particular characteristic that helps to better understand cultural subjectivity. In these novels Freyre presented homoeroticism as the center of the new patriarchal order. This homoeroticism presents a combination of masculine and feminine traits that are erotically oriented toward men. Furthermore, race is constructed via gender and directed toward this homoeroticism. Women appear as biological, "racial," or archetypal mothers, who function as part of repressed desire in the Oedipal triangle, as they are the only connection to desire in the father's absence.

Dona Sinhá and its second part *O outro amor* narrate the story of two young men who fall in love with each other. José Maria, Dona Sinhá's son, is the "effeminate" homosexual boy who falls in love with Paulo Tavares, a strong masculine *mestiço* (in Portuguese, mixed race, i.e., black and white). Although they never become sexually involved, Paulo Tavares escapes his object of passion by leaving the Brazilian state of Pernambuco for France. Paulo's departure represents happiness for Dona Sinhá,

José Maria's religious and domineering mother, who wants her son to devote his life to the Catholic church. After becoming a priest, José Maria becomes ill from tuberculosis and dies. When he finds about José Maria's illness, Paulo returns from Europe to find that his best friend is dead. Also, Paulo confronts his father's death. In an act of despair, he asks Dona Sinhá to marry him, but she refuses. At the end, he leaves for France again. In *O outro amor*, Freyre narrates the story of Paulo's "second love," an exiled Brazilian young woman called Maria Emília, and their travels together through Europe. In this text, Paulo is transformed into a divided subject, caught "between" the desire to learn about Europe and his longing for Brazil. His *saudade* or nostalgia for Brazil becomes a complex metaphor. Paulo feels *saudade* for his former lover, particularly for their erotic/"brotherly" relationship. He also wants to return to Brazil's "maternal waters." Upon returning, he sees Brazilian culture with "new eyes," recuperating his other half (José Maria/Brazil), the part of himself that he had been missing for so long. Meanwhile, Maria Emília, after suffering two abortions, cannot bear Brazilian tropical diseases and dies of yellow fever. Symbolically, Paulo's desires have been displaced in his desire for an "effeminate" other (José Maria). Brazil as a *pátria* becomes a motherland/fatherland in which the masculine and the feminine coexist.[4] Although Paulo and José Maria never sexually consummate their union, these novels prove that masculine alliances are necessary ties for Brazilian nation-building projects. Women, on the other hand, are presented as essential archetypes (i.e., the strong mother, the sea) whose bodies—though influential for men's desires—have to be erased or excluded from the nation. Therefore, homoeroticism and homosexuality as factors in the "ontological condition of the young poet" construct a subjective map of the self that is necessary in order to represent national culture and identity (Cruz Malavé, *El primitivo implorante*, 90).

In Freyre's novels, the theme of repressed homosexuality must be understood in the context of his views regarding national culture and subjectivity. As he expresses these views in other essays and conferences from the 1940s and 1950s, repressed homosexuality becomes analogous to what Benedict Anderson calls "the ideal fraternity and comradeship" of national projects (7). Therefore, homosociality defines a particular way of understanding Brazilian nationhood. For Freyre, homosocial alliances are linked to the erotic. In this sense, erotic desire, even if sublimated, opens a "threshold" of ambiguity, fragmentation, and hybridity that subscribes to Freyre's imaginary of culture. Both homosociality and homoeroticism, though different aspects of relations between men, appear integrated in these novels as ways of understanding politics and culture. In this sense, Freyrian continuous exchange of social relations and sublimated erotic fantasies between men—from the homosocial to the homoerotic—makes possible the cultural reconciliation of opposites in Brazilian culture.[5] For Freyre, Brazilian nationhood, politics, and culture are, therefore, reproduced through this model.

In his 1947 conference "O Camarada Whitman," Freyre makes a call for humanism, fraternity, and a new manhood (85, 98). This view of *humanismo* and *americanismo* was linked to Whitman's homosexuality. In this sense, Whitman's homosexuality or bisexuality, as Freyre constructed it, has—contrary to the "maneira debochada do Verlaine e do Wilde" (Verlaine's and Wilde's mocking way)—an ethical character, a type of sublimation that puts together poetry and politics (95, 97). The balance between poetry and politics makes Whitman a "masculine" and "feminine" man, a Narcissus capable of loving himself through others and, at the same time, "able to penetrate their mysteries" (94). Freyre's comment on Whitman's "equilibrium of masculine and feminine energies," therefore, mirrors his own identity as a "masculine/ feminine man," that is, as a writer.

Discourses of virility and manhood evolve in Europe concurrently with discourses of modern nationalism (Mosse 7). By questioning his own masculinity, Freyre articulates an intricate process of identification and self-validation with the other. In these models, a third term, "the governing fiction of the social," has always been included (Fanon 213–15). Through this social recognition the body plays a central role, because from the performative character of identity politics (i.e., race, sexuality, gender) we can represent culture as a continuous exchange of "love" and "power" relations (Butler; Foucault). For these intellectuals, national politics is a ritual of interpretation and self-validation that focuses on two problematics: first, in questioning their own national cultures, particularly the ways in which they work with or against specific sociopolitical agendas; and second, in challenging fixed Western views of politics and cultural identities.

Race, gender, and sexuality represent national identities from a particular positionality. For Freyre, "writing culture" becomes a subjective and partial process that is constantly questioning representation (Clifford

7). In his novels, race and gender share as tropes of difference "the arbitrariness of cultural prescriptions . . . a similar structure of identity categories whose enactments and boundaries are culturally policed" (Ginsberg 13). Also, while race and gender are defined "within the terms of a hegemonic cultural discourse," as I will discuss later, sexuality creates a space for positioning new subjects (Butler 3). This particular view comes from Freyre's sociological theories, in which he affirmed that "quase não há sexo puro, como quase não há raça pura" (there is almost no pure sex, just as there are almost no pure races) ("O que W. L. disse das mulheres," 181). Writing against European racist theories about hybrid and/or "backward" civilizations, Freyre embraced Freud's concept that culture and civilization originate from the repression of desire (Freud, "Civilization and Its Discontents," 722–71). To liberate culture's double character as artifice and content—"cultura como artifício e como conteúdo"—the social *pessoa* (person) has to fulfill his or her individual desires. Finally, in Freyre's texts, sexual desire for the other marks representation while it puts identity at risk. Paradoxically, this is the only way to create the boundaries of the subject.

In Brazil, as in the United States, slavery creates a discourse on race, gender, and sexuality that problematizes fixed notions of cultural identity (Cunningham; Ginsberg). The white master's masculinity reproduces the partiarchal model of social control. As Elaine K. Ginsberg has argued, "At the same time, to insure the reproduction as well as the purity of his whiteness, the white man also needed to exert control over the sexualities of both the white woman and the black man, effectively enslaving the former and emasculating the latter" (Ginsberg 5). In the case of the black man, the white Father becomes the Law in itself that has to be abolished to acquire a sense of self. Thus, black men needed to take antipatriarchal positions against their white masters and, in order to "kill" them, they had to consolidate a homosocial alliance (Cunningham 123–25). For Freyre, cultural subjectivity is based on this homosocial alliance that erases racial lines to build a "national brotherhood." Paradoxically, it also has to "kill" European master narratives symbolically to constitute a new narrative order. Freyre shares the same contradictory relationship with the Law of the Father as the former slave men. A new "femininity/masculinity" is the way to rewrite and displace this order, which instead of creating a phallocentric male subject, falls into a "third" space, a gap, a "neither nor" (Cruz Malavé, "Toward an Art of Trans-vestism," 147).

I also believe that in these homoerotic novels the constant transposi-tion of racial, sexual, and gender identities problematizes representation while creating a strategic positionality vis-à-vis ethnocentric models of representation. This strategic positionality plays a central role in Freyre's incorporation of a "marginal" voice. He used to called himself "um marginal da literatura" (a literary outsider) ("Como e porque sou . . . ," 178). The "sissification" of writing, essential for understanding national projects in Latin America, is "an active mediation in the exchanges be-tween colonizer and colonized, a role or type ready to qualify, modify, taint, neutralize and even trap—at least into an illusion of domina-tion—whomever and whatever attempts to occupy him/her or his/her territory" (Piedra 375). Fiction and ethnography are part of Freyre's "am-biguous" friendship with literature, what he used to call "meus amorios contra natura" (my affairs against nature), and his apparent submission to European models, which he continuously refers to as relational, frag-ile, and contested masculinity (Ramírez 52–55).

Although based on erotic love, these masculine alliances are also very problematic given their extreme ambivalence about race, class, and sex-ual difference. In this sense, they pose "uma subjetividade outra" (an/other subjectivity) that, as in Adolfo Caminha's homoerotic novel *Bom-crioulo* (1891), "presents every stereotype from a society that saw the Black influence as a dangerous force" (Lopes 71). Even though José Maria is not a black man like Caminha's protagonist, Amaro, his rearing by black slaves makes him "polluted," effeminate, and homosexual. Just like miscegenation, homosexuality becomes another "symptom" of Brazil-ian cultural projects, giving them certainty as ideology because, as Slavoj Žižek has argued, in ideological discourses, "one point contradicts the other, but they coexist at the same time" (21). Although in the late 1950s the influence of Marxist theories in Brazil began to deconstruct the ide-ology of "racial democracy," it remains one of the most important par-adigms for understanding the nature of Brazilian national discourses.[6]

Even though race, gender, and sexuality are key topics for understand-ing and deconstructing Brazilian national and cultural projects, some Brazilian intellectuals appear to be uncomfortable addressing these is-sues. I can only speculate on various reasons for this discomfort. First, they feel that Brazilianists around the world are particularly obsessed with these subjects in order to construct Brazil as a country where "anything can happen." Second, Brazilian intellectuals are tired of Brazil's colonized image as an "exotic" other, as well as Brazil as a space of difference in relation to discourses of race and sexuality.

At the same time, Brazil has constructed its own social and discursive difference from other countries such as the United States, where some of the major socioanthropological interpretations of Brazil—including Gilberto Freyre's and, more recently, Roberto Da Matta's—are written from a comparative perspective between both countries.[7] Nevertheless, since the late 1970s, poststructuralist and feminist theories have influenced a great number of ethnographic works by Brazilian and U.S. academics who openly explore the relationships between racial, political, and sexual identities in contemporary Brazil.[8] Identity politics has helped to deconstruct older myths of Brazilian national culture and identity. As part of this process, it has been necessary—even for these poststructuralist works—to revisit Gilberto Freyre's ideologies of Brazilian culture, politics, and representation. Furthermore, these critics have to understand them from Freyre's particular perspective, that is, as fictions.

Being in Love: Fictions of Culture

> And thus he loves, but he knows not what; he does not understand and cannot explain his own state; he appears to have caught the infection of another's eye; the lover is his mirror in whom he is beholding himself, but he is not aware of this.
>
> —Plato, *Phaedrus*

This section focuses on the transposition of racial, gender, and sexual identities in Gilberto Freyre's *Dona Sinhá e o filho padre* (hereafter, *DS*) and *O outro amor de Dr. Paulo* (hereafter *OA*), as well as on the way these texts construct a Brazilian cultural subjectivity. I want to show how they locate cultural subjectivity in a liminal space, a site that Freyre relates to the homoerotic. This location appears as a longing for other men, a desire that acts more as a "cultural fantasy" of integration with "the same."[9] This displacement of homoerotic desire permits the character of Paulo to begin a book that interprets Brazilian culture, and this homoeroticism that Freyre sees as a combination of masculine and feminine traits is presented as a necessary path to writing where the metatextual character of both novels starts from this authorial relationship of femininity and masculinity. The narrative has a double character; while history is described as a strong feminine woman, fiction acts as a *desvio* (treachery, deviation): "A História como que me surpreendera a querer traí-la, entregando-me aos namoros com a Ficção; e antes que se consumisse o desvio como que me fazia voltar aos seus braços femininos, porém, fortes, absorventes e imperiais" (*DS*, 17) (It was as though History had surprised me in the act of deceiving her by flirting with Fiction, and before the act of treachery could be consummated, had brought me back to her feminine, but strong, enveloping, imperious arms) (*Mother and Son* [hereafter *MS*], 21). In other words, José Maria's repressed homosexuality is the *desvio* or condition that enables the narrative to exist.

Repressed homosexuality could also be explained in two other ways. First, as Edilberto Coutinho has stated, it is presented as Paulo's "erotic experiment," a transitory state that initiates him into manhood and adulthood, which ends when he marries Maria Emília.[10] A close reading of both novels shows not only the importance of the relationship between Paulo and José Maria, but also that Paulo's *saudade* for José Maria is a catalyst for his return to Brazil and his writing. Maria Emília, his *outro amor* (other love), acts as a substitute love who does not erase his desire for José Maria. Furthermore, Paulo's attraction for men is present until the end of the novel.

Dona Sinhá e o filho padre starts with an Unamunian twist. Freyre, as a character, openly discusses the novel's plot with the "real" Dona Sinhá, a rich widow from the northeast who is very upset after reading in a newspaper that her biography and the tragic life of her son will soon be published as a novel in Rio de Janeiro. Dona Sinhá's recriminations open the novel and will have important consequences for the love affair between the two young men: "O Senhor está abusando do meu nome. Não se faz isto com uma senhora" (*DS*, 3) (You are insulting my name. One doesn't do that to a lady) (*MS*, 3).[11] As the narrative develops, this powerful femininity becomes a crucial perspective in the text.

Both the biological and the "racial"/other mother (black nanny) are pivotal characters because José Maria is raised by his black nanny, Inácia. As Freyre has written before, it is the contact with this other mother and young black slaves that marks a "coming-of-age" narrative (i.e., sexual, sociocultural) of the Brazilian nation because "it was through his nurse that the child received the influences of the slave hut, absorbing with his first nourishment the germs of all the African diseases and superstitions" (*Casa Grande,* 372). Blacks simultaneously have a civilizing/corrupting mission in Brazilian national culture that, although analyzed in both novels, is more present in *Dona Sinhá's* bildungsroman.

Thus, the feminine, as a central element for fiction, reassures the love affair between Paulo and José Maria. And although their relationship reproduces the heterosexist patterns of patriarchy—presenting Paulo's aggressive masculinity and José Maria's passive femininity—these characteristics are central conditions for Paulo's writing. In this sense, Paulo's future book wants to "balance" masculine and feminine influences. In this portrait of the feminine, maternal love is a protective and controlling influence. For the narrator, José Maria's passivity comes from Dona Sinhá's protective love for her son:

> [Dona Sinhá] não gostava que tocasse no seu meninozinho nu ou para mudar as fraldas nem mesmo a negra Inácia, que a acompanhara do engenho . . . [Ele era] Alvo como um menino—Deus de presepe. Enxuto. Cabelinho alourado quase como o da mãe. A própria piroquinha, uma piroquinha de Menino-Jesus. Sinhá o contemplava como a um Menino-Jesus. Tratava-o como a um Menino-Jesus. A proporção que o menino foi crescendo, foi enchendo-o de fitas azuis como a um Menino-Jesus vivo. Foi deixando que o seu cabelo crescesse como o dos anjos e o das meninas. (*DS,* 26)

> [She did not like anyone to touch her little naked baby, not even black Inácia, who had come with her from the plantation as a wedding present from her father and in whom she (completely) trusted absolutely. He was pure as a Baby Jesus lying in a manger. So fine, with hair almost as light as his mother's. Even his little penis was just the kind that a Baby Jesus would have. Sinhá would gaze at him as though he really were Baby Jesus. She treated him as though he were one. And as the little boy grew, she covered him with blue ribbons as though he had been a real live Baby Jesus, and let his hair grow long like the hair of angels and little girls.] (*MS,* 33)

This ironic comparison with baby Jesus is important for José Maria's characterization because he is baptized "Maria" after the Virgin Mary. Thus, the religious foundational family and the future effeminate boy come together in Freyre's construction of a national imaginary. José Maria's devotion to the Virgin Mary stems from a promise that Dona Sinhá makes to the Virgin after her son falls ill with diarrhea. Juxtaposing Freud's anal stage with religious devotion, Freyre shows two complementary types of love and exchange: body/corporeal and religious/social. Freud, in fact, has analyzed anal eroticism as the first form of narcissism and as a stage that "creates an important reaction of the ego against the others" (166). For Julia Kristeva, the Virgin Mary, as an archetypal feminine power, "must have been experienced as denied power... a kind of substitute for effective power in the family and the city but no less authoritarian, the underhand double of explicit phallic power" ("Stabat Mater," 45).

This phallic power has been duplicated and syncretized in José Maria's devotion to the Virgin Mary because Inácia tells him stories about Iemanjá, the Yoruban goddess of the sea: "E temia a água funda: um temor misturado com uma vaga vontade de descer um dia ao seu mistério, é claro que protegido por Iemanjá" (*DS*, 28) (He feared the deep water, but mingled with his fear was a vague desire to descend to its mystery— protected of course by Iemanjá) (*MS*, 35). As Natalia Bolívar argues, Iemanjá and other Yoruban goddesses are part of a rigorous and phallic power. She describes them as "mujeres impetuosas, fuertes y rigurosas... que son justas y tienen un alto sentido de las jerarquías" (95) (impetuous, strong and rigorous women... with a strong sense of hierarchies).[12] Although José Maria receives his education from Dona Sinhá's controlling law, Inácia's "other" influences give him an emotional language in the form of syncretic religious devotion. Therefore, as Freyre suggests in *Casa Grande,* African languages and cultures influence the emotions and sexuality of the white lads (307–8).

José Maria discovers his sexuality in the water:

Pois a verdade é que já há algum tempo quando sozinho, no banho morno, ele dera para brincar com a piroca, amolegando-a como se fosse um passarinho, apertando-a como se fosse um dos peixinhos do seu aquário. (*DS*, 32)

[For the truth was that for some time now, whenever he was alone in his warm bath, he had taken to playing with his penis, patting it as though it were a baby bird or squeezing it as it though it were one of the little fish in his aquarium.] (*MS*, 40)

His own eroticism makes him desire to hear more oral African tales and to incorporate African words to his language. José Maria's encounters with Seu Tonho Pescador are part of this education: "(Seu Tonho) se deliciava em contar histórias da mãe de água aos pescadores mais moços"

(*DS,* 39) [(Seu Tonho) liked to tell stories about the Lady of the Water to the young fishermen] (*MS,* 50). These homosocial contacts have a sexual and erotic character that are part of a discovery of black otherness, not outside, but inside himself: "Seu pecado de brincar com a 'tetéia' talvez tivesse qualquer coisa de pecado africano. Feitiço. Mandinga. Quem lhe poderia trazer um pouco de luz sobre um assunto para ele tão escuro talvez fosse Inácia" (*DS,* 36) (Perhaps his sin of playing with his "pretty little penis" had an African sin about it, something of witchcraft, voodoo, black magic. Perhaps Inácia would be able to throw some light on the subject) (*MS,* 46). Although this quote has a strong ironic component, José Maria, influenced by Inácia's education, has made an/ "other" discovery in himself. Although Dona Sinhá is sexually repressive by separating him from the other black half of his identity, he learns about his sexuality through his relationship with Inácia (i.e., Africa, the sea).

Mães pretas like Inácia have been problematic for national projects in colonized and former slave societies because, as mother figures, they were presented as the carriers of sickness and racial contamination in colonial situations (Ramos; Stoler). In this sense, Freyre has separated from the *mãe preta* the "spiritual"component of the black race. At the same time, it is this contact with the black woman or man that produces the *desvio* (i.e., José Maria's homosexuality) in Brazilian national subjectivity. In this sense, the narrative shows that Inácia "sexualizes" José Maria with her blackness. And even though she is not sexually active, the contact with her body "deviates" José Maria. Although women's sexualities—as well as open homosexuality—threaten fraternal or "social" bonds between men, they are still necessary to build the "abject" of desire (Kristeva, *Poderes de la perversión,* 7–20). On the other hand, homosocial contacts are allowed because they provide forms of social knowledge. This explains how Paulo's and José Maria's long conversations with black fishermen give them new forms of knowledge: "Aprendeu com os pescadores do Largo a conhecer peixes... colecionou conchas deliciando-se em admirá-las" (*DS,* 65) (The Largo fishermen taught him so much about fish... he collected shells, he loved to look at them with a sensous admiration) (*MS,* 84). José Maria's repressed homosexuality, a half-subjectivity, is controlled by both the church and his phallic mother, who substitutes and mocks the name of the Father.[13]

Having a less complex profile than José Maria, Paulo Tavares shows masculine attributes and aggressive intelligence. Whenever José Maria's intuitive intelligence feels confused, Paulo responds in a protective way. As a masculine "performer," Paulo is José Maria's guide to manhood. In school, Paulo becomes his guard, protecting him from other boys who constantly refer to him as *Sinházinha* (Missy/Little Sinhá):[14]

> Perigosa amizade, essa, desde o início como o seu toque de amor ou o seu não sei quê de sexo. Com o seu pouco de amor proibido, proibidíssimo até, no tempo a que se refere a história, que aqui desajeitadamente se conta, embora ao rapaz protetor, já avançado em suas leituras, consolasse o fato de ter havido outro tempo ilustre, no passado humano, em que o normal era os Josés Marias serem protegidos pelos Paulos Tavares. (*DS*, 42)

> [There was something about that perilous friendship that smacked of forbidden love—very strictly forbidden indeed, in the time to which this awkwardly told story refers, although it must have been of some consolation to the youthful protector, already advanced in his reading, to know that there had been another time, an illustrious time in history of man, when it had been the normal thing for José Marias to be protected by the Paulo Tavareses.] (*MS*, 53)

Paulo Tavares, José Maria's protector and stronger side, is also an incomplete young man, socially and culturally. In this sense, their relationship presents Greek patterns of social love where men, as Foucault has analyzed, were part of an ideal reciprocity of social and cultural spaces (202–14). For the Greeks, pederasty as an educational and intellectual exchange was seen as a reflection about morals, aesthetics, and philosophical models (214). In his courtship, Paulo's brotherly love for José Maria will provide the "teaching and mastering of social and citizen truths" (Foucault 241). Consequently, kissing each other becomes their way to sign this social contract:

> Até onde terão ido as relações de protetor com protegido, de Paulo com José Maria, nos dias em que a amizade entre os dois se confundiu com atração sexual de um pelo outro? Não é fácil dizê-lo agora. Não seria a Gaspar, muito menos a Dona Sinhá que confessaria o próprio Paulo ter um dia perdido de todo o tino e beijado furiosamente na boca o seu franzino protegido: o fato vem apenas anotado, de modo um tanto cabalístico, no diariozinho de José Maria guardado pelo tio. A verdade é que a esse beijo e talvez a esse agarrado se teriam sucedido outros beijos

e outros agarrados, embora, pelo que sei dos dois, de Paulo e de José
Maria, os agarrados não tenham ido nunca a extremos de realização
sexual: só a antecipações de atos irrealizados. (*DS*, 45–46)[15]

[To what extent did the relationship between protector and protégé,
betweeen Paulo and José Maria, progress, in the days when the friendship between the two was mingled with sexual attraction? It is not easy
to tell now. Paulo would not have been likely to confess to Gaspar, much
less to Dona Sinhá, that one day he had lost his head and kissed his frail
protégé passionately on the mouth. The fact was merely noted, rather
cabalistically, in José Maria's diary, which his uncle has kept. There was
no doubt that the kiss (and perhaps the hug) had been followed by other
kisses and other hugs; although from what I know from both Paulo and
José Maria, the hugs had probably never gone to the extreme of sexual
fulfillment but had only anticipated uncompleted acts.] (*MS*, 57)

In this quote the narrator describes the kiss in various ways. The
erotic moment is first written "cabalistically" in José Maria's diary. Thus,
fiction opens itself to this "other" written text. Various narrative voices
comment on the scene with a celebratory tone; they are full of complicity, putting rumor and gossip between voyeurism and irony. A voyeuristic narrative follows this short relationship that ends when Paulo leaves
for Paris and José Maria enters a Catholic seminary. The latter would
subsequently fall ill with tuberculosis, and the former would return
only to find both his father and his best friend dead. Yet, this sorrowful
comeback represents an act of self-recuperation: "De sua parte sentia-se
restituído a um Brasil materno que de algum modo já vinha-lhe fazendo
falta entre franceses apenas fraternos *e entre francesas nem todas frater-
nas* (*DS*, 110; emphasis added) (For his own part, Paulo felt that he had
been restored to a maternal Brazil that he had missed while living
among Frenchmen who were fraternal at best *and Frenchwomen who
were not always fraternal*) (*MS*, 144).

This ironic quote shows the double character of *saudade*, which in-
tertwines fraternal love with maternal tenderness. In this sense, for writing national texts the fraternal community has to assimilate "maternity," as "mother nature," into its discourse. Therefore, rediscovering
nature is Paulo's return to maternal archetypes: "Ele sentia com o corpo
inteiro dentro daquela água de mar docemente morna como que restituído às fontes ou às raízes . . . Eram águas para ele maternas" (*DS*, 140–
41) (With his whole body immersed in that gentle, warm, ocean water,

Paulo felt as though he had been restored to the source, the root, of all that was deepest in him. To Paulo those waters were maternal) (*MS*, 185). At this moment, to restore/substitute his desire for José Maria becomes Paulo's main objective: "Muitas francesas beijara nos seus vários anos de Europa...Mas de nenhuma lhe ficaria na mémoria uma sensação de beijo igual à que recolhera um dia, no colégio, dos lábios de José Maria (*DS*, 164) (Paulo had kissed many Frenchwomen in the course of several years in Europe...None of their kisses, however, had left in his memory a sensation as intense as that he had received one day in school from the lips of José Maria) (*MS*, 217).

To recuperate José Maria, Paulo asks Dona Sinhá to marry him, but she rejects the offer. In this scene, Paulo's intentions to "find a mother" are really clear. But Sinhá is not an archetypal mother; therefore, these "natural waters" form part of a desire that is never fulfilled. Paulo's desire, then, comes together with the one for his absent father. Desiring the father and Dona Sinhá's controlling, negative love influence Paulo's exile, transforming them into *saudade* and patriotic love. *Saudade* becomes similar to the phallic anxiety created after the mother's repression and produces an incomplete subjectivity because, as Daniel Gerber suggests:

> Lejos de prometer la plenitud, el falo es la marca de la castración que hace del viviente un sujeto deseante, exilado del ser. Exilio del ser sin retorno posible, con una sola alternativa: explorar nuevas tierras en el intento de reencontrar la patria que no puede sino perderse. (Gerber 122)

> [The phallus as the mark of castration, instead of creating a completed subject, creates a desiring subject who is exiled from his own self. An exiled subject with no possible return and who has only one alternative: to explore new lands trying to find his fatherland (motherland) that is permanently lost.]

That is the reason why writing becomes Paulo Tavares's entrance to what Lacan has identified as the symbolic. In *O outro amor do Dr. Paulo*, the narrative explores Tavares's friendship with a group of Brazilian exiles in Paris. Through the descriptions of Paulo's travels, the narrative continuously contrasts northern European civilizations with Mediterranean ones. Although Paulo's romance with Maria Emília produces his *outro amor*, he never forgets his first passion, José Maria. Even though Maria Emília fits the model of an "ideal Brazilian woman," and is presented, as

I will show later, as a "masculine woman," Paulo longs for José Maria's "feminine" manhood.

The first part of this novel is a description of Paulo's *saudade* for José Maria. In the second part, we have a description of Paulo's travels with his lover and her family through Europe. Influenced by Hegelianism, Bergsonian philosophy, and Romanticism, this journey is a recollection of the national character of cultures.[16] For Paulo, intuition and chaos have triumphed over "logical European cultures," suggesting that the latter represents his prior conception of Brazil. Paulo Tavares's transformation after José Maria's death and his visit to Brazil now have an ethnographic gaze constructed by his own unfulfilled desire. He starts writing a new book, *Um brasileiro na Grécia,* a comparison of Europe and Brazil. In Paulo, the "penetrating intellect" of the ethnographic gaze constitutes itself as a desiring and aggressive subject that portrays ethnography as a "feminized" field (Killick 78, 83–85). Yet, and this is a crucial difference, Paulo Tavares's gaze openly responds to the "narratives of Western penetration," an important aspect that problematizes the roles of interpreter/interpreted (86). Thus, this gaze has "aggressive" and "passive" qualities that are at the same time "affective" and "affected." Paulo's desirous gaze is part of what Kate Altork has described as a "highly subjective process, affected deeply by bringing to play all of the senses" (115). Emotions created by his desire for José Maria consolidate an/other form of knowledge built as a "partial truth" because it does not assume totality and completion (Haraway 193).

Paulo's desire marks this project even though the writing of this experience is informed by both his return to Brazil with Maria Emília and their collaborative writing of a new book titled *Um brasileiro revê o Brasil.* This interpretation of Brazil "com fundamentos helênicos" (with foundations of Greek civilization) obliterates Maria Emília because it is written "com a tentativa de reconstituição de um seu amor de homem já de quase quarenta anos que seria mais uma sua grande aventura de personalidade à procura de si mesmo e do que lhe faltava de um Brasil, para ele, paradoxalmente um tanto helênico" (*OA,* 120) (with the intention of restoring him with the love of a forty-year-old man, his new adventure, an incursion into his personality and subjectivity that would lead to the discovery of what he missed from Brazil, a country that has always been for him paradoxically Greek in its nature). In this sense, the Greek foundations of Brazilian culture are laid when, after starting their writing project, Maria Emília dies and the book is never finished. An unfinished book is what influences a final displacement that creates a split subjectivity.

In this sense, *rever* (to rediscover) Brazil from the perspective of a lived European experience is what creates a new sense of cultural subjectivity:

> De acordo com uma sua idéia já antiga, ver era bom; rever melhor. Revendo agora ao Brasil, numa extensão da sua viagem anterior, já anos realizada, ele como que vinha verdadeiramente descobrindo uma terra e uma gente que sendo a sua, só poderia ser descoberta por um nativo com alguma coisa de estrangeiro nos seus modos de observar o *déjà vu*. (*OA*, 203)

> [According to his age-old idea, discovering was good but rediscovering was even better. Rediscovering Brazil now with the knowledge provided by that journey completed many years ago, he realized that he was finally discovering a land and people that, while they were his, could only be discovered with the eyes of a native and the qualities of observation of a stranger as if it were *déjà vu*].

By transforming *saudade* into *déjà vu*, the narrator/Paulo analyzes his country with a more critical and intellectualized gaze, one that comes from an "in-between" position in which desire and patriotic love are part of a displacement. In this sense, Paulo Tavares educates himself into patriotic love after he kissed José Maria and exiled himself in Europe: "Que se processara então em Paulo Tavares, tão respeitoso do amigo mais jovem? Passara a considerá-lo, sublimado um afeto ante outro, um irmão mais moço que não tivera e sempre desejara ter. Passou a amá-lo idealmente" (*OA*, 33) (What happened with Paulo's respect for his younger friend? He started to sublimate one affection after another and ended thinking of him like the younger brother that he had always wanted. He was his ideal love). Writing an interrupted book is, therefore, an act of sublimation and displacement (as desire and exile). National imaginaries are then constructed by this need for completion of a "possible" narrative. For Paulo Tavares, writing transforms itself into the search for the other part of his subjectivity, becoming the embodiment of a "masculinized femininity." We can see Maria Emília's influence in the book as the final substitution, because she is presented as a "masculine woman." Freyre's narrator in *O outro amor* stresses that Maria Emília's liberal upbringing gave her "boyish" and "tomboy" qualities:

Entretanto essas meninas criadas com tantos cuidados . . . quase sempre,
achavam jeito de gozar de liberdades aparentemente só de meninos.
Trepavam em árvores. Armavam arapucas para apanhar passarinhos.
Montavam a cavalo. Viam escondidas brigas de canários e até de galos.
Tinham meios secretos de se afirmarem e serem um tanto livres. (*OA*, 56)

[In the meantime these little girls that were brought up so carefully . . .
had opportunities that most of the time were reserved for young lads.
They climbed up trees. They built cages to capture birds. They rode
horses. They used to hide to watch canary and even cockfights. Quietly
they used to affirm their freedom.]

Consequently, masculinity is the most important quality in order to
construct an idealization of the feminine, whereby Maria Emília is vali-
dated, in comparison to European women, as "um novo tipo de mulher" (*OA*, 57) (a new type of woman). Nevertheless, her death reflects
the fact that the ideal "cultural fantasy" is a feminine man rather than a
masculine woman.

At the end of the novel, this fantasy becomes a reality, when a mature
Paulo Tavares has a platonic relationship with the attractive Russian
dilettante Diaghilev.[17] This young Russian man, a ballet producer, who
started "uma renovação dos tradicionais ballets . . . sacolejando o mundo
inteiro com uma nova expressão de arte" (a revolution in traditional ballets . . . shaking the entire world with this new art expression), hides an
important secret: "Dizia-se que os jovens que transformava em grandes
bailarinos, os transformava em amantes como se fossem mulheres. Bissexual" (*OA*, 229) (They said that he used to transform into lovers the
young men he trained for ballet and to love them like women. Bisexual).
Diaghilev's character is an allegory for Paulo's final psychological alliance between art, homoerotic desire, and sexuality. Brazilian national
difference, seen also as the "other" ballet that closes the novel, presents a
racially mixed country projected into a brilliant future: "Um ballet com
dançarinas de todas as cores. Brancas, pardas, negras e morenas" (*OA*,
241–42) (A ballet with ballerinas from every race. White, mixed, blacks,
and mulattas). Although the novel ends in the 1920s, Paulo Tavares dies
in 1913. His story is recalled in a flashback by his friend Camargo at the
beginning of the novel in 1937, the year when Brazilian populist leader
Getúlio Vargas inaugurated the Estado Novo.[18] While national politics
and culture find their "completion" in the figure of the populist father
or dictator, Paulo Tavares presents the paradoxical condition of the na-

tional writer: a desire for an/other that wants to be assimilated inside, as part of the same. It is in this threshold of ambiguity, in which the desire for the other is marked by the erotic, that Freyre defines the homoerotic. This particular view of desire between men keeps homosexuality as a major abjection, while it addresses the realms of completion, in the cultural fantasy of the nation.

Brazilian Homoerotics, Cultural Subjectivity

> E homem fantasiado de mulher que, à sombra de tal fantasia freudianamente significativa, não se exagere ou em remelexo de corpo ou em acréscimo artificial às próprias formas para ostentá-las como sua maior identificação com uma desejada figura de mulher?
> —Gilberto Freyre *Modos de homem e modas de mulher*

> [And who is the man who influenced by that significant Freudian fantasy of dressing up as a woman does not exaggerate his body movements and would love to have artificial implants to see himself as his desired fantasy woman?]

In Gilberto Freyre's fiction, the symptom of the nation emerges from a desire for completion, particularly one driven by a homoerotic text. Nationalism is reconfigured through a narrative of desire that ends up consolidating male alliances. This cultural subjectivity writes national culture through the transposition of gender and sexuality. In both of these novels, the "performative" character of "writing the nation" is constructed from the "performative" character of gender and its constant transposition (Bhabha, "DissemiNation," 299). Gender appears as "an identity tenuously constituted in time, instituted in an exterior space through a stylized repetition of acts" (Butler 140). Nationalism is seen as displacement, substitution, and a constant longing for equilibrium. Masculinity becomes an enunciative position that creates a social-historical and cultural genre as well (Bhabha, "Are You a Man or a Mouse?" 58). Therefore, national writers find that patriotic love is like masculinity: a displacement, a constant search for validation. As Homi K. Bhabha has suggested, the absence of the Father displaces another type of shared anxiety, *amor patriae:* "Holding onto this anxiety about the domestic scenario of rattish father-love, its compulsion and doubt, I want to displace it onto another kind of anxious love—*amor patriae*—the naturalist, phallic identification with the service of the nation" (ibid., 59).

Freyre represents nationhood by validating his writing and subjectivity through this phallic love, while the absent figure of the Father is a form of identification that slips away continuously. This "phallic peripherality" splits national love because "the national subject is then founded on the trace of the father's absent presence in the present of the mirror, whereas the mother's immanent 'over'-presentness is supplemental— marked by the overbearing shadow of the Father—but more clearly held in the line of vision" (ibid., 60). This anxiety constructs national subjectivity as a discursive order always in the border between identity and representation (ibid.). For Freyre, race and repressed homosexuality are the location of these liminal sites that, paradoxically, also constitute the same traits that define the Brazilian national imaginary. In *Dona Sinhá,* racial discourse associated with feminine characters, homoeroticism, African matriarchal myths of Yoruban religion, and archetypal images (i.e., Inácia, José Maria, Iemanjá, the sea) propose a series of signifiers linked to sexuality and the body. At the same time, the consolidation of masculine bondings in *Dona Sinhá* and *O outro amor* transforms *saudade* and Maria Emília's death into an ideal Brazilian "polis" form of racially uncontaminated patriotic love that is projected into the future. Even though femininity is manipulated to cultivate masculine bondings that will create a new manhood which goes against older forms of patriarchy, Freyre feels *saudade* for that absent father figure. Even in the erotic and cultural fantasies of strong, masculine women such as Dona Sinhá or Maria Emília, the narrator wants to restore his control. As the liberal son wanting to restore his power against the old patriarchy, Freyre longs for new forms of social power. Paulo, his alter ego, has understood his Brazilian reality with foreign eyes, a central fact for nation-building projects.

Homosexuality and the contact with the black race exemplified in Paulo's coming-of-age "initiations" into social life are essential for defining Brazilian national projects. Displacing and relocating them as signifiers is the key for "representing" the symptom of Brazilian cultural subjectivity. Threatened by the fluidity and temporality of the same racial signifier that constitutes them, Brazilian national discourses construct a cultural ideal model based on male bonding. Through this model, the mother, as reproductive subject, is seen as an abject, while the father becomes an absent presence that is desired continuously. These Brazilian homoerotic narratives locate the dangers of racial miscegenation in the woman's body because, as Laura Doyle has suggested, she is a figure in which sex and race converge (21). As other theorists have argued, for Gilberto Freyre, Brazilian narratives about culture are oriented toward a masculinity that needs homoeroticism as a creative source for writing (Benzaquen). Like other postcolonial intellectuals, Freyre describes a problematic epistemological journey inside the realms of subjectivity and power from a position that combines a privileged gaze with a new sense of brotherhood, a sensitive masculinity. In this journey, the figure of the "sissy" creates the "other" as a subjective liminal position because, as Freyre confessed in *Dona Sinhá*, José Maria, more than a character, is that other half of himself who "existed in the ancestors of some of us and still exists within ourselves" (52).

Notes

This essay is an English translation of a chapter of my *Travestismos culturales: literatura y etnografía en Cuba y Brasil*. My grateful thanks to Gilberto Blasini, César Braga-Pinto, Francine Masiello, Candace Slater, Silviano Santiago, Julio Ramos, and the editors of this anthology for their valuable comments on this essay.

1. All translations are mine unless otherwise indicated.

2. *Mães pretas* or black nannies have been very important in the analysis of slave societies in Latin America and the Caribbean. As in the U.S. South, the "nanny" or "mammy" played an important role as member of the household. It was she who breast-fed and raised the white children for generations. For many nineteenth-century Brazilian writers, the nannies appeared as ambivalent characters who were "dangerous" and necessary for the family. It was believed that their presence would "corrupt" the white children with their bodies, stories, language, and sexual overtones, and at the same time they were seen as mother figures whose power was undeniable. Gilberto Freyre romanticizes this relationship between nannies and children, maintaining these contradictions. Slavery as an economic exploitative system recreated these stereotypes and myths of female disorder, based mainly on fears of miscegenation. See Freyre, *Casa-grande e senzala;* Stoler, *Race and the Education of Desire;* Ramos, "A Citizen Body."

3. Owing to the political atmosphere of the times and the controversial criticism of his sociological work, these works were received as minor literary experiments. From 1964 to 1984, Brazil experienced a military dictatorship. Although the first ten years of the dictatorship were repressive for Marxist politics, guerrillas, and leftist intellectuals, particularly from São Paulo, Gilberto Freyre continued publishing his works. See Carlos Guilherme Mota, *Ideologia da cultura brasileira 1933–1974* (São Paulo: Editora Ática, 1990); 54–83. Although Freyre was seen as conservative by the new political and intellectual elite, some of his works published after 1964 were important analyses of this new "cultural" moment of Brazilian politics, and *aber-*

tura to international and transnational capitalism. See Gilberto Freyre, *Modos de homem e Modas de mulher.*

4. For Freyre's uses of the masculine as an ambiguous site for explaining national culture, see Ricardo Benzaquen de Araujo's excellent essay "Guerra e Paz: Casa Grande e Senzala e a obra de Gilberto Freyre nos anos 30" (1994).

5. For the purpose of this reading, I will use both the terms *homosocial* and *homoerotic.* Homosociality will refer to social interactions between men. Homoerotic will refer to the spaces in which there is physical contact of a sexual nature or with sexual overtones.

6. See Do Valle Silva and Hanselbag, *Relações raciais no Brasil contemporâneo;* Thomas Skidmore, *Neither Black nor White, Race and Nationality in Brazilian Thought* (Durham, N.C.: Duke University Press, 1993); and Florestan Fernandes, *A integração do negro na sociedade de classes,* vols. 1–2 (São Paulo: Editora Ática, 1978).

7. For a comparative perspective between Brazil and the United States, see Roberto Da Matta and David J. Hess, *The Brazilian Puzzle: Culture on the Borderlands of the Western World* (New York: Columbia University Press, 1995) and Roberto Da Matta, *Carnival, Rogues and Heroes: An Interpretation of the Brazilian Dilemma,* trans. John Drury (Notre Dame, Ind.: Notre Dame University Press, 1991).

8. About homosexuality and masculinity, see Nestor Perlongher, *O negocio do michê em São Paulo: A prostituição viril* (São Paulo: Brasiliense, 1987); Luiz R. Mott, *Escravidão, homossexualidade e demonologia* (São Paulo: Icone, 1988); Helio Silva, *Travesti* (1993); João Silvério Trevisan, *Perverts in Paradise (Devassos no paraíso),* trans. Martin Foreman (London: Gay Men's Press, 1986); James N. Green, *Beyond Carnival: Male Homosexuality in Twentieth Century Brazil* (Chicago: University of Chicago Press, 1999); Dário Caldas, ed., *Homens: comportamento, sexualidade, mudança, identidade, crise, vaidade* (São Paulo: SENAC, 1997); Peter Fry, *O que é homossexualidade* (São Paulo: Brasiliense, 1991); and Richard Parker, *Bodies, Pleasures and Passions: Sexual Culture in Contemporary Brazil* (Boston: Beacon Press, 1991) and *Beneath the Equator: Cultures of Desire, Male Homosexuality and Emerging Gay Communities in Brazil* (New York: Routledge, 1999). From a feminist perspective, see Ruth Landes's pioneering work from 1947, *The City of Women* (Albuquerque: University of New Mexico Press, 1994); Sonia Alvarez, "Politicizing Gender and Engendering Democracy," in *Democratizing Brazil* (New Haven: Oxford University Press, 1986); Carmen Barroso and Christina Bruschini, "Building Politics from Personal Lives: Discussions on Sexuality among Poor Women in Brazil," in *Third World Women and the Politics of Feminism,* ed. Chandra Talpade Mohanty, Ann Russo, and Lourdes Torres (Bloomington: Indiana University Press, 1991), 153–72; Angela Gilliam's essay "Womens Equality and National Liberation," in *Third World Women and the Politics of Feminism,* 215–36; and Joana Maria Pedro and Miriam Pillar Grossi, *Masculino, Feminino, Plural, gênero na interdisciplinariedade* (Florianópolis: Editora Mulheres, 1998).

9. Paul Gilroy's term *homophilia* applies to masculine alliances in these novels, because it refers to social love between men and also to "love of the same" (quoted in bell hooks's essay "Feminism as a Persistent Critique of History: What's Love Got to Do with It?" In *The Facts of Blackness: Frantz Fanon and Visual Representation,* ed. Alan Read [London: Institute of Contemporary Arts, 1996], 76–85). This "love of the same" relates directly to Plato's *Symposium* and the theory of the androgynous in which men who were "originally attached" to other men love men and boys be-

cause "they are valiant and manly, and have manly countenance and they embrace that which is like them" (Plato, "Symposium"). Also, for Freyre, this love has a social and ethical form. It is obvious that Freyre's view of homosexuality was heavily influenced by his readings of Sigmund Freud, but also by the works of Carl Jung and, particularly, Alfred Adler. But Freud seems to be his major influence, especially his notions of culture as repression of desire and bisexuality. In one of his interesting notes from an article about homosexuality and neurosis, Freud tells one story that could be used for Freyre's allegories of national brotherhood: "Once I met two twin brothers who had a very strong libido. One of them was very fortunate with women, and had many sexual encounters. The other followed in his footsteps for a while, but it was so uncomfortable to become a rival of his brother, and to be compared with him during those intimate moments, that he solved this situation by becoming a homosexual. In this manner, he cleared the way for his brother" (234); see Freud, *Ensayos sobre la vida sexual y la teoría de las neurosis,* 19–44. See also R. W. Conell, "The Science of Masculinity," in *Masculinities* (Berkeley: University of California Press, 1995), 3–44.

10. Although present in the novels, Edilberto Coutinho's theory seems to ignore the complex connection between writing, culture, (repressed) homosexuality, and national politics not only in Freyre's works but in other Brazilian literary texts as well. One of the most important novels in Brazilian literature, *Bom-crioulo* (1891) by Adolfo Caminha, is a "foundational fiction" of homosexual and interracial love. Pathology, sickness, and "sexual depravation" are part of Caminha's Naturalist narrative, which focuses on the "dangers" of racial and sexual alliances between blacks and whites. Thus, homosexuality is an important topic for Brazilian writers. In the specific case of Freyre, I am also using homosexuality as an important theme, with no intention of discussing his sexual preferences. To understand his uses or misuses of homosexuality and the feminine I will quote some statements from Freyre's diary in Europe, *Tempo morto e outros tempos,* in which he uses homoerotic images to subvert European masculine fantasies of colonial domination. Homosexuality is, then, the site in which these encounters between national culture and politics converge: "Cortejado não só por lindas inglesinhas como por mais de um louro inglesinho, desde que estou na Inglaterra. Sinto-me um pouco um Romeu moreno entre louras e Julietas de toda espécie. . . . Em Oxford não são de todo raras as danças de rapazes com rapazes: danças animadas por muito vinho do Porto que para os ingleses é o vinho dos vinhos. São danças que às vezes terminam em beijos e abraços. A verdade, porém, é que tais explosões não sejam tão freqüentes, aqui, como na Alemanha de após-guerra. Aí ao mito da 'raça de senhores' corresponde muito masoquismo sexual da parte de alemães jovens, dos mais senhoris que parecem deliciar-se em ser machucados por morenos ou por exóticos. Em Oxford o que se encontra é, antes, a tendência para intensas amizades de rapazes com rapazes semelhantes às que existiam —suponho eu— entre os gregos platônicos. Podem ter às vezes alguma coisa de homossexual. Mas, quase sempre —é o que me parece— um homossexualismo transitório (Since I have been here in England I have been courted not only by beautiful young English ladies but also by young blond men. I feel like a sort of dark-skinned Romeo surrounded by blond women and Juliets of every kind. . . . In Oxford it is not strange to see a young man dancing with another young man: in these dances Port wine is continuously imbibed, because the English believe that Port wine is the best of wines. These are dances that sometimes end with plenty

of hugs and kisses. It is true that this behavior is not as common here as it was in post-war Germany. There the myth of "a superior race" developed a sort of sexual masochism in young German men, even in the more superior ones, who loved to be "punished" in practices of sexual bondage by dark-skinned "exotic" men. In Oxford, what you find is a type of Greek platonic friendship between young men. Sometimes they could be homosexual. But it seems like a transitory homosexuality) (quoted in Edilberto Coutinho, *A imaginação do real: uma leitura da ficção de Gilberto Freyre* [Rio de Janeiro: José Olympio, 1983], 169). See also Ricardo Noblat, "Entrevista com Gilberto Freyre," *Playboy* (São Paulo) 5: 56) (March 1980): 27–34, 96–105.

11. All the English translations of *Dona Sinhá e o filho padre* are from the English edition, *Mother and Son: A Brazilian Tale*. All translations to *O outro amor do Dr. Paulo* are mine.

12. For Cuban ethnographer Lydia Cabrera, Iemanjá/Yemayá also has a double identity of feminine and masculine energies that is called Yemayá-Olokún, the sea and the ocean. See Lydia Cabrera, *Yemayá y Ochún: kariocha, iyalorichas, y olorichas* (Miami: Ediciones Universal, 1996).

13. As Gilberto Freyre has described in *Casa Grande e Senzala,* the father not only controlled his family and his *fazenda,* but also influenced the local politicians and the church with his power (196–200). The novel portrays the late 1890s, the time of the decadence of the patriarchal regime.

14. In Portuguese, "Sinhá" was the corrupted version of *senhorinha* and used for the daughter in the *casa grande* or patriarchal sugarhouses. José Maria is called *Sinházinha* (translated as "Missy" in Barbara Shelby's translation) and this literally means "Little Sinhá" or "the daughter of Sinhá." This nickname reflects José Maria, as the "daughter of Sinhá," and does not have any referents leading to the paternal order. The narrator says: "Sinhá, viúva e só, distante da parentela dos engenhos ... criara, na verdade no filho único a sua imagem" (*DS,* 26) (Sinhá as a lonely widow so far from her family in the sugar mills reared her only son in her image) (*MS,* 32). As the "son of Sinhá," he is outside the paternal structure, a fact that puts him in a marginal/unidentified position (sexually, socially, economically).

15. As Silviano Santiago discussed with me in an informal interview, the original manuscript of this novel contained more homoerotic scenes, but Freyre had to eliminate them for fear of public and/or personal censorship.

16. Henri Bergson was a French philosopher from the 1920s who influenced the French avant-garde movements. His "intuitive" philosophy was very influenced by Freud and the artistic currents of those years presented a world in which psychological and corporal intuition was more important that the logical order of science and history.

17. An obvious reference to Sergei Diaghilev.

18. Starting the novel's flashback in 1937 is important because that is the year in which populist leader and president Getúlio Vargas founds the Estado Novo (1937–45). In this sense, writing the national becomes an allegorical image of a political system that "leveled" regional interests that were fighting for political power. Therefore, in this final equilibrium of masculine and feminine forces, the populist patriarch or head of state is the father figure. From the Estado Novo as an ideal regime for intellectuals such as Freyre, Mônica Pimenta Velloso quotes, from the *Estadonovista* journal *Cultura política:* "A originalidade do regime é personificada na figura de Vargas, que encarna e concretiza os 'desejos' do povo ... sua maior originalidade

consiste no fato de ter sido previsto por um homem que teve a coragem de proclamá-lo dando-lhe corpo. *Na realidade ele já existia no íntimo de cada um, na alma mesma da Nação como um desejo latente e impossível*" (84; emphasis in the original) (The regime's originality is personified in the figure of [Getúlio] Vargas, who embodies and concretizes the "wishes" of the people . . . whose originality consists in the fact of having been foreseen as a man who had the courage to proclaim himself, giving himself body. *The truth was that he already existed inside of us, in our Nation's soul, as a latent and impossible desire*) (Mônica Pimenta Velloso, "Cultura e poder político: uma configuração do campo intelectual," in *Estado novo: Ideologia e poder* [Rio de Janeiro: Zahar, 1982], 84).

Works Cited

Altork, Kate. "Walking the Fire Line: The Erotic Dimension of the Fieldwork Experience." In *Taboo, Sex, Identity, and Erotic Subjectivity in Anthropological Fieldwork*, ed. Don Kullick and Margaret Wilson. London: Routledge, 1995. 107–39.

Anderson, Benedict. *Imagined Communities: Reflections on the Origins and Spread of Nationalism*. New York: Verso, 1992.

Arinos de Melo Franco, Antonio. "Uma obra rabelaisiana." In *Casa-grande e senzala e a crítica brasileira de 1933 a 1944*. Recife: Companhia Editora de Pernambuco, 1985. 81–88.

Arroyo, Jossianna. "El cuerpo del esclavo y la narrativa de la nación en *Casa Grande e Senzala* de Gilberto Freyre." *Lucero: A Journal of Iberian and Latin American Studies* 4 (1993): 31–42.

———. *Travestismos culturales: literatura y etnografía en Cuba y Brasil*. Pittsburgh: Iberoamericana, 2002.

Benzaquen de Araujo Ricardo. *Guerra e paz e a obra de Gilberto Freyre nos anos 30*. Rio de Janeiro: Editora 34, 1994.

Bhabha, Homi K. "Are You a Man or a Mouse?" In *Constructing Masculinity*, ed. Maurice Berger, Brian Wallis, and Simon Watson. New York: Routledge, 1995. 57–68.

———. "DissemiNation: Time, Narrative and the Margins of the Modern Nation." In *Nation and Narration*. London: Routledge, 1991. 291–322.

Bolívar, Natalia. *Los orishas en Cuba*. Havana: Unión de Escritores, 1990.

Butler, Judith. *Gender Trouble: Feminism and the Subversion of Identity*. New York: Routledge, 1990.

Chaterjee, Partha. "Nationalism as a Problem in the History of Political Ideas." In *Nationalist Thought and the Colonial World: A Derivative Discourse*. Minneapolis: University of Minnesota Press, 1986. 1–35.

Clifford, James. "Partial Truths." In *Writing Culture: The Poetics and Politics of Ethnography*, ed. James Clifford and George E. Marcus. Berkeley: University of California Press, 1986. 1–26.

Cruz Malavé, Arnaldo. *El primitivo implorante: el "sistema poético del mundo" de José Lezama Lima*. Atlanta: Rodopia, 1994.

———. "Toward an Art of Transvestism: Colonialism and Homosexuality in Puerto Rican Literature." In *¿Entiendes? Queer Readings, Hispanic Writings*, ed. Emilie L. Bergmann and Paul Julian Smith. Durham, N.C.: Duke University Press, 1995. 137–67.

Cunningham, George P. "Called into Existence: Desire, Gender and Voice in Frederick Douglass's *Narrative* of 1845." *differences: Journal of Feminist Cultural Studies* 1:3 (1989): 108–36.

Da Matta, Roberto. "Para uma antropologia da saudade." In *Conta de mentiroso: sete ensaios de antropologia brasileira.* Rio de Janeiro: Rocco, 1993. 17–34.

Do Valle Silva, Nelson, and Carlos Hanselbag. *Relações raciais no Brasil contemporâneo.* Rio de Janeiro: Rio Fundo, 1992.

Doyle, Laura. *Bordering on the Body: The Racial Matrix of Modern Fiction and Culture.* New York: Oxford University Press, 1994.

Fanon, Frantz. *Black Skins, White Masks.* Trans. Charles Lam Markman. New York: Grove Press, 1967.

Foucault, Michel. *The History of Sexuality.* Vol. 2, *The Use of Pleasure.* Trans. Robert Hurley. New York: Vintage Books, 1990.

Freud, Sigmund. "Civilization and Its Discontents." In *The Freud Reader,* ed. Peter Gay. New York: Norton, 1995. 722–71.

———. *Ensayos sobre la vida sexual y la teoría de las neurosis.* Madrid: Alianza Editorial, 1988.

Freyre, Gilberto. *Casa-grande y senzala: La formación de la familia brasileña bajo el régimen de la economía patriarcal.* Caracas: Ayacucho, 1985.

———. "Como e porque sou e não sou escritor." In *Como e porque sou e não sou sociólogo.* Brasília: Universidade de Brasília, 1968.

———. *Dona Sinhá e o filho padre.* Rio de Janeiro: José Olympio, 1964.

———. *Masters and Slaves: A Study in the Development of Brazilian Civilization.* Trans. Samuel Putnam. Berkeley: University of California Press, 1986.

———. *Modos de homem e modos de mulher.* Rio de Janeiro: Editora Record, 1986.

———. *Mother and Son: A Brazilian Tale.* Trans. Barbara Shelby. New York: Knopf, 1967.

———. "O Camarada Whitman." In *6 Conferências em busca de um leitor.* Rio de Janeiro: José Olympio, 1965. 85–113.

———. *O outro amor do Dr. Paulo.* Rio de Janeiro: José Olympio, 1977.

———. "O que W.L. disse das mulheres." In *Artigos de jornal.* Recife: Mozart, 1935. 81.

———. "Serei um escritor obsceno?" In *Alhos e bugalhos: Ensaios sobre temas contraditórios: de Joyce a cachaça de José Lins do Rego a cartão postal.* Rio de Janeiro: Nova Fronteira, 1978. 178.

———. *Sociologia: Introdução a seus principios.* Vol. 1. Rio de Janeiro: José Olympio, 1945.

Gerber, Daniel. "La represión y el inconsciente." In *La reflexión de los conceptos de Freud en la obra de Lacan.* Mexico City: Siglo XXI, 1983. 81–169.

Ginsberg, Elaine K. "The Politics of Passing." In *Passing and the Fictions of Identity.* Durham, N.C.: Duke University Press, 1996. 1–18.

Haraway, Donna J. "Situated Knowledges: The Science Question in Feminism and the Privilege of Partial Perspective." In *Simians, Cyborgs, and Women: The Reinvention of Nature.* New York: Routledge, 1991. 183–202.

Killick, Andrew P. "The Penetrating Intellect: On Being White, Straight and Male in Korea." In *Taboo, Sex, Identity, and Erotic Subjectivity in Anthropological Fieldwork,* ed. Don Kullick and Margaret Wilson. London: Routledge, 1995. 76–106.

Kristeva, Julia. *Poderes de la perversión.* Mexico City: Siglo XXI, 1988.

————. "Stabat Mater." In *Tales of Love,* trans. Leon S. Roudiez. New York: Columbia University Press, 1987. 45.

Lopes, Francisco Caetano. "Uma subjetividade outra." In *Toward a SocioCriticism: Luso-Brazilian Literatures,* ed. Roberto Reis. Tempe: Arizona State University Press, 1991. 67–74.

Mosse, George L. *The Image of Man: The Creation of Modern Masculinity.* New York: Oxford University Press, 1996.

Piedra, José. "Nationalizing Sissies." In *¿Entiendes? Queer Readings, Hispanic Writings,* ed. Emilie L. Bergmann and Paul Julian Smith. Durham, N.C.: Duke University Press, 1995. 370–409.

Plato. "Symposium." In *Lysis, Phaedras, Symposium: Plato on Homosexuality,* trans. Benjamin Jowett, notes by Eugene O'Connor. New York: Prometheus Books, 1991. 103–57.

Ramírez, Rafael L. *Dime capitán: reflexiones sobre la masculinidad.* Río Piedras: Huracán, 1993.

Ramos, Julio. "A Citizen Body: Cholera in Havana (1883)." *Dispositio* 19:46 (1994): 179–95.

Silva, Helio. *Travesti: a invenção do feminino.* Rio de Janeiro: ISER, 1993.

Sommer, Doris. "Irresistible Romance." In *Foundational Fictions: The National Romances of Latin America.* Berkeley: University of California Press, 1991. 1–30.

Stoler, Ann L. *Race and the Education of Desire: Foucault's History of Sexuality and the Social Order of Things.* Durham, N.C.: Duke University Press, 1995.

Žižek, Slavoj. "How Did Marx Invent the Symptom?" In *The Sublime Object of Ideology.* London: Verso, 1989. 11–54.

CHAPTER FIVE

Fictions of the Impossible

Clarice Lispector, Lúcio Cardoso, and "Impossibilidade"

Severino João Albuquerque

> In some way each of us offers up his life to an impossibility. But it is
> also true that the impossibility ends up by being closer to our fingers
> than we are ourselves.
>
> —Lispector 1986: 343

In a key passage of *Epistemology of the Closet*, Eve Kosofsky Sedgwick
addresses the important, and highly ironic, role the closet has played in
Western culture in general, as one of its most productive tensions in the
past one hundred years or so, providing culture with breadth and even
a certain consistency and longevity. Although she acknowledges the
risks inherent in such a claim and takes pains to remark on the ills entailed by the closet, Sedgwick asserts that it has been "inexhaustibly productive of modern Western culture and history at large" (68). The closet,
or "the regime of the open secret," as she sometimes calls it, with its
limiting and contradictory rules regarding privacy and openness, the
public and the private, knowledge and ignorance, has contributed significantly to the formulation of key issues concerning value and epistemology in contemporary society.

Proust's figure looms large in this discussion: one of the chapters of
Epistemology concerns itself with Proust and references to the French
novelist are found throughout the book. The epigraph to the chapter
(chapter 1) I draw upon the most is a passage from Proust's *The Captive*
that has considerable relevance to my topic.[1] There are important factors
approximating Marcel Proust (1871–1922) and Lúcio Cardoso (1912–1968)
in matters of sensitivity and taste, sexuality, lifestyle, and literature.

With a marginalized sexuality manifested throughout their writing and their lives, both writers exemplify how figures of homosexuality function at the limits of narrative (with homoerotic incidents hidden in plain sight) and at the borders between public and private discourse (as seen in their letters and diaries, for example). And perhaps most important, both men preceded the "invention of the homosexual," which evolved between the Wilde trials and Stonewall, but whereas Proust lived in a society that was central to and contemporaneous with that process, Lúcio survived as other in a world that was itself peripheral to this invention, and other key developments in twentieth-century thought.

In a society such as Brazil—subaltern and dependent, on the one hand, and carnivalizing and cannibalistic, on the other—the notion of inversion holds a key place. Mindful of the widely discussed views of Bakhtin and Da Matta on carnivalization in general, and of Richard Parker on the particular of homosexuality in Brazil,[2] I proceed to use the pertinent ideas put forth by Sedgwick in *Epistemology* and Judith Butler in her article "Imitation and Gender Insubordination."

Sedgwick rejects the traditional, homophobic "inversion trope," that is, the concept of "inversion" as "anima muliebris in corpore virili inclusa" (a woman's soul caught in a man's body) or vice versa, because it is grounded on the perpetuation of the idea of an essential heterosexual desire, the attraction between male and female, regardless of the sex of the bodies housing such elements (*Epistemology,* 87). Related to this notion, but in part contradictory to it, is the trope of "gender separatism," which, according to Sedgwick, "tends to reassimilate to one another identification and desire, where inversion models, by contrast, depend on their distinctness" (88).

The complex relationship between the two models in the last one hundred years (since the foundation in 1897, by Magnus Hirschfeld and others, of the German movement for homosexual rights) is crucial for an understanding of gender asymmetry, oppression, and resistance (ibid.). Of foremost interest to me here is the fact that, if one considers that the "gender inversion" topos posits the male homosexual's tendency to identify with the heterosexual woman, Lúcio's self-imaging vis-à-vis Clarice Lispector could only lead to a relational impasse.[3] Furthermore, because Lúcio never had a strong and stable relationship with another male homosexual,[4] his only outlets were either what I call "relacionamentos de sensibilidade" (aesthetic friendships) with Octávio de Faria and later,

Walmir Ayala, for example, or else, fortuitous encounters that only increased his sense of guilt and sin, as witnessed in some passages of his
Diário completo.

In her analysis of the homosexual individual's alledged inversion and
imitation of the opposite heterosexual gender, Judith Butler appends a
long discussion to the axiom "Gender is a kind of imitation for which
there is no original" (which she prefers to reword into "a kind of imitation that produces the very notion of the original as an effect and consequence of the imitation itself"). She later concludes that mere inver-
sions are impossible, for "the entire framework of copy and origin
proves radically unstable as each position inverts into the other and
confounds the possibility of any stable way to locate the temporal or
logical priority of either term" ("Imitation," 22). Elaborating on the idea
put forth by Derrida in "The Double Session" (included in *Dissemination*), that inversion is to be understood through a careful study of
mimetic displacement, Butler asserts:

> If the structure of gender imitation is such that the imitat*ed* is to some
> degree produced—or, rather, *re*produced—by imitation, . . . then to
> claim that gay and lesbian identities are implicated in heterosexual
> norms or in hegemonic culture generally is not to derive gayness from
> straightness. On the contrary, imitation does not copy that which is
> prior, but produces and inverts the very terms of priority and
> derivativeness. (21)

It is my contention here that the relationship between Clarice Lispector and Lúcio Cardoso constitutes an excellent framework for an examination of the interplay among derivation, (re)production, and inversion
in the core of mid-twentieth century Brazilian cultural construction.

When she met Lúcio Cardoso in the early 1940s (he was twenty-eight
and she about twenty years old in 1940), Clarice Lispector was embarking on a career that would, three decades later, give her a prominent
place in Brazilian letters. The ambiguity she immediately sensed in Lúcio's figure was to be a crucial element both in the attraction she felt for
him and in the development and expression of her fictional world.[5] A
relationship gradually developed that was based on affinities beyond
the literary realm and that soon revealed the duplicity and ambivalence
that Teresa de Lauretis identifies as central to female desire and its entwined passivity and action (1984: 156), and at the same time confirmed

Butler's contention regarding the instability of "the entire framework of copy and origin."

Thanks to the many masks behind which she hid and by means of which she simultaneously revealed herself, Clarice Lispector composed a mystique of ambiguity throughout her entire life. Through reticence, evasion, indirection, and conflicting information found in her spoken and written texts, Clarice cultivated uncertainty regarding her age (giving different birth dates to different interviewers), nationality (calling herself alternately Russian, Ukranian, Brazilian, *nordestina* [northeastern Brazilian]), ethnic background (whether or not she considered herself Jewish), physical appearance, political and other personal opinions, and so forth. Such uncertainty included her sexuality, which was not discussed, especially not in writing, until the 1990s, not only because she consistently refused to talk about it, but also because she was assumed to be heterosexual.[6] But her intense attachment to women—especially toward the end of her life—was well known. Among such liaisons, two are particularly well known, the first with her nurse Siléa Marchi (who was hired after Clarice suffered severe burns in a 1966 fire at her home), and more important, the second, with the writer Olga Borelli, who introduced herself to Clarice in 1971 and stayed with her until Clarice died in 1977.[7]

Having mastered earlier in life the art of dealing with what Hélène Cixous sees as a major obstacle in dealing with difference,[8] Clarice approached Lúcio Cardoso as "the same that is not," a source that would provide her with clues to production and derivation.[9] Lúcio's presence is strongly felt as image and as foil in two of Clarice's short stories written in 1940–41 and published posthumously in *A bela e a fera* (Beauty and the beast). In the suggestively titled "História interrompida" (Interrupted story), the female narrator remembers the figure of W., whom she had longed to marry one day. Becoming aware of his cold detachment, she tried in vain "achar a fórmula que pudesse salvá-lo" (to find the key to his salvation) (Lispector 1979a: 18). Attempting to justify W.'s coyness, the woman admits to having tried to convince herself to accept the truism "destrói-se tudo em torno de si, mas a si próprio e aos desejos (nós temos um corpo) não se consegue destruir" (16) (we destroy everything around ourselves but our identity and our desires [for we do have a body] we cannot destroy).

The idea of the impossibility of developing a relationship with an equal, with "a same that is," grounds the story "Obsessão" (Obsession), in which Daniel, who is apparently based on Lúcio (Barbosa 1993b: 184), kindles in Cristina not only an attraction that she feels is "diferente de amor" (other than love), but also something "mais impossível ainda" (more impossible still); "ele me amaria e eu me vingaria, sentindo-me ... igual a ele" (*A bela,* 68) (he'd love me and I'd avenge myself, believing myself to be ... like him). Unable to feel (let alone be) like Daniel, Cristina breaks up with the object of her desire. Returning to Jaime, the husband she had left for Daniel, she resumes a hopeless situation, for Jaime in his turn "adivinhava-me diferente dele" (82) (sensed that I was different from him).

Among the letters Clarice sent Lúcio,[10] the oldest still extant, dated Belo Horizonte, July 13, 1941, closes with an intriguing postscript: "Esta carta você não precisa 'rasgar'" (Carelli, *Corcel de fogo,* 44) (this one you don't need to "destroy"). This comment suggests strongly that there were previous letters and that they carried the sender's request that they be destroyed. Whether or not Lúcio followed Clarice's instructions is unknown, but the absence of any letter prior to the one just quoted suggests they were indeed destroyed. Although the verb *rasgar* appears in quotation marks (and it is not clear why),[11] one assumes that Clarice might have been concerned with the compromising content of her letters to Lúcio, which possibly included declarations of sensuality and love, for, as Clarice herself explained years later,

> ele fora a pessoa mais importante da minha vida durante a minha adolescência. Naquela época ele me ensinava como se conhecem as pessoas atrás das máscaras, ensinava o melhor modo de olhar a lua.... Em tantas coisas éramos tão fantásticos que, se não houvesse a impossibilidade, quem sabe teríamos nos casado ("Lúcio Cardoso," 244).

> [in my adolescent years he had been the most important person in my life.... At that time he taught me how to get to know people hiding behind their masks, taught me the best way to look at the moon.... We were so wondrously alike that, had it not been for the impossibility, we might have married each other, who knows.]

Curiously enough, although Clarice was twenty-one years old when she wrote that letter from Belo Horizonte, she uses the term *adolescence* in this 1969 reminiscence, possibly to cover up discrepancies about her age.[12] But what really matters here is Clarice's use of terms such as *im-*

possibilidade (impossibility) or, a few lines earlier in the same text, "sua vida misteriosa e secreta" (his secret, mysterious life) as a euphemism for Lúcio's homosexuality.

The relationship remains strong as the decade progresses, surviving even Clarice's marriage to another man in 1943, the diplomat Maury Gurgel Valente. Clarice's persistence remains equally strong, as she tries to topple Lúcio's reticence and self-imposed barriers, as shown in the following passages from a letter dated Belém do Pará, February 6, 1944: "Eu só falo de mim porque nem sei o modo de abordar você" (I speak [write] only about myself because I wouldn't know how to approach your inner self); and, revisiting the conversation they had had as they said good-bye in Rio before she departed on this trip, Clarice alludes to what may have been the core of their problem: "Quando eu telefonei para você pra me despedir fiquei aborrecida com um engano seu. Eu disse que nunca tinha podido chegar mais perto de seus problemas porque você nunca deixava" (Carelli, *Corcel do fogo,* 44) (When I called you up to say good-bye I was upset with a misperception of yours. What I really said was that I had never been able to get closer to your problems because you never allowed me to).

It would be another decade and a half until Clarice came to terms with the impasse occasioned by this essential difference. By then she was writing *A maçã no escuro* (1961) (*The Apple in the Dark* [1967]), a key text in her fictional output. The search for understanding of the other is central in *A maçã no escuro,* as it is in much of Clarice's works. Here, however, the discussion is framed around the notion of impossibility. Martim, the male protagonist so rare in Clarice's fiction, must reshape his identity in the wake of a personal crisis, and he can only do this through a "gesture of rupture" (Cixous 61), a crime, for he believes he has murdered his wife. In Nancy Gray Díaz's analysis: "At this elemental stage of self-awareness, the process of re-establishing an identity functions as perception and cognition of otherness" (94). In order to reach that stage, the quality of impossibility must be recognized. In Cixous's long piece on *A maçã no escuro,* understanding of the other is described as a temptation, for understanding tempts one "to take or to absorb" (65), a process that entails accepting that "there is no love but in the relay of love" (ibid.). The odd courtship of Martim and Vitória is presented in terms of "victory of failure" and "failure in victory," with Martim being victorious in his failure for "he maintains the impossible

in impossibility," that is to say, although he does not succeed in understanding others, he constantly strives to move toward others (67). The
issue is further explained through a close reading of a short text by Clarice,
"É para lá que eu vou" (included in *Onde estivestes de noite?* [1974])
("That's Where I'm Going," in *Soulstorm* [1989]). In this piece, which,
Cixous believes, contains the infinite in a nutshell (69), Clarice sums up
the notion of the impossible as the understanding that in the very an-
nouncement of a thing lie the limits to its existence; it is the recognition
of the impossible that signals the existence of the impossible. Similarly,
"Movement toward reality is what constitutes reality" (74) and "The
goal is the movement toward, not the arrival" (77). Language is key in
this movement, though reaching communication with the other—leap-
ing from "I" to "you"—is an impossibility. And it is through this movement—through writing—that one, the writer, attempts to dissolve borders and arrive at the limits of the other.

Among the critics, the Clarice–Lúcio relationship is for the most part
ignored,[13] even in a major work such as Marta Peixoto's significantly titled *Passionate Fictions* (1994); and in the most often quoted biographical study of Clarice Lispector (Borelli), Lúcio's name appears only three
times, and only because it is used by Clarice herself in letters to her sisters (134–37). In some cases, the relationship is only alluded to; critics
will mention, for example, the fact that it was Lúcio who suggested to
Clarice the Joycean title *Perto do coração selvagem (Near to the Wild
Heart)* for her first novel, published in 1944. Earl Fitz refers to Lúcio as
"friend, mentor and confidant at the Agência Nacional" (25); pages earlier, "colleague" is used in lieu of "confidant" (5). Not even the best study
of Lúcio Cardoso's life and works tackles the *impossibilidade* issue.[14] Although the book includes a chapter on the relationship at hand, Carelli's
account of the situation leaves much to be desired, not only because it
evades Lúcio's homosexuality, but also because it essentially ignores fundamental questions of self and other, inversion, and gender (re)presen-
tation and (re)production. Titled "A paixão de Clarice," the short chapter
(eleven pages, of which more than half are taken up by long quotations
from letters and diary entries) skirts the crucial issues, as does the entire
book. There is throughout the work a noticeable unease with homosexuality; not once do such words as *homosexual* or *gay* appear in the biographical half of the book, and *homosexuality* occurs once, although it
is used not by Carelli but in a quotation from Lúcio's diary. This entry

from the late 1950s (Cardoso, *Diário completo*, 255) suggests that by then Lúcio had overcome his resistance to spelling out the term, signaling an at least partial acceptance of his homosexuality—a condition Clarice had often tried to name. One such occasion was the postcard she sent Lúcio from Naples, dated September 30, 1944; the card shows a bust of Antinous and a message from Clarice:[15] "Transmito-lhe agora esse Efebo da Itália. Até parece um pouco com você. . . . Não me esqueça" (Carelli, *Corcel de fogo*, 46) (From Italy I now send you this Ephebe. He even looks a little like you. . . . Don't forget me).

Writing in the 1980s, Carelli seems to have been less at ease with the subject of Lúcio's homosexuality than Clarice was almost half a century earlier.[16] Thus, instead of approaching the issue from an angle that might leave room for a consideration of homosexual panic and repression and acceptance, Carelli couches his reading in pathological terms:

O "mal" que o aflige não deixa de estar ligado ao que a psiquiatria chama de esquizofrenia, essa psicose caracterizada por uma desagregação do psíquico que está na origem de uma ambivalência dos pensamentos e dos sentimentos, bem como de uma conduta paradoxal devido à perda do contato com a realidade. (Ibid., 224)

[His "affliction" is related to what in psychiatry one calls schizophrenia, a psychosis that is defined by a psychic disintegration that lies at the center of both an ambivalence of thinking and feeling, and of a paradoxal behavior resulting from a loss of contact with reality.]

Still beating this unfortunate path, Carelli turns to Lúcio's fiction, whose tortured nature he explains in these terms: "o mal profundo das criaturas cardosianas está ligado à indefinição do pai e à onipresença da mãe" (ibid.) (the profound affliction of Lúcio Cardoso's creatures is related to the indefinition of the father and to the dominating presence of the mother).[17]

And thus Mario Carelli, a French critic of Italian descent, writing toward the end of the twentieth century, though probably convinced of the cutting-edge nature of his critical praxis, was in fact falling prey to, and perpetuating, the same prejudices held by most French critics dealing with Rimbaud, Proust, Gide, Genet, and others, up to about 1970. The alleged discretion, good taste, and respect for other people's right of privacy were in fact attempts to disguise a considerable uneasiness about, if not repugnance for, the subject of homosexuality. In the case of Lúcio Cardoso, the matter is complicated further by the novelist's reticence to accept his own homosexuality, which he saw as a kind of flaw or sin, and which prevented him from writing openly about it in the diary or elsewhere. Thus, even his most autobiographical novel, *Dias perdidos* (1943), evades the issue of homosexuality. As for the *Diário completo*, while earlier entries show that Lúcio was aware, as was Proust, of the role played by "lies" (see note 1), evasion, and the closet ("O que aprendemos, é como nos ocultar. . . . O que ocultamos, é o que importa, é o que somos"; entry for September 15, 1949 [*Diário completo*, 20]) (What we do learn is, how to hide. . . . What we hide is what matters, that's who we really are), writings closer to the end of the volume ring defensive and apologetic, as does this entry from March 17, 1951:[18]

> Se de nem tudo falei, se sobre aquilo que provavelmente constituiria o interesse do público mais numeroso calei-me ou apenas sugeri o que devia ser a verdade, é que um arrolamento constante de fatos sempre me pareceu monótono e sem interesse para ninguém. A questão sexual, por exemplo, que alguns leitores provavelmente reclamariam, que adiantaria estampá-la, destituída de força, apenas para catalogar pequenas misérias sem calor e sem necessidade? (169)

> [If I did not write about everything, if I was silent about or only suggested what should be the truth, it's because a constant cataloging of facts has always seemed dull to me and devoid of interest for anyone else. Sex, for example, a subject some people would probably expect to read about, what good would it do to record it, bereft of any impact, only for the sake of cataloging minor miseries without affection or justification?]

Still, as though Lúcio suddenly sensed the vast importance of what was being left out, the next-to-last paragraph in this same entry surprises the reader for its revelatory, if rather succinct, nature:

> Este Diário é uma súmula de remorso e de consciência culpada. Tenho agora outro remorso, é o de não ter ido até o fim, de não ter perseguido até à fronteira, as sombras que sempre me acenaram de lá. Renuncio, mas sem fé no bem que pratico. (Ibid.)

> [This diary is a compendium of remorse and of a guilty conscience. I now have another remorse, for not having gone all the way to the end, for not having pursued to the limit the shadows that have always beckoned me from the other side. I am resigned to this, but I have no faith in the good I practice.]

Seemingly impervious to any abjection regarding homosexuality,[19] Clarice persevered with Lúcio throughout the 1940s but seems to have been silent afterwards. Her silence may be explained by a number of factors, including weariness, geographical distance (those were the days of long sojourns abroad in the company of her diplomat husband), and the lack of response (in both senses of the term, "reply" and "reaction") on the part of Lúcio, who had by then embarked on a decade-long journey of drinking that led to the stroke that paralyzed him in 1962 and finally to his death in 1968. In fact, a 1950 letter Clarice sent from Torquay, England, to one of her sisters, already suggests her waning interest in Lúcio; referring to Julien Green, Clarice writes that the French novelist "foi minha paixão por muito tempo" (cast a very strong spell on me for a long time), to which she appends a parenthetical comment that may be read as an oblique reflection on her relationship with Lúcio: (também as paixões literárias vão se apagando, sem se saber por quê)" (Borelli 1991: 138) (literary passion, too, will fade away, for reasons unknown).[20] Years later, after Lúcio's first stroke, there was a rapprochement, with courteous visits, and Clarice's encouragement of his newly discovered talent for painting. Unable to speak or write, but having regained use of his left hand, Lúcio took up painting first as therapy and later as a career. Clarice attended at least one of his vernissages, at Rio de Janeiro's Galeria Goeldi on May 19, 1965 (column by Léa Maria, *Jornal do Brasil*, May 21, 1965); also in attendance were other major names in Brazilian arts and society, including Carlos Drummond de Andrade.

A more careful study will consider "Clarice's passion" not in the terms in which Carelli approaches it in his eponymous chapter, nor in the identically titled, and existentialism-seeped, works by Benedito Nunes (1987) and Berta Waldman (1993), but rather, by resorting to "uma subjetividade outra" (a different subjectivity),[21] an approach that would allow for the situation of someone who finds herself caught in a relational impasse at a time and in a society pervaded by the gender-inversion topos and its profound ramifications.

"Clarice's passion" is thus best understood as the situation wherein one desires an other "that is" and "that is not"; therefore, when a production and/or derivation attempt is made, one is confronted with the *impossibilidade* issue. The resolution of such an impasse was beyond Clarice's powers, as were, gradually, the problems attending her marriage,

and the control of her demons; the one thing that was still perhaps under her control was her writing, through which she could express her
vision of the complexity and multiplicity of being, a task that has been
called "travessia do oposto" (contrary crossing)—the subtitle of Olga
de Sá's 1993 book on Clarice. Sá's choice is an allusion to the message
Clarice writes to the "possíveis leitores" (eventual readers) of her 1964
novel, *A paixão segundo G.H.* (*The Passion according to G.H.*) (1988).

The aforementioned 1969 *crônica* or reminiscence Clarice wrote in
the form of a letter to Lúcio after his death (or, to be more precise, written at some point between Lúcio's death on September 23, 1968, and
the publication date in Rio de Janeiro's *Jornal do Brasil,* January 11, 1969)
is the only extant document or written testimony recording Clarice's
reaction to the loss of Lúcio. It is interesting to note that throughout the
letter, Clarice changes the nominal addressee (the ultimate addressee
being, of course, the implicit reader of the *crônica*): initially, the letter is
addressed to Lúcio as *você* (informal you, singular), but in subsequent
paragraphs Lúcio is now a third person, *ele* (he) (third paragraph), *esse
homem* (that man) (fifth paragraph), or *Lúcio* (last paragraph).[22] The
distancing afforded by the use of different, and more distant, pronouns
and nouns suggests Clarice's attempts to accept the departure of her
once possible lover. To the best of my knowledge, there is no other written documentation of Clarice's reaction to Lúcio's death, but we do
know that in general the death of those who were dear to Clarice took a
heavy toll on her, which may explain the delay in the publication of the
elegiac *crônica.*

The *impossibilidade* issue leads almost inevitably to speculation regarding "a vida inteira que podia ter sido e que não foi" (an entire life
that could have been and wasn't), to quote another knower of *impossi-
bilidades.*[23] What if there had been no *impossibilidade?* What if Lúcio
had not led his "secret, mysterious life"? What if these two people who
got along wondrously well had indeed married each other? Clarice Lispector was fascinated by speculations and contrary-to-fact situations; in a
crônica dated November 14, 1970, she speculates about what her life
would have been like had her family emigrated to the United States instead of Brazil:[24]

> Se minha família tivesse optado pelos Estados Unidos, eu teria sido
> escritora? em inglês, naturalmente, se fosse. Teria casado provavelmente
> com um americano e teria filhos americanos. E minha vida seria

interamente outra. Escreveria sobre o quê? O que é que amaria? Seria de que Partido? Que gênero de amigos teria? (1984a: 499)[25]

[If my family had chosen to go to the United States, would I have been a writer? I'd write in English, of course, had I become one. I'd have married an American man and would have had American children. My life would have been altogether different. What would I write about? What would I love? What political party would I belong to? What kind of friends would I have?]

A definitive understanding of the "true nature" of Clarice and Lúcio's relationship may not be attainable, at least not more than a general consensus about its importance. Carelli uses the term *vestígios* (traces) to describe what evidence is available. He is correct up to a point, but we do have several letters and other documents and texts, and besides, personal interviews with those who knew the authors can yield a wealth of new information.[26] Of foremost importance here, though, is the fact that queer readers of Brazilian culture must not be deterred by challenging research or other attempts at distracting them from their goals.

Leaving aside interpretations as simplistic as unrequited love and even a little more complex, as a vicariously experienced love affair,[27] a more compelling reading of the problematic relationship would include an element of *aprendizagem* (apprenticeship; learning) on the part of Clarice as she faced a certain new reality, that of queerness, an element that was to clearly imprint several of her future characters. Through Lúcio's mediation, Clarice experienced the impact of a situation Judith Butler describes as one in which

the parodic or imitative effect of gay identities works neither to copy nor to emulate heterosexuality but rather, to expose heterosexuality as an incessant and panicked imitation of its own naturalized idealization. (22–23)

The Lispector-Cardoso relationship is important because it sheds light on the intersection of anxieties (if not panics)—sexual, social, political—at the center of intellectual production in mid-twentieth-century Brazil. The consequences of crises (in the sense of "turning points" or "crucial steps") occasioned by their encounter were significant for their respective careers, but so far it is evident that in their personal and professional life, the outcome was far from negligible, and the sometimes contradictory reverberations generated by such crisis left them better prepared to face and make sense of the challenges and conflicts entailed by the *im-possibilidade* riddle.

Notes

I wish to acknowledge with gratitude the assistance I received while researching this essay at the Fundação Casa de Rui Barbosa, Rio de Janeiro; special thanks are due Júlio Castañón Guimarães at the Setor de Filologia, and Eliane Vasconcellos, Rosângela Rangel, and the staff at the Arquivo-Museu de Literatura.

1. "The lie, the perfect lie, about people we know, about the relations we have had with them, about our motive for some action, formulated in totally different terms, the lie as to what we are, whom we love, what we feel with regard to people who love us . . . —that lie is one of the few things in the world that can open windows for us on to what is new and unknown, that can awaken in us sleeping senses for the contemplation of universes that otherwise we should never have known" (quoted in Sedgwick, *Epistemology of the Closet,* 67).

2. Equally well known are the two more traditional notions of inversion, the Freudian and the Marxist views. As the deceptively disinterested language of *Three Contributions to the Theory of Sex* puts it: "There are men for whom the sexual object is not woman but man, and there are women for whom it is not man but woman. Such persons are designated as contrary sexuals, or better, inverts, and the situation of such a relationship is called inversion. The number of such individuals is considerable, although it is difficult to estimate them accordingly" (Freud, "Inversion. Invert," 86). In the Marxist view, "the conception of ideology as the 'inverted' consciousness [is] determined by what is itself an inverted social and historical reality. Thus, the capitalist market, a real set of relations, inverts the underlying reality of production relations by giving the appearance of a free and equal interaction to what is at base an unequal, coerced process of exploitation" (Larsen 1990: xxiii).

3. Their relationship has parallels with that of English painter Dora Carrington and Bloomsbury writer Lytton Strachey (depicted in a 1995 film directed by Christopher Hampton); a Latin American parallel is found in the relationship between Mexican writers Antonieta Rivas Mercado and Manuel Rodríguez Lozano (I am indebted to my colleague Vicky Unruh of the University of Kansas for bringing the latter relationship to my attention).

About this type of relationship in general, see Malone (1980) and Whitney (1990). Both authors use "life stories" put together from questionnaires and interviews with people who are or were involved in this type of relationship. Both books thus provide an abundance of personal detail but are disappointing in their inability to offer any theoretical insights. See also Carol A. Warren, "Women among Men: Females in the Male Homosexual Community," *Archives of Sexual Behavior* 5 (1976): 157–69; and Rebecca Nahas and Myra Turley, *The New Couple: Women and Gay Men* (New York: Seaview Books, 1979). A more openly queer approach is taken by Camilla Decarnin in "Interviews with Five Faghagging Women," *Heresies* 12 (1981): 10–14.

4. Although such "gender-separatist" relationships were not impossible in Lúcio's time, intense social pressure prevented them from forming or lasting very long.

5. The attraction of the Jew for the Other, especially at the historical moment of the Holocaust in Europe, needs to be taken into account here; Clarice's fascination

with Lúcio's traditional, *mineiro* (from the state of Minas), right-wing Catholic family background denotes her desire to belong fully in her adopted country. I am grateful to Silviano Santiago for helping me formulate this interpretation (interview, Rio de Janeiro, August 15, 1996).

6. Nádia Battella Gotlib remarks that as late as the 1970s Clarice was still adamant in her refusal. To interviewers, who often asked her to talk about her love life, she had the same answer: "É segredo" (It is a secret) (Gotlib, "Ser ou não ser," 320).

7. The relationship has often been alluded to, but critics have always shied from presenting it as a love affair. To the best of my knowledge, it was not until 1995 that a critic referred to Borelli using a term ("Lispector's longtime companion") strongly associated with homosexual relationships (Vieira 1995a, 104). The phrase has had wide currency as a code term for homosexual partners (see, for example, its use in AIDS obituaries in the 1980s).

8. "Our problem, when we want to write, speak, evoke the other, is how not to do it from ourselves. . . . In a relationship to the other, there is everything that is not of the same, of the same that is not, and of the other that he or she is" (Cixous 44).

9. As a man, Lúcio was to Clarice "a same that is not," but as a gay man he was simultaneously "a same that is." Clarice's possible bisexuality further complicates the issue. In a consideration of "the same that is not," one should also bear in mind Sedgwick's discussion of *The Portrait of Dorian Gray*, and especially her remarks about the "linguistically unappealable classification of anyone who shares one's gender as being 'the same' as oneself, and anyone who does not share one's gender as being the Other" (*Epistemology*, 160). Clarice Lispector had an active interest in Wilde's novel; she made passing references to it in her writings and later translated and "adapted" it to Portuguese (Wilde 1974). (I examine this translation/"adaptation" in "Reading Translation Queerly: Lispector's Translation of *The Picture of Dorian Gray*," *Bulletin of Hispanic Studies* 76 [1999]: 691–702.)

10. So far twenty letters from Clarice Lispector to Lúcio Cardoso have been located and cataloged; they were written between 1941 and 1947 (Barbosa 1993b: 183–84). The originals are in the Arquivo Clarice Lispector, Museu de Literatura, Fundação Casa de Rui Barbosa, Rio de Janeiro. Of those letters, Carelli ("Vestígios") includes seven in their entirety and three, partially. An issue (number 9) of the journal *Remate de Males* reproduces in facsimile three letters each from Clarice to Lúcio, and from Lúcio to Clarice. It seems that these three letters from Lúcio to Clarice are the only ones that survive. Clarice's son, Paulo Gurgel Valente, confirms that this is indeed the case (telephone interview, August 16, 1996). Could it be that these are the only letters Lúcio ever wrote to Clarice? Did this polite man of letters fail to reply to the at least twenty letters he received from Clarice, this at a time when letter writing had not yet succumbed to the exigencies and distractions of modern life? Or did Clarice destroy the other letters she received from him? It should be pointed out that Lúcio always delayed replying to her letters, which occasioned all kinds of complaints from her, from admonitions not to be "preguiçoso" (lazy) ("Correspondência" 219) to humorous pleas (in Carelli, *Corcel de fogo*, 47). In what concerns delay and delayed response, it may be fitting to consider the following remarks by Joanna Russ, albeit in a very different context (that of pornography in *Star Trek*): "We have . . . sexualized our female situation and training, and made out of the restrictions of the patriarchy our own sexual cues. For example, women wait. . . . Thus, the endless analyses of motives and scruples for pages and pages, a delay that is in itself erotically

arousing, since it's a sexualization of what is or was presented to us as 'the real thing' for women. ([Camilla] Decarnin has suggested . . . that this waiting be taken metaphorically, as related to women's need for long 'foreplay' in order to achieve orgasm.) Women must not initiate sexual activity. Thus the enormous plot conventions which finally free the lovers to be sexual, in which that lack of responsibility is itself exciting, an intensifier of arousal, vulnerability, and emotion made out of condition" (86–87).

11. Knowing exactly "why," according to Nádia Battella Gotlib, is yet another impossibility. Writing about Clarice's approach to the filing of her own personal papers and her general attitude toward anything autobiographical, Gotlib maintains that Clarice worked from an epistemological assumption: "já que conhecer é impossível, que se caminhe à beira do 'quase'" ("Ser ou não ser," 314) (since knowing is impossible, let us tread at the edge of "almost"). The experience of such limitations, Gotlib argues, led Clarice to "um estilo de agir que lhe permitia divisar o universo do impossível e também dele se alimentar" (315) (a way of being that allowed her to discern the universe of the impossible and also to thrive on it).

Responding to my query about the Clarice-Lúcio relationship, Gotlib remarked on the fact that what we see in the problematic relationship, as in so much of Clarice's biography, is, to a large degree, bits and pieces, lacunae and questions, and deliberate indefinitions. Clarice reseachers should therefore make connections and draw tentative conclusions as best they can (telephone interview, August 27, 1996).

12. Clarice's birth certificate (that is, a statement taken from her father by a Recife notary public) has 1920 as year of birth (facsimile in Varin 84).

13. Two recent biographies of Clarice Lispector (Gotlib 1995; Ferreira 1999) are an exception. In both works, Lúcio is mentioned quite often (especially toward the beginning of each book) and several pages are dedicated to the relationship. Lúcio's homosexuality is clearly mentioned in Gotlib (but not in Ferreira), although no effort is made to delve deeper and consider questions of gender production and duplication.

14. Carelli, *Corcel de fogo;* the title is a phrase in Clarice's "Lúcio Cardoso," a *crônica* written in letter form eulogizing Lúcio, first published in *Jornal do Brasil,* January 11, 1969 (Lispector, *Descoberta,* 243–45) and reprinted in Cardoso 1991 (786–87).

15. Antinous was the young lover of Hadrian, Roman emperor from A.D. 117 to 138. Antinous's legendary beauty and Hadrian's devotion to the memory of his deceased young lover fomented Roman art for centuries; see, among others, Boswell (1980: 84–86). Lúcio Cardoso's fascination with the story of Antinous and Hadrian only grew after he discovered Marguerite Yourcenar's *Les Mémoires d'Hadrien,* which he read in French. Lúcio wrote at least one poem inspired by the youth, the sonnet "Antinous" (original at Arquivo-Museu de Literatura, Casa de Rui Barbosa).

16. Carelli's Portuguese text was published in 1988; his doctoral dissertation, "L'Univers romanesque de Lúcio Cardoso," which includes most of this material, was defended in 1986 at the University of Paris III (Sorbonne Nouvelle).

17. The reader is confronted again with the noun *mal,* which also appears in the preceding quotation (where it is in quotation marks to signal Lúcio's repeated use of the term in the *Diário completo* [9]). Regarding the meaning of this Portuguese noun ("disease," as in "Mal de Parkinson," for example; or the opposite of good, as in "o Bem e o Mal" [Good and Evil]), its use in connection with homosexuality denotes intolerance and (self-)oppression.

18. The *Diário completo* consists of two sections: the first (totaling 167 pages, and dedicated to Walmir Ayala) covers the two-year period from August 1949, to March 1951, when Lúcio was most intensely dedicated to his diary writing; the second part (totaling 133 pages, and dedicated to Octavio de Faria) includes the shorter and more sporadic entries he wrote in the decade from May 1952 to October 1962. These were, of course, the passages Lúcio selected for publication; many pages and paragraphs of his notebooks were deleted or destroyed during that process; he also mentions having lost or discontinued other diaries in his youth (*Diário completo*, 5–6). Part I was originally published in 1961; the *Diário completo* was published posthumously two years after his death. Lúcio also wrote diary entries and general reflections on life and art in other notebooks; two of these, short and undated, have been published: "Diário de terror" and "Pontuação e prece," the former in *Revista Senhor* (Rio de Janeiro), November 1961, with a different title, "Diário proibido: Páginas secretas de um livro e de uma vida" and also in Carelli 1985 (68–75) and Cardoso 1991 (743–49); and the latter in Carelli 1985 (75–77) and Cardoso 1991 (751–53). Still unpublished is "Diário de bordo," a four-page manuscript filed (along with the originals for *Diário completo* and "Diário de terror") in the Arquivo Lúcio Cardoso at the Fundação Casa de Rui Barbosa in Rio de Janeiro. Good studies of Lúcio's diaries are Carelli 1985; Guy Besançon, "Le Journal intime de Lúcio Cardoso," *Cahiers du Monde Ibérique et Luso-Brésilien (Caravelle)* 52 (1989): 73–90; and Egon de Oliveira Rangel, "Em torno do discurso e da perversão," *Cadernos de Estudos Linguísticos* 19 (1990): 159–72.

19. Kristeva comments that "it is . . . not lack of cleanliness or health that cause abjection but what disturbs identity, system, order. What does not respect borders, positions, rules" (4).

20. This is yet another affirmation on Clarice's part of her enormous admiration (enthusiastically shared by Lúcio) for the work of Julien Green, the French novelist who, like Proust and Lúcio, led his own "vida misteriosa e secreta." Teresa Virginia de Almeida studies the two writers from a comparative approach in her Ph.D. dissertation, "Lúcio Cardoso e Julien Green: Transgressão e culpa" (University of São Paulo, 1990).

21. I am using here the title of Francisco Caetano Lopes Jr.'s study of three gay-themed Brazilian novels of different eras, Adolfo Caminha's *Bom-crioulo*, Lúcio Cardoso's *Crônica da casa assassinada*, and Silviano Santiago's *Stella Manhattan* (Lopes Júnior 1991). In *Bom-crioulo* (1893), reputedly the first openly gay novel in the Americas, "several gender alignments and realignments are in operation, and they represent other levels of displacement that include class and race relations that, in their turn, point to even more complex and ideological alignments" (Bueno 95). Both *Crônica* (1959) and *Stella Manhattan* (1985) are predicated on gender's performative element, the latter in its eponymous character, who "dramatizes through his own body the many contradictions of a writing that, produced on the fringes of the Western world, anthropophagically swallows its enemies" (Lopes Júnior 1991: 412), and the former in the youngest of the Menezes brothers, the cross-dressing Timóteo, whom I consider in a work in progress tentatively called "Timóteo's Divinity: Gender, Transgression, and Performance in *Crônica da casa assassinada*." Lopes Júnior also published a shorter version of this essay in the journal *Brasil/Brazil* ("*Stella Manhattan*: Uma sujetividade outra," *Brasil/Brazil* 5 [1991]: 54–78). See Susan Canty Quinlan's essay in this volume.

22. It is likewise interesting that in the next-to-last paragraph, *você* becomes Lúcio's sister, Maria Helena Cardoso, whom Clarice urges to write a book about Lúcio. Maria Helena complied with Clarice's suggestion by writing *Vida-vida* (1973). The book, written between two other works by her—an autobiography (1968) and a largely autobiographical roman à clef titled *Sonata perdida* (Rio de Janeiro: Nova Fronteira, 1979)—covers almost exclusively the years of Lúcio's illness.

23. Manuel Bandeira (1886–1968), a lifelong bachelor, was a kind of unofficial poet laureate of Brazil at the time Clarice and Lúcio started their literary careers. A member of an older generation and a participant in several literary movements, Bandeira was always supportive of both Clarice and Lúcio. The quote is a famous line from "Pneumotórax," a 1930 poem in which Bandeira playfully laments the limitations tuberculosis had set on his life. Rubem Braga casts Bandeira and Lispector as unnamed characters in his *crônica* "O poeta e os olhos da moça"; in Maria José Barbosa's account, "Braga retells Bandeira's story of passing by Lispector and her fiancée *[sic]* in Flamengo at the precise time that Bandeira felt desperately lonely and unhappy because of an unrequited love. He had the strong feeling that she understood his pain" (in Marting 220–21).

24. The piece is titled "Esclarecimentos: Explicação de uma vez por todas." I am indebted to Roselena Nicolau's informative essay "Misteriosa Clarice" (1994) for drawing my attention to this *crônica,* which Gotlib also examines (1995: 113–15).

25. One cannot but take note of Clarice's choice of terms here, when she could have used other words such as *tipo* and *espécie;* in Portuguese, *gênero* can mean "type/kind," "genre," and "gender."

26. Ironically, Carelli speaks of "traces" in the same piece in which he reproduces several previously unpublished letters Clarice and Lúcio wrote each other ("Vestígios").

27. Of no small relevance to this matter are the following remarks Richard Bernstein makes (in his review of Dan Hofstadter's *The Love Affair as a Work of Art*) with regard to the expressions of love in the letters Proust wrote to Jeanne Pouquet, who was married to his best friend: "Was Proust writing those letters to conceal the illicit, homosexual love he felt for his friend, Gaston de Caillevet? Mr. Hofstadter, as always resisting simple explanations, does not answer this question, but he does make a virtue of the impossibility of doing so" (Bernstein 1996).

Works Cited

Barbosa, Maria José Somerlate. 1993a. "Biographical Statements and Criticisms." In *Clarice Lispector: A Bio-Bibliography,* ed. Diane Marting. Westport, Conn.: Greenwood Press. 220–21.
———. 1993b. "Published Letters to and from Clarice Lispector"; "Biographical Statements and Criticism." In *Clarice Lispector: A Bio-Bibliography,* ed. Diane Marting. Westport, Conn.: Greenwood Press. 183–90.
Bernstein, Richard. 1996. "In Love with the Lore (or Lies?) of Love Affairs." *New York Times.* February 14. C-2.
Borelli, Olga. 1991. *Clarice Lispector: Esboço para um possível retrato.* Rio de Janeiro: Nova Fronteira.

Boswell, John. 1980. *Christianity, Social Tolerance, and Homosexuality: Gay People in Western Europe from the Beginning of the Christian Era to the Fourteenth Century.* Chicago: University of Chicago Press.

Bueno, Eva Paulino. 1994. "Caminha, Adolfo." In *Latin American Writers on Gay and Lesbian Themes: A Bio-Critical Sourcebook,* ed. David W. Foster. Westport, Conn.: Greenwood Press. 94–100.

Butler, Judith. 1991. "Imitation and Gender Insubordination." In *Inside/Out: Lesbian Theories, Gay Theories,* ed. Diana Fuss. New York: Routledge. 13–31.

Cardoso, Lúcio. 1970. *Diário completo.* Rio de Janeiro: José Olympio.

———. 1985. "Diário de terror" and "Pontuação e prece." "Écrits intimes de Lúcio Cardoso." *Cahiers du Monde Hispanique et Luso-Brésilien (Caravelle)* 45: 68–75, 75–77.

———. 1991. *Crônica da casa assassinada.* Ed. Mario Carelli. Madrid and Brasília: Consejo Superior de Investigaciones Científicas/Conselho Nacional de Pesquisa.

Cardoso, Maria Helena. 1968. *Por onde andou meu coração?* 2d. ed. Rio de Janeiro: José Olympio.

———. 1973. *Vida-vida.* Rio de Janeiro: José Olympio.

Carelli, Mario. 1985. "Écrits intimes de Lúcio Cardoso." *Cahiers du Monde Hispanique et Luso-Brésilien (Caravelle)* 45: 63–78.

———. 1988a. *Corcel de fogo: Vida e obra de Lúcio Cardoso, 1912–1968.* Trans. Júlio Castañón Guimarães. Rio de Janeiro: Editora Guanabara.

———. 1988b. "Vestígios de um 'amor impossível': Clarice Lispector e Lúcio Cardoso revelam em suas cartas dados importantes da gênese de suas obras." *Folha de São Paulo* 605 (August 20): 9–11.

Cixous, Hélène 1990. *Reading with Clarice Lispector.* Ed. and trans. Verena Andermatt Conley. Minneapolis: University of Minnesota Press.

de Lauretis, Teresa. 1984. *Alice Doesn't: Feminism, Semiotics, Cinema.* Bloomington: Indiana University Press.

Díaz, Nancy Gray. 1993. "A maçã no escuro." In *Clarice Lispector: A Bio-Bibliography,* ed. Diane Marting. Westport, Conn.: Greenwood Press. 93–97.

Ferreira, Teresa Cristina Montero. 1999. *Eu sou uma pergunta: Uma biografia de Clarice Lispector.* Rio de Janeiro: Rocco.

Fitz, Earl. 1985. *Clarice Lispector.* Boston: Twayne Books.

Foster, David W., ed. 1994. *Latin American Writers on Gay and Lesbian Themes: A Bio-Critical Sourcebook.* Westport, Conn.: Greenwood Press.

Freud, Sigmund. 1958. "Inversion. Invert." *Freud: Dictionary of Psychoanalysis.* Ed. Nandor Fodor and Frank Gaynor. Greenwich, Conn.: Fawcett. 86–87.

Fundação Casa de Rui Barbosa. 1989. *Inventário do Arquivo Lúcio Cardoso.* Rio de Janeiro: Ministério da Cultura; Fundação Casa de Rui Barbosa.

Gotlib, Nádia Battella. 1995. *Clarice, uma vida que se conta.* São Paulo: Editora Ática.

———. 1997. "Ser ou não ser autobiográfica (A propósito de Clarice Lispector)." In *Navegar é preciso, viver: Escritos para Silviano Santiago,* ed. Eneida Maria de Souza and Wander Melo Miranda. Belo Horizonte: Editora da Universidade Federal de Minas Gerais; Salvador: Editora da Universidade Federal da Bahia; Niterói: Editora da Universidade Federal Fluminense. 314–22.

Hofstadter, Dan. 1996. *The Love Affair as a Work of Art.* New York: Farrar, Straus and Giroux.

Kristeva, Julia. 1982. *Powers of Horror: An Essay on Abjection.* Trans. Louis Roudiez. New York: Columbia University Press.

Larsen, Neil. 1990. *Modernism and Hegemony: A Materialist Critique of Aesthetic Agencies.* Minneapolis: University of Minnesota Press.

Lispector, Clarice. 1970. *Near to the Wild Heart.* Trans. Giovanni Pontiero.

———. 1979a. "História interrompida." In *A bela e a fera.* Rio de Janeiro: Nova Fronteira. 13–21.

———. 1979b. "Obsessão." In *A bela e a fera.* Rio de Janeiro: Nova Fronteira. 41–82.

———. 1984a. "Esclarecimentos: Explicação de uma vez por todas." In *A descoberta do mundo.* Rio de Janeiro: Nova Fronteira. 498–99.

———. 1984b. "Lúcio Cardoso." In *A descoberta do mundo.* Rio de Janeiro: Nova Fronteira. 243–45.

———. 1986. *The Apple in the Dark.* Trans. Gregory Rabassa. Austin: University of Texas Press.

———. 1988. *The Passion according to G. H.* Trans. Ronald W. Sousa. Minneapolis: University of Minnesota Press.

———. 1989. "Correspondência." *Remate de Males* 9: 211–25.

Lopes Júnior, Francisco Caetano. 1991. "Uma subjetividade outra." In *Toward Socio-Criticism: Luso-Brazilian Literatures,* ed. Roberto Reis. Tempe: Center for Latin American Studies, Arizona State University. 67–75.

———. 1994. "Santiago, Silviano." In *Latin American Writers on Gay and Lesbian Themes: A Bio-Critical Sourcebook,* Ed. David W. Foster. Westport, Conn.: Greenwood Press. 410–13.

Malone, John. 1980. *Straight Women/Gay Men: A Special Relationship.* New York: Dial.

Marting, Diane E., ed. 1993. *Clarice Lispector: A Bio-Bibliography.* Westport, Conn.: Greenwood Press.

Nicolau, Roselena. 1994. "Misteriosa Clarice." *Jornal do Brasil* 29 (Rio de Janeiro): B-1, 2.

Nunes, Benedito. 1987. "A paixão de Clarice Lispector." In *Os sentidos da paixão.* São Paulo: Companhia das Letras. 269–81.

Peixoto, Marta. 1994. *Passionate Fictions: Gender, Narrative and Violence in Clarice Lispector.* Minneapolis: University of Minnesota Press.

Russ, Joanna. 1995. *Magic Mommas, Trembling Sisters, Puritans and Perverts: Feminist Essays.* Trumansburg, N.Y.: Crossing Press.

Sá, Olga de. 1993. *Clarice Lispector: A travessia do oposto.* São Paulo: Annablume.

Sedgwick, Eve Kosofsky. 1990. *Epistemology of the Closet.* Berkeley: University of California Press.

Varin, Claire. 1987. *Clarice Lispector: Rencontres brésiliennes.* Laval, Quebec: Éditions Trois.

Vieira, Nelson. 1995a. "Clarice Lispector: A Jewish Impulse and a Prophecy of Difference." *Jewish Voices in Brazilian Literature.* Gainesville: University Press of Florida. 100–150.

———. 1995b. *Jewish Voices in Brazilian Literature.* Gainesville: University Press of Florida.

Waldman, Berta. 1993. *Clarice Lispector: A paixão segundo C.L.* 2d. ed. São Paulo: Editora Escuta.

Whitney, Catherine. 1990. *Uncommon Lives: Gay Men and Straight Women.* New York: New American Library.
Wilde, Oscar. 1974. *O retrato de Dorian Gray.* Trans. and adapted by Clarice Lispector. Rio de Janeiro: Tecnoprint/Ediouro.

Interviews

Nádia Battella Gotlib (telephone interview, August 27, 1996)
Paulo Gurgel Valente (telephone interview, August 16, 1996)
Silviano Santiago (Rio de Janeiro, August 15, 1996)

Part II
On Subjects, on Sex

CHAPTER SIX

Loving in the Lands of Portugal

Sex in Women's Fictions and the Nationalist Order

Ana Paula Ferreira

Toda a gente sabe amar,
Nas terras de Portugal.
Toda a gente namorou,
Na volta de um arraial.[1]

[Everyone knows how to love,
In the lands of Portugal.
Everyone has courted
On returning from a fair.]

On the Way Back Home: Luso Promises of Reward

Some time before António de Oliveira Salazar's *Constituição Política do Estado Novo* (Political Constitution of the New State) was published, on April 11, 1933, theoretical models of nationalist womanhood, in the making since at least the preceding decade, begin to appear.[2] They are found mostly in speeches and pamphlets that reduce to a caricature or demonize feminist ideals as the sine qua non of endorsing the dictator's plans for the moral reconstruction of the Portuguese family. The latter is considered the basic unit of what is to become the new corporate state. In line with other European fascisms, propagandists of Salazar's Estado Novo primarily ascribed to women-as-mothers the mission of nationalist moral regeneration.[3] They were to keep the family unit undivided by working at home as primary mediators of the traditional values of nation, of empire, and, above all, of "os interesses morais e espirituais da raça" (the moral and spiritual interests of the race [Vasconcelos 38]).[4]

In order to distinguish such a course of action from what could be regarded as "teorias!" "utopias!" "heresias" (theories! utopias! heresies [ibid., 39–40]), terms implicitly referring to contemporary fascist propaganda on woman and family, Salazar's early accolades tend to call upon the historically determined grandeur of the nationalist mission awaiting the Portuguese. In one symptomatic instance, it becomes, in fact, explicitly associated with the bold exploits of the navigators who found the sea route to India in 1498, as sung by Luís Vaz de Camões in the national epic, Os Lusíadas (1572).[5] Just as the navigators, on the way back home from Calecut, were rewarded by the gods with nymphs in the poem's mythic "Ilha dos Amores" (Island of Love), so too the boldness, as well as the sacrifices, expected from the Portuguese in honoring the New State's constitution would be justly rewarded. This reward would be in the form of "um Portugal maior, uma era nova, um Estado Novo, uma União Nacional, um império colonial português" (a bigger Portugal, a New Era, a New State, a National Union, a Portuguese Colonial Empire [ibid., 40]).

This enthusiastic supporter of Salazar's constitution, Pestana de Vasconcelos, does not take his specious syllogism so far as to explicitly compare Portuguese women of the early 1930s—the primary subject of his speech on the topic "O conceito do lar e da família no Estado Novo" (The concept of home and family in the New State)—with the homebound heroes in Vasco da Gama's fleet, as featured in canto 9 of The Lusiads. Yet, the parallel looms there, at the closing of one of the many proposals for the moral and political reconstruction of the "família portuguesa" (Portuguese family) as microcosm of the nation (ibid., 20). It is thought to be the basic vehicle of "terapia nacional" (national therapy [Martins]) resulting from the democratic excesses of the First Republic.[6] By literally and metaphorically going back home, to occupy the center of family life, women become here the privileged synecdoche for all Portuguese compelled to return to (and close themselves in) their home-nation.

Here lies the crux of the emphatically suggested historical continuity between "the lusiads" represented by Camões and those of now, embarking upon another phase of yet the same epic course. That, in one case, "the lusiads" call upon the image of would-be ardent and virile seafarers who had decisively opened the route to the Portuguese empire, and, in the other, the sacrificial, submissive women bearers and reproducers of the renewed imperial order, seems to be of no concern. After all, navigators of yesteryear and mothers of today would all share the same goal of defending the "interesses morais e espirituais da raça" (moral and spiritual interests of the race [ibid., 38]). Even if one rejects a literal reading of the "Island of Love" respite featured in canto 9 of *The Lusiads*, one cannot but wonder about its rhetorical implications as far as racial essence and new nationalist morality are concerned. I am referring to the kind of "rewards" that the *lusos*, now supposedly enclosed in the sacred Portuguese family-home, should expect from their compelled identification with a foundational poetic scene involving the symbolic prize of casual, orgiastic sex, outside of marriage, with artfully seductive nymphs in faraway seas.

Before tackling the discursive productivity of this moral paradox in closer theoretical terms, it may be important to note that Camões's epic poem was officially hailed and taught as the Portuguese book par excellence throughout the duration of Salazar's New State. It is noteworthy that at least on one occasion before the official inception of the regime in 1933, during the backlash against feminism and against all forms of democracy represented by the First Republic, reading of *The Lusiads* was prescribed to "modern" (i.e., feminist or pseudofeminist) Portuguese women. Given exclusively to foreign readings and influences, they were thought to be in urgent need of developing "um forte sentimento nacional" (a strong national sentiment [Guimarães 145]). "Neste momento" (At this moment)—adds the inflammatory, satirical author of *Saias curtas* (1925)—"em que nós todos parecemos acordar para um novo destino de glória e de imortalidade—essa obra ficará bem nas suas mãos" (146) (when we all seem to be waking up to a new destiny of glory and immortality—that book will look good in your hands).

It so happens that the hands of Portuguese women—the very few who were presumably reading at the time[7]—are not merely to hold the stylistically challenging Renaissance epic; they are also to hold other, simpler books—not all of which are pious examples of saints and martyrs, nationalist renditions of historical feats and heroes of the Fatherland, or treatises on "domestic economy."[8] Those other books are of "feminine" love verse—not necessarily of the nationalist kind cited in the epigraph at the beginning of this essay—and, especially after the second half of the 1930s, collections of short stories and novels written by women, centered on women, and, for the most part, to be consumed by women—those who were supposed to be the main physical and ideological reproducers of the "God-Fatherland-Family" trilogy of values, largely disseminated by the propaganda poster titled "Salazar's Lesson" (in *Cartazes* no. 72).

Whether or not such books of fiction observe and pass on that lesson is a different story, but one that warrants pursuing a theoretical understanding of the question posed earlier. What can one make of a nationalist program of regeneration that sends women back home to be wife, mother, and the primary mediator of morals for the greater good of the Portuguese imperial home-nation, while, at the same time, holding up as mirror of "the spiritual and moral interests of the race" an epic poem that features, in canto 9, as elsewhere, the apparently uncontrollable, enlightening force of sexual love?[9]

Following Foucault's seminal argument against the widespread notion that power, working primarily through the social institution of the bourgeois family, represses sexuality, it can be asserted that the discursive currency given to woman and the family throughout the making of the New State puts into motion a specific construct of nation-sex that structurally binds and yet threatens the process of national reimagining and imperial rebuilding. This construct may be envisioned along the terms of *lusosex*—and not simply because the title of the present collection suggests it; for, one must bear in mind the fact that the fascist appeal to a Lusitanian spiritual and racial essence (and, notably, "interests") calls upon and privileges the foundational *lusosex* intertext emblematized in the national epic poem, *The Lusiads*.

As will be examined with reference to representative fictions by women writers, discourses constructing *lusosex* crystallize in negotiation with prescriptions for a new sexual morality, propagated, though not homogeneously, by the New State's "elites of the word" (Baptista 193).[10] Straddling an equivocal "no" to sex (including nonreproductive sex within marriage [ibid., 201–2]) and what Foucault would describe as an "incitement" to tell about the bodily pleasures of the "nation's various definitional others" (Parker et al., 5), women in particular, such discourses live off this productive power-knowledge contradiction. They may be said to constitute the central nexus of a nationalist "system of alliance" (Foucault) that depends on the representation of a threatening, sexy difference: the "secret" of sex inhabiting within the *luso* family-nation. This difference is summoned forth to be put under surveillance and control, but also to be enjoyed, in the very sensuous materiality of literary discourse—or in word made flesh.[11]

Consistent with other fascist and protofascist discourses, that figure of potential community disorder inherent to *lusosex* is the hysterical or sexualized bourgeois woman (Theweleit 367). She is the *luso* "other," who takes the place and displaces, within the corporate state's microcosm of the family, the late-fifteenth-century adventurous (read "adulterous"), Lusitanian seafarer and his male progeny. The epic sexual wanderings of the latter persist in the national(ist) imagination as historical premium of human divination and therefore binders of the "large aggregate of men, healthy in mind and warm of heart, [creating] the kind of moral conscience which we call a nation" (Renan 20). By contrast, the mere shade of an active sexual demand in the proverbial daughter of Eve is chastised under the brand of a sentimental, shameless individualism endangering family, nation, and empire. Such denouncements begin to take shape at the end of the nineteenth century, and continue into the 1920s. They appear in both progressive, including Republican feminist, and conservative diagnosis of national "degeneration."[12] The sensationalized phenomenon of the liberal-feminist "new woman" and Freud's theories on sexuality and on femininity further contribute to help congeal during the 1930s the paradoxical tenor of a network of discourses that variously produce the feminine or feminized "other" on which the ideological cohesion of *lusosex* in vain attempts to rest. The body of fictional works written by women and centered on the "woman's condition" that emerges for the first time in the history of Portuguese literature after the institutionalization of Salazar's New State is an important, albeit critically unrecognized, part of such a network.[13]

The Angel of the Hearth Claims Her Rewards

In complicity with, reacting against, or placed at the margin of nationalist propaganda that dictates woman's place in the Portuguese family, the works in question manifest a consistent preoccupation to dramatize the cultural and class determinants of the bourgeois woman's psychosexual desires and experiences. Critically appropriating the script of romance disseminated during the 1920s and early 1930s mainly through the editorial success of so-called feminine poetry, women's fiction published from the mid-1930s on continues the critique of what Eça de Queiroz pointed out, in 1872, as "o mundo do sentimento" (the world of sentiment) to which idle, socially unproductive Portuguese women are confined (Queiroz 131). In doing so, they call attention to how long-standing cultural and moral conventions are reinforced by the state's imposed ideology of feminine difference.[14] More important, they show how such patriarchal, sexist (and, of course, heterosexist) beliefs turn the family home into a sort of hotbed for transgressions and resistances of various kinds. And thus these fictions tend to denounce women's continued dependency on both the conventional family structure and the constrictive myth of romantic love. Cases in point, both published in 1935 and illustrating two hypothetically contrasting ideological positions are Alice Ogando's *Pena maior* and Maria Lamas's *Para além do amor*.[15]

Pena Maior, by the prolific translator of pulp romance, poet, drama-tist, writer of fiction and children's literature Alice Ogando (1900–1981), bespeaks the author's intelligent, opportunistic strategy to attract a ready-made "feminine" reading public of romance while still a striving woman writer.[16] The second of the author's first two first novels, both published in 1935, is an equivocal text on several accounts, exploiting the contro-versies of the period regarding femininity and feminism, ideal woman-hood, and maternity.[17] From a historical-literary perspective, it may be considered a transitional work, placed between the momentous institu-tional stimulus to confess, or elaborate, *lusosex* in novelistic form, and the thematic evocation of the sexy strand of feminine poetry from the preceding decade. The latter became culturally infamous owing to its insistence on thematizing the standard ploys of heterosexual love (and the ironies thereof), but also to the fact that it brought into Portuguese literature the first representations of lesbian eroticism.[18]

Although not overtly mentioning the work of either Freud or his dis-ciples or critics, it is obvious that *Pena maior* follows the ideas publi-cized throughout the 1920s and early 1930s on the topic of female sexu-ality. Couched in the unpretentious, simple language and linear structure associated with the genre of romance, the novel outlines what Freud describes as "the third very circuitous path" (1961: 189) of a woman's ac-quisition of "normal" female sexuality. Summarily put, Freud describes how a potentially bisexual person of the female sex comes to accept and identify with castration, subsequently taking on the social-cultural place assigned to her in the Oedipus complex, and going on to acquire the characteristics of socially and culturally accepted femininity. Ogando, however, problematizes the basic Freudian plot by implicitly calling attention to the missing links of economics, class ideology, and historical-cultural context in conditioning this process.

Centered on the coming of age of a young woman educated in a religious boarding school for the upper class, *Pena maior* initially presents the budding of an adolescent lesbian relationship between the fragile, innocent, and passive "feminina" Clara, the protagonist, fatherless since age six, and her stronger, wiser, actively loving "viril" friend Luiza. The relationship is broken when Clara's widowed mother—still young, desirable, but "resignada" (resigned) with the fate of keeping her supposed "dever maternal" (maternal duty)—forces her daughter into a marriage of convenience with an older man, who is to save her from the prospect of economic ruin. The remainder of the novel follows Clara through the pain and "repugnância" (repugnance) of her sexual violation, whose perpetrators—both her mother and her husband—she courageously confronts; her unwanted pregnancy and failed attempts to seek an abortion; the rejection of Luiza's desire to establish sexual intimacy, her lesbian love now characterized as "abnormal" by association with other known such cases; and the protagonist's seduction by her husband's young, sensitive, and idealist friend, Paulo Duran, who embodies for her the solution to her emotional and sexual dissatisfaction. The novel ends with Clara's ambiguous moral "purificação" (purification), when, upon the birth of her symptomatically dead son, she realizes the redemptive effect of maternal love and finally makes peace with her previously abhorred biological mother. While in such a state of apparent feminine grace, she deliberately pushes aside the painful memory of her husband and fantasizes about the son who her absent lover, temporarily gone away to work as an engineer in colonial Africa, one day will give her.

The irony of this ending, as of the plot in general, cannot but lead the reader to reflect on the nature and subject(s) of the *pena* fictionalized in Ogando's novel. By playing on the double meaning of that noun, denoting "sentence" but also "pain," *Pena maior* suggests how woman's "worst pain" is not only a consequence of the social and cultural "sentence" that she submit to "castration, copulation, and childbirth," thereby attaining (according to Freud) the masochistic characteristics of femininity (Mitchell 114). As if in reply to official messages proscribing women's work outside the home,[19] Clara's story indicates that in addition to traditional patriarchal myths imposing motherhood as a woman's only

role—and glory—in life, her "worst pain" is directly related to economics and to class ideology.[20] This is something that Clara herself denounces when she blames her mother for using her as a form of "capital
acumulado que se põe a render" (55) (added capital put into investment).[21]
Even if not "resigned," like her mother, to the fate of being an object of
use-value to a husband-master simply out of "medo da miséria" (37)
(fear of misery), Clara follows the same hypocritical thought and socially accepted path. Luiza escapes this predicament, but perhaps only
because she has the economic means to do so, and assumes her lesbian
sexuality irrespective of its potentially marginalizing consequences.[22]

   Although Clara openly questions her mother's rationalized acceptance of woman's role and denounces marriage as a business contract
not based on mutual love, her chosen form of resistance is questionable. Whether for reasons of sexual orientation or not, she refuses
Luiza's love and protection, but does not attempt to secure any means
of self-sufficiency. She merely flees the humiliation of sex with her husband by seeking an adulterous romantic relationship. The man-savior
who sweeps her off her feet—no actual sex is mentioned, but then again
Clara is pregnant—may, in fact, prove to be nothing else than a new
master, not coincidentally in new colonialist guise. For all the personal
transgression that her love affair may entail, in the end, Clara stands as
the great metaphor for the (domestic) land awaiting the future national
rule and cultural order that the engineer is already off reinstating in
colonial Africa. In this context, the original masters—Clara's husband,
in one case, and the rightful owners of African lands, in the other—are
swiftly erased from the scene.

   The ideal script of romantic love, uniting "the tender affectionate
feelings and the sensuous ones" (Freud 1961: 49), through which the
novel's protagonist attempts to affirm herself in opposition to the business contract of marriage turns out to be possible in only two culturally
and morally proscribed relationships: that represented by Luiza's unrequited lesbian love for Clara, and that of the affair in which the latter
opts to embark with her husband's friend. Does *Pena maior* suggest that
lesbianism and adultery are the inevitable dangers faced by an institution that, in the context of the Estado Novo, officially decrees women's
subservient status as reproducers of the "interesses morais e espirituais
da raça" (moral and spiritual interests of the race)? Is the enactment of
fantasies—not to mention the psychosexual, ultimately culturally con-

ditioned need for romantic love—what is to be expected of would-be angels in the hearth left to claim their long-withheld "rewards"? Ogando does not necessarily answer these questions. Unwittingly or not, she raises them by configuring the "worst sentence" of those from whom is being taken all sense of independent subjecthood and self-determination; all right to emotional and sexual fulfillment irrespective of a sanctioned institution; and all say on how to contribute actively toward their community outside the multiple confines of the "Casa Portuguesa" (Portuguese [family] home).

In *Para além do amor,* Maria Lamas (1893–1983) takes the ambivalent frame of thought that characterizes *Pena Maior* to clearer ideological terms in tune with the author's stance of feminist, nonpartisan opposition.[23] A respected journalist, feminist activist, and pacifist; editor of the influential woman's magazine *Modas e bordados* (1928–48); writer of poetry, critical essays, short fiction and novels, and children's literature; and author of two ambitious works, *As mulheres do meu país* (1950) and *A Mulher no Mundo* (2 vols., 1952 and 1954), Lamas is unquestionably one of the most important all-around public figures among the generation of women born at the turn of the twentieth century, who began their publishing careers in the 1920s and early 1930s. *Para além do amor,* her first novel published under her own name,[24] lays out the early argumentative grounds that inform the author's lifelong example of personal, professional, and political contributions to women's emancipation. By focusing on what her contemporary Maria Archer (1905–82) would describe as "o problema da mulher casada" (1953) (the problem of the married woman), Lamas's daring novel posits the need to talk about, attempt to understand, and help overcome the silent plight of, particularly, the bourgeois and upper-bourgeois alienated wife and mother. For Lamas, this plight cannot be conceptualized apart from the larger frame of reference of the socioeconomic division of classes, nor from the ideologies or the concrete, individual efforts that purport to better the fate of the have-nots.

In an explanatory preface to her novel, Lamas defends in an emotive, melodramatic tone the seriousness and social-moral relevancy of her novelistic enterprise. Perhaps in an attempt to distinguish her work from the genre of sensationalist romance for feminine mass consumption, she begins by asserting that her sole objectives are "ser sincera e ser mulher" (7) (to be sincere and to be a woman). She goes on to bring the reader to identify with the cultural construction implied in this dyad. Like the author herself in the act of writing, the female reader is neither "sincere" nor "a woman" naturally, that is, without deliberately positioning (and constructing) herself as such in the act of reading. This rhetorical strategy enlisting a reasoned, though still affective type of reader response may also be directed at the male reader, inasmuch as it calls upon the challenge—as Jonathan Culler famously put it—of "reading as a woman" (49).

This, of course, does not mean eroding the feminist notion of a "common female experience." In fact, Lamas upholds the ideological authority of the position of the "leitora" (woman reader), who is assumed to be able to recognize and identify herself with the novel's heroine. The latter lives,

> com a alma torturada por mil interrogações, em luta com o meio ambiente e consigo própria, numa ânsia constante de Verdade e de Beleza; uma alma onde *todas nós, mulheres,* encontraremos muito das nossas revoltas inconfessadas, das nossas ilusões, dos nossos sonhos e da nossa dor. (7; emphasis added)

> [like a soul tortured by a thousand questions, fighting with her environment and with herself, constantly anxious for Truth and Beauty; a soul in which *all of us, women,* will find many of our undisclosed rebellions, our illusions, our dreams, and our pain.]

Rejecting the anticipated criticism of "doutrinária" (indoctrinating), Lamas goes on to state that her only intention is "lembrar aos indiferentes a necessidade de ter uma fé que se traduza numa aspiração de nobreza, justiça e bondade" (8) (to remind the indifferent of the need to have a faith translated into aspirations of honorability, justice, and goodness). In effect, *Para além do amor* demands to be read (theoretically at least) as a consciousness-raising novel. It represents a fictional personal trajectory that professes to illustrate, speak to, and ultimately intervene in the actual dramas afflicting the class of contemporary Portuguese women to whom it is addressed.

The novel is structured as the autobiographical account of a thirty-something educated and sensitive upper-bourgeois woman named Marta, who evokes the story of the adulterous love affair that changed the course of her life. This evocation takes place while she waits, in a state similar to the fluster she felt right after giving birth to her son, for the return of her ex-lover (72), the architect Gabriel de Sá. The latter lives abroad and only occasionally visits Portugal. It is during an earlier such visit, occurring sometime in an undisclosed temporal past, that they meet for the first time amid the idyllic scenery of the fashionable Buçaco spa. Marta goes there, while her husband and son travel throughout Europe, in search of a remedy for the repeated spiritual and emotional crisis that afflicts her. Her permanent dissatisfaction and "vácuo da minha alma" (28) (emptiness of my soul) are attributed to the superficiality of conventional life as a rich lady in Lisbon society. This is also the cause of disillusions resulting from occasional love escapades that prove to be nothing but "a Mulher e o Homem, vivendo abstractamente um minuto de instinto" (37) (Woman and Man, living aloofly a minute of instinct). Soon to be *the* man of her life, the politically radical, idealist, but bitter architect Gabriel de Sá, with residence in Berlin, is also apparently in search of inner peace in Buçaco. The basic ideological contradiction in his character surfaces here for the first time, because the spa is an environment associated with the bourgeois class that Gabriel so despises and that Marta herself represents. More than a third of the novel is dedicated to the unfolding of the protagonists' feelings and thoughts as she comes to know her companion during their encounter.

The remainder of the narrative follows the course of Marta's life in Lisbon, once she is reunited with her family and maintaining a clandestine love affair. Her proposal for a divorce is met with the violent wrath of the man, who reasserts that he is in charge of her life and is not about to face the social scandal that her "aventura engendrada pelo [seu] histerismo de mulher" (134) (adventure engendered by [her] woman's hysteria will bring him). Prompted by the spiritual, emotional, and ideological enlightenment that her continuing love affair with Gabriel brings her, Marta takes a very different course of resisting action. She begins by defending the workers in her husband's factory, after a bomb incident (152). Unexpectedly, her husband not only supports her involvement in his work, but requests that she alert him to any problems of injustice at the factory, and, finally, invites her to implement programs of social assistance for the workers (161, 164). She is thus able to sublimate her previous nervous, melancholic disorder and, superficially at least, reconcile herself with the institution of marriage. The thesis of the book is synthesized in the last few pages, where Marta's "renúncia" (renouncement) concerning individual, egotistical love is presented. She proudly announces that her "sacrifício" (sacrifice) in refusing to accompany Gabriel de Sá, now being invited to work in America, has transformed her into a deserving, "mulher forte capaz de amar ainda para além do amor, sem egoísmo nem cobardia" (204) (strong woman, capable of loving beyond love, without selfishness or cowardice). From this basis, she expects his departure to mark not the conventional ending of a love affair, but a new beginning in their respective, geographically distant lives: they are to remain forever "unidos" (united) in the common goal of "esclarecer outras almas" (enlightening other souls) and thereby lessen the "império do sofrimento humano" (205) (empire of human suffering). Considering Marta's maternity-like excitement before the imminent arrival of Gabriel at the beginning of her narration, it is tacitly suggested that the future periodic reunions between the estranged lovers are limited to being the birthing ground of ideology and social action—a point to which we will return shortly.

It is, of course, ironic that for all his cold, scientific, ideological perspective on revolutionary struggle, Gabriel is never represented doing anything concrete to bring about the communist utopia he so vehemently defends in front of Marta. She, on the other hand, is inspired by a "sentido de religiosidade" (sense of religiosity), dictating the need for "espiritualidade" (spirituality) in all socially oriented undertakings (165), a position that brings about concrete changes in the lives of the workers in her husband's factory (173–75). Marta even seems to be on the way to transforming or humanizing the husband/master himself, who becomes receptive to and further supports his wife's good deeds (176, 181). As the biblical resonance of the main characters' proper names implies, Gabriel's function in the story is merely that of an announcer, who comes from an outer sphere, literally and figuratively speaking—here, the "heaven" represented by Berlin and the philosophy of scientific materialism. Evoking the traits of Lazarus and Mary's sister in the scene of Lazarus's resurrection, Marta is presented as a progressively strong woman who chooses to attend to her duties rather than to follow what to her seems a pseudodivine, abstract word (i.e., Gabriel's revolutionary talk). The female protagonist, in fact, continues to perform "feminine" activities—albeit very different ones—to ensure that the immediate earthly needs of herself, her husband, and her family, and, finally, the workers as simultaneously part of the family of man and of the "Portuguese family," are at least partially met—in contrast to waiting for the materialization of what seems a complicated and far-fetched plan of communist salvation. By having Gabriel de Sá go off to America after the love interlude with Marta, the author is likely to be further pointing to his ideological incoherence (already signaled with his presence in the Buçaco spa). At the same time, Lamas stresses the importance of Marta's way—faulty and paternalistic, to be sure, but perhaps the only possible way—of intervening in (or appeasing?) the class struggle as an ideologically revamped bourgeois wife and mother.

Fulfilling the promise laid out in the novel's preface, the novel's plot delineates the course of a woman's experience from self-indulgence and "indifference" to sociopolitical awakening and, finally, to humanitarian social action. Bearing in mind the overall Freudian grid that informs Lamas's (as Ogando's) representations of femininity, Marta's trajectory follows the maternal predicament of a full-blown "feminine sexuality." It shows, moreover, what for Freud is the necessary renunciation of sexual love for cultural and social progress (Freud 1961: 59–60), an idea more fully developed in his *Civilization and Its Discontents*. Yet, with or without Freud, that exemplary process of "sublimation" comes dangerously close to echoing the fascist-nationalist ideology of woman as asexual guardian of the nation and family. It must be remembered that all seems to end well in Marta's home, once she finds a socially positive cure for her bourgeois civilizational "discontent." Short of this reading, which would put into question Lamas's oppositional literary intentions, Marta's path toward unselfish, community-oriented dedication of self is likely to stand as a (contextually necessary) pretext for what may be considered an unsettling—and unsettled—feminist statement concerning a woman's right to enjoy her own person, her own body, her own sexuality. The text suggests to what an extent this enjoyment is accessible, even if constrained and dislocated by culturally ingrained, Freudian, and/or fascistic (and heterosexist) myths of femininity and womanhood.

The ideological primacy given to the issue of woman's sexuality in Lamas's novel is ultimately indicated by the fact that, even after her "renunciation," the protagonist excitedly looks forward to the visit of the only man who seems to have brought her full spiritual, emotional, and sexual satisfaction. From Marta's perspective, her past disappointing love affairs, which are said to answer solely to basic "instinto" (instinct) masked as romantic love (37), follow the pattern initiated by her initial experience as a married woman—a phenomenon that illustrates the experience of most women (75). Gabriel's scientificist standing on the issue is unequivocal: woman's problem is really everyone's problem, in that "[f]alseamos a vida com a preocupação de espiritualizar o instinto, e de transformarmos em romance de amor o que não passa, em geral, dum fenómeno fisiológico" (91) (we falsify life with the preoccupation of spiritualizing instinct, and so we transform in a love romance what is purely a physiological phenomenon). Lamas's third novel, *A ilha verde* (1938), forcefully reiterates this same point from the perspective of a liberated foreign woman who vacations in one of the hypertraditionalist islands of the Azores archipelago. What this suggests is that such foreign theoretical views and/or ways of conduct are directly opposed to the accepted cultural experience of ordinary Portuguese women, culturally compelled to "spiritualize instinct." Marta's initial belief that woman's only possible fulfillment is through romantic love is, therefore, meant to stand as an antiexemplary norm to be denounced. Marta's story serves, in fact, as a vehicle for Lamas to demonstrate how traditional marriage, supported by an officially imposed morality, enters into conflict with the long-standing cultural myth of romantic love to simultaneously restrict and stimulate women's sexuality in repressive rather than liberating ways.

From the beginning of the novel, the narrator establishes a basic relation of comparison and contrast between her position of, albeit painful and contradictory, resistance and those women who live in "uma tristeza humilde e resignada" (a humble and resigned sadness), those who conform, renounce, and submit, despite many a "revolta íntima" (29) (intimate revolt). Whether she pretends to justify her sexual detours and/or articulate a reasonable cause for her own "intimate revolt," the point is that the topic of marriage is brought up in myriad commentaries that echo one basic thesis: "O casamento devia ser a união de dois seres ainda para além do amor, mas não passa, em geral, duma sociedade sentimentalmente falida" (124) (Marriage should be the union of two beings even beyond love, yet it is generally nothing more than an emotionally failed society). Her husband, representative of a broader class of bourgeois males, is criticized for such emotional failure on the grounds of his lack of tenderness and sensitivity, his authoritarianism, his adulterous love affairs (73–74). Women, too, are blamed for this: on the one hand, they enter into marriage with uninformed, sentimental expectations of full, everlasting love and/or socioeconomic promotion (121); on the other, remaining aloof from their husbands' work and public lives, they become complicit with the patriarchal order that reduces them to "frívolas" (frivolous), dependent objects of men's pleasures and social standing (137–38). No one should be surprised, then, as Gabriel's feminist sister claims, at the "escândalos frequentes, dos divórcios cada vez mais numerosos, das aventuras em que as mulheres casadas comprometem os nomes dos maridos" (122) (frequent scandals, the divorce rate steadily growing, married women who compromise their husbands' names in [adulterous] adventures). It would seem that as many women follow this latter route as those who, contrary to Marta, conform, renounce, and submit. Or better, no distinction should be made between the former and the latter, for apparently all women are victims of the same basic problem: "looking for love in all the wrong places," as the popular song says—and perhaps even more so when those "places" have a place in Salazar's Portugal.

Conclusion: "What exists is only that which the public knows to exist"[25]

Verbalizing what in Ogando's novel is only equivocally suggested, in *Para além do amor,* Lamas shuns both the institution of marriage and the alternative institution of adultery (in the culturally accepted guise of romantic love). The author seems to criticize the enactment of pure "instinct" as a solution to women's hunger for love beyond or outside of the morally imposed contentment of marriage and motherhood. Consequently, at a superficial level, the obvious implication of Lamas's text may be that women should give up the desire of ever attaining full personal satisfaction and, like Marta, dedicate themselves to altruistically serving the needs of others—preferably the socially underprivileged. After all, according to a Freudian view of the matter, such giving up of desire signals the "general feminine tendency to ward off sexuality" (Freud 1961: 69). Nevertheless, is maternity all there is to Marta's excitement in anticipation of Gabriel's presence—which also, not incidentally, marks the beginning of her writing activity? Her culturally conformed—and constructed—exhibition of feminine renunciation is, in fact, very distant from her initial overwhelmingly physical desire for Gabriel, symptomatically associated with Marta's experience of sexual awakening to a nun's kiss while in religious school (32, 42).[26] Marta's subsequent desire for sexual gratification appears to be erased once she identifies with the qualities of unselfishness, goodness, and altruism brought about by love (79). It is further erased in face of the privileged literary model of adultery as the only relationship where "a espiritualidade dum grande amor" (114) (the spirituality of a great love) may be enjoyed. And, finally, Marta's sexual desire is suppressed once she draws upon her acculturated maternal role and transfers to others the "spirituality" to which her sexuality is reduced, if only at the level of public verbal representation.

Although Ogando's *Pena maior* does not posit a social(ist) "beyond love" prescription for solving the "problema da mulher casada" (Archer 1953) (the problem of the married woman), her novel insists on denouncing the absence of emotional and spiritual involvement and, expectedly, of women's sexual fulfillment in the traditional marriage contract. Similarly to Lamas, Ogando too presents a female character who resists what is not only an unsatisfactory but also an unbearable marital relationship, entered upon against her wishes, by taking on a lover.

Through their adulterous relationships, Clara and, particularly, Marta achieve some degree of affirmation of selfhood, some degree of ("instinctual" or not) self- and sensuous/sexual gratification that, at least in principle, excludes procreation. Yet, they both end up associating their potential enjoyment as individuals with the ploy of maternal sensation and/or love: Clara waits for her lover to come back from Africa and give her a son; Marta waits for her lover to come back from America and, in a way, *be* her son. The omnipotence of the Freudian phallic script of feminine sexuality would not be so disturbing here were it not for the fact that, among other things, the grand finales of both novels are embarrassingly imperialistic as well as nationalistic. The parallel is obvious: the new engineer of the African colonies does his job too in the new (nationalist) ordering of the motherland; communist or capitalist, the architect prodigal son always returns to the original design of his motherland.

In spite of Clara's and Marta's stepping out of one of the roles assigned to them by convention, they still identify womanhood with motherhood, using the latter to justify, to authorize, even apparently to eulogize their answering to their demand for sexual love. As a representative of those women who conform, renounce, and submit while sustaining "intimate revolts," Clara's mother adduces maternal duty to defend what, in her case, amounts to a selfish, egotistical, and fully sensuous desire to enjoy a world of riches. She is, indeed, portrayed as the "bad mother," who is apparently not purified by maternal love because she is a mother by cultural-social and physiological fate. Does this mean that the "good mother" is only likely to be the one who chooses that as premium of the spirituality to which her sexual desire has been culturally reduced, as supposedly happens with Clara?

"[A] Mãe sofre sempre pela Mulher" ([T]he Mother always suffers for the Woman), Lamas has her fictional character, Marta, state in *Para além do amor*. She explains that women are taught "o 'dever' de ser felizes" (the 'duty' of being happy) through wifehood and, especially, maternity; the reality, however, is that maternity offers them only "dor e um sentimento divino" (pain and a divine sentiment). By contrast, men as fathers enjoy "liberdade de amar" (76) (freedom to love). Now, this is a daring, virtually revolutionary thought in a political context that imposes the conscious, deliberate identification of woman-as-mother for nationalist (and fascist) objectives, namely, those of regeneration. This is the regeneration of morals as well as the regenerated reproduction of a "race" left dissolute in part by the "modern" (or feminist) women who, since the turn of the century, made their appearance in Portuguese public culture (Silva). (Evidently, this is also the period when the Portuguese nation, and the nationalists within it, deal with the shame [feeling of castration?] of having fallen behind England and Germany in the run for the African continent.) By pointing out what in "the Woman" is lost to "the Mother," concretely, the enjoyment of her sexuality—as the father enjoys his—Lamas does point to the possibility of her text being read otherwise, but only by those whose own interests would so warrant it. These may include the wife-mother to whom Lamas overtly appeals and who Ogando ambiguously assumes to be among the potential readership of her *Pena maior*. This virtual reader is the theoretical figure who would embody the possibly "worst sentence" of ideal womanhood as guardian angel of traditional morals in what came to be known as the "sagrada família portuguesa" (holy Portuguese family).

Can women, the ideal defenders of the "moral and spiritual interests of the race," to quote Pestana de Vasconcelos (38), be phantomed in terms of the sensuous and erotic delights that, following the fascist logic of historical and spiritual continuity, presumably await them, as they awaited the bygone Lusitanian seafarers? Despite their differences of perspective and of implied or explicit literary intentions, both Ogando and Lamas, through the stories of their female protagonists, and, above all, through their own gesture of public intervention in the culture and the politics of their day, seem to think so. They reclaim, after all, the unsettling, menacing voice of *lusosex* that no piece of fascist propaganda on woman and the family is able to foil over. For neither the model of the nuclear family "corresponderia às realidades do período" (Baptista 194) (would correspond to the realities of the period) nor, even less so, would women strictly abide by the role imposed by Catholic, fascist-nationalist, and, especially, the dictator's own personal brand of feminine asceticism.[27]

Appendix: Selection of Women's Fiction Published between the Mid-1930s and Mid-1940s

Irene Lisboa (1892–1958)   *Esta cidade!* (1942; stories)

Maria Lamas (1893–1983)   *Para além do amor* (1935)
                             A ilha verde (1938)

Adelaide Félix (1896–1971)   *O grito da terra* (1936)

Aurora Jardim (1898–1988)   *Uma vida de mulher* (1939)
                             Ressaca (1943)

Maria Archer (1899–1981)   *Três mulheres* (1935)
                             Ida e volta de uma caixa de cigarros
                             (1938)
                             Ela é apenas mulher (1944)
                             Filosofia de uma mulher moderna (1950;
                             stories)

Alice Ogando (1900–1981)   *O amor dos outros* (1935)
                             Pena maior (1935)

Raquel Bastos (1903–84)   *Destino humilde* (1942)
                             Aquele que veio de longe (1942)

Manuela Porto (1912–50)   *Um filho mais e outras histórias* (1945;
                             stories)

Patricia Joyce (b. 1913)   *Anúncio de casamento* (1947; stories)

Notes

1. Fernanda de Castro, *Danças de roda* (1921; in Sampaio 93). Fernanda de Castro (1900–1994) married journalist António Ferro (1895–1958), appointed director of the National Secretariat of Propaganda by Salazar in 1933. All translations are my own.

2. António de Oliveira Salazar (1889–1970) was appointed prime minister in 1932 by President General António Carmona, head of the military junta responsible for the coup that brought to an end the First Republic in 1926. Salazar's *Political Constitution of the New State* defines the authoritarian, corporative form of government that was to rule over Portugal and its colonies in Africa until 1974, when a democratic revolution headed by a military elite overthrew the New State.

3. For an informative study of the concept of nationalist regeneration as it applies to Portuguese fascism, see Proença (1987). See Cova and Pinto for a brief analysis of Salazar's position regarding women in comparision with other European fascist dictatorships.

4. In the same vein, see also, for example, Lima and Esteves—both of whom explicitly honor Salazar's political slogan "For a Greater Portugal!"

5. For a recent English translation of the poem, see *The Lusiads*, trans. Landeg White (1997).

6. The political and social upheavals, as well as the rampant economic crisis, that affected the First Republic (1910–26) are denounced by many a conservative as the obvious result of democratic politics and Enlightenment ideals in general. More often than not, the supposed disarray of morals is blamed on "modern" bourgeois women, who do not abide by the traditional role of dutiful mothers and housewives. See, for example, Ferreira (1932), Ferro, and Guimarães.

7. In 1930, 69.9 percent of women and 52.8 percent of men were illiterate (Proença 1997: 62).

8. These, together with folklore and ethnography, represent the main areas of nationalist education intended for women, so as to lead them to identify with and commit themselves to the pillars of Salazarist ideology: "God, Fatherland, Family." See Ferreira (1994) for an overview of the components of national education.

9. For an excellent study of how sexual love figures in *The Lusiads* and in the poet's other lyrical works, see Macedo.

10. See Baptista for an informative overview of the values and images of the family circulating from 1933, the year in which the new constitution went into effect, until 1940, when an agreement between the New State and Rome issued the abolishment of divorce between those married by the Catholic church.

11. The foregoing theoretical argument is inspired primarily on my reading of Foucault (esp. 105–11).

12. I have studied elsewhere the array of discourses that construct this "other" of the Portuguese nation at the end of the nineteenth century, and subsequently as part of the backlash against feminism during the First Republic (see Ferreira 1998, 1999).

13. It is important to note that despite the unprecedented number of fictional texts (novels and short-story collections) published by women in the period between 1935 and 1949, they have not received critical attention and have never been

republished. I have begun taking up this task in the critical anthology *A urgência de contar: contos de mulheres dos anos quarenta*.

14. The famous proviso to article 5 of the 1933 constitution withdraws women from the sphere of citizenship and the (supposed) "igualdade de direitos perante a lei" (equality of rights before the law) on the grounds of "differences" resulting from "a natureza da mulher e o bem da família" (woman's nature and the good of the family) (*Constituição*, 4–5).

15. See the appendix for a selective list of representative works of fiction published between the mid- to late 1930s and 1940s. Included there are novels and short-story collections that refer in whole or in part to the topic of women's sexualities. Titles are not in chronological order, but follow instead the order of each author's date of birth. Only the titles discussed in this essay (or referred to in notes) are included in the works cited.

16. The material, emotional, and moral difficulties experienced by a young, single woman in her attempts to become a professional writer are fictionalized in Ogando's 1938 novel *O meu sonho de papel*. The author became, in fact, widely read by (conceivably) female mass audiences, with hundreds of what appear to be romance titles published under various pseudonyms and under her own name. She was eventually recruited to serve as mouthpiece of the regime on the National Radio (Emissora Nacional).

17. Also published in 1935, her first novel, *O amor dos outros*, apparently takes delight in representing a "virile," independent, professional woman pianist, who resists the contract of marriage and confronts public opinion on her summer love affair with a reputedly male-chauvinist sculptor. The last two pages of the novel describe her sudden change of heart about marriage, or about "what people will say" (i.e., she abides by convention).

18. The poetry of Judith Teixeira (1880–1959), most of it featuring explicitly lesbian love, has only recently been republished (Teixeira 1996). Her collection of short novels, also featuring lesbian love, *Satânia* (1927), has never been republished. The most well known and artistically accomplished of the women poets representing heterosexual love is Florbela Espanca (1894–1930). Of all the women writers who begin their careers after the mid-1930s, Maria Archer (1905–1982) is, without doubt, the one who most insistently calls attention to nonreproductive sexualities marginal to the institution of the family.

19. For positions against women's work and "competition" with men, see, for example, Esteves; Lima; Vasconcelos; and Castro. This type of propaganda is further disseminated, after 1936, through the activities of the fascist women's group OMEN (National Initiative of Mothers for National Salvation).

20. It might be noted that, according to Freud, woman's "worst pain," including that of the lesbian woman, would be "renouncing all hope of motherhood" (1961: 149).

21. This is insistently denounced by Maria Archer in several of her short stories. See, for example, "Emprego de Capital" and "Sujeição," in *Filosofia de uma mulher moderna*.

22. It is evident that with respect to the topic of lesbianism, as all else, Ogando follows the moralizing, Naturalist trend epitomized in French literature by Victor Marguérite's controversial novel *La Garçonne* (1922).

23. Although she never enlisted in a political party, Maria Lamas was repeatedly imprisioned for her subversive activities as a pacifist, a feminist, and an oppositional voice to the regime. In 1962, at the age of sixty-eight, she went into exile in Paris, where she remained for seven years (Fiadeiro 13–16).

24. Maria Lamas had previously used the pseudonym Rosa Silvestre in a number of short fiction pieces and in her first novels, *Diferença de raças* (1923) and *O caminho luminoso* (1930).

25. "Politicamente só existe aquilo que o público sabe que existe." This is the famous slogan by Salazar, during the inauguration of the "National Secretariat of Propaganda," previously known as the "National Secretariat of Information," reinforcing the activities of the Committee of Censorship, officially founded in 1933 (in Rodrigues 76).

26. Besides the Freudian subplot possibly present here, as in the case of Ogando's *Pena maior,* this incident might point to the questionable "morals" that are directly or indirectly taught in religious schools, attended by bourgeois girls who are supposed to become the future model Portuguese women.

27. It is important to note, in this regard, that, contrary to other fascist regimes that exploited the erotically charged figure of the dictator to mobilize the masses—including, of course, women—see, for example, Reich; Theweleit; and Spackman. Salazar's strategy of identification and control of the population rested on his modest, virtually "matronly," public profile (Belo, 263–79).

Works Cited

Archer, Maria. 1950. *Filosofia de uma mulher moderna.* Porto: Livraria Simões Lopes.
———. Entrevista. 1953. "Diga-nos a Verdade." *Diário de Notícias,* January 16. Arquivo Diário de Notícias, n.p.
Baptista, Luís Vicente. 1986. "Valores e imagens da família em Portugal." In *A mulher na sociedade portuguesa: Visão histórica e perspectivas actuais. Actas do colóquio.* Coimbra: Instituto de História Económica e Social, Faculdade de Letras da Universidade de Coimbra. 191–219.
Belo, Maria. 1987. "O Estado Novo e as Mulheres." In *O Estado Novo: Das origens ao fim da autarcia, 1926–1959,* vol. 2. Lisbon: Fragmentos. 263–79.
Camões, Luís Vaz de. 1997. *The Lusiads.* Trans. Landeg White. Oxford and New York: Oxford University Press.
Cartazes de Propaganda Política do Estado Novo (1933–1949). 1988. Lisbon: Biblioteca Nacional.
Castro, Augusto de. 1933. *Sexo 33 ou a revolução da mulher (idífios e ironias).* 2d ed. Lisbon: Empresa Nacional de Publicidade.
Constituição Política da República Portuguesa e Acto Colonial. 1936. 2d ed. Lisbon: Livraria Moraes.
Cova, Anne, and António Costa Pinto. 1997. "O Salazarismo e as mulheres: Uma abordagem comparativa." *Penélope* 17: 71–94.
Culler, Jonathan. 1982. "Reading as a Woman." In *On Deconstruction: Theory and Criticism after Structuralism.* Ithaca, N.Y.: Cornell University Press. 43–63.
Esteves, Alberto. 1932. *A Família.* Coimbra: n.p.

Ferreira, Ana Paula. 1999. "Nationalism and Feminism at the Turn of the Century: Constructing the (M)Other of Portugal." *Santa Barbara Portuguese Studies* 3: 123–42.

———. 2002. *A urgência de contar: contos de mulheres dos anos quarenta.* Lisbon: Editorial Caminho.

———. 2001. "'Tell Me the Mother You Had': Anti-Feminist Discourses and the Making of The Portuguese Home." In *Global Impact of the Portuguese Language,* ed. Asela Rodriguez de Laguna. New Brunswick, N.J., and London: Transaction Publishers. 127–43.

Ferreira, Cândida Florinda. 1932. *A Mulher na família e na sociedade contemporânea.* Lisbon: Casa Portuguesa.

Ferreira, Isabel Alves. 1994. "Mocidade Portuguesa Feminina: Um ideal educativo." *Revista de História das Ideias* 16: 193–233.

Ferro, António. 1979. *Leviana: Novela em fragmentos com um estudo crítico do autor* [1921]. 4th ed. Lisbon: Roger Delraux.

Fiadeiro, Maria Antónia. 1993. "Maria Lamas: Uma Mulher em Pessoa." In *Maria Lamas 1893–1983.* Lisbon: Presidência do Conselho de Ministros, Instituto da Biblioteca Nacional e do Livro. 11–16.

Foucault, Michel. 1990. *The History of Sexuality.* Vol. 1, *An Introduction.* Trans. Robert Hurley. New York: Vintage Books.

Freud, Sigmund. 1961. *Civilization and Its Discontents.* Trans. James Strachey. New York and London: W. W. Norton.

———. 1963. *Sexuality and the Psychology of Love.* Ed. Philip Rieff. New York: Collier Books, Macmillan Publishing Company.

Guimarães, Luís d'Oliveira. 1925. *Saias curtas.* Lisbon: Empresa Internacional Editora.

Lamas, Maria. 1923. *Diferença de Raças.* Lisbon: Portugália.

———. 1930. *O caminho luminoso.* Lisbon: Sociedade Nacional de Tipografia.

———. 1935. *Para além do amor.* Lisbon: Editorial "O Século."

———. 1938. *A ilha verde.* Lisbon: Editorial "O Século."

Lima, Pires de. 1932. *Feminismo e Feministas.* Porto: Edições Germen.

Macedo, Helder. 1980. *Camões e a viagem initiátrica.* Lisbon: Moraes Editores.

———. 1998. "Love as Knowledge: The Lyric Poetry of Camões." Unpublished MS.

Marguérite, Victor. 1922. *La Garçonne.* Paris: Flammarion.

Martins, Moisés de Lemos. 1986. "Uma Solidão Necessária à Ordem Salazarista: A Família como Terapêutica Nacional." *Cadernos de Ciências Sociais* 4 (April): 77–83.

Mitchell, Juliet. 1975. *Psychoanalysis and Feminism: Freud, Reich, Laing and Women.* New York: Vintage Books.

Obra das Mães Pela Educação Nacional. 1938. Orientação e Fins. Lisbon, OMEN.

Ogando, Alice. 1935a. *O amor dos outros.* Lisbon: Editorial "O Século."

———. 1935b. *Pena maior.* Lisbon: Empresa Nacional de Publicidade.

———. 1938. *O meu sonho de papel.* Lisbon: Livraria Civilização Editora.

Parker, Andrew, Mary Russo, Doris Sommer, and Patricia Yaeger. 1992. "Introduction." In *Nationalisms and Sexualities,* ed. Andrew Parker, Mary Russo, Doris Sommer, and Patricia Yaeger. New York and London: Routledge. 1–18.

Proença, Maria Cândida. 1987. "O conceito de regeneração no Estado Novo." In *O Estado Novo: Das origens ao fim da autarcia, 1926–1959,* vol. 2. Lisbon: Fragmentos. 257–62.

———. 1997. *História: O Estado Novo. Materiais para Professores.* Instituto de Inovação Educacional. Lisbon: Ministério da Educação.

Queiroz, Eça de. 1946. "Estatuto Social de Portugal em 1870." In *Uma campanha alegre das farpas,* 6th ed., vol. 2. Porto: Lello & Irmão. 105–31.

Reich, Wilhelm. 1970. *The Mass Psychology of Fascism.* Trans. Vincent Carfagno. New York: Farrar, Straus & Giroux.

Renan, Ernest. 1990. "What Is a Nation?" In *Nation and Narration,* ed. Homi K. Bhabha. London: Routledge. 8–22.

Rodrigues, Graça Almeida. 1980. *Breve história da censura literária em portugal.* Biblioteca Breve, vol. 54. Lisbon: Instituto de Cultura e Língua Portuguesa.

Sampaio, Albino Forjaz de. 1935. *As melhores páginas de literatura feminina (Poesia).* Lisbon: Livraria Popular de Francisco Franco.

Silva, Maria Regina Tavares da. 1992. *Feminismo em Portugal na voz de mulheres escritoras do início do séc. XX.* 2d ed. Lisbon: Comissão Para a Igualdade e Para os Direitos das Mulheres.

Spackman, Barbara. 1996. *Fascist Virilities: Rhetoric, Ideology, and Social Fantasy in Italy.* Minneapolis: University of Minnesota Press.

Teixeira, Judith. 1927. *Satânia.* Lisbon: Livraria Rodrigues Editores.

———. 1996. *Poemas.* Lisbon: &etc.

Theweleit, Klaus. 1987. *Male Fantasies.* Vol 1, *Women, Floods, Bodies, History.* Trans. Stephen Conway. Minneapolis: University of Minnesota Press.

Vasconcelos, J. A. Pestana de. 1933. *O conceito do lar e da família no estado novo.* Coimbra: Imprensa da Universidade.

CHAPTER SEVEN

Not Just for Love, Pleasure, or Procreation

Eroto-Racial, Sociopolitical, and Mystic-Mythical Discourses of Sexuality in Pepetela's A geração da utopia

Russell G. Hamilton

Pepetela's *A geração da utopia* qualifies as a landmark novel, not only for Angolan literature, but also for Lusophone African and, indeed, Portuguese-language writing in general. Moreover, since its publication in 1992, the novel has stirred up controversy—much, though not all, of it stemming from its portrayal of explicit sex. There is, of course, a history of sexuality in the literature of Angola, Cape Verde, Guinea-Bissau, Mozambique, and São Tomé e Príncipe. On the other hand, until around the mid-1980s, explicit language and scenes of sex were virtually absent from the corpus of Lusophone African literature.[1]

In order to locate *A geração da utopia* in its sociohistorical context, I cite what I believe to be the most plausible explanations as to why discourses and the depiction of sexuality occur implicitly, if at all, in Lusophone African works written before the 1980s. With respect to the immediate preindependence period, one explanation is simply that prevailing Portuguese cultural conventions and social interdictions militated against the use of overt sexuality in the literary expression of the then African colonies. Moreover, the official state censorship that prevailed in the colonies under the Salazar dictatorial regime applied not only to what the authorities deemed politically subversive, but also to what they considered to be an affront to public morality.

Another explanation, particularly with respect to works produced by socially conscious writers during the waning decades of colonial rule and the first years of Lusophone African independence, has much to do with a basically puritanical, socialist ideology that eschewed sexual explicitness in cultural expression. Both before and immediately after independence, many militants, including writers, tended to view the depiction of explicit sex as bourgeois, antirevolutionary frivolity or hedonistic obfuscation.

Beginning in the late 1940s and increasingly during the 1950s and 1960s, literary manifestations of cultural affirmation, social protest, and combativeness on the part of engagé writers did result, in both the colonies and Portugal, in a number of works glorifying black and mixed-race women. A not insignificant body of poems of the preindependence period exalts an archetypal woman who emerges as a nativistic symbol and an emblem of the rising sentiments of cultural resistance and nationalism among black, mixed race *(mestiço)*, and white intellectuals. In this literature of exaltation and celebration exist love and other intimist poems characterized by discourses of sensuality with overtones of eroticism.

Viriato da Cruz, one of the founders, in the late 1940s, of the Movimento dos Novos Intelectuais de Angola (Movement of Angola's New Intellectuals), wrote in his poem "Namoro" (Courtship):

Sua pele macia—era sumaúma...
Sua pele macia, da cor do jambo, cheirando a rosas
sua pele macia guardava as doçuras do corpo rijo
tão rijo e tão doce—como o maboque...
Seus seios, laranjas—laranjas do Loge
seus dentes...—marfim...[2]

[Her soft skin—silky down of the Kapok tree...
Her soft skin, the color of the rose apple,
her soft skin, smelling of roses, held all the sweetness of her firm body
as firm and sweet—as the *maboque* fruit...
Her breasts, oranges—oranges from Loge
her teeth...—ivory...]

The tropical fruit imagery of preindependence works such as Cruz's "Namoro" heralded, as I discuss presently, the more overt eroticism of some recent postcolonial, Lusophone African poetry. Along with the glorification of the black and mixed-race woman (i.e., the *mulata*, the *morena*), the latter colonial period also gave rise to a literature, again consisting mainly of poems, of an agonistic, eroto-racial nature. Some of the most notable writing of that period deals with the sexual exploitation of the subjugated woman, as depicted, for example, in these lines from "Mulato," by Rui Knopfli, a Portuguese poet born and raised in Mozambique:

Venho cansado e tenho
fome de mulher. Sou branco.
Escolhi-te. Hoje durmo contigo:
Um ventre negro de mulher
arfando, a meu lado arfando,
o cansaço, o espasmo
e o sono. Nada mais.
Amanhã parto. E esqueço-te.
Depressa te esqueço.
    E teu ventre? (28)

[I arrive tired and I hunger for
a woman. I am white.
I chose you. Today I sleep with you:
A woman's dark belly
heaving, heaving next to me,
then lassitude, spasm,
and sleep. Nothing more.
Tomorrow I depart. And I forget you.
    And your belly?]

The Portuguese word *ventre* can mean "belly" or "womb." The poet thus plays on this double meaning to dramatize the possibility of a child born as a result of this brief sexual encounter between the dominant white male and the subjugated black female.

In a similar vein, there are preindependence poems that capture the eroto-racial angst of the black or *mestiço* male. In "A sombra branca," by Mário António, an Angolan poet, the persona addresses a black or mixed-race woman:

Quando choraste, Rosa, nos meus braços,
Quando, vencida, me rogaste amor,
Forçados foram todos os abraços
Porque a branca entre nós se veio pôr!

Ela, a branca, tolheu o meu desejo
Da Lua vinda numa noite igual,
Quando arfante, sem pejo, descobriste
O tropical maboque do teu seio. (33)

[Rosa, when you cried in my arms,
When, in surrender, you pleaded for my love,

All of my caresses were forced
Because the white one placed herself between us!

She, the white one, thwarted my desire
Having arrived from the moon on a night like this,
When you, breathing hard, without shame, bared
Your breasts with their tropical scent of the *maboque* fruit.]

As in lines from Viriato da Cruz's "Namoro" quoted earlier, the sensual, tropical fruit imagery of Mário António's oneiric "A sombra branca" constitutes one of several harbingers of the "liberation," beginning in the 1980s, of the language of Lusophone African poetry. The political *abertura* or "opening up," which, to varying degrees beginning in the late 1980s, swept all five Lusophone African countries, has contributed significantly to a cultural ambiance that seems to have inspired contemporary writers to engage in greater experimentation with form as well as content.

One of several representative products of this period of politically inspired aesthetic liberalization in Angola is "O mamão" (The papaya), an epigrammatic, erotic poem written in 1984 by Paula Tavares:

Frágil vagina semeada
pronta, útil, semanal.
Nela se alargam as sedes
    no meio
    cresce
    insondável
o vazio ... (15)

[Fragile vagina, sown,
beneficial, ever available.
In it thirsts expand
    and at its center
    there looms,
    unfathomable,
the void ...][3]

Along with the eroticism of tropicalist sensuality that increasingly delineates the discourse of Angolan and Mozambican poets, images and themes of racial erotica have emerged in this most recent preindependence period. The social liberalization that allowed for greater use of erotica in recent postcolonial poetic expression also set the scene for the discourses of sexuality for contemporary prose works, most notably *A geração da utopia.* Before analyzing the role of explicit sexual discourses and situations contained in the novel, I should note that starting with its title, which has multiple meanings and connotative values, Pepetela's novel is socially and politically provocative. The literal English translation of the title is "The generation from utopia"; but it can also be rendered as "The utopian generation." On a more connotative level, reflecting the work's underlying epistemological intentionality, the title conveys the sense of a generation that believed in and sought to bring about utopia, in the Marxian sense of the term.

Over a period of nearly thirty years, members of the generation depicted in Pepetela's four-part saga believed, with varying degrees of conviction, in the possibility of bringing about an egalitarian society through revolution. This overriding conceptual sense of utopia determines the thematic dynamic and has much to do with the role that sexual relationships play throughout the narrative.

"A Casa (1961)," the novel's first part, refers to "A Casa dos Estudantes do Império" (CEI) (The House of Students from the Empire), a social organization established in Lisbon in 1944. Although Angolans founded the CEI, the House rapidly became a meeting place for students from all of the then African colonies, with even a few from the Asian lands of Goa, Macao, and East Timor. Moreover, a number of Portuguese students and intellectuals, among them members of the then clandestine Communist Party, made common cause with Africans and Asians from those territories officially known as the *Ultramar*. Indeed, by 1961 the CEI, established, ironically, with the approval of the colonialist Salazar regime, had become the headquarters for discussions and literary activity revolving around a coming new political and social order.

The year in which part one of the novel unfolds is significant because on February 4, 1961, supporters of the MPLA (People's Movement of the Liberation of Angola) stormed a Luanda jail in an attempt to free political prisoners. And on March 15, 1961, elements of UPA (Union of Angolan Peoples, later renamed FNLA—National Front of the Liberation of Angola) initiated an armed rebellion in northern Angola.[4] During that pivotal year, among those young Angolans who belonged to the so-called Utopian Generation were, in the order in which their names appear in the narrative, Sara, Aníbal, Malongo, and Vítor Ramos. Consistent with the author's penchant for the allegorical, as demonstrated in earlier works, several of the novel's characters bear sobriquets relating to the broader context of that sought-after new political and social order.[5] In time, Vítor, presumably because of his visions of "worldwide" revolution, would take "Mundial" as his nom de guerre. Aníbal would come to be known as "o Sabio" (the Sage). But it is Sara and Malongo, without nicknames and, for that matter, surnames, who play central roles in "A casa," especially with respect to discourses of sexuality as manifestations of the racial, social, and ideological tensions that attend the idealism of a generation.

In 1957, Malongo had arrived in Lisbon from his native Angola to study and to win a slot on Benfica, one of Portugal's major soccer clubs. So great is Malongo's devotion to the sport that he neglects his studies and, as a result, fails to graduate from high school. Moreover, unlike Vítor Ramos, his roommate, as well as many other African students in Lisbon, Malongo eschews politics. Besides being a dedicated soccer player, Malongo is also an inveterate womanizer, and this in spite of being all but engaged to Sara. His rationalization for his unrelenting attempts to have sex with Denise, a twenty-year-old French student, helps establish the racial-erotic themes that inform the experience of the African male in Europe: "pôssas, não podia perder a oportunidade de comer uma francesa" (27) (hell, I wouldn't lose out on the chance of sleeping with a Frenchwoman).

The passages describing Malongo's sexual encounters with Denise contain some of the most explicit language and scenes in this novel, and, indeed, in all of Lusophone African literature. Some readers of *A geração da utopia* have been taken aback by this explicitness, perhaps even shocked by what they see as gratuitous, salacious details, and offended by what may seem unabashed pandering to prurient interests. Indeed, some readers might wonder why the author dwells at length on Malongo's at first unsuccessful attempts to have intercourse with Denise. These same readers might ask why the narrator then offers a similarly detailed account of the couple's heavy petting in the privacy of Denise's bedroom. The answer begins to emerge when we next find the lovers in a nearly empty movie theater, where, in the only relative privacy of the last row, Malongo succeeds in bringing Denise to orgasm without engaging in intercourse. When she offers to return the favor, he refuses, vehemently asserting: "Não gozo com isso. Só sexo no sexo, sou um tradicionalista" (30) (I don't reach orgasm that way. With me, it's sex organ in sex organ; I'm a traditionalist). Ironic though it may seem, in view of his willingness to perform a sexual act in a public space, Malongo is indeed a "traditionalist" in the sense that he holds to a patriarchal imperative.[6] To accept Denise's offer would mean to be the submissive partner, a role that would subvert Malongo's need to control. What takes place in the movie theater is, in effect, a kind of foreplay that leads to the successful conquest, in the "traditional" fashion, when the couple returns to spend the night in Denise's apartment.

As concerns the social themes and ideological context of part I, both Malongo's calculated lust and his drive to excel on the soccer field serve as metaphors for the colonized in the land of the colonizer. In other words, Malongo is, ironically, the slave Caliban seeking to dominate in the land of the master Prospero; symbolically, sexual and athletic prowess constitutes means to that end. Thus, the implied author boldly confronts and elaborates on some time-honored racial-erotic stereotypes and myth. Concomitantly, the explicit terms and graphic scenes of sexual encounters possess socially redeeming value, as it were, in the work's aesthetico-ideological design.

The relationship between Malongo, the womanizer, and Sara, the one-man woman, constitutes a complex set of social, racial-erotic, as well as eroto-racial, and political contradictions with respect to the groups of students from Angola and elsewhere in the empire who share in common their "exile" in Portugal. When the landlady sees Malongo leaving Sara's room early one morning, "[a] portuguesa se escandalizava que ela, uma médica, dormisse com um negro. E na sua casa" (28) (the Portuguese woman was scandalized that she [Sara], a doctor, would sleep with a black man. And in her house). When together on the streets of Lisbon, the interracial couple endures the hostile stares of passersby. If Sara and Malongo are violating a social taboo, there is also the matter of social class. Sara is the daughter of wealthy parents; Malongo, on the other hand, comes from humble origins. And whereas Sara is nearing the end of her medical training, Malongo has flunked out of secondary school. Moreover, Sara subscribes to the anticolonialist political agenda of the utopian generation. As far as Malongo's commitment to "the cause" is concerned, as Vítor Ramos puts it: "ele não se mete em nada, só manda umas bocas de vez em quando" (15) (he doesn't get involved, he just shoots his mouth off from time to time). What, then, is the attraction that brings Malongo and Sara together as lovers and even friends? The easy answer is sexual attraction, heightened perhaps by the

lure of the "forbidden fruit."[7] Inevitably, of course, there is in the delin-
eation of Malongo much of the stereotypical and mythic: that is, the
athletic, sexually well-endowed, preternatural, lustful, black male: "Sempre foi um apressado, ávido de sexo, pensou Sara. Os preconceituosos
definem-no como um africano típico" (40) (He was always in a hurry,
avid for sex, Sara thought. Those who harbor racial prejudices would
characterize him as a typical African male).

Sara muses, however, that she has no way of knowing whether Malongo is typical or not; he is the first and only man with whom she has
had sex. With sensuous and lyrical abandon, she admits to herself, however, that "Malongo transmitia calor suficiente para evaporar todos os
cacimbos. De cada vez era para ela como a primeira, no deslumbra-
mento da descoberta" (43) (Malongo transmitted enough warmth to
evaporate all of the mists that clouded her existence. Every time was for
her as if it were the first, in that fascination of discovery). The "opposites attract" cliché notwithstanding, consistent with the layers of social
and racial ironies that delineate gender relationships in the novel, a
kind of familiarity based on origins transcends hedonism and the lure
of the exotic in Sara's attraction to Malongo. Their mutual Angolanness
also plays a role in Sara, the high-achieving and socially conscious professional, and Malongo, the high-school dropout and apolitical athlete,
having found each other in the alien environment of the *metrópole*.

With respect to Sara's ethnic origins, in the thirteenth century her
Jewish ancestors had migrated to Portugal and in the eighteenth and
nineteenth centuries her family, on both her mother's and father's sides,
settled in southern Angola. Thus, the descendant of "cristãos-novos"
(i.e., converts to Christianity), several generations of whom have lived
in Africa, Sara feels herself to be as Angolan as Malongo. She muses
about her family's legacy of so-called contaminated blood, both Jewish
and African. As for the latter, Sara believes, although she lacks definitive
proof, that her maternal great-grandmother was a *mulata*. In short,
Sara's roots in the creole city of Benguela legitimize her Angolanness,
especially as a member of a generation seeking utopia.

Parenthetically, it is worth noting that Pepetela, which is both the
pseudonym and nom de guerre of Artur Maurício Pestana dos Santos,
descends from Portuguese who in the nineteenth century settled in
Benguela. Whether or not Pepetela has Sephardic heritage and/or black
African ancestry, he celebrates his hometown as a unique city with a

mixed-race population and creole culture.[8] It is therefore quite consistent with the author's regionalist topophilia, or love of place, that Sara would want to have a child by Malongo. And this child "só podia ser uma mulatinha linda. Nascida em Benguela, para não fugir à tradição. A cidade das acácias não era conhecida por ser o berço das mais belas mestiças de Angola?" (45) (could only be a pretty little mulatto girl. She would be born in Benguela, so as not to deviate from tradition. Was not the city of acacia trees known as the cradle of the most beautiful mixed-race women of Angola?).

If Sara's involvement with her black compatriot is infused with cultural sentimentality and presents a utopian vision of creole eugenics, Malongo also transcends the physical. For him the sexual conquest of European women, including Denise and later, in Paris, a young Dutch-woman whom he follows to Amsterdam, is a form of self-validation on a continent where he meets with real and imagined disdain and rejection. Although Sara is somatically white, and dominating her also represents a form of affirmation for Malongo, she is not "a European."

When Malongo learns that Sara is pregnant, he swells with virile as well as paternal pride. Contradicting Sara's intuition with respect to the baby's gender, Malongo maintains that the child will be a boy, whom he will teach to play soccer and to be Angola's greatest *nguendeiro* (a word of Kimbundu origin meaning "womanizer").

In "A Casa" graphic descriptions of sexuality involve only Malongo, Denise, and Sara. There are, however, allusions to sexuality, if not explicit scenes of sexual encounters, involving Aníbal, one of the other two main characters in this first part of the novel. After Aníbal drops out of the university, he is conscripted into the Portuguese army. When his mobilization to Angola appears imminent, the increasingly militant Aníbal plans to desert and flee to France. And it is Sara who first hides him in her room. She does so without the knowledge of Malongo, whose machismo, Sara confides to Aníbal, would not permit him to accept her sharing her apartment with another man, even though they do not sleep together. Sara sees herself as a mother-protector to Aníbal, whose principles she admires. For all her maternal instincts, Sara admits to herself, however, that she would make love to Aníbal as a ritual akin to an act of communion. In my assessment of part III, I elaborate upon how this urgent, politically inspired arrangement fosters a bond that ultimately results in a sexual intimacy between Sara and Aníbal, when, in April 1982, they meet in Benguela.

Similarly, with respect to sexuality without physical intimacy in the novel's first part, Vítor's involvement with Fernanda is almost idyllically romantic. On a Lisbon beach, Vítor is smitten by a comely, dark-skinned *mestiça* who, it turns out, is an eighteen-year-old nursing student from the south-central Angolan city of Lubango.[9] Fernanda eventually consents to be Vítor's girlfriend, but their love relationship does not go beyond dancing together and a chaste kiss on the cheek, at least with respect to what is described and implied in the text. Fernanda's Portuguese settler father and black mother, who are married, rather than living in a common-law arrangement—which was frequently the case in such liaisons between the dominant settler male and the colonized woman—have raised their daughter and her siblings to respect the prevailing colonial political and social order. In Lisbon, Fernanda avoids the Casa dos Estudantes do Império, which, she has been warned, is a hotbed of communist activity. "A Casa" then comes to a close with a group, including Malongo, Sara, Laurindo, Elias (who will play an important role in the novel's final part), and Aníbal fleeing by car, first to Spain and eventually to Paris (Vítor had made his escape prior to his friends' exodus).

"A Chana" (The savannah), the novel's second part, is set in Angola, in 1972, a little more than ten years into the guerrilla war against colonial rule. Although in the third person, the narrative voice is essentially that of Mundial (Vítor Ramos), who, along with Sábio (Aníbal), has joined the struggle as a guerrilla fighter.

In several flashbacks, the racial-erotic discourse of "A Casa" continues in "A Chana," but in a somewhat different register. This particular register reflects a heightened sense of the juxtapositions between Africa and Europe, as characters such as Malongo struggle for self-affirmation in venues even more socially and culturally alienating than Portugal. Malongo, in an intensified mission to prove himself, continues his sexual conquests and eventually abandons Sara and Judite, their five-year-old daughter. When Aníbal passes through Paris on his way to Algeria, where the MPLA had its headquarters in exile, he learns from Sara that Malongo had departed for Amsterdam in pursuit of the aforementioned Dutchwoman and a career as a cabaret musician.

There are also discourses of sexuality in "A Chana" that either differ markedly from or somewhat alter the tone and substance of those that characterize the novel's first part. Specifically, in "A Chana" a decidedly lyrical language register accompanies the theme of nativism and cultural reaffirmation. The prime example of sexuality as it relates to an affective Angolanness appears in Sábio's account, as told to Mundial, of the *xinjanguila,* a traditional round dance from eastern Angola. Sábio's graphic account of the ceremony and choreography may seem to play to Western stereotypes with respect to African dance: "a pessoa da esquerda, ao vir do centro, te convida batendo os pés ou dando um sacão de anca, ou à tua frente bamboleia o ventre a mimar o acto sexual" (126–27) (the person to the left, upon entering the center of the circle, invites you with stomping feet, gyrating hips, or a grinding belly close to yours in simulation of the sex act). The frenetic, lascivious dancing conveys a meaning that furthers the author's codification and ritualization of modes of sexuality for purposes of enhancing the work's social themes and underlying political statement.

Mussole, a teenager destined to become Aníbal's wife, figures centrally in the erotic dance. And in contrast to the image of the submissive female of the novel's first part, Aníbal exalts in Mussole's aggressive role in the dance as simulated sex act: "é a fêmea que comanda o acto, não pelos movimentos do corpo, mas pelo aspirar profundo dos músculos da vagina" (127) (the female is the one in control, not through her body's movements but through the deep aspiration of her muscular vagina). Sábio refers then to Mussole's dominant role as subtle and "tentacular," and this allusion foreshadows the sexual symbolism of the octopus, the creature for which the novel's third part, "O Polvo," is named.

Muscularity, with reference to both female and male sex organs, serves metaphorically to further the themes elaborated in "A Chana." In this section of the novel, cultural revindication and resistance, an archetypal Angolanness, tellurian symbols, masculinity, femininity, and, conversely, a hermaphroditic sexuality all revolve around and enhance the theme of the armed struggle against colonial rule. Inevitably, the perversion of sex into violence also emerges as a weapon of war and a tool of domination in the novel's second part. Thus, "foi nesse trágico Abril que ele [o Sábio] pressentiu no meio do capim o corpo violado e esquartejado de Mussole" (140) (it was in that tragic April that he [Sábio] foresaw Mussole's violated and mangled body lying in the grass).

Mussole's death occurs in that tragic April of 1972, and "O Polvo," the novel's penultimate section, unfolds ten years later to the month, in a more tranquil, albeit likewise troubled, April. In April 1982 Angola was already seven years and five months into independence. By that year, independence euphoria and postcolonial revolutionary zeal had begun to dissipate. The fabric of the utopian dream had become frayed by a myriad of nation-building problems, exacerbated by a seemingly endless civil war.

As part III begins, Aníbal is found living a kind of self-imposed exile on the outskirts of his hometown, the southern coastal city of Benguela.[10] The ex-combatant lives alone in a beach-side house, and in an ocean grotto dwells the octopus that encompasses several symbolic and totemic meanings. The creature is, first of all, Aníbal's childhood nemesis, which he had sworn to slay. It also represents the indomitable force of nature and a simultaneously appealing and menacing mystery of the sea. Finally, the octopus, with its grasping tentacles and gaping maw, also has hermaphroditic and generally sexual significance.

Aníbal's semireclusive existence in southeastern Angola, far from the politics of Luanda, is ahistorical, atemporal, and intimately linked, physically and symbolically, to the primordial sea. Moreover, in this temporally static and spatially circumscribed context, Aníbal's semiascetic existence does not include celibacy. He in fact exhibits four levels of sexuality. One level is animistic and involves a mango tree, which Aníbal has planted in his front yard and which he calls Mussole: "Ele afagou distraidamente o tronco da mangueira. Sentiu por trás da casca rugosa, a seiva movendo-se com volúpia" (202) (Distractedly he stroked the trunk of the mango tree. He felt beneath the rough bark the sap voluptuously running). In spite of this spiritually sensual bond to Mussole, Aníbal maintains a sexual relationship "of convenience" with Marília, a local woman. This liaison, in satisfying Aníbal's libido, serves as an escapist diversion for one who has all but abrogated his role in the nation-building process.

The third component of Aníbal's sexuality reflects yet another form of escapism. In this configuration, lovemaking is the long-deferred consummation of Sara's and Aníbal's relationship. In 1977, fifteen years after Sara gave Aníbal refuge in her Lisbon apartment and ten years after having seen each other briefly in Paris, they met again in Luanda.

Sara had returned to Angola in 1974, and after independence she established a medical practice in Luanda and also assumed a position in the ministry of health. It is not until the bittersweet April of 1982 that the two old friends and former colleagues in the anticolonialist struggle submit to the mutual physical attraction that had begun nearly twenty-one years earlier. And by making love to Aníbal, Sara finally performs that communion-like ritual she had envisioned two decades earlier when she harbored Aníbal in her Lisbon apartment. Unlike the animal magnetism that Malongo awakened in Sara, she had fantasized sex with Aníbal in other terms: "Faria amor com ele para com ele se fundir, co-mungar. Adormeceu, reconhecendo nessa idéia algo de religioso, vindo talvez do misticismo das origens" (56) (She would make love to him in order to fuse with him, to partake of communion. She fell asleep recognizing that there was something religious in that idea, perhaps arising from the mysticism of her ancestral origins).

Aníbal's and Sara's deferred encounter combines racial erotica with gender juxtapositions and purely physical gratification under a mantle of mysticism, myth, and the transcendentally idyllic. Nearly five pages of descriptive narrative depict the lovemaking in the sensuous environment of the ocean, near the lair of the simultaneously menacing and erotically totemic octopus. The third-person narrator describes, from Aníbal's perspective, the mythical-erotic event, infused with erogenous referents. Later, as they lie sated in each other's arms, Sara recapitulates the progression of events from her perspective. The forty-five-year-old Sara reveals herself to be uninhibited and assertive, in contrast to her submissive relationship, as a twenty-four-year-old, with Malongo. She professes her role in taking the initiative in what, implicitly, was a seduction on Aníbal's part. Sara indulges in a mythically erotic act by licking Aníbal's salty shoulder and uttering a sensuous play on words (the double entendre is, of course, lost in translation): "Cheiras a mar, sabes a mar, sabes amar" (221) (You smell of the sea, you taste of the sea, you know how to make love). Presumably, Sara had journeyed to her native Benguela solely for this idyllic, mystical, escapist, and implicitly therapeutic tryst. Soon after the "communion," she returns to Luanda.

Immediately after Sara's departure another thread weaves itself into the ritualized fabric of Aníbal's sex life. Nina, the seventeen-year-old daughter of a neighboring fisherman, had confided to Aníbal that she needed a man and that he was the most eligible one around. In spite of

Aníbal's fatherly advice and protestations, the virginal teenager persists in her intentions. Nina resigns herself to the fact that Aníbal will not take her as his wife and that eventually she will have to submit to the lustful attentions of Mateus, an older man who lives in town and allegedly has amassed money and material possessions by means of shady business deals. Still, she insists on surrendering her virginity to the man once called Sábio. And, indeed, after first rejecting Nina's advances, Aníbal, under the influence of alcohol, invites the willing Nina to his bedroom: "Ele empurrou-a para a cama. Caiu sobre ela, afastou-lhe as pernas que hesitavam em se separar, penetrou-a. Não foi brutal, apenas firme. Ela gritou ao ser deflorada" (250) (He pushed her onto the bed, threw himself on top of her, with some difficulty spread her legs, and penetrated her. It wasn't brutal, merely resolute. As he deflowered her, she cried out in pain). This brief and brusque encounter stands in marked opposition to the protracted description of Aníbal's and Sara's idyllic lovemaking. And in contrast to Sara's poetically sensual and sensorial approval of Aníbal's adeptness as a lover (i.e., "Cheiras a mar, sabes a mar, sabes amar"), Nina murmurs a pathetic "Afinal não foi bom. Só doeu" (250) (It wasn't good after all. It just hurt).

In spite of the disparity between Aníbal's performances with Sara and then Nina, the two sexual encounters share something in common with respect to the ritualistic and ceremonial. Nina provokes the encounter as a rite of passage and Aníbal rationalizes his acquiescence as, in effect, a social obligation to participate in an act of initiation. Aníbal also professes a rather cynical, didactic objective. The worldly sage, a refugee from paradise lost, tells the doleful Nina that she has the right to be disillusioned, as does he.

Aníbal also rationalizes what Sara had termed his macho behavior toward Marília. Just as he defends his deflowering of Nina as a lesson with reciprocal benefits, he justifies his sexual exploitation of Marília as a quid pro quo: "Marília era apenas um corpo de que se servia. Mas também ela se servia do dele e das suas estórias, estavam pagos" (210) (Marília was just a body that he made use of. But she also made use of his body and his stories; so they were even).

The sexual discourses of "O Polvo" serve as paradigms for the social transformations that took place in colonial times and have occurred in a postcolonial Angola plagued by war. Many of the former believers in a utopian society are now caught up in varying degrees of disillusionment, escapist spirituality and sexuality, and the manipulation of power structures and interpersonal relationships. In some cases, as the novel's final section reveals, some also engage in corrupt behaviors predicated on personal economic gain.

Apropos of collective disillusionment, during their reunion Aníbal, as he distractedly caresses the trunk of the animistic mango tree, confides to Sara that theirs was indeed a utopian generation. They themselves were pure and unselfish, and they wanted to construct a just and egalitarian society. The dream has ended, however, and, Aníbal proclaims that "[a] utopia morreu" (202) (utopia has died). In the epilogue to "O Polvo," Aníbal embraces the trunk of the mango tree; but the sap does not run voluptuously, as it had in the past. April 14, the preceding day, marked the tenth anniversary of Mussole's death. Aníbal surmises, with apparent feelings of guilt, that the tree's "sadness" may well be because of his very nonmystical sexual liaisons with Nina and Marília (the mango tree's sap did run, however, apparently with Mussole's approbation, during his and Sara's mystical tryst).

"O Templo" (The temple), the novel's final section, is set in Luanda, beginning in July 1991. Malongo had returned to Luanda some seven years earlier, and by 1991, with the end of the long civil war and the help of Vítor, now a government minister, he has become a successful middleman for Belgian, French, and Dutch firms. These successful business ventures with European companies may indeed parallel his past sexual encounters with European women. Whether for financial gain or the challenge of sexual conquests, what seems to enter into Malongo's otherwise economic opportunism and lust for power is a continuation of his need for self-affirmation as an African confronting Europe.

In the opening scene of "O Templo," Judite, Malongo's and Sara's thirty-year-old daughter, who is also a physician, visits her father. Judite and Orlando, her economist boyfriend, discuss the prevailing political order and their blueprint for a new Angola. The younger generation's social idealism clashes, however, with the apolitical views and, worse, the venality and opportunistic self-centeredness of Malongo and Vítor Ramos. Vítor, a government minister, also appears at Malongo's home on that July evening to accompany his old friend to Luanda's most popular nightclub.

Luzia, Vítor's wife, who goes with him to Malongo's house, where she proceeds to drink herself into a drunken stupor, is deposited in the guest room to sleep it off until morning. Because of Luzia, however, Vítor and Malongo miss the opportunity to meet the two women they had arranged to meet at the nightclub. Once there, the two friends shun the advances of prostitutes, who not only could ruin their reputation, but who could also be infected with HIV.

Among the revelers in the cabaret's freewheeling environment, Vítor catches sight of Elias on the dance floor. This portly, balding man is the same Elias who, in 1961, also fled to Paris with the group of students "from the empire." During his stay in Lisbon, Elias, a staunch, evangelical Protestant, shunned the Casa dos Estudantes do Império, most of whose members were members or supporters of the MPLA. Although ideologically Elias aligned himself with the rival National Union of the Total Independence of Angola (UNITA), he shunned direct involvement in politics. After fleeing Paris, he made his way to the United States, where he earned a Ph.D. in social psychology. Then, after a stint as a university professor in Nigeria, he returned to Angola as a man with a mission.

Elias's mission gives a bizarre twist to the story's paradigms of sexuality. He identifies himself to Malongo and Vítor as the founding bishop of A Igreja da Esperança e Alegria do Dominus (The Lord's Church of Hope and Joy). The code and credo of this unconventional religious cult, as explained by Elias, lead Malongo to consider the church's economic potential: "essa Igreja vai ser popular e ganhar muito dinheiro. A maralha quer é dançar, beber, foder, sem sentimentos de pecado" (290) (that church is going to be popular and bring in a lot of money. What the masses want is to dance, drink, and screw without any feelings of sin). In other words, besides being a reductio ad absurdum of redemptive hedonism and sexuality, in the eyes of Malongo and Vítor, A Igreja da Esperança e Alegria do Dominus holds out attractive economic possibilities. And the novel comes to an end with a disconcertingly carnivalesque, verbal crescendo in celebration of the power of hedonistic redemption.

At the beginning of this essay I made reference to the controversy that *A geração da utopia* has engendered among readers. I hope to have demonstrated that to the extent that sexual explicitness contributes to the controversy, it plays a key role in imparting artistic vitality to the text's subject matter and its political, socioeconomic, and cultural themes and messages. Racial erotica, along with related eroto-racial components, certainly informs much of the novel, particularly in the first two parts.

Sexuality serves throughout the novel as an instrument of power and control. The telluric and mythical configurations of physical love and hedonistic escapism, in the form of the commodification of sexual pleasures and as a source of redemption and financial profit, gather impact through the author's attention to what some may consider to be salacious details.

Whatever the criticisms leveled against the novel, *A geração da utopia* seems to have struck a responsive chord among a number of Lusophone African writers and intellectuals, especially those who have come of age since independence. João Melo, also an Angolan, is notable among those who published their first works since independence. His *Imitação de Sartre e Simone de Beauvoir* (1998) is a collection of ten short stories set in postcolonial Angola. Several of these stories describe violent sexual, albeit often humorous, encounters between men and women. In the aptly titled "Sexo e violência" sexual passion plays a rather existentialist purpose to capture the story's satire of postindependence nationalism and traditional forms of machismo.

In a similar vein, Rosária da Silva, Angola's first postcolonial female novelist, published *Totonya*. This first novel, unique in both its form and its content, has scenes of explicit sex that make strong, albeit well-crafted, statements of protest against the physical and psychological abuse of women.

Another writer worthy of mention is Abdulai Sila, author of *Eterna paixão* (1994), Guinea-Bissau's first postcolonial novel. Sila figures prominently among those writers and intellectuals from Lusophone Africa who have resonated to the messages inherent in Pepetela's landmark work.[11] Sila, albeit with somewhat less explicitness, also uses sexual discourses to delineate characters involved in agonistic encounters and immersed in parable-like mystifications with social and political implications for developing African nations.

My sense is that the sexual discourses of *A geração da utopia* are essential to the novel's statement about the human condition, as well as the hopes and disillusionment's of a generation. Finally, despite the hedonist escapism the novel's open-ended conclusion, with an invocation of "o Mundo e a Esperança," does indeed suggest that there is hope in the world. This more or less optimistic open-endedness is summed up in the novel's final epilogue: "Como é óbvio, não pode existir epílogo nem ponto final para uma estória que começa por portanto" (316) (Obviously, there can be no epilogue nor period for a story that begins with *therefore*). The nonepilogue epilogue refers to the novel's opening sentence, which begins with the word *portanto*. (Parenthetically, the author observes that when he was a university student in Lisbon, he initiated his response to a professor's question with *portanto*. The professor chided his Angolan student for beginning a sentence with a word that should only be used at the conclusion of a line of reasoning. Pepetela confides to readers that he resolved, at that time, to write a book that opens with *portanto*.)

Notes

1. *Mayombe*, Pepetela's monumental novel, published in 1979, but written some four years before Angola's independence, was daring for its time, not least because of the love relationships depicted between male and female combatants in the Cabinda war theater. Another postcolonial novel in which there appear explicit sex scenes, including a euphemistic reference to cunnilingus, is Cape Verdean writer Germano Almeida's *O testamento do Sr. Napumoceno da Silva Araújo*, published in 1989. Almeida's four subsequent works to date, including three novels and a collection of three long short stories, also contain discourses of sexuality and scenes of explicit sex.

2. "Namoro," written between 1947 and 1950, appears in Cruz's *Poemas (1947–1950)*. The poem also appears in a number of anthologies in the original as well in translation. The original was reprinted, for example, in Manuel Ferreira's *50 Poetas Africanos* (49–50). An English translation appears in *Poems from Angola* (selected and translated by Michael Wolfers); however, the translation of the lines transcribed in this article are mine, as are all other translations.

3. This is a revised version of my translation of the same poem that appears in "The Audacious Young Poets of Angola and Mozambique." That the author is a woman, in a society where female writers are in a distinct minority, makes "Mamão" all the more audacious.

4. The same year (1961), India reclaimed Goa from Portugal.

5. Pepetela's *Mayombe*, Angola's first postindependence novel, comes to mind with respect to allegorical names. The novel's narrator is "Teoria" (Theory), and there are characters called "Mundo Novo" (New World), "Milagre" (Miracle), and "Sem Medo" (Fearless).

6. Ironically, with regard to eroto-racial stereotypes, Malongo is also attracted to the unknown. In rationalizing his attempts to seduce Denise, he asks the rhetorical question: "Então, e o amor livre das francesas?" (27) (And what about the Frenchwomen and their liking for free love?).

7. Some thirty years later, Malongo asks Judite, his daughter, when she and Orlando, her boyfriend, plan to marry. Judite replies: "Agora virou tradicionalista, com estórias de casamento?" (22) (So have you turned into a traditionalist, with this talk of marriage?). There is no real contradiction between Malongo as a self-proclaimed "traditionalist" in matters pertaining to male dominance and a daughter's incredulous question put to a father who did not marry her mother.

8. In the mid-1980s, Pepetela spent a week or so in New Orleans, where, he reports, he felt at home because of that city's creole populations and culture, similar to Benguela's.

9. The author consistently refers, in the novel's first part, to Huambo and Lubango, although at the time that the events took place in "A casa," these cities were officially known, respectively, as Nova Lisboa and Sá da Bandeira.

10. "A Chana" ends with a question regarding Sábio's fate. In an epilogue to that section, the answer is that two months earlier Sábio had died in an ambush. We learn subsequently that although Sábio, the guerrilla commandant, may have ceased to be, just as his generation's utopia has evaporated, Aníbal has survived.

11. Carlos Gomes, a member of Sila's generation, in his preface to *Eterna paixão*, refers to how well Pepetela describes former militants' disillusionment and even corruptibility in *A geração da utopia* (8). See my "Reading Abdulai Sila's *Eterna paixão:* Guinea-Bissau's Premier Novel as Postcolonial Myth, Parable, and Fable" for an assessment of discourses of sexuality and the politics of disillusionment in Sila's work.

Works Cited

Almeida, Germano. 1989. *O testamento do Sr. Napumoceno da Silva Araújo*. Mindelo: Ilhéu Editora.

António, Mario. 1963. *100 Poemas*. Luanda: ABC.

Cruz, Viriato da. 1961. *Poemas (1947–1950)*. Lisbon: Casa dos Estudante do Império.

Ferreira, Manuel. 1989. *50 Poetas Africanos: Angola, Moçambique, Guiné-Bissau, Cabo Verde, São Tomé e Príncipe*. Lisbon: Plátano Editora.

Hamilton, Russell G. 1995. "The Audacious Young Poets of Angola and Mozambique." *Research in African Literatures* (Special Issue: New Voices in African Literatures) 26:1: 85–96.

———. 1996. "Reading Abdulai Sila's *Eterna paixão:* Guinea-Bissau's Premier Novel as Postcolonial Myth, Parable, and Fable." *Luso-Brazilian Review*, 33:2 (Special Issue: Luso-African Literatures, guest ed. G. M. Moser) (winter): 75–84.

Knopfli, Rui. 1962. *Reino submarino*. Lourenço Marques (Maputo): Publicações Tribuna.

Melo, João. 1998. *Imitação de Sartre e Simone de Beauvoir*. Luanda: União dos Escritores Angolanos.

Pepetela. 1979. *Mayombe*. Lisbon: Edições 70, para a União dos Escritores Angolanos.

———. 1992. *A geração da utopia*. Lisbon: Publicações Dom Quixote.

Sila, Abdulai. 1994. *Eterna paixão*. Bissau: Ku Si Mon Editora.

Silva, Rosária da. 1998. *Totonya*. Luanda: Brigada Jovem de Literatura de Angola.

Tavares, Paula. 1985. *Ritos de passagem*. Luanda: União dos Escritores Angolanos.

CHAPTER EIGHT

Border Writing, Postcoloniality, and Critical
Difference in the Works of Orlanda Amarílis

Phyllis Peres

A massive uprooting of dualistic thinking in the individual and
collective consciousness is the beginning of a long struggle, but one
that could, in our best hopes, bring us to the end of rape, of
violence, of war.

— Gloria Anzaldúa 1987

The Other of the West, the Other of man: one is never installed
within marginality, one never dwells outside it. . . . Otherness has its
laws and interdictions. It is by assuming the moment of rupture and
of negativity that underlies feminist practices, and by questioning
everything finite, put forth as a given, or reduced to the simplicity of
essences, that these texts open the space for critical difference. What
is at stake is not only the hegemony of Western cultures, but also
their identities as unified cultures; in other words, the realization
that there is a Third World in every First World, and vice-versa.

— Trinh T. Minh-ha 1989

Postcolonial Border Writing

To understand the works of Orlanda Amarílis, we must first address the
author's national identity and her inscription into a national literature.
After all, Amarílis was born in 1924 in colonial Cape Verde at a time
when Cape Verdeans were considered citizens of the metropolis.[1] A naturalized Portuguese who has been living mainly in Portugal since her
marriage to the late writer and critic Manuel Ferreira, she writes narratives that are situated in both the archipelago and the European main-

land. The seemingly facile question of her national identity—well, is she a Cape Verdean writer? a Cape Verdean born Portuguese writer? a diasporic Cape Verdean writer? a postcolonial Cape Verdean writer?—generally has solicited pat responses. Orlanda Amarílis is unquestioningly called Cape Verdean and/or homogenized into the postcolonial trans-Lusitanian discursive melting pot.[2]

Orlanda Amarílis was associated with the short-lived journal *Certeza* (two issues published), but it was only in 1974 that she published her first book of short stories, *Cais-do-Sodré té Salamansa*. She has since published two other collections, *Ilhéu dos pássaros* (1983) and *Casa dos mastros* (1989). All three works were published in Portugal, further complicating the issue of the writer's national identity.

Obviously, this attention to Orlanda Amarílis's "national identity" calls attention to the larger question of what it means to be a diasporic writer, or a postcolonial border writer. Writing on the border signifies a specific position of subjectivity, and, as Trinh T. Minh-ha reminds us in her work on postcolonial feminism, the recognition of writing as a practice located at the intersection of subject and history.[3] In Amarílis's case, that position straddles borders of nation, race, class, and gender, and her works illustrate the negotiation of identities in the so-called postcolonial world.

To call Orlanda Amarílis a postcolonial border writer places her in the context of recent critical work on both border and postcolonial writing. The latter has come under particularly heavy fire as a term that indicates a passage from the colonial past without accounting for colonialism's impact on political, social, economic, and cultural relations in the present. Ella Shohat's "Notes on the Post-Colonial" problematizes the "post" as part of a "narrative or progression in which colonialism remains the central point of reference, in a march of time neatly arranged from the pre to the post, but which leaves ambiguous its relation to new forms of colonialism" (107). Not only does the term *postcolonial* obscure the continuities of colonialism, but it also implies an uncontested temporal border, which puts the colonial narrative safely in the past while simultaneously privileging it as the center of reference. Writing in the same special issue of *Social Text* as Shohat, Anne McClintock similarly criticizes *postcolonial* as a singular term "organized around a binary axis of time rather than power" (88). For McClintock, the term become especially monolithic and unstable in relation to women for whom "post-colonialism has been a history of hopes postponed" (92).[4]

This criticism of the "post" is especially provocative given the suppos-edly liberating condition of postcoloniality and, more specifically, the postcolonial subject. By questioning the "liberating" effect of the free-dom of formal colonialism, one can then critique the postcolonial pe-riod as marked by regenerated colonial relations (neocolonialism).[5] For "postcolonial" critics, this has often meant the radical critique of both elitist modes of expression and the exclusive inscription of elite subjects.[6] Studies of the "post" condition emphasize the overlapping boundaries of central and marginal cultures with due emphasis on hybridity and syncretism. Shohat points out that "hybridity and syncretism allow ne-gotiation of the multiplicity of the identities and subject positionings which result from displacements, immigrations and exiles without polic-ing the borders of identity along essentialist and originary lines" (108). As I will discuss shortly, these terms *(hybridity* and *syncretism)* must also be questioned as possible figures for the consecration of hegemony, particularly as concerns cultural studies on Lusophone Africa.[7]

I borrow the term *border writing* from Gloria Anzaldúa's critical texts on mestiza consciousness. In *Borderlands/La Frontera,* Anzaldúa elabo-rates a plural consciousness of the borderlands based on often conflict-ing Anglo and Mexican knowledges. She defines a consciousness of "be-ing on the border" that simultaneously reads its own ambivalences and contradictions and enables Chicanas to act collectively with strength and authority. As Chandra Talpade Mohanty emphasizes in "Cartogra-phies of Struggle," Anzaldúa's borderland consciousness is that of a his-torically specific place, the U.S.–Mexican border, which privileges mul-tiplicity as a historical and geographical agent (1991: 37).

Calling Amarílis a postcolonial border writer recognizes both the cri-tique of the "postcolonial" and Anzaldúa's politics of borderland con-sciousness. In this context, I use the term *border writing* to indicate a practice of negotiating border territories that may or may not overlap in terms of spaces, hierarchies, centers, and peripheries. Amarílis's type of postcolonial border writing negotiates the multiplicity of *caboverdia-nidade* (Cape Verdeanness), specifically in regard to women's agency and subject positionings. The borders are many and encompass identity con-structs of gender, nation, race, and class, as well as the false sequentially of colonialism and postcolonialism. Her narratives problematize the sanctity of territory, so that border crossing—indeed, living on many borders—becomes the central focus of Cape Verdean womanhood.

Amarílis's narratives resonate with the ambiguities of other Cape Verdean writing as a practice long concerned with representations of identity. In this sense, the previously mentioned *Certeza,* along with *Claridade* (1936–60), mark significant points in Cape Verdean literary-cultural history. Initially influenced by Portuguese neorealism and Brazilian northeast regionalism, the *claridosos,* as well as *Certeza's* collaborators, participated in the definition of Cape Verdean subjects in direct opposition to the object status of Cape Verdeans in colonial Portuguese discourses.

Certain persistent features remain from those roots of Cape Verdean literature. The textualization of *caboverdianidade,* or a distinctly Cape Verdean ethos, is characterized by what Angolan writer Mário de Andrade termed *insularidade,* the seemingly closed universe of island space and time. The depictions of insularity are about the conflicts between the desire to remain and the necessity to leave because of devastating economic and climatic conditions, the border crossings to exile and alienation in the Cape Verdean diaspora.[8]

As border writing, Amarílis's narratives problematize the complexities, contradictions, and negotiations of identity in the lives of Cape Verdean women of different races, religions, cultures, and classes. Her practice decenters the first world's monolithic construction of third-world woman, or what Chandra Talpade Mohanty defines as "the 'Third World Difference'—that stable, ahistorical something that apparently oppresses most if not all of the women in these countries" (1984: 355). In fact, Amarílis's negotiations for plural subjectivity break down the preconceived homogeneity of the accepted dyad of first and third worlds, especially in regard to the false universalizations of the "postcolonial other" or the "postcolonial woman."

This study will examine the open spaces of difference in several of Amarílis's short stories. Essential to my readings of her texts as postcolonial border writings are their expressions of *insularidade* (insularity), exile, diaspora, and (alie)nation. The stories in question are set in colonial and postcolonial contexts, or perhaps, less problematically put, in pre- and postindependence times. Set in relation to the violence of both colonialism and neocolonialism, Amarílis's border writings negotiate the positionalities and plural identities of Cape Verdean womanhood.

Border Crossings: Salamansa, the Metropolis, and the *terra longe*

As Russell Hamilton notes, the title of Orlanda Amarílis's first group of stories, *Cais-do-Sodré té Salamansa* (1974), echoes the textual concerns with departure and arrival—Cais-do-Sodré in Lisbon and the beach of Salamansa in Cape Verde (178). In such stories as "Cais-do-Sodré" and "Desencanto," Amarílis uses transitory spaces as metaphors for the dislocations and questionings of Cape Verdean identity. Andresa, in "Cais-do-Sodré," has a chance meeting with another Cape Verdean woman in the train station that precipitates a questioning of her new Portuguese self.

By the end of the story, Andresa decides to accompany the other woman to Caxias, but only after she recalls common territories and their Cape Verdean past. The movement toward Cape Verdean identity is underscored as Andresa changes seats and, by extension, also position; she originally sits next to an Englishwoman before seeking out Tanha on the train. The ending, however, remains somewhat ambiguous: Andresa's identity crisis is resolved only for the duration of the train ride to Caxias. Furthermore, this resolution comes about through a subjective reworking of a past that is distanced in both time and space and viewed through diasporic lenses.

The ambiguity of women's subjectivity also is the subject of "Desencanto," in which an unnamed Cape Verdean woman's own *desencanto* begins with the daily ritual to get to work—the familiar faces and impersonal exchanges. Her lack of name is essential because she is recognized as an individual neither by herself nor by the metropolitan society. At the end of the story, however, she is named by the metropolitan male, who refers to her as a *mulata* in a sexual innuendo to his friend. The woman, who has felt some sense of liberation in this anonymous daily movement, at once recognizes her recolonization in terms of gender and race.

This realization is telling of Amarílis's critique; no matter what name or identities the Cape Verdean woman attempts to give herself, the colonizer always has his own name for her to describe his fascination with the exoticized and colonized other; in this case, *mulata*. The Cape Verdean woman who has defined herself negatively (by what she is not) and has avoided being identified with her African side so as not to be taken for "one of them" will nevertheless always be perceived in the metropolis as the "other." Her space of exile is doubled; all pretense of identification with the colonizer has been ruptured, and at the end she finds herself "sem amigos, sem afeições, desgarrada" (64) (without friends, without affection, lost).[9]

The territories of exile have many boundaries, not always metropolitan, as is evident in "Salamansa," the closing story of the 1974 collection. Baltasar, a Cape Verdean living successfully in Portugal, is visiting his sister back in São Vicente. In the garden of her house, Baltasar is drawn to the memory of his past relationship with Linda. As Gregory McNab discusses in his analysis of "Salamansa," Baltasar's recollections reveal a relationship of possession and exploitation. Baltasar, who sought out and maintained the liaison while he was courting his future wife, is drawn to the memory and the need to discover Linda's fate after twenty years.

Within that recollection, however, Linda has moments of empowerment in which she crosses the boundaries of gender constructed by the male. Baltasar, for example, is fascinated by her masculine way of smoking and by the fact that she has left her married lover because of his sexual kinkiness. Linda, even in her colonized situation, makes certain choices, which Baltasar perceives as part of her "masculine side." His fascination with this side of her enhances what he believes to be his domination. In the final moments of their relationship, however, Linda reveals exactly which part of her body he rules:

> Subindo a roupa até á cintura, curvou-se mostrando a polpa cheia e, batendo repetidas vezes nas nádegas com a mão espalmada, desatou em berraria. "Aqui, aqui, aqui é que mandas em mim." (119)

> [Pulling her clothing up to her waist, she bent over and exposed her full flesh while repeatedly slapping her buttocks with the palm of her hand and bellowing, "Here, here, here, is where you rule me."]

Baltasar's enraged reaction is to kick Linda, although in the end he flees from her, exhausted and defeated.

Prompted by his memories to discover her whereabouts, he questions Antoninha, his sister's servant, who reveals that she is Linda's niece and that Linda has emigrated to São Tomé. As Russell Hamilton points out, within the Cape Verdean diaspora, only São Tomé, no farther geograph-

ically than Portugal, is considered the *terra longe:* "A 'terra longe' é sinó-
nimo da emigração coerciva e penosa, ao passo que Europa e América
representam a emigração livre e a promessa de um regresso feliz" (178)
(The far-off land is synonymous with the coerced and painful emigration, while at the same time Europe and America represent free emigration and the promise of a happy return). Baltasar is shocked by this news
and wonders at her decision. As McNab aptly concludes, her emigration
was "the almost logical continuation" of the sexual and economic exploitation that Baltasar's recollection reveals—but which he cannot
comprehend.

McNab's detailed reading of "Salamansa" effectively opens critical
spaces of sexual difference, which point to a domination, which is not
only masculine but also determined by class relations. Building on that
reading, my own counters the self-image of Baltasar, the successful em-
igrant with his mental picture of Linda in São Tomé, the so-called *terra
longe.* Baltasar, himself a colonized subject living in the metropolis, is
dislocated in the present-day São Vicente. He imagines a past time,
place, and position that he dominated. This domination by the colonized petit-bourgeois male over the colonized working-class female is
played out in terms of possession, rule, and mastery. Was he ultimately
defeated as Linda reveals the borders of his own colonization?

Moreover, Antoninha, the servant, is undoubtedly Linda's present counterpart, the colonial reality to Baltasar's recollected daydream of dominance. Of Linda's bloodline, Antoninha, too, declares: "Eu também
qualquer dia vou pâ S. Tomé" (121) (Someday I'll also go to São Tomé).
When Baltasar questions her about that statement, he is really asking
the Linda of twenty years ago. Antoninha's response—"Sabe, esta nossa
terra está nhanhida" (You know, our land is nothing)—prompts Baltasar
to imagine his return to what is now his home, Portugal.

In this sense, Orlanda Amarílis's first narrations of the borders of the
Cape Verdean diaspora return full circle to the Cais-do-Sodré. For Andresa, in the collection's first story, the memory of São Vicente reconstructs one positioning, however provisional, of Cape Verdean identity
and affinity. In "Salamansa," the recollection reveals the patterns of Portuguese colonization that have determined the violence of class and
gender relations in Cape Verde. Faced with the stark reality voiced by
the female domestic servant, Antoninha, Baltasar cannot act within the
constructs of present-day Cape Verde. The story's last images reveal this

impotence; Antoninha's *coladeira* (regional song) in Cape Verdean Creole transports Baltasar to the beach at Salamansa with the smells, tastes,
and visions of the past. But in the end, Baltasar leaves the garden and
retreats into the big house where his identity as master over Antoninha
remains privileged, at least for the moment.

In "Salamansa," as well as in "Cais-do-Sodré," positionalities of subjectivity that have been fragmented in the diaspora are re-formed through
recollections of a seemingly unified and insular Cape Verdean identity.
The narratives, however, problematize those very images of identity;
what began as a memory triggered by the smell of jasmine in the garden
in Salamansa opens spaces for the rupture of a unified vision of the
past. Moreover, at least in "Salamansa" and "Desencanto," as women negotiate their subject positionings, the many borders become apparent
not only as ambivalent spaces, but also as sites of conflict and contestation.

Ilhéu dos Pássaros and "Thonon-les-Bains"

Published almost a decade after *Cais-do-Sodré té Salamansa, Ilhéu dos
Pássaros*'s narratives also negotiate subjectivity, but here largely through
contradictory and violent postcolonial spaces. The women's struggles
for agency along the many borders of gender, race, class, and nation are
more clearly acts of contestation than in the earlier stories, but are no
less ambivalent, whether represented as taking place in Cape Verde or in
the newly defined diaspora.

In a 1984 article (included in *Africanidade*, 1985), Brazilian critic Maria
Aparecida Santilli describes the female subjects of *Ilhéu dos pássaros* as
women who are alone, whose existence revolves around the absence (or
eventual presence) of the male other. The islands here are significant as
indicators of desired feminine territory, topographic markers that reflect
the insular space of *caboverdianidade*. The title's "ilhéu dos pássaros"
(island of the birds) appears in the epigraphs to the seven stories as a
sentinel or lighthouse and ultimately as the guardian of insular time
and space as well as an image guide (again through both space and time)
to the problematic attempted recuperation of plural identities.

Ultimately, Santilli's critique of *Ilhéu dos Pássaros* questions the colonizing perception of feminine territory as limited by the absent or present male. She focuses on the women's negotiations of Cape Verdean
identities, particularly in her analysis of "Luna," in which the title character is doing research at the university in Ile-Ife, Nigeria. Santilli claims

that, as an intellectual, Luna attempts to "superar a relatividade do poder social e a dependência da mulher ao casamento, pela via cultural" (109) (to overcome the relativeness of social power and woman's dependence on marriage by opting for culture). In Nigeria, Luna soon discovers the same relations of inequality played out in the academic world, as well as the regenerated exploitation of the third world. In the birthplace of the Orixás, she buys necklaces in a boutique owned by a young American woman, and at the hotel near the airport sees postcolonial relations revealed at a party attended by multinationals: "A Europa e o imperialismo ficavam para além daquela porta. Deste lado era a exploração" (59) (Europe and imperialism were behind that door. Exploitation was on this side). In contrast to this neocolonial departure, Luna projects her return to postcolonial Cape Verde as the realization of her identity as a Cape Verdean intellectual woman: "nada ela receava. Tinha o passe e a senha" (64) (she did not fear anything. She had the pass and the password).

For Luna, the "ilhéu dos pássaros" is that link to ethnocultural memory and the guide through her journey of self-discovery. What is even more significant, however, is that her positioning is projected within an imaginary community, a dream of postcoloniality and nation that eludes marked boundaries or hierarchies.[10] It is a construction of imagined subjectivity that attempts to link past and present in a recuperation of the postcolonial nation as a liberating site for women's agency.

The realities of this recuperation are questioned, however, in several other stories in *Ilhéu dos Pássaros,* ones that take place in postcolonial Cape Verde or in the diaspora. Perhaps nowhere is the questioning of postcolonial subjectivity as liberating so jarring and complete as in "Thonon-les-Bains." Here, Piedade's exile is quite different from Luna's; she is a Cape Verdean guest worker in a small French town on the Swiss border. In this story, Amarílis divides the narration between the islands and Thonon-les-Bains, between the expectations of Piedade's mother nh'Ana and the realities of the daughter's exile. Given the economic hardships of the archipelago, nh'Ana plans to send all of her daughters to Europe in the care of their half brother Gabriel, who already works in a ski factory. The money that her children send will be used to open a store, because, as she tells Piedade's godmother, "a vida aqui já não podia continuar como era" (Life here cannot continue as it was). The first part of "Thonon-les-Bains" focuses on the letters that Gabriel and Piedade send nh'Ana. While the mother grasps at the image of her daughter marrying a Frenchman—"assim iam ter os seus filhos de cabelo fino e olho azul ou verde" (and so she would have children with straight hair and blue or green eyes)—the children's letters reveal the conditions of their exile. Piedade, too, works in the ski factory, gluing labels and cleaning skis. In the mornings, she cleans the hotel in exchange for the "caveau da escada no corredor" (stairwell in the hall) where the owner lets Piedade and Gabriel sleep. Her fiancé Jean (described as both French and Swiss) is significantly older, separated from another woman, and far too serious for Piedade.

The shift from Cape Verde to Thonon-les-Bains centers precisely on the time in which Piedade begins to have second thoughts about her upcoming marriage. At Gabriel's birthday party, she dances to the *sambinhas* and *coladeiras* with a Cape Verdean male. Although she spurns the advances of the latter, Jean locks Piedade in the bathroom, where he slits her throat. The police do not arrest Jean, but instead force Gabriel and his Cape Verdean friends to leave Thonon-les-Bains. Upon his return to Cape Verde, Gabriel at first tries to downplay the violence of the metropolis, but as nh'Ana's image of Europe remains confined to dreams of economic prosperity and whitening through miscegenation, he finally ruptures that imagined space: "Emigrante é lixo, mãe Ana, emigrante não é mais nada" (25) (An immigrant is garbage, mother Ana, an immigrant is nothing).[11] Santilli focuses on precisely this postcolonial reordering in the first world:

> Piedade enquanto mulher, na transposição de contextos sociais, identifica-se, assim, com as minorias marginalizadas ou submetidas numa sociedade qualquer onde a força do trabalho não dá consequentemente, o acesso ao direito da voz. (108)

> [Piedade, although a woman, within this transposition of social contexts, identifies herself with the marginalized minorities or people submissive to whatever society where the workforce does not give access to the right of a voice.]

I would add that Piedade is murdered precisely because of her negotiated identity, which her fiancé cannot accept. Her actions at the party are indicative of this aspect of her identity, for not only does her dancing demonstrate a "joyous affirmation of her Cape Verdeaness" (McNab 1987: 65), but it is with whom she dances that is the most likely offense to Jean. Piedade, "numa euforia nunca vista, agarrou uma toalha de rosto, atou-a abaixo da cintura e reboulou as ancas" (22) (in a euphoria never before seen, grabbed a face towel, wrapped it below her waist, and began to shake her behind), in a dance not only expressive of *caboverdianidade,* but also of her own sexuality, expressed in ritualized movements. She chooses to express her identity not with Jean, but with the Cape Verdean, Mochinho.

Her dancing at Gabriel's birthday celebration is a repetition of the customary evening gatherings among Cape Verdean workers in Thonon-les-Bains where Piedade also dances. Jean, who does not dance, watches from the corner with a fixed smile, somewhat symbolic of a moribund ex-colonizer sitting out the dance of continued Cape Verdean cultural resistance.

Moreover, in the context of "Thonon-les-Bains," this dance of *caboverdianidade*—and, I would argue, *africanidade*—constructs inroads into the space of a former metropolis. This postcolonial space, once deemed impenetrable, has become the site of third-world territories, and, in the company of the Cape Verdeans, it is Jean who is the Other. Piedade conceals this aspect of her identity from Jean, but dances her *caboverdianidade* with her compatriots. On the night of the murder, Jean removes Piedade from the main room, from the borders of Cape Verdean territory, and takes her to the bathroom to kill her. At first, Piedade suspects that his motives are sexual and attempts to reconcile this violation with her upcoming marriage.

McNab emphasizes that Jean's action—the slitting of Piedade's throat—is careful, deliberate, and ritualistic, "as he would an animal at slaughter" (65). When the Cape Verdeans at the party break down the bathroom door, they find her "degolada como se de um porco tratasse" (24) (with her throat slit as if she were a pig). Obviously, Jean does not take her virginity, but rather her womanhood, her humanity, and her life. If he is unable to reconstruct colonial territory along the borders of *caboverdianidade,* his actions at least attempt to redefine the dominant constructs of gender. Jean does, indeed, violate Piedade, but it is the violation of a Cape Verdean woman whose dance of identity was reaffirmed by her Cape Verdeans in the space of exile. Jean cuts with a knife, not his penis; he ravages her voice, not her vagina.

The ending of "Thonon-les-Bains" underscores the imagined construct of the Cape Verdean diaspora to those who remain in the islands.

When Gabriel returns home to explain Piedade's death, his two younger female cousins fantasize about immigrating to France with him. Gabriel will go back to Switzerland, to a meeting in a train station with a man who will get him a job in a bar. Unlike the final journey that Luna takes to map out an imagined Cape Verdean community, Gabriel's return to exile is expressed in terms of loss of identity and humanity. In contrast to Luna, whose imagination of agency is secured by the proper *passe e senha* (pass and password), Gabriel's crossing is one made to uncommon ground, and, as he remarks, "ainda temos de marcar as palavras da senha" (26) (We still have to remember the password).

A casa dos mastros and "Maira da Luz"

The jarring violence of regenerated colonial relations in "Thonon-les-Bains" echoes in the title story of Orlanda Amarílis's 1989 collection *A casa dos mastros*. The setting is not the postcolonial Cape Verdean diaspora but the islands, as Violete is about to enter a marriage of convenience with Augusto. Like Piedade, she answers back, but here in the form of an ultimatum: "Se fizeres casa na vizinhança da tua mãe não me caso contigo" (43) (If you set up our house in your mother's neighborhood, I won't marry you). Augusto, ever the reluctant bridegroom, takes Violete at her word and never returns.

Violete's actions are above all attempts to negotiate agency, both within the upcoming marriage of convenience and within the male-dominated insular community as a whole, immediately represented by the family house, the "casa dos mastros." In his introduction to the collection, Pires Laranjeira identifies the house with monarchical and republican masts as the center of paternal power (11).

As there are no established means to contest the male domination within the insular community, Violete's reactions to the violent exploitations are often turned against other women, or against herself. She is publicly humiliated when her friend Bia Vitória comments on her father's latest affair. Violete's immediate response is to break off her friendship with Bia Vitória. As she nears her home, she is filled with the desire to punish someone. The ambiguities of negotiated subjectivity are made manifest in Violete's violent actions as she confronts her father. Unable to strike him, she grabs his cane and beats her stepmother. Her real aim, however, is one of disclosure, so she screams out loud. Unable to shout down domination, however, or even to speak it, Violete turns against another woman—both her godmother and stepmother—who ultimately dies from the attack.

The rest of the story follows Violete's further attempts to negotiate agency along the borders of patriarchy and insularity. At the church where Violete tries to give her confession, Padre André rapes her. The confessional scene mirrors the moment of Piedade's murder, when she justifies what she suspects will be her loss of virginity with the property domains of marriage. Here, a faint Violete finds the priest on top of her, but she ultimately works through her sobs and prayers to mystify the rape as a moment of liberation. The church—as an institution, one of the principal bearers of patriarchal hegemony in the Portuguese colonies—here becomes the site of Violete's continued violation. Along the contradictory borders of the insular community, she transforms her rape in the territory of male patriarchy into a rite of passage to womanhood.

Violete also is raped by her cousin Alexandrino when she ties to confide that her stepmother did not die from a fall, as her father has led the community to believe. Here too, as in "Salamansa," published fifteen years earlier, the language of male domination follows that of colonization and possession. In *A casa dos mastros*, however, Violete once again turns the violation into future meetings with her cousin, which she provokes. Confined in the insular community, Violete's attempts at negotiating agency are met repeatedly with sexual violence. She remains trapped within the territory of domination and equates acts of sexual violence with the recognition of her sexuality.

A final rape, however, silences Violete. She wakes up one night to find a man on top of her and, once again, she transforms the violation. When Violete realizes that the man is her father, she loses her voice and never speaks again. The father disappears, but is actually hidden in the top floor of the "casa dos mastros," and Violete daily assumes her position by the window where she comes to resemble a mummy. The house—center of paternal power—remains her prison while she faces outward, half-hidden, half-exposed, to the patriarchal community that has mummified her.

Violete's silencing and mummification, here the patriarchal response to her attempted negotiations of subjectivity, find their counterpart in "Maira da Luz," the last text of *A casa dos mastros*. Amarílis opens this narrative with an epigraph that relates the title character's possible dreams:

Se acaso preguntassem a Maira da Luz qual a sua premonição quanto ao futuro, ela responderia: "Vou ser médica. Vou usar uma bata branca como a de doutora Maria Francisca. Mandarei construir um hospital novo e uma maternidade. No hospital haverá raios x e untravioletas; e ondas curtas. E a roupa da cama dos doentes será mudada todos os dias. Na sala de operações terei um bom anestesista e as melhores enfermeiras. E nenhum doente morrerá nas minhas mãos por incúria ou desleixo." Estes eram os sonhos de Maira da Luz. (118)

[If by chance someone asked Maira da Luz what she thought her future held, she would respond, "I'm going to be a doctor. I will use a white lab coat just like Dr. Maria Francisca. I will order a new hospital built and a maternity hospital as well. In the hospital there will be X rays and ultra-violet lights and shortwaves. And the patients' sheets will be changed every day. In the operating room, I will have a good anesthesiologist and the best nurses. No sick person will ever die in my care from not being cured or from neglect." These were Maira da Luz's dreams.]

The use of the subjunctive and conditional tenses puts Maira da Luz's voicing in a hypothetical mode: if she were asked, then this is what she would have answered. In fact, "Maira da Luz" too is representative of Amarílis's texts of attempted articulation of Cape Verdean womanhood, the mapping of identity along border spaces.

"Maira da Luz," set in recent colonial Mindelo, begins with a rite of passage into the male-dominated high school. Here the negotiation of identities is marked by Maira da Luz's intellectual and personal ties with her classmates and is played out against the foreshadowing of upcoming political unrest and a break from Portugal. One of her teachers is denounced by a *mondrongo* (Portuguese) for speaking against the fascist Portuguese state, because on various occasions he has praised the English system, and the metropolis orders the school closed. At that moment, Maira fears that if she is forced to abandon her studies, her life will stop, because her parents cannot afford to send her to school in Portugal.

Although the school reopens, Maira's unvoiced dreams of becoming a doctor are cut short when her uncle emigrates and her father, who is eighty-two years old to her mother's forty, dies. Unable to continue her studies, Maira applies for a teaching position but is shocked into reality when she is placed at Tarrafal de Monte Trigo and will have to leave Mindelo, the center of intellectual activity in colonial Cape Verde.

Maira's metamorphosis from adolescence to womanhood finally takes the form of a Kafkaesque transformation. Her dreams cut short, she abruptly becomes a disgusting bug and is stomped by her school rival Cesarina. In this somewhat heavy-handed ending, Cesarina—she of the masculine imperial name—comes looking for Maira, most likely to rub the latter's face in her miserable destiny. Maira pleads for recognition but cannot even hear her own voice: "Nem de grilo, nem de formiga era. De som a alcançar audição nenhures, ainda clamou: Estou, Cesarina! Sou eu!" (126) (She wasn't even a cricket or an ant. With a sound that reached no ears, she kept on clamoring, "Here I am, Cesarina! It's me!"). Cesarina, who had arrived on the first day of school to brag of the seven new cotton dresses that her mother had ordered her, spots the newly transformed Maira and, with the declaration "pois eu a bichos faço assim" (ibid.) (this is what I do to bugs), crushes the "bicho nojento" (nauseating bug).

Heavy-handed though its ending may be, "Maira da Luz" culminates in a pattern familiar in Amarílis's border writing. Here the wealthier Cesarina, filling in for the colonial male patriarchy, stomps the now-voiceless Maira and along with her the future identity of Cape Verdean womanhood. The last lines of the story—also the last lines of Amarílis's latest book—write the epitaph of this lost identity: "E assim selaram a casa porque a D. Eufémia enloqueceu e a Maira da Luz tinha desaparecido sem deixar rastro" (127) (And so they sealed up the house because Dona Eufemia went crazy and Maira da Luz had disappeared without a trace).

Conclusion

Maira da Luz may indeed disappear without leaving a trace, but not from the larger space of Cape Verdean womanhood within the borders of Orlanda Amarílis's writing. As is the case with Amarílis's other female subjects, she is recuperated, here, in the story's epigraph. This is, in a sense, her trace, the articulation of her unvoiced dreams, her negotiated subjectivity, the expression of her womanhood that was so violently stomped into the ground.

Orlanda Amarílis's own expressions of Cape Verdean womanhood are wrought with the contradictions of the colonial past that for more than five hundred years determined the relations of class, race, and gender, both in the islands and in the diaspora. Her border writing opens critical spaces for the problematization of postcolonial identities; indeed, it questions the very validity of the "postcolonial" as a liberating condition. Her female subjects are recolonized at every step as they seek to negotiate the boundaries of Cape Verdean womanhood in the diaspora, in the islands, in academia, in the confessional, in their homes, in their families, and in their discourse. And they are murdered, raped, gagged, mummified, stomped, and silenced.

Amarílis writes back against the postcolonial patterns of exile and domination. Piedade may think that she dances her Cape Verdean identity in postcolonial France, but the territory is neocolonial and ultimately male, even in her brother's planned revenge. Her voice is literally ripped out, at that very moment in which she recognizes that she really should have been dancing only for herself. Violete, as well, is violently rendered voiceless. At the end of her story she is positioned as the quintessential colonial woman in the window, but here the image of the exoticized other is turned upon itself as she is cloistered and mummified in the patriarchal house.

The negotiations for female subjectivities in Amarílis's writings are always problematic and question the ambiguities of the Cape Verdean ethos at every step. This questioning is, perhaps, never clearer than in the character of Luna Cohen who, at the end of her story, dreams her return to Cape Verde as the conquest of female territory within the postcolonial imagined community. Luna is an intellectual and the daughter of Jewish immigrants to the islands. In a way, Amarílis's story of "Luna Cohen" writes the beginnings of imagined hybrid national space in a tracing back to the populating of the Atlantic islands five centuries earlier by Jews and New Christians expelled from the Iberian Peninsula. Here, however, the dislocation is chosen as location, and Luna's claiming of territorial boundaries becomes a trope of imagined postcolonial nation.

Ultimately, Luna's imagining of community is no less problematic than Amarílis's other narratives of negotiated positionalities, which inhabit the borders of race, class, gender, and nation constructs. Linda's contestations do emerge, even through the lens of male memory. Piedade's dance leaves a trace across the borders of reconstituted community that is as indelible as her blood. And Maira da Luz's voice is ultimately reconstituted even as it echoes in a space removed from the stomping ground of colonial Mindelo to the borders of Amarílis's own writing, where these Cape Verdean women's expressions of subjectivity are finally privileged as contestations to the violence of the many colonialisms.

Notes

1. Cape Verde achieved independence in 1975 following a protracted liberation struggle against Portugal.

2. See, for example, Fernando Mendonça's articles on Orlanda Amarílis on the use of *crioulo* in Amarílis's writing within the context of Portuguese-language literatures.

3. In *Woman, Native, Other: Writing Postcoloniality and Feminism,* Trinh T. Minh-ha describes ethnic feminist writing as weaving into language "the complex relations of a subject caught between the problems of race and gender and the practice of literature as the very place where social alienation is thwarted differently according to each specific content" (1989: 10).

4. McClintock contends that *postcolonial* cannot describe the present situation in which women do two-thirds of the world's work, earn 10 percent of the world's wages, and own less than 1 percent of the world's property. In this sense, women's political relation to the nation—even in this "postnationalist" era—is still submerged in social relations of marriage. See also Cynthia Enloe's chapter "Nationalism and Masculinity" in *Bananas, Beaches and Bases: Making Feminist Sense of International Politics.* Enloe argues that the histories of nationalist movements are always filled with gendered debate, which later is masked by nostalgic patriarchal interpretations of nationalism, masculinized memory, and hope.

5. *Neocolonialism,* like *postcolonialism,* still privileges the colonial as the center of reference. The term, however, is in many ways preferable in that it emphasizes new forms of colonial relations at play in the so-called postcolonial world. As a theoretical term, Shohat points out that it makes more sense to speak of neocolonizers and the neocolonized than of postcolonized and postcolonizers (107).

6. In this vein, the importance of the Indian Subaltern Collective cannot be minimized. The principal target of the Subaltern Collective's critique was, of course, bourgeois historiography's inscription of the bourgeois leaders of the Indian independence movement as the subject of history and the Indian masses as unquestioning followers. Enabling the subaltern to speak and be heard not only critiqued elitist conceptual frameworks, but also posited the views from the bottom up. See, for example, Ranajit Guha's study "The Prose of Counter-Insurgency." The most extensive critique to date of the "strategic essentialism" of the Indian Subaltern Collective has come from Gayatri Chakravorty Spivak, especially in "Can the Subaltern Speak?"

7. Shohat argues quite convincingly that the postcolonial's celebration of hybridity must always be problematized and related to regenerations of colonialism. She reminds us that colonial discourse also celebrated hybridity in all of its diverse modalities (forced assimilation, internalized self rejection, cultural mimicry, etc.) and that hybridity therefore is subject to the same critique as post-colonialism (110).

8. Manuel Ferreira defined the term "a diaspora caboverdiana" (Cape Verdan diaspora) as one of bitterness and nostalgia within exile (69). In cultural-demographic

terms, the Cape Verdean diaspora has created what Raymond Almeida has termed a "transnational Cape Verdean community." Of the estimated nearly one million Cape Verdeans worldwide, more than half live outside of the islands, with more than four hundred thousand in the United States alone and fifty thousand in Portugal.
9. Unless otherwise indicated, all translations from the Portuguese are mine.
10. The reference to an "imaginary community" alludes to Benedict Anderson's writings on nationalism and the construction of "horizontal comradeship" as commitment to the imagination of nation.
11. Gabriel's statement—"emigrante é lixo" (an immigrant is garbage)—is reminiscent of the closing lines of Lima Barreto's *Clara dos Anjos* (1923), the story of a young *mulata* in postabolitionist São Paulo. Clara falls in love with Cassi Jones, the sleazy white bad boy of *modinhas* (Brazilian popular songs of the era), and when she becomes pregnant she turns to Cassi's mother for help. She is, of course, rejected and cursed in racial terms, and the closing words of the novel—"Nós não somos nada nesta vida" (We are nothing in this life)—rupture the Brazilian republican model of modernity through whitening.

Works Cited

Almeida, Raymond. 1995. *Festival of American Folklife*. Washington, D.C.: Smithsonian Institution.

Amarílis, Orlanda. 1983. *Ilhéu dos Pássaros*. Lisbon: Planato Editora.

———. 1974. *Cais-do-Sodré té Salamansa*. Coimbra: Centelha.

———. 1989. *A casa dos mastros*. Lisbon: ALAC.

Anderson, Benedict. 1983. *Imagined Communities: Reflections on the Origin and Spread of Nationalism*. New York: Verso Books.

Anzaldúa, Gloria. 1987. *Borderlands/La Frontera*. San Francisco: Spinsters/Aunt Lute.

Enloe, Cynthia. 1990. *Bananas, Beaches and Bases: Making Feminist Sense of International Politics*. Berkeley: University of California Press.

Ferreira, Manual. 1977. *Literaturas africanas de expressão portuguesa*. Vol. 1. Lisbon: Instituto de Cultura Portuguesa.

Guha, Ranajit. 1983. "The Prose of Counter-Insurgency." In *Subaltern Studies II: Writings on South Asian History and Society*, ed. Ranajit Guha. Delhi: Oxford University Press. 62–101.

Hamilton, Russell. 1984. *Literatura africana, literatura necessaria*. Lisbon: Edições 70.

Laranjeira, Pires. 1989. "Mulheres, Ilhas Desafortunadas." Preface to Orlanda Amarílis, *A casa dos mastros*. Lisbon: ALAC. 9–11.

Lima Barreto, A. H. 1978. *Clara dos Anjos*. São Paulo: Editora Brasiliense.

McClintock, Anne. 1992. "The Angel of Progress: Pitfalls of the Term Post-Colonialism." *Social Text* 31/32: 84–98.

McNab, Gregory. 1987. "Sexual Difference: The Subjection of Women in Two Stories by Orlanda Amarílis." *Luso-Brazilian Review* 24: 59–68.

Mendonça, Fernando. 1983. "Orlanda Amarílis." *Revista de Letras* 23: 63–70.

———. 1984. "Orlanda Amarílis, uma escritora de Cabo Verde." *Vértice* 44: 44–53.

Mohanty, Chandra Talpade. 1984. "Under Western Eyes: Feminist Scholarship Colonial Discourses." *Boundary* 2:13: 333–58.

————. 1991. "Cartographies of Struggle: Third World Women and the Politics of Feminism." In *Third World Women and the Politics of Feminism*, ed. Chandra Talpade Mohanty, Ann Russo, and Lourdes Torres. Bloomington: Indiana University Press.

Santilli, Maria Aparecida. 1985. "As mulheres-sós de Orlanda Amarílis." In *Africanidade*. São Paulo: Editora Ática. 107–111.

Shohat, Ella. 1992. "Notes on the Post-Colonial." *Social Text* 31/32: 99–113.

Spivak, Gayatri Chakravorty. 1987. "Can the Subaltern Speak?" In *Marxism and the Interpretation of Cultures*, ed. Larry Grossberg and Cary Nelson. Urbana: University of Illinois Press. 271–313.

Trinh T. Minh-ha. 1989. *Woman, Native, Other: Writing Postcoloniality and Feminism*. Bloomington: Indiana University Press.

CHAPTER NINE

"I Was Evita," or *Ecce Femina*

Lídia Jorge's The Murmuring Coast

Ronald W. Sousa

> The effectivity of masquerade lies precisely in its potential to
> manufacture a distance from the image, to generate a problematic
> within which the image is manipulable, producible.
>
> —Mary Ann Doane

In a number of passages in the second, and principal, part of Lídia Jorge's 1988 novel *A costa dos murmúrios* (*The Murmuring Coast*), the speaker recalls scenes, of some years earlier, in which she found herself in what can only be called desirous contemplation of another woman, the overaptly nicknamed "Helen of Troy," beautiful wife of her new husband's superior officer.[1] The contemplation reaches the point, toward the novel's end (233 [222–223]), where, acting on a powerful attraction involving a complex attitude toward that other woman, she fondles Helen's leg, and an erotic (same-sex) encounter of sorts ensues. On the path to the encounter, which is the culminating point of one of the novel's main narrative strands, the speaker refers to Helen in terms such as the following: "a beautiful woman; nude she resembled a dove . . . ; it was . . . her legs, her breasts" (65 [68]); "she could be the body serving as the abstraction of Beauty, Innocence, and Fear simultaneously" (88–89 [90]); "her wet-looking dress rippl[ed] on her body" (101 [102]); "her body parts, her foot, her leg, her arm, her neck, expanded separately, as if looking for a place to display themselves" (165–66 [161]).

It is fair to say that the most frequently employed narrative situation in the novel is the scene in which the speaker contemplates Helen. In its iteration it is so persistent as to pose itself as a kind of question: "What (all) is going on in this recurring situation?" Even the speaker, in effect, poses questions in that vein: during one of the gaze scenes, she pointedly asks herself, "but what was [Helen] an abstraction of?" (88 [90]) (for similar questioning, see also, e.g., 101 [102], 230 [220]).

So that these passages may be properly contextualized, a few general observations are in order. First, *A costa dos murmúrios* consists of two parts, the first being a short story called "Os gafanhotos" (The Locusts) and the second being a series of nine sections, marked only with Roman numerals, in which the speaker, Eva Lopo, in an associative exposition, recalls the events dealt with in the preceding short story—events in which she participated—as well as other, related happenings of the time the short story refers to. Second, that set of reminiscences is produced, some years after the actual events, in relation to Eva's actual reading of the short story (we and she must be thought of as reading "The Locusts" simultaneously). Moreover, that reading/reminiscence is carried out in the presence of the (male) author of "The Locusts," to whom, in the process, Eva intermittently addresses herself (he, by contrast, never speaks). Third, Eva's recollections, taken as a whole, piece together a pattern that demonstrates the inadequacy of the narrative presumptions that principle the short story—and, it is repeatedly suggested, traditional linear narrative in general. Indeed, the last gesture in the novel involves Eva's "handing back, annulling 'The Locusts'" (274 [259]). I have elsewhere postulated that

> the novel's very division into a polished short story and an uncoordinate set of reminiscences about what is not, and cannot be, represented in that story... designates a realm of what might be termed historical contingency ever exceeding the reach of narration. (Jorge 1995: vi)

It is, then, in an associative process of memory with multiple implications for narrative, that Eva—at the time of the represented events, significantly, the (presumably naive) new army bride "Evita"—recalls engaging in sexual/sensual contemplation of Helen. Such a narrative arrangement, of course, makes it impossible definitively to separate choices made in the process of recollection from the actions and motives attributable to the "recalled" scenes—makes it, then, impossible on most scores definitively to separate the retrospective speaker Eva from the represented Evita (punctuation in the novel rarely functions as a separator of the two positions; indeed, it generally furthers their conflation). In summary terms, what is presented to us must be seen as involving a mature Eva recalling herself contemplating another woman, wife of the (also overaptly named) Captain Jaime Forza Leal, her husband's superior officer.[2] Indeed, the very tone suggesting an attitude of contemplation requires the presence of the gap between Eva and Evita for its realization, because, more often than not, Evita cannot be pictured as stopping to gaze at Helen; instead we get the sense of contemplation from the later recollection by Eva of impressions usually formed by Evita during interaction.

We are left to ponder what all the reasons for the repeated attitude of contemplation might be—as, apparently, is Evita as well. Or is it Eva who wonders about what sort of explanation might be adduced for this attraction, about why it is so important to her as to recur frequently in these recollections of years later, about what question(s) it poses. The tone in which Eva's remarks are produced suggests that Evita is in some important respects little more than a character in her memories, that she, Eva, has come to some understanding in the intervening years, and that that understanding underpins her reaction to "The Locusts." (There is certainly an irony in the fact that she becomes "Eve" after gaining knowledge.) Indeed, her repeated assuring of us, and herself, that "I was Evita" serves, along with other functions, to suggest a distance between her past and present selves and an attitude of experience-based knowledgeability with regard to the recalled events. (As the distinction between the two is not always central to the issues to be examined in this essay, I shall henceforth use the composite term "Ev/ita," unless at a given point the distinction between the two is either obvious or crucial for my argument.) It is, implicitly, the short-story author's burden— and ours as readers—to seek to understand something of that understanding that Eva fashions retrospectively in reaction to the reading that she and we have just completed.

It is the aim of this essay to inquire into the significance of that recurring contemplation and its role in the reaching of that understanding. In this novel, which actually problematizes the possibility of traditional novel narrativity—by proceeding in associative fashion, developing one issue until it crosses with another, dropping it, then taking it up again when another associative link presents itself—that inquiry will necessarily be bound up with such issues as how this series of scenes of contemplation articulates with others of Eva's associations to characterize aspects of the recalled events without attempting to put them in the form of a linear(izable) narrative. Indeed, although the second part of *A costa dos murmúrios* clearly proceeds in rough chronological order, there is little specification of sequentiality among passages, and thus no large-scale sequential relationships can be definitively established. The relationships in the novel thus pose problems of several orders.

It should be clearly understood that it is not my aim to "read" the novel or to account for its overall thematics or narrative structure. This inquiry is instead aimed narrowly at exploring the implications within the novel pattern of the set of recalled scenes referred to above.

Our understanding of Eva's understanding—whatever the precise epistemological status that might be ascribed to the latter—must, then, involve wider issues as well, for access to which a second set of orienting observations is necessary. First, the novel's scenario is the coastal Mozambican city of Beira during the colonial wars; the time is, then, probably, the 1960s.[3] Second, the relationship between Evita and Helen—as, presumably, that among the many military wives represented—is bound up with the reason for their presence in Beira, namely, their husbands' involvement in an attempt to defeat the African enemy militarily. Third, in that environment, relationships—between males and females in particular, but in fact all relationships—are brokered by what I have elsewhere called a *blatant* phallocentric symbolic economy, an economy ratified by "possession of the female body" (Sousa 1997). By "phallocentric symbolic economy" I mean to refer to issues ranging from the represented language of military strategy and accomplishment, to the cloistering of army wives when their husbands are away in battle, to the ostentatiously paraded battle scar of Forza (in this respect a Coriolanus figure), to discourse about Portuguese superiority to the Africans (and the Portuguese military's prized links to the South African regime of the time), to the epic discourse of Portuguese national history and national identity (principally articulated in a ludicrous lecture titled "Portugal within and beyond Its Borders Is Eternal" given by a caricaturesquely blind army officer (218–27 [209–17]), all the way to dogged insistence on the necessity of authoritative establishment of univocal meaning in general (for these connections, see Sousa 1997). It is clear by inference that the male-authored "Locusts" that Eva's recollections critique is of a piece with that phallocentric symbolic economy (as, of course, is an analysis such as the one I am carrying out now, try though I might to proceed associatively rather than authoritatively).

It is in some relationship to both that economy and the Evita-to-Helen contemplative gaze that, as the continuation of the "encounter" scene introduced earlier, Helen makes the proposition to Evita that the two of them "take revenge on them." The full phrase in Portuguese is "vamos vingar-nos deles?" (236 [225]). The "revenge" is to be taken by their engaging in sexual relations. The *eles* (masculine) upon whom the revenge is to be taken are their husbands in particular and the soldiery— and associated military/war ideology—in general. The proposal, as the very words in which it is uttered make clear, comes not principally in a sexual or even an individual-psychological mode, but rather in some measure as the symbolic-level initiative for a kind of solidarity and ful- fillment in the face of the obvious sociosymbolic strictures the two women face. And while "revenge" (an act of opposition) is clearly the pri- mary sense of the verb in context, unlike its English cognate, *vingar-se* also means "to vindicate oneself," "to affirm oneself"—acts potentially of self-constitution in any mode, not necessarily in a mode of opposition.

How, then, are we to understand the recurring contemplative gaze so clearly but problematically linked to the sociosexual dimensions of this complexly presented symbolic economy, developed in so associative a manner as to render problematic any standard cause-and-effect analysis in the area of narrative emplotment, and carried out to the terminus we have seen? And what are its implications? One route that might carry some weight in exploring those issues, albeit perhaps only in schematic terms—that is, as source of useful procedures and points of compari- son—is provided by the considerable and continually developing criti- cal tradition involving the "gaze," much of it deriving from psychoana- lytically oriented criticism of (Hollywood-style) film.

From the pioneering work of Laura Mulvey on, treatment of the "gaze" in film criticism has operated on the basis of a relatively stable—one might call it "canonical"—analytic paradigm derived from a reading of Freudian and Lacanian psychologies.[4] Recent work (some of it by Mul- vey) has come as much to question, complexify, or in various ways rela- tivize the paradigm as it has merely to reproduce it in theory or in analytic practice. Terms constituent of the paradigm are such as the spectatorial gaze, which Mulvey sees as socially legitimized and socially framed scopophilia. The gaze necessarily involves either its subject's identification with "gaze"-ing/desire to possess its object (operations of power) or its subject's identification with that object/desire to be the object of the "gaze" (operations of passivity). As is well known, the terms come gender-typed: the object of the gaze is female, while the first subject is male, the second, female. The "subjectness" of the two subjects is thus markedly divergent, a problem resolved by the assertion that "subjecthood," now no longer primarily a positional designation, but rather one having to do with power, is denied the female by dint of this very mechanism: looking is said to be constructed—in dominant film practice, if not in wider social venues as well—as a masculine activity involving a distancing from and power over the object, while being looked at is constructed as a feminine activity involving what might be called "closeness-to-the-image" or "closeness-to-self." This paradigm is seen as operating in a close relationship to the productive/reproductive processes of subject construction in society at large—that is, there is a positive correlation between the first subject and social constructs of the masculine and between the object/second subject and constructs of the feminine. And, with respect to its place in the theorizing of film spectatorship, the paradigm is seen in a complex, positively correlated relationship with other subject-constructing, or subject-locating, functions of the filmic text as plot and cinematographic conventions and techniques, especially the technical "location" of the spectator, though this second set of processes and the elements of the basic gaze paradigm can at times be seen to dislocate each other.

Some questions about this paradigm are the following: What, exactly, is the relationship between gendered construction of film spectatorship and the wider construction of gender? Where and how fully—if at all—do the proposed norms of film spectatorship operate with actual film spectators viewing actual films? How can we think such possibilities, "open" within the paradigm, as, say, nonidentificatory "female" spectatorship (see Doane, Stacey) or the possibility of a lesser rigidity in definition of gender and/or in the fixing of subject and object positions (see, e.g., Brown)?

In relation to *A costa dos murmúrios,* several correlations with the basic paradigm and with the critical uses to which it has been put can be registered. Ev/ita's gaze, often manifestly scopophilic in its verbal presentation (e.g., 166 [161]), is regularly cast in a position like that of the theoretical film spectator's gaze, manifesting itself thus by representing

Helen as, for example, "putting her clothes back on pensively, as if she were supposed to be seen from different angles by a pensive public" (ibid.), or as "playact[ing]" (44 [50]); that is, in her diction, Ev/ita manifests the sense that she is dropping in on Helen's private world, à la Mulvey's film spectator. At the same time, she sees Helen as someone whose actions, like those of the film actor/actress, are carried out in some degree of awareness of spectatorship; indeed, the repetition of the word *pensive* in this quote (the English recapitulates the original Portuguese on this point) suggests a complex interaction between Helen as object of the spectatorial gaze and the spectator—generic but not genderless (being, by this logic, male)—that she projects to receive her actions. Moreover, the diction of acting and of the (female) film star is one of the structuring discourses in several of the gaze scenes.

All of this is contextualized, and thus reinforced, by the fact that Evita moves to a great degree in "female" circles in the rarified colonial military setting of *A costa dos murmúrios,* and we therefore see the women playing their assigned roles: acting as helpmeets and caretakers for their soldier husbands, engaging in domestic labor, preparing their appearance for their husbands (with minute and exhaustive attention to their hair). In this environment, the central, passive location of the female body is emphasized. And that emphasis is reinforced in several specific events: for example, an episode of a stillbirth in which the army-wife expectant mother suffers permanent bodily harm, all of which is vehemently blamed on the local—that is, non-European—medical care system (173–75 [168–71]); and the elaborate cloistering done when husbands are gone, a practice to which Helen loudly proclaims excessive adherence (e.g., 91–92 [92–93], 97–99 [98–100]).

Indeed, the sense is created that the location of the female body is crucial here, as anchor of the symbolic economy, as "cause" of the entire conflict, all the more so as it is a "European" female body in this non-European locale. It is as though the Hotel Stella Maris in which the army wives are quartered (ironically, the remnants of a luxury hotel from the heyday of colonial splendor) was a sanctuary established against an alien world, a world to be ventured out into, even paid attention to, only at the individual's peril (e.g., 60 [64], 77–78 [79–80]). This same arrangement is inversely readable as well: as physical and sociosymbolic imprisonment within a system that requires that imprisonment as a cornerstone of its very order. And moving outside the sanctuary/prison into the world of the non-European other is equivalent to challenging that order.[5] It is noteworthy that Evita both quietly refuses to accept many of the strictures and refuses to stay within the assigned sanctuary— and eventually has an affair with a local man while the groom is away on a campaign. Also, her close relationship with Helen (they meet at Forza's house, which is away from the Stella Maris)[6] comes to provide a kind of woman-to-woman bond that helps to unmask, for Ev/ita if not for Helen, the arbitrary brutality of the military actions that their husbands carry out in the name of the greater logic. In some sense, their collaborative "discovery" of their symbolic location and the terms that maintain it play a role in the buildup to the encounter scene.

An important question within this highly freighted frame involves the nature of the gaze repeatedly cast: is Ev/ita Mulvey's "male" spectator engaging in a power relationship, does she somehow still end up playing the identificatory "female" role, or does she—perhaps because she is otherwise ambiguously constructed as "female"—vary from the paradigm that equates the gaze and maleness? The immediate answer would seem to be the latter—for reasons of complexity if none other. Ev/ita has a dual view of Helen, a view that she herself often describes as alternately "material" and "abstract" (see, e.g., 88 [90]). With the "material" Helen she sets up an identificatory relationship: she identifies with the woman she sees as mundane, self-absorbed, dependent, dominated, and fearful. It is, however, the "abstract" Helen at whom she "gazes" and to whom she is attracted, the beautiful, seemingly perfect, slightly aloof female movie star Helen who behaves in an extravagantly "female" manner—hence, again, the more than simply sexual nature of the attraction. Indeed, the denouement of the "encounter" scene asserts as much, for to Helen's proposal Evita replies:

> I can't, Helen. If I got close enough to you to touch you I would come apart into blood-colored mud. Nature, or maybe just the priest to whom I was sent in my childhood . . . keep me from touching you for any reason other than pure contemplation. . . . We would have to return to our first nursing to correct this defect. Or even earlier, because I have no body part that can bury you under marble, Helen of Troy. What I love in you cannot be buried in earth nor does it aspire to be. Men, yes, they make me happy because they bury me in the earth and make me mortal. I want to have a man on me so I can feel mortal. . . . Between you and me, identity is a mirror that reflects us and implacably isolates us. (236 [225–26])

The gaze relationship with the "abstract" Helen is, then, a complex one. It is clearly here, not in the "material" realm that there comes the strong attraction, the desire to "touch" Helen, albeit in "pure contemplation." The initial temptation is to see it as a kind of intense, "pure" identification and thereby to confirm the canonical paradigm, albeit in terms in which some sort of metaphorical reversal must be presumed. That solution, however, runs afoul of both the "material" diction of the gaze scenes and the very fact that they continue on—indeed, build in expression of desire—up to the encounter scene.

The argument for some collapse of the gaze into identification is all the more tempting, however, as another principal strand of the gaze relationship with the "abstract" Helen is precisely an identificatory one. Evita identifies with the abstract Helen, blatant symbol of the female— and, in this social environment, the "cause" of the war:

> "Do you know what your name means?"
> Helen of Troy started laughing—"No, I don't."
> "No one has ever said '*Haec Helena*' to you?"
> "No, never," she said with innocent eyelashes batting . . .
> "Saying '*Haec Helena*' is the same as saying 'There's the cause of the conflict.' Do you like that?" (69 [72])

The formulation, read in relation to the canonical gaze paradigm, makes the passive object of desire also the cause of the action—an arrangement that, as has been observed often enough, locates agency in the desiring subject while simultaneously setting the object up as a pretext for the action. The phrase "haec Helena" is, however, a verbally complex one, more so in the context of its use here. *Haec* (*i* [locative particle] + *ce* [demonstrative suffix]) must be seen potentially as (1) reflexive in effect (in Latin, *hic homo,* for example, functions as an emphatic first-person singular [masculine] subject pronoun), (2) demonstrative in both simple and emphatic deictic uses (the latter being much like *ecce,* "behold" [also *i* + *ce*], save that *ecce* points outward), or (3) distributitively demonstrative: "this" *(haec)* is the "Helen" of this particular "conflict"—a usage wherein "Helen" becomes, through a metaphorization conditioned by the demonstrative itself, little more than a common noun. The last two options are patent in the passage: Helen of Troy is pointed to verbally, but also made a metaphor for any female/object/ cause. And the last option, coupled with the first, combine subtly to indict Evita as well: she is, in terms of the European-female-body-centered symbolic economy of the milieu depicted in the novel, obviously an/other "Helen"; the deictic finger—whether conceived of as a *haec* or as an *ecce* matters not—points equally to her.

Ev/ita's "gaze," then, at a minimum, complexifies the canonical spectatorship paradigm: to be sure, she "identifies"—on multiple scores—with Helen, thereby occupying the "female" role(s) of object and of passive "cause." But she does so without leaving off a male-typed "subjective" voyeurism constructed around a desire that builds to the encounter scene. As a matter of fact, it is quite possible to read the successive "gaze" scenes in a way that would suggest that Helen becomes increasingly aware of Evita's voyeuristic desire and increasingly "plays" to this one specific member of her "pensive public"—that, in the final analysis, Evita actually solicits Helen's proposition. (If that is the case, then the complexity of the attraction has been at least partially communicated to Helen, for she clearly does not interpret it as principally sexual, seeing the proposed encounter as, at least in some considerable part, an active overcoming of gender-linked prohibitions.) This is, then, an arrangement in which "identification" is not wholly opposite to what the canonical paradigm sees as a desire to possess.

To be sure, the female-to-female gaze is not defined in the canonical paradigm, but it is obvious that in *A costa dos murmúrios* the gazer does not control the interplay as "he" should. There is power displayed, but it does not seem to relate canonically to possession of the object. And the entire arrangement is grounded in a complex, ongoing interaction between the two women that is less an action explainable within a complex of gendered relations than a re-action to that complex. The matter, to say the least, requires further exploration. One route is to go into some of the work that complexifies the "gaze" paradigm, especially that work that inquires into the questions surrounding female spectatorship, to do so more fully cognizant now even than before that we are seeking terms to think from, not a simple explanatory blueprint.

A useful beginning for such exploration might be to move attention to the "object" of the gaze, namely, Helen of Troy. "After all," we should ask ourselves, "what kind of 'passive cause' is it who talks back, who asks for what she needs in the situation, and whose view of that need exceeds the social norms that define 'passive causes'?" It is, after all, Helen herself, in a dramatic role reversal (unless we explain it by reading Evita as soliciting the response), who asks: "Shall we take revenge on them?"

Helen is in fact the source of several surprises—so much so that as the second part of the novel progresses it becomes increasingly difficult to know exactly how to take such phrases as the "innocent eyelashes batting" that comes with Helen's answer to Evita's question about her nickname. For example, we learn that she has had a lover—whom Forza had mercilessly beaten and finally killed and dumped into the sea when the relationship was discovered (214–17 [204–8]). Helen greatly laments that lost love. And when Forza is away in battle, Helen spends great amounts of "cloistered" time thinking in detail about the perils he is facing and about his chances for survival. She even goes through elaborate pseudostatistical processes, using the army's working estimates of likely casualty rates in what is, mathematically speaking, a "magical" process using numbers, to try to determine his chances. It is only toward the end of the novel that we realize that Helen is wishing for, even calculating odds on, Forza's death, not his survival (208–10 [200–202]). Still in all, we are never allowed to see Helen as deliberately subversive of the paradigms that define her; we never know for sure about the "innocent eyelashes batting."

The most consistent reading is to conclude that Helen acts in manners contrary to a desire to be the object of the gaze only in some unreflective way when equally self-serving needs to blunt discomforting aspects of that object status intervene. But these distinctions are probably beside the point. I have elsewhere argued that Helen can be described as so completely inapposite to the entire logic that seeks to inscribe her in the dominant order, principally in failing to internalize it, that we have to see her position as an ironic one that she in effect occupies unironically (Sousa 1997). Through her actions, Helen of Troy thus suggests that total, fulfilled acceptance of the status of object of the gaze is a questionable concept, but she *evidences* no cogent opposition to the order that seeks to locate her there, the order of which she, by nickname, is the quintessential anchor. (In other words, the name "Helen of Troy" becomes pointedly ironic.)

To whom, however, is the suggestion made about the questionable status of the object? To us as readers, of course, but, I think to Ev/ita as well—and, I would argue, prioritarily. Many passages, among them the last one cited earlier, suggest that she "reads" Helen more or less as I do here in the process of relating her to us. "Innocent eyelashes batting" amounts, then, to a sample of discourse from Ev/ita's reading of Helen's complex pattern of behavior. But what sort of reading is this? And to what ends? Such questions force us back to the gaze scenes with a new set of questions: What does it mean to play the role of an object? Where does the necessarily reflective nature of "playing a role" come into conflict with traditionally conceived "object" status? How can the two coexist? In this regard, another significant text from the "gaze" critical tradition will be schematically useful, namely, Mary Ann Doane's "Film and the Masquerade."

Doane: "the masquerade's resistance to the patriarchal positioning would lie in its denial of the production of femininity as . . . presence-to-itself" (80–81); that is, Doane, conceiving of "masquerade" as woman's "acting out" (in terms stereotypical if not exaggeratedly so) of the role she is assigned, in effect posits that the female/object in the classical paradigm of film criticism is constructed precisely around the tension expressed in such questions as these. One way of recasting that conclusion is to say that the supposedly conflicting terms are in fact all present simultaneously, that the playing of the role of the "to-be-looked at," of the "cause," potentially always involves both canonically conceived "identification" with the assigned role and something like the distance constituent of the supposedly "masculine" gaze, that playing the role of object can never be collapsed into simple object status. In effect, the female role thus conceived involves, at some level, the role-player's seeing herself playing the role. For present purposes, these considerations enable a reading of Helen of Troy that says that she is necessarily aware at some level of the doubled nature of her position and acts out that nature, though—arguably—she never comes to grips with it. Such an outlook also enables the suggestion that Ev/ita, in her gaze/recollection, can quite accurately be seen as gazing at Helen not only as a flesh-and-blood person and as the incarnation par excellence of the role assigned to her (that is, to Ev/ita), but also at the role itself seen through its incarnation—hence perhaps the ultimate ironic implication of the nickname "Helen of Troy" (though with assumption of it, "Helen of Troy" seems to merge with the Trojan horse).

Let us illustrate with a passage:

> The Captain opened the trunk and told his wife to feel a certain something that he had in there wrapped in burlap. He wanted her to guess what it was by touching it.
> "It's tools!" she said.

"No!"

She tried again. "It's the parts for a table." It was obvious she knew what the burlap hid, but she pretended not to know; it was all playacting.

"No again!"

"It's a part for the boat's engine!"

"Oh, come on now, you're wrong again." Pretending to give up, the Captain pulled the burlap off and revealed four weapons. Helen of Troy pretended she was scared, and with a hand over her mouth she began running across the sand while the Captain called out to her. The beach was deserted and the red flag was flapping in the wind, as were Helen's clothes as she ran. "Here!" the Captain said, and whistled. At the whistle Helen of Troy started to come back, with a scared look, zigzagging, pretending to be afraid of seeing the weapons. (45 [50])

The speaker/gazer is, of course, the recollective Ev/ita. The almost caricatural scene (blatantly "phallic" weapons, Helen as trained animal) serves to depict Forza's virtual conditioning of Helen's role-playing when they are together (this is but one of several juvenile-seeming scenes between the two). The scene's very caricatural character, coupled with the speaker Ev/ita's obvious interpretations of the two participants' motivations (repetition of the verb *pretend*), suggest that Ev/ita is noting the roles in the abstract, that in the processes of observation/recollection she is in fact analyzing the roles themselves. Thus, while Helen plays her role when it is necessary and does otherwise when it is not, Ev/ita is fascinated by Helen as a sign of her-self (Ev/ita) and is involved simultaneously in both the role-playing and its examination.

This, of course, is precisely the pattern described by the sum of the scenes of contemplation: they involve a kind of identification, on the one hand, with the "material" Helen and, on the other hand, with the "abstract Helen," a process akin to the canonically "male" gaze in that it operates at an "analytic" distance but variant from it in that it recognizes that its object is also itself. In this sense, Helen is blatantly Ev/ita's assigned self: the quintessential object—but also the quintessential masquerade. In effect, Ev/ita has to see the "innocent eyelashes batting" as her own as much as they are Helen's. Hence her multifaceted attraction to Helen—and the latter's partially correct understanding of that attraction. If this is still to be called "identification" with the object, then it is, at least potentially, a different, more complex "identification" than the one presumed in the canonical gaze paradigm, for it contains reflexive elements in its very constitution. (It might be noted, by contrast, that the principal male characters, Forza and Luís Alex, the groom, show no such analytic complexity directed to themselves in their identification with the gaze.)

If we now return to some of the wider entailments of Evita's "contemplation" of Helen, we can see, first and foremost, that being looked at through what we might now call a "metagaze" that proceeds from an undefined position within the phallocentric economy (though the coining of a term such as *meta-identification* would be more nearly appropriate) redefines the justificatory "cause"—of the war, of the military culture portrayed in the novel, and of the nationalistic ideology outlined in relation to that portrayal—thereby causing those constructs to implode; that is, through an entrance provided by work with assigned gender relations, an entire edifice is subverted: in Eva's recollections, key constituent constructs of that edifice are pushed analytically to a point where they are no longer sustainable as propositions.

Within the texture of *A costa dos murmúrios,* while the hypersymbolic Helen unconsciously stands for "something other" than the system that locates her at its core, in an even more subversive mode, the speaker/gazer Ev/ita actually quite reflectively stands "somewhere else" altogether. She stands in a place fashioned by her reflective awareness of assigned object status, of "other" understanding that that awareness provides her, and of the analytic possibilities that such understanding opens up. Moreover, the very fact that the novelistic process must be seen as originating from that "other" space as it retrospectively dismantles the inherited constructs of gender, war, and nationality makes it clear that *A costa dos murmúrios* also, in its very novelistic practice, proposes—indeed, to some degree instantiates—something to succeed those imploded constructs.[7]

To be sure, the narrowly political among those constructs had been historically rejected in the years between the time of the novel's setting and the time of its writing and publication. This novel, however, would seem to go beyond seeking replacements in kind for those narrowly political constructs to proposing a wide revamping. In the simplest of terms, that revamping would seem to rest on an openness to modes of understanding not committed to univocal interpretation and its investment in social power, the cultivation of the multiplicity of "other" options available when one succeeds in getting beyond the sway of authority-based epistemology.

It is ultimately that potential that lies at the end of the novelistic associative chain that has been followed out in this essay. It all starts with a gaze.

Notes

1. Because, in the ensuing pages, I reproduce passages from the English translation (Jorge 1995), initial reference will be to that text, with corresponding references to the Portuguese original (Jorge 1988) appearing afterward in brackets. Because of the digressive/repetitive character of the novel, many references are selected rather than exhaustive.

2. On the symbolic dimensions of the relationship between the two couples, as well as, incidentally, on the question of historical contingency, see Sousa (1997). That title, a lightly revised version of a text created for oral delivery, represents on several fronts the forerunner of the current project and therefore will be referred to several times here.

3. Lídia Jorge knew the place and time, having lived in Beira at the end of the war era; see, for example, the interview she gave in *A ponte do afecto* (51–62).

4. See Mulvey (1975). I cite this text to stand for a line of critical production, of which it is the usually acknowledged starting point, that is now so vast that its representative bibliography would be huge indeed. The terms I employ and the manner of their use are drawn from the developing tradition, and thus are not always exactly Mulvey's. Moreover, I tailor my presentation to my present purposes, which are in some important ways—having principally to do with the different media involved—inapposite to their use in the critical tradition.

5. On colonial discourse and the female body generally, see Mills, especially 57–63 and the related bibliography. Some relevant work has been done on this issue in relation to North American female captivity narratives (see, e.g., Castiglia 3–4 and Derounian-Stodola and Levernier 47).

6. The irony here is that Forza, in an attitude of hypervigilance, sees the female gossip in the Stella Maris as potentially subversive. Thus, for the fiercest proponents of the established order, the sanctuary is itself insufficiently a sanctuary (67 [70]).

7. Criticism has identified an abiding interest in the problem of Portuguese cultural identity as a constant in Jorge's work (see, e.g., Bulger).

Works Cited

Bulger, Laura F. 1984. "*O cais das merendas* de Lídia Jorge—Uma identidade cultural perdida?" *Colóquio/Letras* 82: 51–57.

Brown, Jeffrey A. 1997. "'They Can Imagine Anything They Want . . .': Identification, Desire, and the Celebrity Text." *Discourse* 19:3: 122–43.

Castiglia, Christopher. 1989. "In Praise of Extra-Vagant Women: *Hope Leslie* and the Captivity Romance." *Legacy* 6:2: 3–16.

Derounian-Stodola, Kathryn Zabelle, and James A. Levernier. 1993. *The Indian Captivity Narrative, 1550–1900.* New York: Twayne.

Doane, Mary Ann. 1982. "Film and the Masquerade: Theorizing the Female Spectator." *Screen* 23:3–4: 74–88.

Jorge, Lídia. 1988. *A costa dos murmúrios.* Lisbon: Dom Quixote.

———. 1995. *The Murmuring Coast.* Trans. Natália Costa and Ronald W. Sousa. Minneapolis: University of Minnesota Press.

Mills, Sara. 1991. *Discourses of Difference: An Analysis of Women's Travel Writing and Colonialism.* London: Routledge.

Mulvey, Laura. 1975. "Visual Pleasure and the Narrative Cinema." *Screen* 16:3: 6–18.

A ponte do afecto: entrevistas. 1990. Ed. Nelson Saúte. Maputo, Mozambique: BJ.

Sousa, Ronald W. 1997. "The Critique of History in Lídia Jorge's *A costa dos murmúrios,* or Helen of Beira Meets Luís of Troy." *Cincinnati Romance Review* 16: 135–43.

Part III
Brazilian Performativities

CHAPTER TEN

Supermen and Chiquita Bacana's Daughters
Transgendered Voices in Brazilian Popular Music
César Braga-Pinto

> I owe it to you to have discovered homosexuality, and ours is indestructible. I owe you everything and I owe you nothing at all. We are of the same sex, and this is as true as two and two are four or that S is P.
>
> —Jacques Derrida (1987)

> Meu amor,
> Tudo em volta está deserto, tudo certo.
> Tudo certo como dois e dois são cinco...
>
> —Caetano Veloso, "Como 2 e 2"

"Everyone knows the pain and the delight of being what one is" (Cada um sabe a dor e a delícia de ser o que é), sings Gal Costa in Caetano Veloso's "Dom de Iludir" (Gift for deluding).[1] Pain and delight (or pain and pleasure) in this case are not opposites, but rather define what is commonly called "identity." According to Derrida's citations of Nietzsche, "pain is something other than pleasure," "it is not the opposite of pleasure," and "one might perhaps characterize pleasure in general as a rhythm of small painful excitations" (1987: 408). But if pleasure is a kind of *rhythm* that is produced only as it differs from itself, what can the pleasure of identity be, that is, the pleasure of being who you are? For a number of Brazilian musicians, and for Caetano Veloso in particular, identity and its pleasures have been repeatedly presented as the rhythm of painful and delightful acts of stripping and disguising oneself, the interplay between revealing and concealing sexual differences. This rhythmic presentation of identity, which is also a form of repeated withdrawal, is not only the work of pleasure itself, but may constitute that which we usually call "desire."

Transgendered Voices

The "being" in Caetano's "Dom de Iludir" is, in principle, "woman," because the song is a response to the male voice who speaks in "Pra Quê Mentir" (Why lie?), by Noel Rosa (1910–37). The man addresses a woman who, according to his judgment, does not know how to lie and, therefore, is not fully a woman: for she cannot fulfill what *he* considers to be every woman's inherent and universal gift for deceiving. Her (Caetano's) response, on the other hand, argues that men's urge to explain and to tell the truth is in fact nothing but another way of deluding. Both songs expose the constructions of gender and the failure to or the pretense of satisfying these constructions, and further relate each gender's performance to the art of delusion or concealment. Whereas Noel Rosa's song addresses women from the viewpoint of someone who believes himself capable of seeing beyond appearances, Caetano's song suggests that the demand for truth, and therefore the demand for identity, defines men's own deceitful identity.

In a very (Fernando) Pessoan fashion, the pretense in each case is, moreover, also the poet's or the singer's gift for pretending and deceiving.[2] For the supposedly male voice created by Noel Rosa became famous in the early 1950s when a woman, Aracy de Almeida (1914–88), recorded the original song, just as the female voice in Caetano's response acquired a new tone when Caetano himself, (after Gal Costa's recording), impersonated it (in *Totalmente Demais*, 1986). Each rendition inevitably suggests that the feigned pain or delight is in reality an emotion that not only the dramatis personae, but also each composer and interpreter feels. In Brazilian popular music, the unstable relationships between the genders of the composer, the singer, and the "I" in each song constantly blur the boundaries of gender presentations. When pretense is a fundamental part of the game, it ultimately serves to reveal as much as it apparently conceals. Somewhere between the public and the private, it seems that Brazilian popular music has been the perfect place for artists (and consumers) to express and, at the same time, conceal "the delight and the pain" of sexual identities.

It is no wonder that rumors would have us believe that Aracy de Almeida, the "male" voice in Noel Rosa's song, was a lesbian, and that

Caetano is either gay or bisexual. Transgendered voices have been present in Brazilian music for many decades, particularly after the 1960s.[3] And rumor has never ceased to circulate concerning the homosexuality of the most important figures who have subsequently entered the Brazilian popular music scene: Gal Costa, Gilberto Gil, Maria Bethânia, Simone, Marina Lima, Ney Matogrosso, Zizi Possi, Milton Nascimento, to name just a few. Most of these artists have consistently refused to open the door to their closets, but have kept their windows open—not only for all insects to fly in, as another song ("Janelas Abertas n° 2") by Caetano suggests, but also so that the public eye might fantasize about the clothes hanging in those closets, and whom those artists would or would not entertain in their beds. In the case of Caetano, it is said that once, when a reporter asked him if he was homosexual, he simply responded that he would not kick Mick Jagger out of his bed.

To be sure, despite the sexual ambiguity of these artists and the public's interest in this ambiguity, the heterosexist tradition in Brazil cannot be dismissed: the delight of the macho persists, and he is obviously not the one who suffers the pain in sambas like Noel Rosa's "Mulher indigesta" (Indigestible woman): "Ai que mulher indigesta, merece um tijolo na testa" (This woman makes me sick, she deserves a brick on the head); in Lamartine Babo's somewhat nonsensical and comical "Só dando com uma pedra nela" (The only way is to throw a stone at her) (1932): "Mulher de setenta anos / já cheia de desenganos / que usa setenta gramas / de vestido na canela / Só dando com uma pedra nela / Só dando com uma pedra nela" (A seventy-year-old woman, so full of disenchantment, who wears seventy grams of dress on her shin; the only way is to throw a stone at her); or in Geraldo Pereira's samba "Na Subida do Morro" (Climbing the hill), interpreted by the prototype of the *malandro*,[4] Moreira da Silva—even if one might argue that these artists' machismo is undermined by their own implicit self-mockery:

Na subida do morro me contaram
que você bateu na minha nega.
Isso não é direito,
bater numa mulher que não é sua:
deixou a nega quase crua no meio da rua,
a nega quase virou presunto.

[As I was climbing the hill
I was told that you beat up my (black) woman.

This is not right, beating a woman who is not yours:
you left her almost raw in the middle of the street;
The woman almost turned into a piece of ham (slang for "corpse").]

Brazil's long history of machismo, with its varying degrees of violence, could be illustrated by many other popular songs by composers
such as Lupicínio Rodrigues and Ataulfo Alves, the author of a gallery
of submissive female characters among whom figure Guiomar, Emília,
and, of course, Amélia, the famous "mulher de verdade" (real woman).
Similarly, more or less homophobic songs have been popular among
all social classes, from Luiz Gonzaga and Humberto Teixeira's classic
"Paraíba masculina, muié macho sim sinhô" ("Paraíba," 1950) (Masculine "Paraíba," yes sir, a macho woman),[5] to recent, supposedly funny
songs by, for example, the band Mamonas Assassinas, containing lines
mocking gays and that have delighted teenagers and their parents alike,
such as "Abra a sua mente / Gay também é gente" (Open your mind,
gays are people too) (Gay Robocop).[6] Yet, even homophobia seems to
be ambivalent in Brazil, and can suddenly turn into tolerance, as in Tim
Maia's "Vale Tudo," where at first he sings: "Vale tudo / Vale o que vier /
Vale o que quiser / Só não vale dançar homem com homem / e nem
mulher com mulher / O resto vale!" (Anything goes, whatever it may
be, whatever you want—except men dancing with men or women with
women—anything else is OK), but finishes with what can be interpreted
as a call for wider—including sexual—liberation: "Atenção: liberou geral /
Agora vale tudo!" (Attention! Now it's total freedom, now everything
goes!). It was perhaps an act of perverse political reinterpretation that
made this apparently homophobic song a favorite among gay audiences
even though Tim Maia's own gender presentation was unambiguously
male and heterosexual. A new twist to this ambivalence was added when
Sandra de Sá, who is known to be a lesbian, recorded her own version
of "Vale Tudo."[7]

The heterosexist tradition in Brazil came under fire in the 1960s with
the international counterculture and civil rights movements, and by the
1970s even Chiquita Bacana's daughter was ready to proclaim in a famous song: "Entrei pro Women's Liberation Front" (I became a member of the Women's Liberation Front).[8] "Chiquita Bacana's daughter," as
is well known, is not really a woman, but a fictional character created
and impersonated by Caetano Veloso, and a playful response to a 1940s
carnival song in which Chiquita Bacana was supposed to be a daring

woman from Martinique who dressed in nothing but a banana peel.[9] Few Brazilian artists have displayed a public image that blurs the limits of sexual identities as often and as effectively as Caetano has, both in his records and on stage. Through Caetano's parody, the carnivalesque song stands out like a fruit basket on the head of a drag queen.[10]

Other male composers of Caetano Veloso's generation also wore disguises and were cross-dressers, often using the feminine "I" to refer to themselves in their songs, just as many women impersonated men when they sang. This has occurred at least to some extent because, traditionally in Brazil, men are the ones who compose, whereas most women only perform the songs. Particularly prior to the 1960s, female performers often adapted the gender in the lyrics to their own gender, even if this radically altered the meaning or disrupted the rhymes of a song. This still seems to be the case in most other countries. In the United States, for example, Frank Sinatra sang "The Girl from Ipanema," but Ella Fitzgerald—and, more recently, Crystal Waters—sang "The Boy from Ipanema." Just as it was rare to find women composers, it was likewise quite uncommon for a man to perform if he did not compose. In the 1950s, Cauby Peixoto was one of the few male singers in Brazil who did not compose and, curiously enough, his name stood out for being the only male name on the list of greatest singers of his time: Ângela Maria, Dalva de Oliveira, and Emilinha Borba, to name a few. In an interview in a Brazilian newspaper, Cauby—who has a low, Sinatra-like voice—himself acknowledged: "If you pay attention to my interpretation, you can feel that it is feminine, it's a woman singing in a man's voice. There is a woman who takes control over me when I sing" (quoted in Sanches). This rigid division between male composers, on the one hand, and female performers (intérpretes, in Portuguese), on the other, has contributed to the development of new, ambivalent forms of discourse, at times skillfully manipulated by both composers and performers. Until the 1960s, when (male) composers wrote lyrics specifically for women to sing, these women seemed to be expressing their own female subjectivities. But then more and more women began to retain the genders found in the original lyrics when they performed songs in which the composers either referred to themselves in the masculine, or else declared their love for a woman. These songs could thus be understood as though a woman were performing a male role, but also as the expression of lesbian love. Similarly, when male composers recorded those songs intended for female performers to sing, they could not avoid being perceived as men in drag, or men who loved other men. Brazilian singers, as well as composers, both female and male, have since started to play with the multiple possibilities of such utterances. The acceptance of transgendered voices allowed, for example, an otherwise sexist song written by Erasmo and Roberto Carlos to acquire, in the voice of Marina Lima, a strong homosexual connotation: "Você precisa de um homem pra chamar de seu / Mesmo que esse homem seja eu" (You need a man to call your own / even if this man is me). Marina Lima mimetically appropriated the male composers' lyrics to express the gender dynamics present in what seems to be a particular lesbian relationship. Furthermore, by displacing the author's sexist words through repetition, the singer staged an act of imposture on two levels. First, the singer's gender presentation was redefined by her performance of a man's discourse; then, as the lyrics suggest, the "I" is a subject whose gender is (or perhaps refuses to be) constructed as "male" ("even if this man is me") in response to the other person's desire ("you need a man to call your own"). Through this double imposture, the performer ultimately reveals, rather than conceals, something about her sexuality, thus reinscribing her pain and delight in the open-ended negotiation of identities.

Concealing has also been an alternative way of revealing one's identity for Ney Matogrosso, who acquired his fame by performing almost in drag, covering his face and half-naked body with paint, and singing in a high-pitched voice. Ney Matogrosso launched his career as the lead singer of the band Secos e Molhados with the famous and extremely ambiguous "O Vira," by João Ricardo (*Secos e Molhados*, 1973), a mixture of rock and roll and Portuguese folk tune (namely, the *vira*) that he performed half-naked, moving his hips and feathers at the same time as he ironically demanded: "Vira, vira homem, vira vira / vira vira lobisomem" (Turn into a man / turn into a werewolf). Years later, Ney Matogrosso still used this kind of irony and humor to construct an image of his sexuality, even when his lyrics apparently denied homosexuality with lines such as "porque eu sou é Homem / Homem com H" (because what I am is a Man / a Man with an M) and "Telma, eu não sou gay / o que dizem de mim são calúnias / meu bem eu mudei!" (Thelma, I'm not gay / what they say about me is all calumny / oh baby, I've changed!) ("Telma"). The contrast between these lines and his high-pitched voice and androgynous presentation not only makes the lyrics utterly ironic, but also allows them to convey precisely the opposite of what they would denote in a different context or in the voice of another performer. By exposing the limits of closeted identity, Ney Matogrosso can thus affirm his own homosexuality without essentializing it. In other words, he discloses his homosexuality by representing it always under erasure, or as a (mock) heterosexuality.

The meanings produced in the slippage between the performer's gender (or sexuality) and those of the poetic voices they perform depend on the context defined not only by the artist, but also by the media and the public. Ney Matogrosso's and Marina Lima's unstable representations of gender and sexuality are present both in the lyrics they sing and in the image they construct and perform. Conversely, although Chico Buarque is one of the composers who has most often written songs for female singers to perform, and subsequently recorded them, while always retaining the feminine "I," his heterosexual image is seldom questioned. Because he has constantly displayed conventional signs of a heterosexual marriage and a "masculine" lifestyle (he likes to play soccer, for example), the contents of his songs hardly affect the way in which his personal life is perceived. Thus, as odd as it may sound, Chico Buarque can sing a song such as "Folhetim" (first recorded by Gal Costa) and play the role of a female prostitute, without revealing much about his own sexuality: "Se acaso me quiseres / Sou dessas mulheres que só dizem sim . . . / e te farei vaidoso / supor que és o melhor / e que me seduz" (If by chance you desire me / I'm the kind of woman who always says yes . . . / and I'll make you so proud / supposing that you are the best / and that you seduce me). In addition, the female persona is only one in a gallery of characters Chico has created and sometimes impersonated throughout his career, such as the mother of a street kid ("Meu guri"), the submissive wife ("Com açúcar, com afeto"), a number of macho husbands and *malandros,* and so on. As with a Shakespearean actor, the impersonation of various social types, regardless of their gender, race, or social class, is characteristic of Chico Buarque's performance, and does not necessarily reflect his own sexual or social positions, nor does it radically change the way he is perceived by his public. To be sure, some degree of ambiguity remains, regarding both the artist's identity and the identity of the character he impersonates. The prostitute performed by Gal Costa in "Folhetim" is not quite the same as the one performed by Chico Buarque, and, moreover, each artist is certainly revealing or suggesting quite different aspects of her or his own personality. And depending on the context that he creates in each case, Chico Buarque and his characters may reveal a greater deal of ambiguity, as when he and Caetano Veloso play the roles of two lesbians in Chico's own "Bárbara."[11] But, unlike Caetano, whose public performance can hardly be dissociated from his own identity, Chico not only can impersonate a number of characters, but also seems to have taken upon himself the responsibility of speaking for other subjects and, in particular, for the subaltern. Presently, however, as minority voices begin to find expression in and outside of the musical sphere, Chico's role as a legitimate representative for silenced Brazilians—that is, as the spokesperson for all subaltern groups—seems to have lost its original force. Yet, he is still largely associated with the democratic ideal, and his political activity has never been reduced to the realm of his artistic performance. On the contrary, he has presented the private domain as largely inflected, if not defined, by his deep identification with democratic values and institutions.[12]

Gilberto Gil's case is somewhat different from Chico's, in that he rarely performs female characters in his songs, or represents other subalterns—perhaps because he is himself a black man. Yet, Gil has occasionally expressed his identification with other excluded groups, such as the poor and sexual minorities. In his song "O veado" (literally, "The deer," but colloquially, the Brazilian equivalent of "The faggot"), for example, it is not necessarily his own sexuality that is in question when he makes an explicit homage to gay men. Yet, as in several other instances, in this song Gil attempts to articulate that which also seems to be his own subjectivity, in such a way that, not unlike Chico Buarque's, his concerns with and adhesion to pluralist values become entangled with his activity of self-fashioning. But whereas Chico Buarque could be said to articulate his own subjectivity through a discourse in which the commitment to Brazilian democracy and human solidarity prevails, Gilberto Gil most frequently expresses that which appears to be his private concerns or desires in such a way that it may provide the pluralistic imperative with a language of contestation that is based on one's desire for self-fashioning.

In terms of sexual identity, for example, Gil has often depicted himself in such a way that one can picture him as a bisexual man without conflicts, as in his "Fé-Menino" (Faith-boy):" "vou levando cada vez mais jeito / Bela menina, minha sina / Cada vez mais / Belo menino, meu destino" (each day I've got more of a knack for it / pretty girl, my fate / each day more / pretty boy, my destiny); or as in his song "Tradição" (Tradition): "Menino que eu era e veja que eu já reparava / numa garota do Barbalho / Reparava tanto que acabei já reparando / No rapaz que ela namorava" (I was just a boy, and see how I already noticed / a girl from the Barbalho neighborhood / I noticed her so much that I ended up noticing / the boy who was her boyfriend). By representing himself as a (possibly, but not necessarily) bisexual man, he does not speak for others—nonetheless his lyrics can become the site of identification for alternative (homo- or hetero)sexualities. Gil's songs can offer a new language of contestation and lend themselves to reinterpretation precisely because they do not claim to be representative and, moreover, because their meanings are never univocal. "Pai e mãe" (Father and mother), for example, is a complex and multilayered song that suggests an Oedipal relationship with both the mother and the father, thus reflecting an ambiguous and unresolved relationship with both men and women:

Eu passei muito tempo
Aprendendo a beijar outros homens . . .
como beijo meu pai.
Eu passei muito tempo
Pra saber que a mulher
que eu amei, que amo, que amarei,
será sempre a mulher
como é minha mãe.

[I have spent much time
Learning how to kiss other men . . .
the same way I kiss my father.
I have spent much time
before I learned that the woman
whom I loved, love, and will love,
will always be that woman
who is just like my mother.]

One of Gilberto Gil's best-known and most influential works is "Super-homem, a canção" (Superman, the song). Contemporary to the film *Superman, the Movie,* the song is also a reference to Nietzsche's *Übermensch,* and has often been perceived as a manifesto for alternative male sensibilities. In addition, it has served to support male bisexuality, as it popularized the notion that every man has and should cultivate his "feminine side":

Um dia,
vivi a ilusão de que ser homem bastaria,
que o mundo masculino tudo me daria
do que eu quisesse ter.
Que nada!...
Minha porção mulher que até então se resguardara,
é a porção melhor que trago em mim agora,
é o que me faz viver....
Quem sabe...
O super-homem venha nos restituir a glória,
mudando como um deus o curso da história
por causa da mulher.

[One day,
I lived the illusion that being a man would suffice,
that the masculine world would give me everything
I wanted to have.
But not at all.
My woman portion, which had so far been kept hidden inside,
is the best portion that I have in me now,
it's what makes me live
Perhaps...
Superman might come to restore us to glory,
Changing the course of history like a god
for the sake of women.]

"Super-homem" has become a sort of hymn for gays, bisexuals, or heterosexual men who in one way or another contest the masculinist order and want to express an alternative sensibility along with their allegiance to women. Although at the time it was released it could indeed have represented a promise of new gender performances in a gynocentric future, today its phallocentric perspective has become apparent not only in the idealized construction of *mulher/melhor* (women/best), but also in the notion that a female portion (in which the "feminine" seems to be essentialized) may serve the improvement of what ultimately remains male. Gilberto Gil's "new man" incorporates female subjectivity in the same way that, years earlier, Gil himself—and in the 1970s he

was not alone—looked at Eastern philosophy as a redemptive alternative to the corruption of the West.

Caetano's "Equivocal Sex"

Caetano Veloso is the performing artist of his generation who most
effectively articulated the complex constructions of sexuality and gender presentation. Much more than Gilberto Gil, Caetano always seems
to be implicated in everything he sings, even (or especially) if the "I" in
a song happens to be a female character, such as the previously discussed
women in "Dom de Iludir" and "A Filha da Chiquita Bacana." More
than any other Brazilian artist, in his case, one can hardly disassociate
the private from the public realms, or the biographical from the literary.[13] Thus Caetano consistently leaves much room for interpretation in
his self-fashioning of sexuality and gender. The inside cover of his most
experimental album, "Araçá azul" (1973) (Blue tropical fruit tree), ambiguously stated: "Um disco para entendidos" (a record for people who
understand—*entendidos* also being an allusion to those who knew
about and contested the military dictatorship in Brazil, as well as being
the argot used by "gay people" to refer to themselves). Considering the
experimental character of the album—the worst-selling work of Caetano Veloso's whole career—and that the album in fact does not have
any other allusions to politics or homosexuality, one might argue that
the sentence is meant primarily as a statement regarding the avant-
garde qualities of the project; but for audiences who have traditionally
been invisible, the double entendre most certainly worked as a rare site
of identification. At any rate, the theme recurs throughout Caetano's
poetic production, and is almost an obsession in his only feature film, *O
cinema falado* (1986). Although he has constantly avoided overtly stat-
ing whether or not he has had homosexual relationships, he has continuously represented his sexuality, and even his gender, as that which Derrida has called the "undecidable." In a song called "Branquinha" (Little
white girl), Caetano (almost) defines himself as follows:

Eu sou apenas um velho baiano,
um fulano, um Caetano, um mano qualquer.
Vou contra a via, canto contra a melodia, nado contra a maré./ . . .
Esse mulato franzino, menino, destino de nunca ser homem não.

Esse macaco complexo, esse sexo equívoco, esse mico-leão...
                                            (*Estrangeiro,* 1989)

[I am just an old *baiano,*
a John Doe, a Caetano, any old brother.
I go in the wrong direction, I sing against the melody, I swim against the
    flow....
(I am) this frail mulatto, a boy, doomed never to be a man;
this complex ape, this equivocal sex, this lion-tamarin...]

Caetano has often expressed his identity not as that which dares not say its name, but as something that cannot be named. As these lyrics suggest, identity is an "equivocal" sign, an always inadequate signifier for something that cannot be pinned down. However, one might ask, isn't it exactly such a space of equivocal identity that defines the impossible category that has been recently referred to as "queer"? Caetano would probably agree with Judith Butler when she states that "it is precisely the *pleasure* produced by the instability of those categories which sustain the various erotic practices that make me a candidate for the category [lesbian] in the first place" (1993b: 308; emphasis in the original).[14] Thus, for Caetano, sexuality can only be expressed in the form of an undecidable question, as he explicitly proclaims in his song "Eu sou neguinha?" (Am I a *neguinha?*):

Eu era o enigma, uma interrogação
olha que coisa mais que coisa à toa, boa boa boa boa...
a me perguntar: Eu sou neguinha?...

totalmente terceiro sexo totalmente terceiro mundo
terceiro milênio carne nua nua nua nua.
                                            (*Caetano,* 1987)

[I was the enigma, a question mark,
"tall and tan and young" and so vain and so good, so good, so good...[15]
and asking myself: am I a *neguinha?*...

Totally third sex, totally third world,
third millennium, naked flesh, so naked, so naked, so naked.]

The term *neguinha* (literally, "little black woman"), which in Salvador is used as a term of endearment as well as argot for "gay man," in Caetano's song translates the impossible sexual and racial identity it seeks to define, while at the same time refusing to present itself. Meanwhile, Caetano can take pleasure in passing for the "girl from Ipanema" herself, another absent sign that, rather than fixing a referent, simply passes by. Identity, for Caetano, cannot be presented because all signs are unstable and the constant producers of other signs: "e o mesmo signo que eu tento ler e ser / é apenas um possível ou impossível em mim, / em mil, em mil, em mil" (and the same sign that I try to read and be / is only one possible or impossible one in me / in a thousand, a thousand, a thousand). Every attempt at defining identity as "one" thus exposes the thousand possibilities that have to be excluded or repressed for its constitution. The song suggests that one self always conceals and unfolds one thousand selves: "em mim, em mil, em mil." For Caetano, identity, like pleasure, is never *self-identical,* but is an interminable relationship with the other's desire. And indeed, according to Derrida's reading of Freud:

> Pleasure, if it is found, the tendency to pleasure and the mastery of the PP [pleasure principle] thus would have their proper place between the two limits of the without-pleasure, stricture and discharge, preparation and end, desire, if you prefer, and its final fulfillment." (397)

Identity is always in a rhythmic relationship to desire, and therefore it is always directed toward an elsewhere. The pleasure (or pain) of identity takes place between the fulfillment of the self and its complete loss into otherness. It is constituted as the differential presentation of oneself toward the intepellation of the other's desire: "o quereres está em estares sempre a fim / do que em mim é de mim tão desigual" (Your desire resides in always longing for that which, in myself, is always so dissimilar to myself) ("O quereres," first recorded in *Velô,* 1984). As such, it can never be delivered, but only promises deliverance. For Caetano, this ambiguous withholding and offering of the self is what makes what one is at the same time painful and delightful. It is also what makes visibility impossible, and yet necessary.

Caetano repeatedly proposes to represent his own sexual identity as constituted by a restrictive, rather than liberating, pleasure of the undecidable, that is, as the pain and the delight of a visible invisibility. But as such a process of self-fashioning takes place precisely in the boundaries of the public and the private, Caetano seems aware that undecidability risks becoming mere undefinition and therefore may reinforce the hegemonic heterosexuality. Caetano is thus faced with the ethical problem that concerns the presentation of his own private, undecidable identity, and the demand for decision and visibility as a form of political action. In his most recent work, identity calls for a naming, though Caetano still refrains from even provisionally situating himself in relation to any particular name. Identity categories sometimes appear as something foreign, fixed, artificial, and, not surprisingly, associated with (North) American identities:

> Veados americanos trazem o vírus da AIDS para o Rio no carnaval
> Veados organizados de São Francisco conseguem controlar a propagação
>   do mal.
> Só um genocida em potencial—de batina, de gravata ou de avental—
> Pode fingir que não vê que os veados—tendo sido o grupo-vítima
>   preferencial—
> Estão na situação de liderar o movimento para deter a propagação do
>   HIV.
>> ("Americanos," in *Circuladô ao vivo*, 1992)

> [American fags bring the AIDS virus to Rio during carnival.
> Organized fags from San Francisco manage to control the spread of the evil.
> Only a potential mass murderer—in a cassock, a tie, or an apron—
> Can pretend not to see that fags—having been the preferred victims—
> Are in the position to lead the movement to contain the spread of HIV.]

If *veados* here refers first and foremost to American gays, it is because Caetano, like many Brazilian intellectuals, sees the urge to categorize as something "typically" American. However, Caetano recognizes that it is the (alleged) Brazilian lack of any clearly defined category that makes the demand for civil rights so difficult:

> Para os americanos branco é branco, preto é preto,
> (e a mulata não é a tal).
> Bicha é bicha e macho é macho, mulher é mulher e dinheiro é dinheiro
> E assim ganham-se, barganham-se, perdem-se, concedem-se,
>   conquistam-se direitos
> Enquanto aqui embaixo a indefinição é o regime
> E dançamos com uma graça cujo segredo nem eu mesmo sei
> Entre a delícia e a desgraça, entre o monstruoso e o sublime.

> [For Americans, whites are whites, blacks are blacks
> (and the *mulata* isn't at all). Fags are fags, straight men are men,
>   women are women, and money is money.
> Thus rights are gained, bargained, lost, conceded, conquered.
> Meanwhile, down here, nondefinition is the regime,
> and we dance with a charm whose secret not even I can understand,

somewhere between delight and disaster, between the monstrous and the
sublime.]

Americanos reflects not only the ways in which the introduction of
(American?) identity categories has become inevitable, but also how
such categories already are, or have always been present in Brazilian
mentalities. The lyrics contrast Americans to Brazilians not as an undecidable question that can be deferred, but as a dilemma that urges resolution. The representation of Brazilian society as a secret, that Caetano
acknowledges not to understand, reflects his own impasse between the
problematic implications of rigid categorization, visibility, and decision, on the one hand, and an all too familiar ideology or regime of
nondefinition, on the other. As the rhythmic presentation of his own
"I" is inscribed in the larger conjuncture of a dancing "we," Caetano
implicates the rhythm of his own "pain and delight" in the drastic
movement between "delight and disaster," between "the monstrous and
the sublime" that characterizes contemporary Brazilian reality. In some
instances of his most recent work, however, Caetano reveals an attempt
at redefining his earlier representations of rhythmic identity. He recognizes the dangers of racial and sexual nondefinition, and does not deny
the inevitable introduction of identity categories, but rather understands
such categories as unstable and necessarily unfulfilled signs. Instead of
simply accepting that "whites *are* whites, blacks *are* blacks" or "fags *are*
fags, straight men *are* men, women *are* women, and money *is* money,"
Caetano introduces a Nietzschean "almost," and replaces the verb *to be*
with an "almost identity" that must remain rhythmic, and yet does not
conceal the name, the slur, the injury:

> a fila de soldados, quase todos pretos
> Dando porrada na nuca de malandros pretos
> De ladrões mulatos e outros quase brancos
> Tratados como pretos
> Só pra mostrar aos outros quase pretos
> (E são quase todos pretos)
> E aos quase brancos pobres como pretos
> como é que pretos, pobres e mulatos
> e quase brancos quase pretos de tão pobres são tratados.
> ("Haiti," in *Tropicália 2*, 1993)

> [the line of soldiers, almost all blacks,
> beating black *malandros* on their necks;

of mulatto thieves and others, almost white,
treated like blacks,
just to show to the other almost blacks
(and they are almost all blacks)
and to the almost white ones, who are poor just like blacks,
How it is that blacks, poor and mulattos,
and the almost white, almost black of poverty, are treated.]

To make a decision—and this is why philosophers have often characterized the decision as a relationship to madness—entails gazing at the
invisible, naming that which cannot be named. This moment and movement of naming and, at the same time, exposing the arbitrary act of
concealment and exclusion that naming always represents is, I believe,
what Ernesto Laclau has called "the logic of the decision taken in an undecidable terrain" (53). If, as Laclau suggests, "the subject is the distance
between the undecidability of the structure and the decision" (54), every
identificatory process or "acquisition of being" is necessarily contingent, and always occurs as an "almost."[16] The presentation of a rhythmic
identity could then be defined as a gesture that reveals a decision and, at
the same time, exposes the plurality of possibilities within the structure
of undecidability.

The tradition of transgendered voices in Brazilian popular music
creates the possibility of new gender presentations. The repeated enactment of a pretense may thus be deployed in order to redefine identity categories. As identity is revealed as pure performance, the repetition of the performance may also redefine the performer's identity. The
result is not simply the concealment of sexual identities behind ambiguous representations. Rather, the performance of a displaced sexual
identity may enable new interpretations or the reappropriation of hegemonic identity categories. Yet, if the artistic performance and displacement of such categories reveal the performative nature of identity, it is
only insofar as the artist becomes implicated in this presentation to blur
the boundaries between the public and the private. Only then can one's
voice translate or become the representation of other voices. And only
then can one, without silencing those other voices, appropriate them
for the articulation of one's own subjectivity. The "translatability" of
gender performances may thus become the site of political struggle and,
at the same time, the sexual politics that one embraces may become the
expression of one's subjectivity. As with Caetano's recent artistic ges-

tures, identities remain equivocal and dissimilar to the categories by which they are defined: they remain as the delightful and painful movement between an always fleeting enigma and an always present signifier.[17]

Notes

I am extremely indebted to Clélia Donovan, Hélio Guimarães, Alexandra Hammond, and Bia Abramo, who carefully read the earlier versions of this article and gave me invaluable suggestions. I would particularly like to mention some remarks made by Bia, who told me about Sandra de Sá's version of "Vale Tudo" and gave me a great deal of the information I used in this article; among her invaluable comments, she pointed out—and she is probably right—that I might not have adequately stressed the relationship between the Brazilian artists I discuss and the international counterculture movement that emerged in the 1960s. Bia has also acutely pointed out the presence of other undecidable identities in Caetano's performances: between the popular singer and the intellectual; the *baiano* and the foreigner; the traditionalist and the avant-garde artist, and so on.

1. All translations are mine unless otherwise indicated.

2. I am referring to Fernando Pessoa's famous poem "Autopsicografia": "O poeta é um fingidor / Finge tão completamente / Que chega a fingir que é dor / A dor que deveras sente" (The poet is a faker / Who's so good at his act / He even fakes the pain / Of pain he feels in fact [translated by Richard Zenith]).

3. It is probable that men who play a female persona belong to medieval Galician-Portuguese lyrical tradition that goes back to the "Cantigas de Amigo." However, it only became widespread and commonly accepted in Brazilian popular music after the 1960s.

4. The *malandro* is, in fact, the impersonator par excellence. For a complete discussion on the *malandro* in Brazilian popular music and his role as frontier character, see Cláudia Matos's *Acertei no milhar: malandragem e samba no tempo de Getúlio*).

5. "Paraíba" is the name of a Brazilian state and for the people who are born there, but it has also become a slang term for lesbians.

6. Humor in itself does not make songs about homosexuality derogatory. However, the only good-humored Brazilian song about homosexuality I know is João Bosco and Aldir Blanco's "A Nível de . . ." (1982). I must add that I am quite aware that I am not doing justice to the complex role of homophobic and sexist songs in Brazilian culture. The reasons why they seem so appealing and, at the same time, funny and transgressive to Brazilian audiences cannot be developed here, and should be the theme of another article.

7. The case of Sandra de Sá may prove that in fact there is a somewhat clearly defined limit between the public display of sexuality in and outside someone's work. Whereas sexual ambivalences are acceptable in songs, they are not always tolerated in the artist's "real life." Recently, Sandra de Sá's record company, WEA, suggested that she, and all other artists who record under its label, stop giving interviews to the Brazilian gay magazine *Sui Generis*, after the latter published an interview in which Sandra de Sá states, without much fuss about it, that she would

like her audience to know that she is "a woman who loves women" (see *Folha de S. Paulo*, November 12, 1996).

8. Bacana in Portuguese generally means "fine," "tops," or "really good." The play on Chiquita Banana, oftentimes the symbol for Brazilians of U.S. interventionist politics in Latin America since World War II, is lost on a U.S. readership, who generally associate Chiquita Banana as a stereotype of Latin American women or a banana.

9. "Chiquita Bacana" was composed by João de Barros and Alberto Ribeiro, and recorded by Emilinha Borba in 1949. See Edigar Alencar's *O carnaval carioca através da música*. I am thankful to Camillo Penna, who gave me this reference. Caetano Veloso's song "A Filha da Chiquita Bacana" is in his album *Muitos Carnavais* (1977).

10. On several occasions, Caetano has created parodic impersonations of Carmen Miranda and expressed a rather ambivalent relationship with that Brazilian icon. In his *Circuladô ao vivo* (1992), he recorded "Disseram Que eu Voltei Americanizada," a landmark of her career (see, for example, the film *Bananas Is My Business*). Caetano also discussed this ambivalent relationship in an article published in the *New York Times* titled "Caricature and Conqueror, Pride and Shame," October 20, 1991.

11. This song by Chico Buarque and Ruy Guerra was recorded in *Caetano e Chico juntos e ao vivo* (1972). The word that reveals the lesbian relationship was censored and deleted from the original recording: "O meu destino é caminhar assim / Desesperada e nua / Sabendo que no fim da noite serei *(tua)*" (It is my fate to walk this way / desperate and naked / aware that tonight I will be yours [the Portuguese words *nua* and *tua* are in the feminine]). A more discerning reader could see the suggestion of homosexuality, or of a homosexual relationship between the two performers in various other moments of the concert/album. In "Ana de Amsterdam," Chico impersonates another female prostitute; in "Atrás da porta," he impersonates a submissive woman; in "Você não entende nada," Caetano sings the famously ambiguous lines "Eu como, eu como, eu como—você . . . não está entendendo nada do que eu digo" (I eat [*comer* in Brazilian Portuguese also means "to fuck"], I eat, I eat—you . . . you are not understanding anything I say). And Caetano further sings, in his "Esse cara" (this guy), the following suggestive lines: "Ele é quem quer / Ele é o homem / Eu sou apenas uma mulher" (He is the one who wants, he is the man, and I am just a woman).

12. Eric Nepomuceno, in the preface to *Chico Buarque—letra e música*, writes about Chico Buarque: "how can one explain this infinite capacity to reproduce, amplify, reconstruct other voices and other lives? How can one understand his way of using his voice to reveal other voices that have been concealed by silence?" (11). And further: "Francisco is a kind of honorary ambassador of the deepest and, at times, utterly lost causes. He has written, with rare brilliance, the record of collective time, of collective memory. He was and still is the reporter of his time, of his people. He has invented impossible lines for love and everyday life. Nobody will ever be able to talk about Francisco and leave aside words such as *generosity* and *solidarity*. Happy and unhappy love stories, dreams and nightmares, men who love women and women who love women, a transvestite who saves a whole city, they all parade throughout his verses and melodies" (15–16). However, it is important to stress that Chico Buarque's position as spokesperson par excellence today seems rather dated, and now re-

veals a problematic, colonizing characteristic. Such a paradox is, I believe, explicit in Chico's recent work. In his most recent album *Para todos* (1993) (For everybody), a number of images represent the faces of men and women of different races and social classes. In the opening song, he defines himself as the synthesis of the "Brazilian man," but at the same time as part of a patriarchal lineage that does not reveal its name, race, or social class ("O meu pai era paulista, meu avô, pernambucano, O meu bisavô mineiro, meu tataravô, baiano" [My father was from São Paulo, my grandfather from Pernambuco, my great-grandfather from Minas, my great-great-grandfather from Bahia]); on the other hand, he inscribes himself in a genealogy of Brazilian popular musicians (Tom Jobim, Dorival Caymmi, Noel Rosa, Cartola, Caetano Veloso, and others) in such a way that in the last line he can conclude: "Sou um artista brasileiro." However, both on the cover and in one of the last pages of Chico's album, one finds, among the faces of many other typical "Brazilians," the reproduction of an old photo of his for a police record and, among other data, his name: Francisco Buarque de Holanda; sex: male; color: white; and his father's name: Sérgio Buarque de Holanda (who is one of Brazil's most eminent intellectuals). In the last song ("A foto da capa"), Chico Buarque explains the picture. His position as the utmost representative of the Brazilian people seems to reveal a crisis, but, I believe, still lacks reflexivity. In fact, Chico Buarque may be inscribed in a lineage of Brazilian intellectuals who, from José de Alencar to Gilberto Freyre, appropriate subaltern subjectivities to construct an image of the Brazilian nation, but also to express their own elitist concerns. For an excellent discussion of this recurrent aspect in Brazilian literature, see Roberto Reis's works, particularly *The Pearl Necklace* (1992).

13. Indeed, Caetano frequently makes references or sends private "messages" to his personal friends or people he admires in his lyrics. See, for example, how he conflates the biographical and the literary in, among other songs, his "Gente" (in *Bicho*, 1977). Here, a line by the Russian poet Mayakovski ("Gente é pra brilhar" [People are supposed to shine] in Augusto de Campos's Portuguese translation), incites the enumeration of several proper names, among which a few (including his own) can be easily identified: "Narina Bethânia Dolores Renata Leilinha Suzana Dedé . . . Rodrigo Roberto Caetano Moreno Francisco Gilberto João . . . Maurício Lucilla Gildásio Ivonete Agripino Gracinha Zezé." Yet, his personal life is by no means dissociated from broader social concerns: "Gente é pra brilhar não pra morrer de fome" (People are supposed to shine, not die of hunger).

14. Judith Butler has further discussed the limitations of self-definition by means of identity categories throughout her influential works, particularly in her *Bodies That Matter*. In the last chapter of that book, for example, she writes: "As much as it is necessary to assert political demands through recourse to identity categories, and to lay claim to the power to name oneself and determine the conditions under which that name is used, it is also impossible to sustain that kind of mastery over the trajectory of those categories within discourse. This is not an argument *against* using identity categories, but it is a reminder of the risk that attends every such use. The expectation of self-determination that self-naming arouses is paradoxically contested by the historicity of the name itself: by the history of the usages that one never controlled, but that constrain the very usage that now emblematizes autonomy; by the future efforts to deploy the term against the grain of the current ones, and that will exceed the control of those who seek to set the course of the terms in

the present. If the term 'queer' is to be a site of collective contestation, the point of departure for a set of historical reflections and futural imaginings, it will have to remain that which is, in the present, never fully owned, but always and only redeployed, twisted, queered from a prior usage and in the direction of urgent and expanding political purposes" (1993a: 228).

15. The first part of this line, "olha que coisa mais," is a clear reference to Jobim's and Vinícius de Moraes's "Garota de Ipanema." In order to render the citation, I used Norman Gimbel's English translation, recorded in 1963 by Astrud Gilberto.

16. And Laclau adds: "If there is need for identification, it is because there is no identity, in the first place. But in that case, that with which I identify, it is not only its own particular content: it is also one of the names of my absent fullness, the reverse of my original lack" (56).

17. This work would not be complete if I did not at least mention the names of two Brazilian artists from the 1980s generation of Brazilian rock whose sexuality became visible and acquired political significance after they contracted AIDS. For Cazuza (1958–90), identity categories were neither a matter of personal decision nor a source of pleasure, as songs such as "Ideologia" suggest: "O meu prazer agora é risco de vida" (My pleasure is now life-threatening). In "O tempo não pára," he further demonstrates the force and the violence of the category: "te chamam de maluco, de bicha, maconheiro, transformam o país inteiro num puteiro" (They call you crazy, a fag, a pothead, and transform the whole country into a whorehouse). The other artist, Renato Russo, was the lead singer of the rock band Legião Urbana, and died on October 11, 1996. Renato Russo planned to adapt Adolfo Caminha's *Bom crioulo* for the opera. He contributed financially to the 1995 World Gay and Lesbian Conference in Rio, and his 1993 solo album, *The Stonewall Celebration Concert*, contains a list of addresses of Brazilian gay and lesbian associations.

Works Cited

Alencar, Edigar. 1965. *O carnaval carioca através da música.* Rio de Janeiro: Livraria Freitas Bastos.

Buarque, Chico. 1993. *Para todos.*

Butler, Judith. 1993a. *Bodies That Matter: On the Discursive Limits of "Sex."* New York and London: Routledge.

———. 1993b. "Imitation and Gender Insubordination." In *The Lesbian and Gay Studies Reader,* ed. Henry Abelove, Michèle Aina Barale, and David M. Halperin. New York and London: Routledge.

Derrida, Jacques. 1987. *The Post Card: From Socrates to Freud and Beyond.* Trans. Alan Bass. Chicago and London: University of Chicago Press.

Gil, Gilberto. 1996. *Todas as letras.* Ed. Carlos Rennó. São Paulo: Companhia das Letras.

Laclau, Ernesto. 1996. "Deconstruction, Pragmatism, Hegemony." In *Deconstruction and Pragmatism,* ed. Chantal Mouffe. London and New York: Routledge.

Matos, Cláudia. 1982. *Acertei no milhar: malandragem e samba no tempo de Getúlio.* Rio de Janeiro: Paz e Terra.

Matos, Maria Izilda S. de. 1996. *Lupicínio Rodrigues: o feminino, o masculino e suas relações.* São Paulo: Bertrand Brasil.

Nepomuceno, Eric. 1989. Preface. In Chico Buarque de Holanda, *Chico Buarque—letra e música*. São Paulo: Companhia das Letras.

Pessoa, Fernando. 1998a. *Fernando Pessoa & Co.* Trans. Richard Zenith. New York: Grove Press.

———. 1998b. *Ficções do interlúdio*. São Paulo: Companhia das Letras.

Reis, Roberto. 1992. *The Pearl Necklace*. Gainesville: University Press of Florida.

Russo, Renato. 1993. *The Stonewall Celebration Concert*.

Sanches, Pedro Alexandre. 1996. "Cauby Peixoto disputou título de maior 'cantora' do Brasil." *Folha de São Paulo*, July 1.

Secos e Molhados. 1973. *Secos e Molhados*.

Veloso, Caetano. 1973. *Aracá azul*. Polygram.

———. 1977. *Bicho*. Polygram.

———. 1977. *Muitos Carnavais*.

———. 1984. *Velô*. Polygram.

———. 1986. *O cinema falado*.

———. 1986. *Totalmente demais*. Polygram.

———. 1987. *Caetano*. Polygram.

———. 1989. *Estrangeiro*. Elektra Entertainment.

———. 1992. *Circuladô ao vivo*. Polygram.

———. 1993. *Tropicália 2*. Elektra Entertainment.

CHAPTER ELEVEN

Cross-dressing

Silviano Santiago's Fictional Performances

Susan Canty Quinlan

> There is something compelling about being both male and female,
> about having an entry into both worlds. Contrary to some
> psychiatric tenets, half and halves are not suffering from a confusion
> of sexual identity, or even from a confusion of gender. What we are
> suffering from is an absolute duality that says we are able to be only
> one or the other. It claims that human nature is limited and cannot
> evolve into something better. But I, like other queer people, am two
> in body, both male and female. I am the embodiment of the hieros
> gamos: the coming together of opposite qualities within.
> —Gloria Anzaldúa 1987: 19

> In truth, neither sex is really mine. . . . I belong to a third sex, a sex
> apart, which as yet has no name.
> —Théophile Gautier 8:29–30

The Placement of Terms

The genesis of this essay rests in understanding the cultural context of
how Brazilian literature might elaborate configurations of sexuality, gender, and sex. The issue of postmodern discussions of otherness (often
marked by discourses of transvestism or *fantasia*)[1] is one that occupies
a central locus in Silviano Santiago's critical and fictional work, whether
in physical, political, or psychological materializations. Inherent in this
discussion of transvestism are the particular ways used to construct the
self and the other, usually in terms of political and national identity
formation and the performance of these configurations within a more

global arena. The novel *Stella Manhattan* and the short story "You Don't Know What Love Is/Muezzin; Você não sabe o que é o amor/Almuaden" serve as examples of this quest, resting as they do on the effects of events that create a sustained tension between reality and fiction.[2]

Silviano Santiago was born in 1936 in the Brazilian state of Minas Gerais but spent much of his adult life in Rio de Janeiro, Paris, and the United States. He has authored five novels, five critical works, several volumes of poetry, and, in 1997, a book of short stories, *Keith Jarrett at the Blue Note*.[3] He has won several literary prizes including the prestigious Jabuti for the best Brazilian novel in 1982, *Em liberdade*. Santiago's literary work received critical attention and praise in France and Germany and, more recently in the United States, with the 1994 publication in English of *Stella Manhattan* (1985)[4] and the translation *The Space in-Between* (2002). Santiago's themes almost invariably include common elements: a multilingual format with English, Spanish, and French juxtaposed with Portuguese, authorial interference within the text, and various types of same-sex relationships, either romantic or intellectual, but rarely sexual. Many times, the relationships within the tales are either overtly or covertly described in political terms: women as other or marginalized as in *Stella Manhattan*, historically homosexual men viewed as cultural icons (Proust, Artaud), the responsibilities of the author and the reader in rendering a work legible, and strong analogies between politics, political histories, and the changing shape of the world.

Although the role of the homosexual in exile and the author-reader relationship in Santiago's fiction have been studied (Lopes; Foster), transvestites and women (often interchangeable) are mentioned only in passing, if at all. However, transvestites in cultural mutations or literary guises signal what Marjorie Garber calls a "category crisis . . . a failure of definitional distinctions, a borderline that becomes permeable, that permits of border crossings from one category (apparently distinct) to another" (16). As feminist scholarship has shown in studies of women writers, transvestites may also be bridges linking discourses of high and popular culture. Santiago, like many Brazilian writers of the 1970s and 1980s, creates a literature that parodies not only himself as author-narrator, but also Brazilian intellectualism and its reverence for Euro-American culture.

In Santiago's fiction, transvestites and women are stereotypically drawn out and shrouded, if not in mystery, then in mysterious circumstances.

As characters, most are, on the one hand, strongly self-aware, and, on the other, suffering a fatal flaw that denies them any real autonomy. These characters appear unexpectedly in the texts in positions of non-specificity, not only as markers of ambiguous sexuality, but as indicators of cultures in decline. Their presence serves to destabilize comfortable notions of binarism showing that "tranvestism is a space of possibility structuring and confounding culture: the disruptive element that intervenes, not just a category crisis of male and female, but a crisis of category itself" (Garber 7).

Transvestism is one of Santiago's alternatives used to describe Brazilian notions of sexuality and culture. Nevertheless, as the term is used in this essay, it includes and signifies more than cross-dressing; it symbolizes what Garber calls the "'third,' a mode of articulation, a way of describing a space of possibility. Three puts in question the idea of one: of identity, self-sufficiency, self-knowledge" (11). In a specifically Brazilian context, the performers or the transvestites themselves are "concentrations of general ideas, representations of and practices of male and female . . . that elaborate the particular configurations of sexuality, gender, and sex that undergird and give meaning to Brazilian notions of 'man' and 'woman'" (Kulick 9). In essence, Brazilian transvestism cannibalizes binary definitions of sex and sexuality, in much the same way that Modernist poet Oswald de Andrade advocated Brazilians cannibalizing other cultures and literature (Kulick).[5]

As Judith Butler, Garber, and Kulick, among others, see it, transvestism is a way of thinking about gender identities and their realities by challenging more than the distinction between sex and gender and, at least implicitly, the distinction between appearance and reality that informs much popular thought about gender identity. As Butler notes:

> If the "reality" of gender is constituted by the performance itself, then there is no recourse to an essential and unrealized "sex" or "gender" which gender performances generally express. Gender is as fully real as anyone whose performance complies with social expectations. (527)

Heterosexuality, homosexuality, and transvestism challenge performative acts as reenactments of social experiences, either to publicly maintain gender within its binary frame or to publicly contradict this essentializing notion (Butler). But transvestism in particular looks at how the body serves as text to publicly define disenfranchisement from the patriarchal, national community and how this textual body "produces within the space of the nation a radical instability that is held in check only by intense degrees of coercion, much of it exercised directly at the level of the body" (Pratt 93).

The construction of selves and identities based on cultural topoi, including literary representations through characters, stories, or themes, considers how knowledge can be socially manufactured in such ways as to avoid circular thought (Garber; Butler). Brazilian society defined itself as hybrid, long before the term had any political or postmodern cachet.

Santiago himself reverts to the images of cannibalism *(antropofagia)* to describe this hybridity, which is in complete conflict with notions of cultural, racial, ethnic, or sexual purity ("O entre-lugar do discurso latinoamericano," in *Uma literatura nos trópicos* [1978]). Santiago's definition of hybridity corresponds to Garber's creation of the "third" as, perhaps, the essence of constructing identities.[6] These constructs read the processes of differentiation; they do not merely look for differences. "Knowledge is unknowable, irreducible difference because difference is not a thing to be recognized, but a process always underway that allows us to favor looking at how truths are produced in order to continually question powerful concepts" (Spivak 128). In simpler terms, the disruptive performance of the transvestite results in a construct that questions anything and everything that had previously been considered known, or given. But, as a word of caution, one cannot just build for differences because one cannot take anything, especially the personal, for granted. In other words, what is important is to view the differences in light of their connection to Brazilian identities and culture infused with its own history, even if the same might be said of other Latin American subjects. Thus, Brazilian culture and Brazilian literature become, in Silviano Santiago's own words,

> a descoberta de que o tecido social é feito de diferenças apaixonadas e
> que a negação das diferenças (com vistas a um projeto único para todos)
> é também o massacre da liberdade individual. (1989: 35)
>
> [the discovery that the social cloth is made out of passionate differences
> and that the negation of these differences (with visions of a single
> project for everyone) is also the massacre of individual liberty.][7]

In one sense, then, this same notion of the "third" shapes and becomes part of the form in Santiago's narratives as he cannibalizes not only his own culture, but others as well, in his process of constructing identities.

It can be argued that there are two sites that separate Brazil from the rest of Spanish-speaking America in terms of literary and cultural production. One, of course, is the mechanism of cannibalization discussed earlier; the second is a sustained position of literary tradition focused on the discovery of Brazil and *brasilidade*. What contributes to the uniqueness of this phenomenon is that in almost every century and/or literary movement, there has been at least one major literary figure who reflects upon an emerging, hybrid Brazilian identity that is a result of the confluence of the European, indigenous, and/or African cultures that are the basis of Brazil's literature.[8] Santiago is merely continuing this process in a more contemporary fashion that happens to have a name, globalization. But Brazil was caught in a global web long before the 1990s. The Portuguese seafarers in the sixteenth century had long since begun a process of miscegenation and transculturation on a worldwide scale, which is crucial for understanding Brazil.

Contextualization

Santiago's fictional work is filled with disruptive notions of history and political processes that form part of conscious choices to mark a plurality of visions. His narrative fiction depends on specific events regarding the status of contemporary Brazilian writing, coupled with critical theories and cultural interpretations that investigate the forms of figurative and linguistic exile or linguistic order, subjects that are often masked, but that are paramount to any study of identity politics that tries to read for differences. Santiago defines his quest as his *entre-lugar* (space in between), a "third" space as he theorizes in the essay "O entre-lugar no discurso latino-americano," a place that challenges static notions of sexuality, gender, and politics and that is at the center of much of his fictional work. It is a place that speaks to the infinite ability to change and to know the other and, through the process of change, to manipulate the power structure that effects the politics of who we are in relation to ourselves and others.

Much of Santiago's fiction that does not revert to a historical past rooted in the 1920s or earlier focuses on the 1960s and 1970s, an era of strong movements for gender identity and gender and sexual freedom.[9] The characters who experience these decades are portrayed as young men or women working to subvert political or gender systems. It has often been noted that the 1960s were an era of liberal hedonism and the 1980s a period of postmodern nihilism. But what if the 1960s were truly a period of social change, at least more change than some are willing to admit, and the 1980s and 1990s were periods that tiredly tried to ignore changes for the better when faced with universal plagues such as ethnic wars, AIDS, and tuberculosis, as well as the repetition of fin-de-siècle depression, coupled by the change of the millennium and all the discordant notes such consequential change implies? What do writers do when they look back and question whether or not the fruits of their life and labor hold any significant meaning? What does it mean to grow older and reflect on the new and the old as both critic and novelist? These questions permeate Santiago's fictional works.

What contributes to the Brazilianness of Santiago's work and seems to be less understood by non-Brazilian audiences, in particular, is the direct relationship between the Brazilian stories of the other and the "otherness" or exile (either physical or emotional) of Brazilian intellectuals during the two decades of the military dictatorship (1964–85), brought about in no small part by U.S. interventionist politics.[10]

The hegemonic misreadings of third-world texts by North American and European critics have had, and continue to have, multilevel repercussions in terms of popular misconceptions by the centers of peripheral cultures and the geopolitical consequences inherent in the relationship between centers and peripheries. From Jean de Léry's impossibly unreal "noble savage" who so influenced Montaigne and helped create the vision of Pindorama or the tropical paradise of Brazil, to Clarice Lispector, who wondered in print how her writing might be received if she had written in English *(Descoberta do mundo);* we see not only the lack of worldwide visibility, but also the lack of prestige associated with that lack of visibility, where language has been a repeated problematic in Portuguese-speaking cultures. Silviano Santiago's use of the space of the "third" (the Brazilian outsider in the United States or France, and, more specifically, the Brazilian homosexual) both enforces and argues against the lack of prestige and visibility; for the protagonists seem to be neither for nor against nationalist ideals, neither for nor against personal responsibilities, neither for nor against linguistic unity. This becomes an active assumption and undermining of hybridity as an essentializing cultural category, a paradoxically dynamic strategy to interact with the rest of the world as an equal.

In addressing transvestism and its relationship to literature and writing, Cuban writer and critic Severo Sarduy indicates that the description portraying the double self, the negation of essentialist notions of only two sexes, and the desire to perform the changes confirm "the very fact of transvestism itself... the co-existence of masculine and feminine signifiers in a single body, the tension, the repulsion, the antagonism created between them" is the basis of writing itself (37). The question becomes one of assuming identities that do and do not belong to oneself and then transcribing those identities to order to be understood or to understand. The author's task becomes one of translating differences, as Sarduy remarks:

> Those places of intersexuality are analogous to the planes of intertextuality that make up the literary object. They are planes conversing in the same exterior, answering and completing, exalting and defining each other: that interaction of linguistic textures, of discourses, that dance, that parody, is writing. (Ibid.)

The act of comingling intertextuality and intersexuality both reflects and redefines the dilemma of defining a Brazilian culture.

Both *Stella Manhattan* and "You Don't Know What Love Is" use innovative, if not always likable, juxtapositions of identity construction in the creation of their protagonists, and both use women as foils or as transvestites to explain the motivations of the homosexual protagonists. These narratives play with the ambiguous nature conferred on the words *male* and *female* in Brazilian cultural discourse and they also demonstrate, to a greater or lesser degree, the performances of sexual, or gender-marked, identities. Santiago reflects otherness and "category crises" within the boundaries of Brazilian cultural reality.

Similarities and Differences

Both texts develop assertions of Brazilian expressions of identity that reject channeling desire and definitions of self in noncontested binary oppositions (homosexual/heterosexual, female/male, bad/good). The relationship of story to history is bound up in both texts, or, in the words of the late critic Francisco Caetano Lopes Jr:

o trabalho poético-crítico-acadêmico de Silviano Santiago tem no seu
bojo, uma reflexão profunda e sistemática a respeito das inter-relações
operadas entre a História . . . e a literatura (estória, . . .). (1991: 56)

[the poetic-critical-academic work of Silviano Santiago has, in the end, a
systematic and profound reflection regarding the operative
interrelations between History . . . and literature (story . . .).]

Santiago's performative representations of transvestites, women described
from a "third" point of view, the author/narrator figure who determines
the more formal and literary aspects linking each text, as well as the
multinational situations of place and linguistic pluralities, help to define
and shape a Brazilian postmodern condition. It is unmistakably true
that current critical models of gender theory, based almost exclusively
on northern European or North American frames of reference, form or
inform Brazilian models.

Both of Santiago's narratives play with the gendering of the words
male and *female* in Brazilian cultural discourse and, of course, play on
the very nature of Portuguese as a gendered language. Both texts incorporate a homosexual male as the central character. Both men are *cario-
cas* who not only live outside of Rio de Janeiro, but in the northeastern
United States (New York and New Haven). Self-reflective narrators who
interrupt the sequential flow of the story to reflect upon the nature of
the process they are transcribing appear in both texts. In fact, in the
short story, the central character is the narrator. Both comment on political situations in Brazil and in the United States, reflecting a third-world
view of the first world. Linguistically, the narratives, written in Portuguese, incorporate a kaleidoscopic mixture of Spanish and English.
Visually, both rely heavily on collages of cinematographic images and
modern art. Transvestites are featured in both texts; Stella herself begins
her story in the novel while a verbal Judy Garland impersonator appears
in "You Don't Know What Love Is."

Santiago employs many forms of popular U.S. culture within each
text: sixties' music, video games, television programs, current events.
Both narratives contrast the cold, inhospitable, and dark urbane landscapes of the northeastern United States with the vibrant and exciting
colors of the Brazilian tropics. If all the characters and images are stereotypes of stereotypes, it is because they are the only way to open up the
cardboard nature of preconceptions.

Differences between the texts, of course, abound, there are two essential ones: first, the short story whittles down the context of the novel to its bare minimum and compensates for what can be called the excesses of *Stella Manhattan* that cause too much estrangement for a reader not intimately connected with Brazil's recent political past; second, the novel creates a strong female character that disappears in the short story. Both stories concern multi-exiled outsiders trying to survive in a world that so far has shown little interest in them. They fit into no preexisting constructions and must create their own identities, however complex or difficult it may be.

Latinos in the United States

Stella Manhattan is a novel that combines suspense, politics, and sex where explicitly transvestite characters such as Eduardo/Stella/'Bastiana and Paco/Lacucaracha interact with the more circumspectly transvestite character of Leila. The action takes place in a space that not only mirrors cosmopolitan Rio de Janeiro and New York, but also permits narrative concerns with identity, exile, and Santiago's own formal experimentation that take place in multileveled contexts. The place of an imagined "United States" in the space of Brazil is a dangerously unknown territory. As one reviewer has noted:[11]

> [I]nstala a ação em Nova York para poder com mais clareza mostrar, tantos os processos libertários da recente historia brasileira, como a americanização que nosso país passava ... [e] ilumina o psiquismo homossexual, também ele à espera de libertação, também ele reprimido pela sociedade vigente. (*Stella Manhattan*, front inside cover)

> [The action takes place in New York in order to be able to show more clearly as much the libertarian tendencies of recent Brazilian history as the Americanization that Brazil underwent ... [and] to illuminate the homosexual psyches waiting for liberation, also repressed by society.]

Just as *Stella Manhattan* is the story of political ennui versus political action, it is also Silviano Santiago's attempt to describe the relationship between history and story in a formal context in a fashion reminiscent of Georges Bataille. For the novel's writer-as-character, however, art will apparently elude this contextualization:

> [A arte] não é nem pode ser norma, é energia desperdiçada mesmo, é alguma coisa, uma ação por exemplo—não importa agora a questão da

qualidade—que a energia humana produz num rompante e que
transborda num vômito pelo mundo de trabalho, pelo universo do útil,
com a audácia e inépcia de alguém que, ao despejar leite numa xícara
para se alimentar pela manhã, deixa que a maior parte do líquido se
desperdice pela mesa. (70)¹²

[(Art) is not and cannot be a norm, it is wasted energy. It can be anything,
for example, an action—here quality has no bearing—that comes into
existence with an outburst of human energy; it is then vomited throughout the world of work, the universe of utility, with the audacity and
ineptness of someone who, on pouring milk into a cup for breakfast, lets
the greater part of the liquid go to waste on the table.] (50)

The novel is divided into three parts and the action is contained within
the space of one weekend in New York City. Narrated time weaves contrasting and confusing webs that disrupt all binary concepts such as
Rio/New York, freedom/subjugation, rightist/leftist politics, heterosexu-
ality/homosexuality, and submission/domination.

Opening with Stella Manhattan herself, there is little in the original
Portuguese to indicate that s/he is a transvestite until the very end of
the chapter. The reader's first introduction to Stella/Eduardo mirrors
the ambiguity and dilemma that will be discussed later in the narrator/
author role. Francisco Caetano Lopes had observed that

Primeiro... começa com a despertar de Stella. Nesta, o leitor ainda não
sabe de quem se trata o personagem: Um homem? Uma mulher'? Um
travesti? [A segunda parte] dá os esclarecimentos devidos ao leitor e
começa a informar-lhe do tom do mistério que estará presente em toda a
narrativa. Desde o início, há a dúvida quanto à sua sexualidade, dúvida
essa que se estenderá na sua estruturação (até mesmo no que diz ao
respeito ao seu futuro desaparecimento). (74 n. 10)

[First... the story begins with Stella's waking up. In this (part) the
reader does not know anything about the main character: A man? A
woman? A transvestite? (The second part) clears up things for the reader
and begins to introduce the mysterious tone that will be present throughout the narrative. From the beginning, there is doubt about Stella's
sexuality, the same doubt that will extend to the entire construction of
sexuality (and what it says about his future disappearance).]

However, Stella is described in flamboyant, if not schizophrenic, detail, such as "como vedete na apoteose final de revista da Tiradentes"
(12) (like a vedette... in a burlesque review at Tiradentes Theater [4])
or "'divina lá vou eu', grita como se já montada numa vassoura de

bruxa, voando mary-poppins por sobre os edifícios" (13) ("here I come divinely," she cries as if mounted on a broom, flying Mary Poppins–like across the sky [4]). The reader can almost presume her female identity to be so exaggerated that she must have assumed the "third" state, transvestism. However, the power of the written image is felt full force when, at the end of the chapter, Stella performs the act of cross-dressing, without actually changing clothes. Santiago has successfully destabilized all of the textual information:

> Faz de conta que amarra um lencinho colorido de Azuma na cabeça para proteger os cabelos da poeira, fazendo turbante com coque atrás; fez de conta que veste vestidinho de chita leve e sem mangas e, for sure, sem cinto, que as carninhas ainda estão duras, duras! E pinça as nádegas de um lado e do outro para comprovar, fingindo que não precebe as gordurinhas do inverno nas ancas. . . . *Sou di-vi-na ou não sou?* (15; emphasis in the original)

> [She pretends to wind a colored scarf from Azuma's around her head to protect her from the dust, creating a turban, tucking the ends in the back to protect her from the dust; she imagines stepping into a short, lightweight and sleeveless calico dress and, without a belt for sure, as her flesh is still firm! She pinches both buttocks as proof, pretending she doesn't see the winter love handles on her hips. . . . *I am deee-vine, aren't I?*] (6)[13]

Just as there are flashes of Stella's metamorphosis within the opening chapter, there are also flashes of events to happen. The traditional, if not joyously happy, carnival song about a woman gardener whose camellias have just died in her garden is juxtaposed with the ironic incantation that closes the chapter: "No love, just fuck/No love/just money./No fuck, just love./No money, just, love" (16).

When we finally meet Eduardo (and his two female alter egos),[14] an effeminate male without any political conviction whatsoever, forced to leave Brazil after his parents discover his homosexuality, we also meet Paco. His friend and mentor, Paco, is an anti-Castro Cuban right-winger whose own homosexuality is as problematic to the right as it is to the left:

> E Paco não podia nem de longe imaginar que Eduardo o dava como exemplo perfeito de bicha assumida. Já se comporta como alguém que não é homem nem mulher. Paco tem estilo. Um estilo que não chega a ser individual, só dele, mas um estilo que recobre, que é resumo e síntese dos gestos e comportamentos tão inventivos de classe. (211)

[It never occurred to Paco that Eduardo held him up as an exemplary faggot, a maricón with a true sense of self. Paco's life was no longer that of a man or a woman. He had style. Not an individual style ... but a style that recuperates and sums up and synthesizes all the inventive gestures and behaviors of an entire class of people.] (158)

What ties these two characters together is their ambivalent, almost innocent, stance regarding the effects of politics and revolution on their lives and their naïveté in the face of their own homosexuality and society's reaction to it. They lack a coherent center as they desperately search for identities and a place to belong. Their emotional immaturity and failure to think things through reflect not only on themselves, but also on the stance taken by many Brazilian and Cuban citizens vis-à-vis dictatorial governments. The state had served as mother, the provider of all things, until they transgressed, and now they are no longer cared for. For Eduardo, moving to a foreign country, with a different language and cultural codes, compels him to depend on Paco as a mother figure even if he considers him stupid: "Lacucaracha parecia um romancista ou pelo menos, ele pensa que seja um romancista ... persegue-se um personagem. É burra ela ... encontrando um sistema que a vai definindo como uma luva. ... Sente tal entusiasmo e tal carinho pelo outro" (214) (La Cucaracha is like a novelist, or in any case she thought she was a novelist, searching for herself ... like a novelist in search of a character. She's stupid. ... She has found a system that fits her like a glove. ... She has such enthusiasm and love for the other [160]).

Ironically, it is New York society that casts them as one, collapsing Brazilian and Cuban identities into one, "Latino." The construct Latino is used because Eduardo and Paco both possess African features, speak with accents, and have trouble communicating in English. Ironically, the communication difficulties are not only with English speakers, but also with each other. Both Eduardo's Portuguese and Paco's Spanish are misinterpreted and misunderstood so that their common language becomes a "third," English, which is then a complete inversion of Latino.

Relishing, fearing, and hating his mother role all at the same time, Paco realizes that there is responsibility, worry, and pleasure in mothering:

Temeroso e feliz, tal um rei mago que vislumbra no céu a estrela que conduz ao salvador, se aproximou delicadamente de Eduardo e lhe tocou os ombros com as duas mãos, girou lentamente o tronco do corpo sentado e sem esforço, deitou a cabeça de Eduardo no seu colo, passando-lhe os dedos pelos cabelos como fazia a sua mãe com ele nas tardes quentes e ensolarados de Havana. La cucaracha sabia certamente que acaba de receber um fardo pesado, muito pesado—os últimos meses de rejeição, sofrimento e solidão de Eduardo—e o seu colo, como uma almofada fofa resguardava o fardo de maiores dores no seu encontro com o mundo.

Nisso a barriga de Eduardo ronronou de fome dando o sinal de alarme e ambos se abraçaram e, como se combinados, soltaram uma desopilante gargalhada, misturando português e espanhol no único desejo de sair para jantar.

"Tu no puedes imaginar, chico me siento feliz, feliz como uma lombriz." (36–37)

[Fearful, yet happy, like the magus who beholds the star that will lead him to the savior, Paco carefully drew near, placing his hands on Eduardo's shoulders and gently turning his body towards him and, effortlessly laid Eduardo's head in his lap,[15] stroking his hair like his mother used to do on hot and sunny Havana afternoons. La cucaracha knew for certain that he had just taken on a heavy burden, a very heavy burden—Eduardo's last months of rejection, suffering and loneliness—and his lap, like a soft pillow, cushioned the burden of greater sorrows along the way.[16]

With this, Eduardo's belly roared with hunger, sounding an alarm and the two fell into each other's arms and as if they had planned it, let out a cheerful belly laugh, mixing up Portuguese and Spanish in their singular[17] desire to go out to eat.

"Tu no puedes imaginar, chico, me siento feliz, feliz like a clam." (You can't imagine, chico, I'm happy, happy...).] (23–24)

This is an uncomfortable role for Paco, a role that implies involvement in another's life, yet it echoes his desire to create a "universal sorority" devoted to the fostering of international sisterhood (215).

The Author and the Text

In the second part of "Primeiro" there is an interlude that includes the performance of an author/narrator and his *leitor/cúmplice* (reader/accomplice) as they construct stories and histories surrounding the creation of this novel:

(Estou de pé detrás da cadeira em que você está sentado escrevendo, e leio no bloco—por seus ombros—essas anotações sobre leite derramado e músicos no metrô que você está jogando no papel em dezembro de 1982, época em que você acredita que já está pronto para um novo romance).

Você se vira para mim e me diz que me despreza agora.

Levo um susto, pois até então tínhamos sido bons amigos—lembra-se do último romance?—unha e carne como se diz? (72)

Você volta ao escritório e recomeça a escrever pedindo a minha ajuda, a minha ajuda na elaboração do romance, pede help. (73)

[(I'm standing behind the chair on which you are seated.[18] As you write, I stoop over your shoulder and read about the spilled milk and the musicians on the metro. It's December, 1982 and you feel that you're ready for a new novel.)

You turn toward me and tell me that you despise me now.

I'm taken aback, until today I was under the impression that we were hand-in-glove, the best of friends—don't you remember the last novel?—tooth and nail as they say. (51)

You return to your desk and continue writing, asking for my help, my help in elaborating the story, you ask for 'ajuda.'] (51)

The author, in fact, does seek advice from the disembodied other as s/he begins to comment on the act of writing itself, vacillating between truth and reality, between fact and fiction. S/he questions whether or not to include a personal anecdote that would anchor the author/narrator in the late 1960s and early 1970s (a sexual experience with a man named David listening to Bob Dylan's early music) and then agrees to the other's suggestion to exclude it entirely, only to put the entire incident back in the novel in the second part titled "Começo: o narrador."

Vira-se para mim e diz que na verdade sou eu quem tem razão e que você realmente não gosta de narrativas autobiográficas. Ficção é fingimento blablabla, o poeta quem diria? é um fingidor. El poeta qua-quaquaqua-quá es un jodedor, eso si. A fucker. A motherfucker. Fode tão-somente pelo prazer de se escrever. Pois isto é tão fodido. The novelist is a fucker who fucks only to be fucked. El novelista es un jodedor que fode só pelo prazer de escrever. (74)

[You turn to me and say that in truth I am right and that you really don't like autobiographical narratives. Fiction is all bla-bla-bla fakery; and what about the poet who said he is a faker?[19] The poet is a quack. Quackery is his trade, quack quack, the poet is a faker, the fucker, that's right, a jodedor. A motherfucker. A fode-jode-fucker, he fucks just for the pleasure of writing. That's why he's so fucked up. The novelist is a fucker who fucks. *El novelista es un jodedor que fode só pelo prazer de escrever.*[20] He fucks only for the pleasure of writing.] (52)

Fiction as fakery, transvestites as fakirs are all signs that point to the postmodern dilemma of relativity, or simply autobiographic and nonautobiographic literature's inability to discern fact from fiction, or, as Sarduy calls it, the meeting of the analogous planes of intersexuality and intertextuality that is writing. The multilayered construction of this section underscores the importance of the transvestite. The literary allusion that forms the basis of the parody is to "Autopsicografia" a poem by the Portuguese poet Fernando Pessoa. Pessoa's own gender/sexual ambiguity,[21] as well as the self-questioning about the act of writing that occurs in the very poem, reflect the author-disguised-as-narrator's dilemma. Also put into play is the colonizer-colonized relationship. Visually this is illustrated by the inability to sustain one language within this paragraph, indicating a category crisis that calls into question textuality/sexuality and the validity of the author-as-chronicler of history, for what s/he constructs must always be story.

Paco's realization of the responsibility of motherhood, the author/narrator's questioning of the veracity of literature, and Stella's ambiguous identity set the stage for constructing the identities of the "third" way of knowing.

The "Other" Transvestite

The third transvestite in this novel is Leila, not only because she is written as if she were male, but also because she represents another, more serious "category crisis," not only disappearing from the text, but also from culture, thus leaving ambiguous gender borders more intriguing, but less knowable. As Garber notes, "The cross-dresser plays a crucial narrative role as that which is mistaken, misread, overlooked—or looked *through*" (187; emphasis in the original). However, unlike most detective fiction where crimes are solved, neither Leila nor Stella is found out and they remain forever looked through.

Leila is a pseudo-predator who is a continually unknown but desirable other, sometimes portrayed sympathetically, sometimes with savagery. She is a victim not only of Brazil's revolutionary politics of the 1960s, but also the frightening side of imagined feminine identity. "Leila não é apenas uma mulher, é um potro selvagem indômito e domado que nasceu no sertão de Minas e foi educado pelas freiras no internato do Colégio Santa Maria, na Floresta" (147) (Leila is not only a woman[22] but a wild mare. Untamable yet tame. She was born in the backlands of Minas and went to boarding school with the nuns at the Colégio Santa Maria, in Floresta [108]).

Leila is coerced into prostituting herself on the street in front of her apartment so that her sexually dysfunctional husband can watch. In order to do so, she must first use a disguise not only for her husband, but also for herself. "Alimentado pelos desencontros e as frustrações, vai renascendo debaixo da pele de Leila *um felino* que, agora sob o signo das águas, se recolhe enquanto aguarda o momento de metamorfose completa" (190; emphasis added) (Stimulated by frustration, Leila feels the feline being reborn, swelling beneath her skin. Contact with water makes her recoil, waiting for the moment of its total metamorphosis) (142).[23] As Leila metamorphoses into the cat, she is quite aware of being objectified through her disguise, by her husband and whoever else she meets. She knows that she is

> [a]quela outra, uma imagem criada para ela sob medida por Aníbal, e que ela recria para ele quando recebe o sinal. Leila é imagem ambulante perambulante que se fixa na superfície do espelho, amiga e desconhecida dela própria—quem você quer ser e não consegue ser. (194)

> [the other woman, the incarnation of the image that Aníbal created for her and which she recreates for him whenever he gives the signal. Leila is a fluid image fastened to the surface of the mirror, she is familiar and yet strange—whom you would like to be and who you never quite become.][24] (144)

Both Leila and Stella are exiled in similar ways and their histories are recounted in richly similar ways. Both characters are misshapen by hegemonic societal attitudes toward sexuality that reduce them to an animal-like status. Leila's subjugation of her own desires and the subsequent cruelty this inspires correlate perfectly with Stella's. It is interesting to speculate on why the only sexual scenes in the novel revolve around Leila. The scenes are brutal, not romantic. Stella's desires are romantic, but her words can be cruel. In order to reconstruct themselves, both characters disappear. Eduardo's disappearance holds some political connotations and his death (or lack thereof) signals his ambiguous nature. Leila's disappearance is no less significant. She is merely written off the page after an encounter with an American male, who surely resembles Rickie, the prostitute of Stella's dreams.

Santiago manages to describe the space in between but leaves us no literal meaning. As Garber notes:

Cross-dressing is about gender confusion . . . about the phallus as consti-
tutively veiled . . . about the power of women . . . about the emergence of
gay identity . . . about the anxiety of economic or cultural dislocation or
recognition of "otherness" as loss. . . . But the compelling force of transvestism in literature and culture comes not, or not only from these
effects, but also from its instatement of metaphor itself, not as that for
which a literal meaning must be found, but precisely as that without
which there would be no such thing as meaning in the first place. (390)

You Don't Know What Love Is/Muezzin

As in any good detective story, "You Don't Know What Love Is" revolves
around a mysterious telephone call from a woman looking for her missing boyfriend and the protagonist's retelling of a surreal dream. The
story opens with a citation from the mystery movie *Sorry, Wrong Number*.[25] "In the tangled network of a great city, the telephone is . . . the
confidante of our inmost secrets" (Santiago 1997: 89) and it is translated into Portuguese as a footnote. The telephone masks or disguises
the user. Coupling the citation with the English version of the story's
title preceding the Portuguese title, the entire title page reads as a parody of today's hegemonic language; Portuguese cross-dresses with English. Santiago's ironic title page sets the tone for the entire story. It is
also noteworthy that Santiago paraphrases the movie plot and reverses
the protagonists. Instead of a woman overhearing telephone conversations of people plotting her murder, our protagonist hears conversations
from someone telling about the supposed murder of someone else.

The narrative voice addresses the protagonist, a Brazilian living in the
United States, as "you," as if he were directing a play. Carlos, the character, begins to question reality on various levels as he is both perturbed
and intrigued by a recurring dream that opens and closes the text, and
by a series of telephone calls from a unknown woman. The story constructs space in a historical present, marked by specificity just as in *Stella
Manhattan*, but it is now thirty years later: the renovation of Ipanema
in 1995 and 1996 is juxtaposed with an ABC news program that speaks
about the Whitewater scandal, the capture of Theodore Kaczyinski, and
Bosnia. Although folk music, cowboys, and political history are extremely
important elements in *Stella Manhattan*, the short story relies heavily
on visual imagery, from a Rauschenberg painting of the Empire State
Building colliding with the Eiffel Tower, to minute descriptions of food
preparation. For Santiago, the juxtaposition of high and low culture

and his ironic use of language are metaphors for category crises of identity formation at both a personal and a cultural level. In remembering his dream, Carlos reflects on these juxtapositions:

> Você pensa deitado à espera dos sons, que a imagem desdobrada de Rauschenberg é a soma do sonho americano da Europa no presente com o sonho europeu da América no passado. Você devaneia, imaginando o encontro desencontrado da utilidade do ferro norteamericano, empilhando milhões de caixotes-escritórios de que o homem neocolonial necessita no século vinte para tocar os negócios da nação e do mundo, com a graciosidade gratuita do velho colonialismo européu. (93)[26]

> [You think, lying down and waiting for sleep to come again, that Rauschenberg's unfolded image is the sum of the American dream of Europe in the present and the European dream of America in the past. You daydream imagining the desultory meeting of the North American iron contraption, stacking up millions of office cubicles that the twentieth-century, neo-colonial man needs in order to conduct the business of the nation and of the world with the gratuitous graciousness of old European colonialism.] (227–28)

Overt transvestism is fleeting and momentary in the story: a male voice on the telephone mimicking Judy Garland, a gay man in uniform, a bisexual male disguised as straight. If *Stella Manhattan* relies on reading through transvestites (Stella, La cucaracha, and Leila) to explain culture, the story relies more heavily on seeing through culture to explain transvestism. The reader is not privileged to know whether Carlos is a transvestite or not, or whether he is a victim, which makes the storytelling more chilling.

Language switches are only reported and not written into the text unless they are proper names in either French or English. Again, the superimposition of the ideology of power and culture: the romantic wanderings along the Seine: the narrator's reveling in the latticework surrounding the old Paris buildings, or bemoaning cold, bureaucratic efficiency of institutions in the United States that are mirrored by the unending snowstorms; and his comments on the ruination of historical locations in Ipanema (France and the United States on top, Brazil on the bottom, with France winning out as in the Rauchenberg painting) are more important than the actual political events as witnessed in *Stella Manhattan*. In the story, the pecking order of nationalities is important to describe the masking and the unmasking of "the third." The importance of this order is played out in the game imagery of the story. The first game includes the imaginary naval battles to determine the superiority of France and the United States over Brazil, as if the winner would receive spoils of war; the inverted pyramid of French, American, Spanish, and Brazilian cultures; gay Brazilians losing lovers; Ipanema battling itself and losing its identity; cold North American cities losing track of people. In all of these cases, the most disempowered is Brazil, either as a culture or disguised as a homosexual male. Carlos, himself, is on the very bottom as a Brazilian homosexual male who faces losing his childhood vision of Ipanema. The second game is that of the telephone call from the mysterious woman and her search for her lost lover, whom she supposes is staying with Carlos. There is no closure to this mystery story. Michael, the lover, does not appear, and Carlos does not really remember meeting him or Catarina. The dream is never fully understood and eventually comes back full circle to end the story on a cautionary note: mixing up Ipanema with the American city, mixing up assimilation with nonassimilation, confusing the identities of the characters and the text itself.

Você sonha com a cidade em que você está morando nos Estados Unidos, como se fosse uma única e sólida nuvem cinzenta, traçada com mechas sujas de algodão, uma nuvem cinzenta, espessa e furadinha como tricô pairando no ar como uma tampa de uma panela de ferro, como uma tampa de bueiro, como um lingote de aço que se espicha e se alonga como um jacaré que abra a bocarra e mostra os dentes brancos pontiagudos que são os flocos de neve que descem, fechando as valas, soterrando as baratas e as ratazinhas famintas, cobrindo os montes de pedras portuguesas, engolindo o mar, sepultando a praia, explodindo os casebres de favela e os edifícios de apartamentos e os jardins, dinamitando as calçadas e as ruas do bairro de Ipanema, apagando também e para sempre qualquer resquício de memória do passado longínquo e de lembrança dos dias atuais. Você procura desesperadamente vislumbrar os amigos nas janelas dos edifícios, os conhecidos caminhando pelas ruas, as babás ninando bebês nas praças, o povaréu boêmios bares pés-de-chinelo, os ricos nos restaurantes da moda, se contentaria até com as imagens que descrevem a batalha naval ipanemense desencadeada pelo prefeito, tudo na vã tentativa de reiniciar uma caminhada despreocupado pelo bairro onde você nasceu, cresceu e não está morando mais. (116–17)

[You dream about the city where you are living in the United States. As if it were a unique and solid gray cloud, braided with dirty strips of white gauze, a gray cloud. Split and perforated like crochet. Hovering in the air like the cover of a cast-iron skillet, like the cover of an air duct, like a steel bar that stretches itself out and elongates like an alligator who opens its jaws and shows its white, sharp teeth that are flakes and more flakes of snow that come down, covering the ditches, burying the cockroaches and the fat, hungry rats, covering the piles of Portuguese tiles,[27] swallowing the sea, entombing the beach, exploding the tumbled down shacks of the favelas[28] and the apartment buildings, and the gardens, dynamiting the sidewalks and the streets of the neighborhood, Ipanema, also and forever putting out any trace of memory of the distant past and memory of the present. You try helplessly to glimpse friends in the window of the buildings, acquaintances walking along the streets, nannies lulling babies to sleep on the plazas, the bohemian crowds in the cheap, dirty bars, the rich in the fancy restaurants of the day, you would be content even with the images that describe the Ipaneman game "Sink the Ship" unleashed by the mayor, all in the vain attempt to reinitiate the carefree walk through the neighborhood where you were born, grew up and where you aren't living anymore.] (240)

The disguises used in the story represent not only real exile but also metaphorical exile from self and from nation. Again, Santiago critiques social culture through human alienation and the inability of individuals to communicate. The telephone, then, is the cross-dresser, the metaphor of meaning.

Begging the Question

Transvestism and its performative aspects are much subtler in the short story, but the two works illustrate many of the same themes. For Santiago, it is impossible for a homosexual ever to construct a self or to become anything but the other unless she or he disguises that self, just as a writer must disguise history in story to preserve both intersexuality and intertextuality. By the same token, cultures must disguise themselves as lacking power in order to attract attention. Brazil will be other than third world when it is read through its mask, as Santiago infers when he quotes Bonnard in the beginning of *Stella Manhattan:* "Não se trata de pintar a vida, Trata-se de tornar viva a pintura" (One is not concerned with painting life. One is concerned with making the painting come to life). Santiago is best when he brings the "world" of the other to life and forces us to read through it.

For the reader, the problem becomes one of translating a kaleidoscope of images that multiply throughout each text. The images result in never knowing what happens to the characters in the final outcome, as the author-as-character in *Stella Manhattan* acknowledges. Leila is written off the page. Eduardo/Stella vanishes into multiple alternatives. S/he either dies or disappears in order to return, disguised as "Billy the Kid" (268) or as a prophetic figure who will return to tell "all" truth. The mysterious Michael never telephones Carlos in "You Don't Know What Love Is," the disembodied voice of Catarina fails to reconnect, and home for the narrator becomes a frustrating battle of city images overshadowed by an overwhelming sense of *saudades*.

Everyone and everything are disguised, no one is who he or she seemed to be at first. The images of Brazil, the United States, Ipanema, Paris, New York, or New Haven become different, yet the same, as all the characters encounter the same difficulties in all places. The stages may move, yet the performers continue, inventing and reinventing disguise after disguise, gender after gender (gender after genre); for Santiago lets us know that not only is a telephone a confidant, but also, in an epigraph to *Stella Manhattan,* that the characters and narrator are disguised and are just as enigmatic as ever:

> narrador e personagens dobradiças, homenagem
> aos *Bichos* de Lygia Clark e
> a *La Poupée* de Hans Bellmer (277)

> [narrator and flexible (female) characters
> in homage to *The Bugs* by Lygia Clark
> and *The Doll* by Hans Bellmer]

But even the epigraphs are disguised. The problem, of course, is in the feminization/masculinization of the narrator/characters in *Stella Manhattan.* Even though in Portuguese *personagem* is one of the few words that has two acceptable genders (*o* and *a*—male and female markers for *the*), that does not change its meaning,[29] *narrador* is definitely masculine (the feminine form is *narradora*). When we see the feminine version of the adjective *dobradiças,* we are required to rework the entire epigraph. In effect, Santiago forces an awareness of gay identity, however problematic. Are we speaking only about the female characters? Is the narrator feminine? And what about the paintings? Is there a reference to *bicha* (Brazilian slang for an effeminate homosexual) in Clark's *Bichos?* Is there more significance to dolls than we realize in Bellmer's *La*

Poupée? In the story, the telephone is merely a machine. Although it may provide disembodied confidences, the voices may or may not be who they say they are. Dreams may or may not be significant. The text, the images, and the characters are all masked in order to question identity. They epitomize Santiago's own struggle for gay space, the "third" space or his *entre-lugar.*

Notes

1. *Fantasias* or "fantasies" refer to the costumes worn as disguises, especially during Carnival. The disguise is used in order to be able to act out as someone else or act as the other. For a Brazilian discussion of costumes, see Roberto Da Matta's *Carnival, Rogues and Heroes* (1991).

2. I will be using George Yúdice's translation of the novel *Stella Manhattan,* except in those cases where I feel the translation is not adequate. Those passages will be marked. I will be using my own translation of the short story in *Urban Voices: Contemporary Short Stories from Brazil.* I will refer to the short story by the title "You Don't Know What Love Is."

3. The original title is in English.

4. The English title is the same, reflecting the novel's crossover personality. The same is true of the short story that bears the English title first and then the Portuguese. Both the short story and the novel are written primarily in Portuguese but with myriad English words and referents. Both works also refer to the substantial Hispanic-American culture in the northeastern United States.

5. For a discussion of Andrade's ideologies, see Mário César Lugarinho's essay elsewhere in this volume.

6. For a fuller discussion of Santiago's positioning, see Fernando Arenas's *Utopias of Otherness: Nationhood and Subjectivity in Portugal and Brazil* (forthcoming from the University of Minnesota Press).

7. All translations not from the novel or the short story are my own unless otherwise noted.

8. For a more extensive discussion, see Earl Fitz and Judith Payne, *Ambiguity and Gender in the New Novels of Brazil and Spanish America* (1993).

9. The women's liberation movement, radical feminism, and the gay liberation movement called for basic freedoms based on sex and gender identification. Most often these movements were essentialist in nature, believing that every woman or every gay and lesbian could derive the same amount of autonomy. What these movements failed to consider fully in the 1970s were issues of race, class, and authoritarianism. More interesting to this study, however, is the lack of discussion about the issue of gender fluidity.

10. See, for example, the film *Four Days in September (O que é isso, companheiro?),* based on the book by Fernando Gabeira, released in 1997 and nominated for the Oscar for best foreign film. The film portrays the political manipulations by the U.S. government and the subsequent kidnapping of the U.S. ambassador to Brazil in 1968.

11. As the reviewer is not mentioned by name, there is every possibility that this quote is from Santiago himself.

12. Both the Portuguese and the English version of the novel use the same title, *Stella Manhattan*. Therefore the page numbers following the Portuguese citations refer to that volume and the page numbers after the English citations refer to the English edition.

13. Yúdices' translation reads: "With a feigned gesture she winds an imaginary red bandana from Azuma's around her head to protect her from the dust; in her imagination she rapidly slips into a sleeveless calico shift. No need for a sash, the flesh is still firm.... *I am deee-vine aren't I . . .*" (6).

14. Of note are the two separate female characters, 'Bastiana, the cleaning lady–comfort figure modeled after Eduardo's maid in Rio, and Stella herself, a complete ingenue.

15. In Yúdice's translation: "gently pulling the seated body toward him, which effortlessly let its head fall on his breast" (23).

16. Yúdice capitalizes La Cucaracha in his translation.

17. In Yúdice's translation: "only" (ibid.).

18. I am using the definite pronoun with the word *chair* instead of the translator's use of "my" as I think the reading is much more ambiguous than Yúdice leads us to believe.

19. Yúdice's translation says "and what about the poet," thereby losing all references to one of the greatest poets in the Portuguese language, Fernando Pessoa. Surely Santiago is referring both to his stature as a poet and to Pessoa's own masking of his homo-bi-a-sexuality. The line mentioned is in the poem "*Autopsicografia*."

20. Yúdice renders this entire sentence in Spanish, thereby losing some of the linguistic cunning of Santiago. I have reverted to the original sentence.

21. See Richard Zenith's essay in this volume.

22. In Yúdice's translation, "Leila is not so much a woman" (108).

23. Yúdice reads: "Stimulated by frustration she feels the rebirth of a feline compulsion swelling beneath her skin" (142).

24. In Yúdice's translation "the woman she'd like to be but never quite embodies" (144).

25. *Sorry, Wrong Number* was originally a radio play by Louise Fletcher starring Agnes Moorehead. This thriller was adapted for film in 1948 starring Barbara Stanwyck and Burt Lancaster and was directed by Anatole Litvak. Stanwyck was nominated for an academy award for her leading role. The movie was remade for cable television in 1989 and starred Loni Anderson. The story involves a rich woman feigning illness who overhears a telephone conversation in which her husband is plotting her murder. The mysterious telephone conversations have obvious parallels in Santiago's story.

26. As both the Portuguese version and the English version carry the same title, the page numbers after the Portuguese citation refer to that volume and the numbers after the English citations refer to that version.

27. Portuguese tiles refer to the intricate stonework designs used in making sidewalks. The Copacabana sidewalk is a good example. This craft is almost always seen only in Portuguese-speaking cultures.

28. Brazilian slums.

29. One may refer to a male character as *a personagem* or *o personagem,* just as one may refer to a female character as *o personagem* or *a personagem.*

Works Cited

Anzaldúa, Gloria. 1987. *Borderlands/La Frontera: The New Mestiza.* San Francisco: Spinster/Aunt Lute.

Arenas, Fernando. Forthcoming. *Utopias of Otherness: Nationhood and Subjectivity in Portugal and Brazil.* Minneapolis: University of Minnesota Press.

Butler, Judith. 1993. *Bodies That Matter: On the Discursive Limits of "Sex."* New York and London: Routledge.

Da Matta, Roberto. 1991. *Carnival, Rogues and Heroes.* Trans. John Drury. Notre Dame, Ind.: University of Notre Dame Press.

Ferreira-Pinto, Cristina. 1999. *Urban Voices: Contemporary Short Stories from Brazil.* Lanham, Md.: University Press of America.

Fitz, Earl, and Judith Payne. 1993. *Ambiguity and Gender in the New Novels of Brazil and Spanish America.* Iowa City: University of Iowa Press.

Foster, David William. 1997. *Sexual Textualities: Essays on Queer/ing Latin American Writing.* Austin: University of Texas Press.

Garber, Marjorie. 1992. *Vested Interests: Cross-Dressing and Cultural Anxiety.* New York and London: Routledge.

Gautier, Théophile. 1973 [1900]. *The Complete Works of Théophile Gautier.* Ed. and trans. Frederick C. de Sumichrast. London and New York: Postlethwaite, Taylor and Knowles.

Kulick, Don. 1998. *Travesti: Sex Gender and Culture among Brazilian Transgendered Prostitutes.* Chicago: University of Chicago Press.

Lopes, Francisco Caetano, Jr. 1991. "*Stella Manhattan:* Uma sujetividade outra." *Brasil/Brazil* 5: 54–78.

Pratt, Mary Louise. 1993. "Criticism in the Contact Zone: Decentering Community and Nation." In *Critical Theory, Cultural Politics and Latin American Narrative,* ed. Stephen Bell, Albert H. LaMay, and Leonard Orr. Notre Dame, Ind.: University of Notre Dame Press. 83–102.

Santiago, Silviano. 1973. *Latin American Literature: The Space in-Between.* Trans. Steven Moscov. Buffalo: Council on International Studies, State University of New York at Buffalo Press.

———. 1978. *Uma literatura nos trópicos.* São Paulo: Perspectiva: Secretaria da Cultura, Ciência e Tecnologia do Estado de São Paulo.

———. *Em liberdade: uma ficção.* Rio de Janeiro: Paz e Terra.

———. 1985. *Stella Manhattan.* Rio de Janeiro: Rocco.

———. 1989. *Nas malhas da letra.* Rio de Janeiro: Companhia das Letras.

———. 1994. *Stella Manhattan.* Trans. George Yúdice. Durham, N.C.: Duke University Press.

———. 1997. "You Don't Know What Love Is/Muezzin; Você não sabe o que é o amor/Almuaden." In *Keith Jarrett no Blue Note.* Rio de Janeiro: Rocco.

———. 1999. "You Don't Know What Love Is/Muezzin." Trans. Susan C. Quinlan. In *Urban Voices: Contemporary Short Stories from Brazil,* ed. Cristina Ferreira-Pinto. Lanham, Md.: University Press of America. 226–41.

————. 2002. *The Space in-Between: Essays on Latin American Culture*. Ed. Ana Lúcia Gazolla. Trans. Tom Burns, Ana Lúcia Gazolla, and Gareth Williams. Durham, N.C.: Duke University Press.

Sarduy, Severo. 1989. "Writing/Transvestism." In *Written on a Body*, trans. Carol Maier. New York: Lumen Books. 118–33.

Spivak, Gayatri Chakravorty. 1988. *In Other Worlds: Essays in Cultural Politics*. London and New York: Routledge.

Part IV

Queer Nations in Portuguese

CHAPTER TWELVE

Small Epiphanies in the Night of the World
The Writing of Caio Fernando Abreu

Fernando Arenas

Caio Fernando Abreu died of AIDS in February 1996 in Porto Alegre, in his native state of Rio Grande do Sul, Brazil. He is considered one of the most important Brazilian writers in the late twentieth century.[1] Caio Fernando Abreu wrote short stories, novels, and plays, and was a well-known journalist for *Estado de São Paulo* and *Zero Hora,* among other print media.[2] His chronicles written for *Estado* are considered by some critics as representative of the Zeitgeist of Brazilian society in the 1980s and early 1990s. He was one of the first Brazilian writers to thematize AIDS and was one of the most outspoken cultural figures with the disease. In spite of his critical stance vis-à-vis monolithic categories such as "gay," "bisexual," or "heterosexual," his antagonism toward the idea of being ghettoized as a "gay writer," and his much stronger preference for a notion of fluid, plural, and interchangeable sexualities, Caio Fernando Abreu's cultural and political contributions are inevitably of great interest to queer communities, in and out of Brazil. At the same time, the author and journalist brought out into the open, as few public figures have done in Brazil until recently, the issue of citizenship and human rights for nonheterosexuals.[3]

Since the mid-1970s and early 1980s, there has been a sizable group of male prose writers and poets in Brazil who have dealt overtly with themes around homo- and bisexuality besides Caio Fernando Abreu, João Silvério Trevisan, Silviano Santiago, Bernardo Carvalho, Herbert Daniel, and poet Valdo Motta, as well other lesser known writers such as Gasparino Damata, Darcy Penteado, Aguinaldo Silva, and Glauco Mattoso.[4] Of this group, both Caio Fernando Abreu and Silviano Santiago are the better-known figures (Santiago is considered one of the most prominent contemporary intellectual figures in Brazil). It is important to point out that the overt thematization of alternative sexualities in Brazilian literature is concurrent with the historical period known as the *abertura* (opening) (which lasted between 1978 and 1984), when the military regime of the time (1964–84) gradually lifted its censorship over cultural production and political expression.

Caio Fernando Abreu belonged to the generation that believed in various ideological and sexual utopias that have been dramatically shattered after major changes in the global and national arenas: on the one hand, the exhaustion of the 1960s counterculture, that, in the case of Brazil, had the particularity of being repressed by the authoritarian and ultranationalistic regime of the late 1960s and early 1970s, and, on the other hand, the very contemporary and ubiquitous threat of AIDS, which has dramatically altered the world's relationship to sex for many years to come.[5] The result is a generalized sense of loss, disorientation, and pessimism, which is the product not only of the contemporary global landscape, but also of a national historical trajectory that has seen many years of authoritarian rule, with all of its well-known political and economic consequences, and an ensuing decade of great insecurity and instability, fraught with frustrated collective dreams, persistently wide socioeconomic inequities, and unlikely saviors. This dynamic is vividly illustrated by the untimely death in 1985 of the charismatic Tancredo Neves (the first democratically elected president after the dictatorship); years of economic stagnation, hyperinflation, and crippling foreign debt; the meteoric rise and fall of Fernando Collor de Mello between 1989 and 1992, involving criminal prosecution on corruption charges;[6] impending ecological disaster in the Amazon (a problem that is not only Brazilian); a lingering and wide socioeconomic gap between the haves and the have-nots, and a dramatic increase in urban violence that is a direct consequence of the great social inequality. All of these elements, which have dominated the recent Brazilian landscape (and continue to do so in varying degrees), constitute the sociopolitical and cultural background of the fiction of Caio Fernando Abreu.

Abreu's fictional production establishes a rich and fluid dialogue with literature, music, and film both from Brazil and from around the world. He creates a complex intertextual web in which musical lyrics, rhythm, and melody, as well as scenes from films, inform fictional plots, and poetry may frame or occupy a prominent place within the geography of a given fictional text. Abreu's writings assume a culturally hybrid location for Brazil in today's globalized world. The cultural referents of the Brazilian nation (Brazilian Popular Music, Afro-Brazilian religion, and Brazilian literature, among others) interact with a multiplicity of referents from the outside (Hollywood films, Portuguese, French, Anglo-American, and Hispanic literatures, and diverse worldwide musical styles, to cite just a few examples) through a dynamically synchronic process of cohabitation and appropriation where the cultural borders between what is considered "foreign" and "native" collapse. Various Latin American critics favor the notion of "appropriation"—among them, Chilean Bernardo Subercaseaux—who is quoted at length in George Yúdice's "Postmodernity and Transnational Capitalism" (8). This model desires to go beyond Manichaean visions of native versus foreign, rejecting any notion of a "pure, uncontaminated" Latin American culture, or the myths of cultural pluralism or essentialism with regard to Latin American identity. Appropriation entails an identity that is rather provisional, fluid, always in the process of becoming. Brazilian cultural identity in Abreu's writings is anything but a fixed, essential entity, unsullied from foreign contamination. The author unabashedly assumes for Brazil a position of liminality as it "negotiates its cultural capital" (ibid., 18) with(in) today's globalized system.

Furthermore, Abreu is also an integral part of a specifically "gay" or "queer" global culture, which is reflected in the literature, film, and music from various parts of Europe, Latin America, and especially North America, which today constitute common points of reference for "gay" or "queer" subjects transnationally. The liminal position that Abreu claims for Brazil within the spectrum of nations of contemporary globalized culture is analogous to a liminal position that the individual subject occupies (i.e., the author or his various individual narrators) as part of an international "gay" culture that cuts across national borders through a variety of mass media and massive population movements (via tourism and immigration), rapidly informing and transforming identity categories and lifestyles, particularly among the middle and upper classes. This transnational "gay" or "queer" culture is yet another alternative imaginary "landscape" composing the contemporary global configuration; it is a layer that cuts across Arjun Appadurai's five dimensions of disjunctive "cultural flows" (ethnoscapes, mediacapes, technoscapes, finanscapes, and ideoscapes), forming its own fluid and dynamic network or "queerscape."[7]

Caio Fernando Abreu's introspective and profoundly lyrical prose is certainly an heir to Clarice Lispector's resplendent writing. There is a clear philosophical dimension to his work, where existential or ontological concerns occupy a prominent space alongside the author's reflections on sexuality. In fact, there are examples within his fiction where frustrated erotic desire or the elusive emotional fulfillment through the other appear as metaphoric expressions of a profound existential anguish. Furthermore, there is often an implicit or explicit reflection on the human condition at the end of the twentieth century. The reflection may present a national, individual, generational, and/or class specificity to it or it may project itself toward the world in general. There is a deep sense of individual and collective pessimism and disillusionment, which is partly the result of the crashing of utopias of various kinds in the past few decades, be they political, sexual, emotional, or even professional. AIDS is seen by the author as one of the most vivid and tragic embodiments of the crashing of the utopia of sexual revolution.

AIDS, according to Abreu, is one of the major facets of contemporary life's insanity, a tragically vivid metaphor of the reality of a contaminated planet. In his last interview published in *O Estado de São Paulo* (see Castello), he reflects about AIDS in ecological terms, articulating what American critic Gabriel Rotello develops exhaustively in his controversial *Sexual Ecology* (1997). Abreu believes that the crisis in the human immune system is analogous to the crisis in the contemporary global ecological system. The author, furthermore, does not glorify the fact of being a person with AIDS, nor does he consider it a heroic or divine experience. He does not hide a sense of tragedy and misfortune that accompanies the disease. Ultimately, though, he believes that in the face of the disease, the human condition is innocent.

Together with Brazilian pop star Cazuza, and writer and political activist Herbert Daniel, Abreu was one of the earliest and most outspoken cultural figures to address the general public in Brazil concerning the AIDS experience. Through interviews, and especially through his poignant and quite personal chronicles collected in *Pequenas epifanias* (1996), Abreu traced the emotional and physiological stages of the disease as they affected him personally. In fact, the experience of AIDS became conflated with his own life and writing owing to the large "pre-posthumous" attention lavished upon him by the media during his final years.[8] He became one of the most powerful and eloquent purveyors of news of the signs of the times, of the countless known and unknown Brazilians and others who have come and gone through the merciless onslaught of the epidemic. However, contrary to the morbid writings of Hervé Guibert, the frenetic urgency of Cyril Collard, or Reinaldo Arenas's desperate cry of victimhood, Abreu's writings, even those about AIDS, reveal a mild, optimistic spirit, despite the endless pain of witnessing the very limits of his own being and that of humanity in general. Most of the time, writings on the subject end inconclusively, pointing to an uncertain future, as well as emphasizing the importance of living (in) the present with passion and hope.[9]

Caio Fernando Abreu's fictional and nonfictional production (between 1988 and 1995)—directly and indirectly—mirrors the various stages the author went through in coping with AIDS, as it affected him personally, as well as the world around him. Given what is known about the progression of the disease within the body, HIV/AIDS has been characterized in terms of stages since the beginning of the epidemic (Sontag). In Abreu's fiction we witness at first the marks of the disease on the body's surface, then the fear of the unknown, as well as the setting in of life's ineluctable uncertainty. Later on, we sense the hovering presence of death, and yet an unwavering commitment to living. In fact, from *Os dragões não conhecem o paraíso* (1988) and throughout his later works, there is a hyperawareness of the limits of life. *Os dragões não conhecem o paraíso*, in particular, is built on an axis of negation or death. Almost all of the stories of this collection reflect upon death ("Linda, uma história horrível" [Beauty, a horrible story], "O destino desfolhou" [Destiny shed its leaves], "Os sapatinhos vermelhos" [Little red shoes], "Dama da noite" [Queen of the night]). However, the collection ends with an affirmation of life: the Chinese ideogram *Chi'en* (which represents the origin of all things) and an ironic quote on happiness by Ana Cristina César that reads "Chamem os bombeiros, gritou Zelda. Alegria! Algoz inesperado" (Call the firemen, shouted Zelda. Happiness! Unexpected hangman).[10] In spite of the profound melancholy that envelops most of Abreu's narratives, they often end with a lingering expression of hope.

Along the rich spectrum of Abreu's fictional writings that thematize AIDS we find "Linda, Uma história horrível" (translated as "Beauty," though more literally it translates as "Beauty, a Horrible Story").[11] The short story, from the collection *Os dragões não conhecem o paraíso* (Dragons don't know paradise) published in the United Kingdom in 1990 under the title *Dragons,* is probably one of the first fictionalized accounts of the AIDS crisis to appear in Brazilian literature. It was one of very few Latin American (and the only Portuguese-speaking) short stories featured in *The Penguin Book of International Gay Writing,* edited by Mark Mitchell (1995). "Linda, uma história horrível" is a symbolic opening to the anthology *Os dragões.* It is in fact a homecoming, the return to a place of origins. The narrator visits his mother, and upon arrival he faces a house in decline. In fact, the house is a mirror image of the narrator, a man in his forties who has AIDS, and his mother, more than twenty-five years older than he. They both display traces of illness, of time. The habitual, tense silences, more than signaling a communication gap, elliptically suggest the deep closeness of mother and son in their different, and yet similar, existential states. There is an evident generational and sexual gap between mother and son, which both tacitly acknowledge and yet remain mutually supportive. Terminal illness in youth (in the case of the narrator) and impending death at old age (in the case of the mother) indelibly unite them. Their family ties are more than blood-related; they are forged out of human solidarity, out of a shared solitude.

Passo da Guanxuma, the locale to which the narrator returns, constitutes an antimythical place of origins, an allegorical representation of contemporary Brazil. Despite the impeachment of Fernando Collor de Mello for corruption in 1992, the implementation of a successful—if not problematic—neoliberal monetary plan *(plano real),* and the election of Fernando Henrique Cardoso (at first a generally well-respected and cosmopolitan president, but now largely unpopular) in 1994, the Brazil that ails has not withered away. The headline "País mergulha no caos, na doença, na miséria" (15) (Country sinks into chaos, disease and poverty [*Dragons,* 3]), so prominent in this short story and so urgent in the Brazil of the 1980s, still echoes on the horizon.

In "Linda, uma história horrível," mother, son, pet dog, house, and country are all subsumed in decadence. The Kaposi's sarcoma lesions on the protagonist's chest mirror the vanishing purple of the living-room carpet and the spots of the near-blind and aging dog. But despite the horizon of ruins, of abjection, there remains a touch of hope, a touch of love that survives out of the links of solidarity between beings—in this case, family members. There lies the touch of beauty in an otherwise "horrible" story:

> Um por um, foi abrindo os botões. Acendeu a luz do abajur, para que a sala ficasse mais clara quando, sem camisa, começou a acariciar as manchas púrpuras, da cor antiga do tapete na escada—agora, que cor?—, espalhadas embaixo dos pelos do peito. Na ponta dos dedos, tocou o pescoço. Do lado direito, inclinando a cabeça, como se apalpasse uma semente no escuro. Depois foi abrindo os joelhos até o chão. Deus, pensou, antes de estender a outra mão para tocar no pêlo da cadela quase cega, cheia de manchas rosadas. Iguais às do tapete gasto da escada, iguais às da pele do seu peito, embaixo dos pêlos. Crespos, escuros, macios.—Linda—sussurrou.—Linda, você é tão linda, Linda (*Os dragões,* 22)

> [One by one, he undid the buttons. He turned on the lamp, so that the room would be lighter and, with his shirt off, began to stroke the purple marks, the same colour as the stair carpet had once been—what colour was it now?—that spread beneath the hairs on his chest. With his fingertips he touched the right side of his neck, tilting his head as if feeling for a seed in the dark. Then he slumped to his knees. God, he thought, and stretched out his other hand to touch the near-blind dog, its coat dappled with pink patches. The same as those on the skin of his chest, beneath the hair. Curly, dark, soft: 'Beauty', he whispered. 'Beauty, you're such a beauty, Beauty'.] (*Dragons,* 10–11)

After the publication of *Os dragões,* AIDS reappears in the novel *Onde andará Dulce Veiga?* (1990) (*Whatever Happened to Dulce Veiga?* [2000]). Set against the backdrop of an apocalyptic São Paulo, *Onde andará Dulce Veiga?* takes place in a city that is falling to pieces, terminally ill. Some of the characters themselves, including the protagonist, have AIDS. In fact, the idea of contamination permeates the narrative as a whole, and comes to symbolize the state of the nation, that is, Brazil in the late 1980s—a nation undergoing one of the worst socioeconomic and political crises of its modern history. In *Onde andará Dulce Veiga?* the reality of the body that is HIV positive or that has AIDS is transferred onto a metaphor of the contaminated nation.[12]

In "Zona contaminada," a hallucinated multimedia spectacle from Abreu's collection of plays, published posthumously under the title *Teatro completo* (1997), we witness a dramatic synthesis of contemporary culture's gallery of all-encompassing horrors (the Nazi Holocaust, AIDS, the threat of nuclear war, the threat of ecological disaster). The author's preoccupation with the state of the Brazilian nation shifts to the global stage, where the well-being of humanity as a whole has been severely compromised like never before. Abreu echoes Susan Sontag, who in the early stages of the AIDS epidemic pointed out that AIDS is one of the central pieces of a series of unfolding disasters of contemporary society on a global scale; in fact, it is "one of the dystopian harbingers of the global village, that future which is already here" (*AIDS and Its Metaphors,* 93). Abreu's play *Zona contaminada* presents a multilayered symbolic structure where an apocalyptic view of humanity's fate in the late twentieth century is counterbalanced by an unwavering faith in the illusion of utopia. According to the character Mr. Nostálgio (Mr. Nostalgic), the illusion of utopia is a necessity in order to continue to humanly exist: "Ilusão, eu já dizia cá com os meus botões, ilusão é tudo que o humano—esse escombro patético—necessita para continuar existindo" (*Teatro completo,* 88) (Illusion, as I was saying to myself, illusion is everything that human beings—such pathetic debris—need in order to continue to exist).[13]

Fear and paranoia have also been an integral part of the AIDS experience from its outset. In Abreu's fiction, the overwhelming fear and paranoia of AIDS are surpassed by the absolute desire and need of the other. The novella "Pela noite" from the collection *Estranhos estrangeiros* (1996), published originally in *Triângulo das águas* (1983)—possibly the first literary work in Brazil to thematize AIDS (Secron Bessa 51)—dramatizes a seemingly endless night of two prospective male lovers in the 1980s in the heart of the anonymous South American megalopolis of São Paulo.[14] Both men struggle to navigate through the turbulent waters of the accumulated fears of contemporary life, in which solitude and AIDS figure prominently, in order to discover the possibility of love.

The possibility of desiring, finding, and loving the other, despite the history of abjection surrounding the disease, as well as the physiological and psychic limits imposed by it, are key to the short story "Depois de agosto," one of the last pieces written by Abreu before his untimely death. According to Marcelo Secron Bessa, this short story stems from the author's own personal experience with AIDS (98). In fact, Secron Bessa stresses the autobiographical thrust that permeates most of Abreu's fiction. "Depois de agosto" appears in the anthology *Ovelhas negras* (1995), a collection of short stories representing different periods of Abreu's writing career that remained unpublished throughout his lifetime. This story recounts the various stages that the protagonist (who has AIDS) must traverse toward his "undeath," that is, from the seemingly irreversible course of the disease and its profound emotional and psychological impact that leads him to feel that "it is all too late," to a turning point in his existence where life, love, and hope, are rediscovered:[15] "Talvez tudo, talvez nada. Porque era cedo demais e nunca tarde. Era recém no início da não-morte dos dois" (257) (Maybe everything, maybe nothing. Because it was too early and never too late. It was just the beginning of their "nondeath"). In one of the most poetic fictional renderings of the experience of AIDS, this short story features a man who comes to revalorize his life through his own inner strength and the promise of the other's love. The certainties of death and life are relativized in this narrative, at the same time as the layer of abjection that has historically enveloped AIDS and those who must endure it, becomes transvalued. The protagonist realizes that in the face of love's promise and of the other's embrace, even in the most dire of life circumstances, it is always early and never too late to live and to love. Even in the most tenuous of horizons within an individual life cycle, the seasons of love can continue on:

> Desde então, mesmo quando chove ou o céu tem nuvens, sabem sempre quando a lua é cheia. E quando mingua e some, sabem que se renova e cresce e torna a ser cheia outra vez e assim por todos os séculos e séculos porque é assim que é e sempre foi e será, se Deus quiser e os anjos disserem Amém. (257–58)

> [Since then, even when it rains or when it's cloudy, they always know when the moon is full. And when it is new and disappears, they know it will renew itself again and will turn full for centuries and centuries, because such is the way that it has always been and will always be, God willing and if the angels will say Amen.]

Sexuality and gender identity categories appear as highly unstable sites of signification in Caio Fernando Abreu's fictional world, where fixed notions of hetero-, bi-, or homosexuality are constantly put into question.[16] Abreu's textual space is populated by subjectivities representing a wide and fluid spectrum of genders and sexualities that escape facile containment within easy binaries. The author rejects any ideological system that may marginalize or exclude difference, or that may preclude the subject from realizing himself or herself emotionally, sexually, and ontologically with whomever he or she chooses. Abreu also makes a case for rethinking the "sexual" borders of the nation-state. Speaking in a variety of forms and registers, the subjectivities that inhabit his fiction underscore the idea of the nation (in this case, the Brazilian nation) as a liminal signifying space marked by a heterogeneity of discourses and tense areas of cultural differences. As Homi K. Bhabha asserts, the nation "becomes a question of otherness of the people-as-one" ("Dissem-iNation," 150), where the difference *outside* against which the nation defines its subjectivity becomes a difference from *within*. This constitutive internal difference marks the nation's finitude as a homogenizing entity. In Abreu's fictional production, nonhegemonic sexual identities will play a key role in destabilizing, renegotiating, and demarcating the borders of the nation-state.

Abreu's best-known short story collection, *Morangos mofados* (1982), was his first work of fiction to bring to the fore questions about sexuality, particularly homosexuality. In *Morangos mofados* there are narratives that feature characters who present a relatively clear sexual orientation, hetero- or homosexual, though always problematized ("O dia que Jupiter encontrou Saturno," "Sargento Garcia" [Sargeant Garcia], "Terça-feira gorda" [Fat Tuesday]). There are also beings who reveal an unclear co-relation between sexual desire and identity, where there are even destabilizing agents such as alcohol that prevent the subject from defining himself or herself sexually or ontologically ("Além do ponto"), or subjects who cannot be located in a binary (heterosexual/homosexual or male/female), given that identities are highly fluid and ambiguous, where even the borders between two beings remain tenuous, suggesting an implosion between the subject and the other ("Os sobreviventes").[17]

At a different register, in *Os dragões* we find the short story "Pequeno monstro" (Little monster), which features an adolescent's initiation into sex. It is the dramatization of a loss of innocence, but at the same time the discovery of self, a powerful moment of freedom and happiness in youth—one of the few encountered in the writings of Caio Fernando Abreu. The young protagonist is spending the summer with his family at a beach home. The boy is in the middle of his rebellious stage, feeling misunderstood and marginalized within the family. He also displays a self-hatred (hence, the *pequeno monstro* nickname that he is given) that starts to dissipate as soon as cousin Alex appears. Alex, interestingly one of the few characters with a name in the entire anthology, is a handsome

college student who joins the family for vacations. His presence unleashes an erotic charge in the young boy that eventually leads to his
first sexual experience. This initiation to sex, and possibly to love, is
overtly and unapologetically assumed as gay. The protagonist lives a
moment of intense self-valorization that escapes any moral constraints.
He feels empowered for the first time after assuming the sexual dimension of his young being. By the same token, the author highly valorizes
this event where the subject, in spite of his innocence—or perhaps because of it—can experience a moment of authenticity, a freedom of
which he will be inevitably robbed. Nevertheless, as ephemeral as this
moment may be, it opens up the possibility of a life assumed in earnest
and lived to its fullest potential.

On the opposite end of the wide spectrum of narratives featured in
the collection *Os dragões,* we find one of Abreu's most powerful short
stories: "Dama da noite" (Queen of the night). Here, the identity of the
protagonist (a "dama" or "queen") is mired in uncertainty. This narrative is the product of an era besieged by panic over the body, fear of sex,
and AIDS. It is an Almodovaresque monologue in very colloquial speech
performed by a forty-year-old woman—or perhaps drag queen—who
lives as a vampire in and for the underworld of the big city nights.[18] The
camp sensibility exhibited in the monologue performed by the actual
dama da noite creates gender ambiguity, which is further heightened by
the word choice in the English translation, "queen." The stage production by Gilberto Gawronski reinforces the gender ambiguity by presenting a completely androgynous character. The monologue, as a performative act, relativizes gender categories and points to their constructedness.
The character speaking may as well be a female prostitute, a male transvestite and prostitute, or a woman posing as a male transvestite and
prostitute. It is a question of packaging, a mask or a figure of simulation—as the character "herself" asserts at the end of the story. But, regardless of the "real" content within the package, the *dama* is a nocturnal being, living precariously at the margins of bourgeois society.

In "Dama da noite," the protagonist addresses an assumed male interlocutor who is twenty years younger. This cross-generational axis on
which this narrative and others by Abreu are constructed ("Linda, uma
história horrível," "O rapaz mais triste do mundo" [The saddest boy in
the world]—in *Os dragões*—and the novel *Dulce Veiga?*) is of utmost
importance in that it deploys a number of key thematic concerns for

Abreu that oscillate between the individual and the collective, the political and the ontological. This interfacing of generations brings together those who came into adulthood in the late 1960s and those who did so in the late 1980s. The former group represents the generation that believed in the possibility of major political and cultural transformations, and who had—in the case of Brazil in the late 1960s—a clearly delineated enemy to fight against. On the other hand, the 1980s generation came into adulthood with AIDS as an inescapable and constantly menacing danger. Furthermore, this generation not only saw the global crashing of the utopias for which the sixties counterculture lived, but, in the case of Brazil, found itself submerged in political and socioeconomic despair. These cultural, political, and epidemiological circumstances are compounded by the fear of aging, together with the idea of growing old amid absolute solitude.

The "Queen of the Night" represents a passionate affirmation of individual values that stand in opposition to hegemonic cultural structures; she encompasses those beings (drug users, transvestites, prostitutes, beings of all sexualities, vampire inhabitants of the night—all in all dragon-queers) who rebel against the notion of a homogeneous and monolithic culture. Dragons constitute the metaphor-synthesis of the anthology *Os dragões.* Dragons are those subjects who inhabit the margins of social space, who contest the hegemonic values of a society steeped in falsehood and artificiality. They encompass—among others—adolescents, drag queens, and, in general, a wide spectrum of (pluri)sexual beings who escape containment within dominant frameworks of sexuality. The term *dragon*—which is used in Abreu's fiction for the purposes of designating alternative subjectivities along a wide and fluid spectrum of genders and sexualities—has certain parallels with the term *queer,* which has been adopted by gay, lesbian, bisexual and transgender political activism in the United States since the 1990s. The term *queer* has undergone a process of reappropriation and resignification—as Judith Butler points out in her classic article "Critically Queer" (1993)—having become (at least provisionally) vacated of its pejorative connotations in English. In a totalizing, yet politically pragmatic gesture, *queer* incorporates (however problematically) distinct groups such as lesbians, gay males, bisexuals, transgendered people, transvestites, and even heterosexual sympathizers whose political positions align with the defiant marginality of the previously mentioned groups. *Queer* disrupts facile binaries in the realms of gender and sexuality that are typically established by hegemonic religious, cultural, and political discourses. Moreover, it undercuts paradigms and expectations that have traditionally governed gender and sexuality categories.

The political parallels between "dragons" and "queers" seem obvious, but the metaphoric richness of "dragons" also evokes a poetic-philosophical dimension within the signifying economy of Abreu's fiction. Dragons belong to the realm of the mythological, as the creatures that in the time of the European navigators and explorers were believed to inhabit the unknown interior of the barely "discovered" lands. These imaginary creatures promised El Dorado, as much as they inspired the deepest fears. For Abreu, dragons are indeed a source of fear in contemporary bourgeois society, but they certainly do not belong (as the title of his anthology states) to the paradise offered by conventional bourgeois life. Rather, they are an archetypal projection of where human beings aspire to be, beyond a society dominated by false values. Their fire possesses a purifying force whereby the subject can struggle for the possibility of forging authentic values and live them openly and constructively. The dragons not only populate Abreu's writings, but they also constitute his fictional attempt at affirming a decentered and tense cultural space. A space, by virtue of its location, is not only defiant, but inevitably vulnerable and fragile, at the mercy of political, economical, juridical, and epidemiological forces over which there is little control.

Queen of the night defies, in a paradoxical way, the highly problematic stability of traditional heterosexual society, as she sets in motion the cultural anxieties that derive from historically dominant discourses around sex and sexuality, that today more than ever, in the age of AIDS, are conflated with discourses of disease. Queen of the night and all that she symbolizes, including the tropical, nocturnal flower, is threatened as much as she is a threat:

> Eu sou a dama da noite que vai te contaminar com seu perfume venenoso e mortal. Eu sou a flor carnívora e noturna que vai te entontecer e te arrastar para o fundo do seu jardim pestilento. Eu sou a dama maldita que, sem nenhuma piedade, vai te poluir com todos os líquidos, contaminar teu sangue com todos os vírus. Cuidado comigo, eu sou a dama que mata, boy. (95)

> [I'm the queen of the night who's going to contaminate you with her poisonous deadly perfume. I'm the carnivorous nocturnal flower who's

going to make you dizzy and drag you to the bottom of her putrid garden. I'm the cursed queen who's mercilessly going to pollute you and infect your blood with every kind of virus. Beware of me—I'm the deadly queen.] (*Dragons*, 84)

On the other hand, the queen of the night is not only about rebellion, she is also about searching. If the utopias of various ideological forms and colors that were so prominent in the cultural landscape of the 1960s and 1970s have faded, there is one utopia that stubbornly remains, albeit tenuously: love. In fact, for Abreu, the utopias of love and God are inevitable, lest the human subject submerge itself in a horrendous pit of absolute solitude. As much as Abreu is aware of the weakening of foundationalist thought in contemporary society, he also recognizes that certain of its expressions—as contingent and provisional though they may be—are still a strategic necessity for our survival as human beings. And so, through the nihilistic haze that looms in the short story "Dama da noite," as throughout most of Abreu's fiction, there is a faint glimmer of hope: the hope of collecting fresh and juicy strawberries amid the contemporary civilizational dump, to evoke the central metaphor of *Morangos mofados*. The strawberries represent the dreams, the utopias of love—all in all, hope. This hope, though, is never unaccompanied by fear, a fear that the queen of the night experiences as a vulnerable child who is left alone and abandoned:

Fora da roda, montada na minha loucura. Parada pateta ridícula porra-louca solitária venenosa. Pós-tudo, sabe como? Darkérrima, modernésima, puro simulacro. Dá minha jaqueta, boy, que faz um puta frio lá fora e quando chega essa hora da noite eu me desencanto. Viro outra vez aquilo que sou todo dia, fechada sozinha perdida no meu quarto, longe da roda e de tudo: uma criança assustada. (98)

[Outside of the wheel, riding on my craziness. Sitting there stupid, ridiculous, couldn't give a shit, solitary, poisonous. Post-everything, you know what I mean? Ultra-gothic, ultra-modern, pure sham. Hand me my jacket, boy, it's bloody freezing out there and when it gets to this hour of the night my spell wears off. I turn back into what I am every day, shut in alone and lost in my room, far from the wheel and everything: a frightened kid.] (*Dragons*, 88)

There is a fundamental ethical dimension in the work of Caio Fernando Abreu that is inseparable from an emotional component, and that is the relationship with the other (in the form of a lover, family, or community). There is a profound creative investment on the part of the author (as well as of his characters) vis-à-vis the "micrological" or more intimate levels of being. The investment in the other that is so strong a thread in Abreu's fiction is implicated with the "philosophical anthropology" of Mikhail Bakhtin, which comprises Bakhtin's notions about self and the other, as well as about being and alterity.[19] As is widely known in the realms of literary and cultural studies, for Bakhtin, the subject cannot be in isolation, and it cannot achieve a degree of self-awareness in the world outside of its relationship with the other. In Bakhtinian thought, communication through dialogue is a fundamental aspect of existence. As stated in Tzvetan Todorov's *Mikhail Bakhtin: The Dialogical Principle* (1984), "it is the human being that exists only in dialogue; within being one finds the other" (xl). Furthermore, Todorov quotes directly from Bakhtin: "to be means to be for the other, and through him, for oneself. . . . I cannot do without the other; I must find myself in the other" (96). Bakhtin arrives at his new interpretation of culture primarily through the analysis of language and the novel. By the same token, his reflections on language and the novel become a philosophical, and even anthropological basis, as Todorov would have it, from which Bakhtin will posit his conceptions of being and *dialogism.*

There is also a confluence of interests between Abreu, Bakhtin, and the philosophical thought of Emmanuel Levinas with regard to the question of alterity.[20] For the late French philosopher, the subject is posited as "coming into being" or into an awareness of its being in the world through a complex of existential layers; for example: its insertion into the world, its solitude, and its mortality. This complex of layers ultimately leads toward alterity or to the other person. Levinas plots a phenomenological itinerary of the subject in which alterity would represent the highest plane. Alterity in Levinas's thought appears boundless and its most absolute expression would be God. There is a fundamental ethical dimension that is related to alterity whereby entering into a relationship with the other, either through a commitment or responsibility vis-à-vis social life or through an erotic encounter, the subject would enter into a "sacred" history. According to Levinas, God passes through the relationship of the subject with the other.

In the fiction of Caio Fernando Abreu, the Bakhtinian notion of the impossibility of being without the other is a crucial reality, but there are historical, ontological, and even physiological layers added to this reality that are connected to a sense of urgency of being owing to impending mortality.[21] In addition, with the loss of hope in the possibility of global change or revolution (of various kinds) or with the loss of faith in totalizing narratives (religious, political, etc.), the other becomes a new utopia. This utopian dimension attached to alterity is to a large extent only implicitly conveyed in the thinking of both Bakhtin and Levinas. On the other hand, the phenomenological in Abreu reveals a near absence of God—though there is at times the memory and nostalgia of its presence or of the faith in it, as well as the paradoxical realization of its necessity as a structuring myth for human existence. The relationship with the other is then posited as a primarily secular instance, still imbued, however, with a sacred aura.

Toward the last years of Abreu's life, the heightened sense of urgency in his fictional production that is connected to the relationship with the other is, in part, the consequence of having AIDS. However, prior to the advent of AIDS, the feelings of disillusionment, disorientation, and solitude that permeate his fiction are already present. These feelings stem from individual, as well as national and global, circumstances. By the early 1980s, Brazil was just leaving behind a lengthy and brutal dictatorship that had shattered the dreams of social revolution and democratization. On the other hand, internationally, the thriving and liberatory 1960s counterculture that survived into the 1970s was displaced by a wave of political, moral, and cultural conformism and conventionality in the 1980s. The AIDS epidemic would eventually become, a posteriori, one of the ideal rationalizations behind this wave. In addition, in this earlier period, Abreu's fiction dramatizes, at an individual level, a profound ontological disjuncture within the subject, expressed in a variety of situations and forms, which in turn informs the social and/or erotic relationship with the other, and the act of literary representation itself (this is most vividly portrayed in *Morangos mofados*). Both the national and global circumstances alluded to partially explain the ontological anguish felt by the subject. After the foregone possibility of social communion and political emancipation, the subject is left orphaned of the utopias that gave sense to an era and to a generation. On the other hand, from a philosophical standpoint, the author is also acutely aware of the impossibility of a unitary and self-identified subject. Such awareness brings about, in Abreu's earlier fiction, a host of solitary and fragmented characters who are located in the heart of anonymous contemporary urban life. Another factor that compounds the sense of ontological anguish that is deeply felt by numerous characters in Abreu's narratives is internalized homophobia, itself a product of societal repression of homosexuality. This is thematized in several short narratives of *Morangos mofados* ("Além do ponto," "Terça-feira gorda," and "Aqueles dois" [Those two]). Homophobia appears as yet another formidable obstacle to self-realization of the desiring subject and the erotic communion with the loved other.

The ontological disjuncture just described deepens in Abreu's later works with the advent of AIDS. At the same time, the need and the desire for the other become greatly intensified. The utopia of the other takes on a central role and literature becomes one of its privileged sites. In this respect, Abreu reveals substantial affinities with other contemporary Luso-Brazilian philosophical fiction writers such as Clarice Lispector and Vergílio Ferreira.[22] The later texts of both of these writers, as well as those of Abreu, exemplify the ways in which existential as well as physiological circumstances of the author become more transparent in the creative process. Literary texts are written with a sense of urgency at the edge of life. They constitute concerted attempts at overcoming life's contingency, while making the final stretch of life more livable. The existence of the literary work itself becomes synchronous to the existence of the writer, the former the reason for being of the latter. This symbiotic relationship is further enhanced by the profound awareness on the part of the writers of living the last years of their lives with terminal illnesses, in the case of Clarice Lispector and Caio Fernando Abreu, and into old age, in the case of Vergílio Ferreira. Throughout Abreu's fiction, the belief in the other is manifested ultimately with great pain and overwhelming solitude. Yet, it is the remaining impulse that may make life more endurable, and death, perhaps, more acceptable. The relationship with the other and its absolute necessity constitute, for Abreu, an ultimate existential horizon for the constitutition of self and society in an era of shattered dreams, accentuated solitudes, and seemingly incurable life-threatening diseases.

> Atrás das janelas, retomo esse momento de mel e sangue que Deus colocou tão rápido, e com tanta delicadeza, frente aos meus olhos há tanto tempo incapazes de ver: uma possibilidade de amor. Curvo a cabeça, agradecido. E se estendo a mão, no meio da poeira de dentro de mim, posso tocar também em outra coisa. Essa pequena epifania. Com

corpo e face. Que reponho devagar, traço a traço, quando estou só e
tenho medo. Sorrio, então. E quase paro de sentir fome. (*Pequenas
epifanias*, 14–15)

[Behind the windows, I seize again that moment of honey and blood
that God, so delicate and swift, placed in my hands, in front of my eyes,
so little used to seeing as of late: the possibility of love. I bow down
thankfully and extend my hand, in the middle of the dust within me,
and I can yet touch something else. It's a small epiphany. With body and
face. I can always redraw it in my mind, trace by trace, when I am alone
and fearful. I smile and my hunger is almost placated.]

Notes

1. Caio Fernando Abreu has been widely translated in Europe, particularly into
French, Italian, and German. So far there are only two works translated into English
(1990a, 2000). With the added visibility and recognition that Caio has gained inside
and outside of Brazil ever since his death, it is highly probable that more of his
works will be translated into English. Meanwhile in Brazil, practically all of his
works (from 1970 until his death) are being republished. Several of his short stories
have also been adapted into performance pieces and several of his plays have been
produced with great critical success. In addition, a major anthology (Riccordi, *Caio
de amores*, 1996) including short stories written by twenty authors from Caio Fernando Abreu's home state of Rio Grande do Sul was published as a tribute to the
author who is considered in his region, as well as in Brazil, one of the most important voices of his generation.

2. For an exhaustive discussion of the work of Caio Fernando Abreu see chapter 3 of my *Utopias of Otherness: Nationhood and Subjectivity in Portugal and Brazil*
(forthcoming from the University of Minnesota Press).

3. Senator Marta Suplicy (from the Partido dos Trabalhadores [Workers' Party])
introduced a bill in the Brazilian Congress in 1996 that would consider a wide-rang-
ing domestic-partnership law granting same-sex couples many of the rights and
responsibilities of matrimony. This bill has since been stalled in the Brazilian Sen-
ate. Meanwhile, by the year 2000, civil rights protections had been extended to gay
men and lesbians at the local and state levels in various parts of Brazil, including the
state of Rio de Janeiro.

4. Brazilian women writers such as Lya Luft (*Reunião de família*, 1982; *As parceiras*, 1986), Márcia Denser (*Muito prazer*, 1982), Leila Míccolis (*Sangue cenográfico*,
1997), Lygia Fagundes Telles (*A noite escura e mais eu*, 1995); Maria Regina Moura
(*Exercício de um modo*, 1987; *Poemas do recolhimento e do frio*, 1996); and Miriam
Alves (in *Enfim nós: escritoras negras brasileiras contemporâneas*, 1994) have been
exploring, in a variety of registers and degrees of intensity, issues regarding lesbian
desire.

The following is a list of pioneering contemporary male Brazilian authors and
literary texts (outside of Caio Fernando Abreu) that overtly thematize homosexuality and bisexuality: Aguinaldo Silva (*Primeira carta aos andróginos*, 1975; *A república*

dos assassinos, 1976; *No país das sombras,* 1979); Gasparino Damata (*Os solteirões,* 1976); Darcy Penteado (*Nivaldo e Jerônimo,* 1981); Herbert Daniel (*Passagem para o próximo sonho,* 1982); Silviano Santiago (*Stella Manhattan,* 1985); João Silvério Trevisan (*Devassos no paraíso,* 1986; *Perverts in Paradise,* 1986); Glauco Mattoso (*Manual do pedolatro amador,* 1986; *Centopéia,* 1999). Devassos no paraíso is an "archaeological" study conducted by João Silvério Trevisan on homosexuality and Brazilian culture since the arrival of the Portuguese in the sixteenth century. Damata, Penteado, Mattoso, and Abreu (with the short stories "Sargeant Garcia" and "Those Two") were all featured in the pioneering anthology of Latin American gay fiction edited by Winston Leyland (*My Deep Dark Pain Is Love,* 1983). Glauco Mattoso is also the subject of a doctoral dissertation by Steven Butterman (University of Wisconsin). Mention must also be made of Malcolm Lowry's introduction to the collection of short stories translated from Spanish and Portuguese in *Under the Volcano* in 1979. This was surely a seminal work.

5. As a result of increased civil resistance against the military junta on the part of workers and students in 1968, the infamous "Ato Institucional n° 5" was put into effect. The result was a "declaration of war" by the military against the opposition (both the armed opposition and its nonarmed expressions). This entailed numerous disappearances of political opponents, strict censorship against intellectuals, artists, and students, university purges, and the flight into exile of important sectors of the Brazilian intelligentsia.

Since 1986, statistics have indicated that Brazil, alongside the United States, has among the highest number of AIDS cases reported outside of Africa and India. In 1998, Brazil ranked fourth on the United Nations' list of infected countries, with 580,000 adult carriers of HIV. According to Dr. Ruth Cardoso, the wife of the president of Brazil, "AIDS is Brazil's second-leading cause of death in people ages 20 to 49" (quoted in Altman). As of 2001, the AIDS epidemic in Brazil had stabilized. The AIDS death rate nationally had been cut by half (Rosenberg 29). This major breakthrough has been possible because of the government's commitment to making AIDS a national priority, which is reflected in its liberal approach toward drug patents in times of national emergency. Thus, Brazil now produces its own affordable anti-AIDS drugs that would otherwise be sold by multinational pharmaceutical companies at exorbitant prices. Anti-AIDS drugs have become widely available in Brazil through a highly organized network of treatment and prevention programs. Brazil's success in curtailing the spread of the disease is also the result of AIDS activism among gays and the existence of six hundred nongovernmental groups that work on AIDS around the country.

6. In December 1994, the Brazilian Federal Supreme Court acquitted Fernando Collor de Mello because it found the prosecution unable to prove its corruption charges against the former president.

7. See Arjun Appadurai, "Disjuncture and Difference in the Global Economy," *Public Culture* 2:2 (1990): 1–23. Appadurai is discussed extensively in Michael J. Shapiro and Howard R. Alker, eds., *Challenging Boundaries: Global Flows, Territorial Identities* (Minneapolis: University of Minnesota Press, 1996), 3–5.

8. I would like to acknowledge Marcelo Secron Bessa for bringing this insight to my attention.

9. The editors are grateful to Rodolfo A. Franconi for bringing to their attention the fact that Caio Fernando Abreu received the most pleasure in the last few

months of his life from receiving cards and postcards with pictures of the sun. The sun was his symbol for life.

10. Ana Cristina César (1952–83) was a lesbian poet who took her own life.—*Ed.*

11. Unless otherwise indicated, all translations are mine.

12. For a full discussion of Abreu's novel *Onde andará Dulce Veiga?* see Fernando Arenas, "Writing after Paradise and before a Possible Dream: Brazil's Caio Fernando Abreu" (1999).

13. In *Tentative Transgressions: Homosexuality, AIDS and the Theatre in Brazil*, Severino Albuquerque provides the most exhaustive study to date of Brazilian theatrical representations of homosexuality as well as AIDS. Here, Caio Fernando Abreu is featured as one of the most prominent contemporary playwrights in Brazil. In his study, Albuquerque also provides a rigorous and in-depth analysis of several of Abreu's plays and theatrical adaptations of short stories and novellas written by Abreu.

14. Renato Farias adapted the novella "Pela noite" for the stage with much success in Porto Alegre and Rio de Janeiro between 1994 and 1996 with Abreu's enthusiastic support (for more details, see Albuquerque).

15. This dynamic gains added potency with the realization that since the late 1990s, people with AIDS, particularly in industrialized societies, can now extend their lives indefinitely with the help of protease inhibitors and various other combinations of drugs that suppress the advancement of HIV. Unfortunately, this was not an option for Caio Fernando Abreu, nor is it an option for tens of millions of people living with AIDS today, especially in Africa.

16. In *Bodies, Pleasures, and Passions* (1991), Richard Parker describes the coexistence of various paradigms within Brazilian sexual culture whereby contemporary imported models coexist with more traditional notions of sexuality and gender. The notion of a "gay community" modeled after what is found in North America, various parts of Europe, Australia, and so on, and coterminus to a political movement, has found echo in elite segments of the larger urban areas of Brazil, at the same time as more traditional notions persist in rural and working-class segments of the population, where sexual acts do not translate into political consciousness and where sexual identity is structured around a vertical axis of active/passive and male/female. In the latter case, from a "gay perspective," the subject would be considered bisexual, but *he* would consider himself to be performing the "male" role regardless of the gender of the sexual object of choice. This model is not exclusive to Brazil, and is still widespread in Latin American and Mediterranean cultures (Almaguer 257; Schmitt 6), and was also common in the United States earlier the last century, particularly in rural areas and among the working classes (D'Emilio 471). Today, the "imported models" from the metropoles have gained greater acceptance and legitimization, at the same time becoming more widespread in countries such as Brazil, while coexisting with traditional models of sexual culture.

In *Beneath the Equator* (1999), Parker updates and expands the arguments in his earlier book by situating his study of Brazilian sexual culture in more concrete socioeconomic and geopolitical terms within the context of industrialization and urbanization in Brazil, together with the process of globalization. He states that local sexual cultures today are caught more than ever in the crosscurrents of global processes of change. Sexual culture in Brazil and elsewhere throughout the world, particularly with regard to same-sex desire, is more the result of the interaction of local prac-tices, international meanings, and world consumer markets.

17. For a thorough discussion of Abreu's *Morangos mofados,* see Fernando Are-nas, "Estar entre o lixo e a esperança: *Morangos mofados* de Caio Fernando Abreu."

18. "Dama da noite" (or "Queen of the Night") was adapted into a performance monologue by Brazilian stage actor Gilberto Gawronski, with French, Portuguese, and English versions. It is said that the first rehearsals took place in the hospital room where Abreu spent some of his last days. The performance piece has since be-come very successful with shows in Lyons (France), Rio de Janeiro, São Paulo, and New York. In 1998, Mário Diamante made a short film version of the solo perfor-mance with Gawronski as the protagonist. For an in-depth analysis of the perfor-mance piece, see Albuquerque 59–65.

19. For a more detailed discussion of the problematic of the "utopia of the other" as it informs the fiction of Caio Fernando Abreu, Clarice Lispector, as well as Portuguese authors Maria Isabel Barreno, Vergílio Ferreira, Maria Gabriela Llansol, and José Saramago, see Arenas, *Utopias of Otherness.*

20. For a philosophical formulation of the concept of being and the other, and the ethical commitment toward the other, see Emmanuel Levinas, *Time and the Other* (originally published in 1947) and *Totality and Infinity* (1961).

21. In the literary works of Bernardo Carvalho (*Aberração,* 1993; *Os bêbados e os sonâmbulos,* 1996) and Silviano Santiago (*Keith Jarrett no Blue Note,* 1996), the "com-munion" with the other that is deeply longed for in Abreu's fiction and ever so ephemerally attained remains elusive and the feeling that prevails is that of resigned solitude in Santiago's narratives and diffuse stoicism in Carvalho's fiction, which, in both cases, AIDS seems to magnify. Santiago posits an existential condition of for-eignness in the subject both at "home" and "abroad," which is as cultural as it is in-trinsically ontological, whereas Carvalho presents a highly globalized world in which characters of many nationalities and cultural backgrounds constantly cross borders, at the same time as they cross each other's paths, ultimately remaining as discon-nected and lonely as ever.

22. For a more in-depth comparative discussion of Vergílio Ferreira and Clarice Lispector, see Fernando Arenas, "Being Here with Vergílio Ferreira and Clarice Lispec-tor: At the Limits of Language and Subjectivity."

Works Cited

Abreu, Caio Fernando. 1982. *Morangos mofados.* São Paulo: Editora Brasiliense.

———. 1983. *Triângulo das águas.* Rio de Janeiro: Nova Fronteira.

———. 1988. *Os dragões não conhecem o paraíso.* São Paulo: Companhia das Letras.

———. 1990a. *Dragons.* London: Boulevard Books.

———. 1990b. *Onde andará Dulce Veiga?* São Paulo: Companhia das Letras.

———. 1995. *Ovelhas negras.* Pôrto Alegre: Editora Sulina.

———. 1996a. *Estranhos estrangeiros.* São Paulo: Companhia das Letras.

———. 1996b. *Pequenas epifanias.* Pôrto Alegre: Editora Sulina.

———. 1997. *Teatro completo.* Pôrto Alegre: Editora Sulina.

————. 2000. *Whatever Happened to Dulce Veiga?* Trans. Adria Frizzi. Austin: University of Texas Press.

Albuquerque, Severino J. Forthcoming. *Tentative Transgressions: Homosexuality, AIDS and the Theatre in Brazil.* Madison: University of Wisconsin Press.

Almaguer, Tomás. 1993. "Chicano Men: A Cartography of Homosexual Identity and Behavior." In *The Lesbian and Gay Studies Reader,* ed. Henry Abelove, Michèle Aina Barale, and David M. Halperin. New York and London: Routledge. 255–73.

Alves, Miriam, and Carolyn Richardson Durham, eds. 1994. *Enfim nós: escritoras negras brasileiras contemporâneas/Finally Us: Contemporary Black Brazilian Women Writers.* Colorado Springs: Three Continents Press.

Altman, Lawrence K. 1998. "At AIDS Conference, a Call to Arms against 'Runaway Epidemic.'" *New York Times,* June 29, national edition, A13.

Arenas, Fernando. 1992. "Estar entre o lixo e a esperança: *Morangos mofados* de Caio Fernando Abreu." *Brasil/Brazil* 8: 53–67.

————. 1999a. "Being Here with Vergílio Ferreira and Clarice Lispector: At the Limits of Language and Subjectivity." *Portuguese Studies* 14: 1–14.

————. 1999b. "Writing after Paradise and before a Possible Dream: Brazil's Caio Fernando Abreu." *Luso-Brazilian Review* 36: 13–21.

————. Forthcoming. *Utopias of Otherness: Nationhood and Subjectivity in Portugal and Brazil.* Minneapolis: University of Minnesota Press.

Arenas, Reinaldo. 1993. *Before Night Falls.* New York: Viking.

Bhabha, Homi K. 1994. "DissemiNation: Time, Narrative and the Margins of the Modern Nation." In *The Location of Culture.* London and New York: Routledge. 139–70.

Butler, Judith. 1993. *Bodies That Matter: On the Discursive Limits of "Sex."* New York and London: Routledge.

Carvalho, Bernardo. 1993. *Aberração.* São Paulo: Companhia das Letras.

————. 1996. *Os bêbados e os sonâmbulos.* São Paulo: Companhia das Letras.

Castello, José. 1995. "Inventário irremediável: Caio Fernando (1949–1996) fala da vida antes da morte." *O Estado de São Paulo,* December 9.

Collard, Cyril. 1993. *Savage Nights.* London: Quartet.

Damata, Gasparino. 1976. *Os solteirões.* Rio de Janeiro: Pallas.

Daniel, Herbert. 1982. *Passagem para o próximo sonho.* Rio de Janeiro: Editora Codecri.

Daniel, Herbert, and Richard Parker. 1991. *Aids: A terceira epidemia.* São Paulo: Iglu Editora.

D'Emilio, John. 1993. "Capitalism and Gay Identity." In *The Lesbian and Gay Studies Reader,* ed. Henry Abelove, Michèle Aina Barale, and David M. Halperin. New York and London: Routledge. 467–76.

Denser, Márcia. 1982. *Muito prazer: contos eróticos femininos.* Rio de Janeiro: Editora Record.

Guibert, Hervé. 1991. *To the Friend Who Did Not Save My Life.* London: Quartet.

Leyland, Winston, ed. *Now the Volcano: An Anthology of Latin American Gay Literature.* San Francisco: Gay Sunshine Press, 1979.

————. 1983. *My Deep Dark Pain Is Love: A Collection of Latin American Gay Fiction.* San Francisco: Gay Sunshine Press.

Levinas, Emmanuel. 1969. *Totality and Infinity: An Essay on Exteriority.* Pittsburgh: Duquesne University Press.

————. 1987. *Time and the Other.* Pittsburgh: Duquesne University Press.

Luft, Lya. 1982. *Reunião de família*. Rio de Janeiro: Nova Fronteira.
———. 1986. *As parceiras*. Rio de Janeiro: Nova Fronteira.
Mattoso, Glauco. 1986. *Manual do pedolatra amador: quenturas & leituras de um tarado por pés*. São Paulo: Expressão.
———. 1999. *Centopéia: sonetos & quejandos*. São Paulo: Ciência do Acidente.
Míccolis, Leila. 1997. *Sangue cenográfico: poemas de 1965 a março de 1997*. Rio de Janeiro: Editora Blocos.
Mitchell, Mark, ed. 1995. *The Penguin Book of International Gay Writing*. New York: Penguin Books.
Moura, Maria Regina. 1987. *Exercício de um modo*. Rio de Janeiro: Rotograf.
Parker, Richard. 1991. *Bodies, Pleasures, and Passions*. Boston: Beacon Press.
———. 1999. *Beneath the Equator*. New York and London: Routledge.
Penteado, Darcy. 1981. *Nivaldo e Jerônimo*. Rio de Janeiro: Editora Codecri.
Riccordi, Paulo de Tarso, ed. 1996. *Caio de amores*. Porto Alegre: Mercado Aberto.
Rosenberg, Tina. 2001. "Look at Brazil." *New York Times Magazine* January 28.
Rotello, Gabriel. 1997. *Sexual Ecology*. New York: Dutton.
Santiago, Silviano. 1985. *Stella Manhattan*. Rio de Janeiro: Editora Rocco.
———. 1996. *Keith Jarrett no Blue Note*. Rio de Janeiro: Editora Rocco.
Schmitt, Arno. 1992. "Different Approaches to Male-Male Sexuality/Eroticism from Morocco to Uzbekistan." In *Sexuality and Eroticism among Males in Moslem Societies*, ed. Arno Schmitt and Jehoeda Sofer. New York, London, and Norwood (Australia): Haworth Press. 1–23.
Secron Bessa, Marcelo. 1997. *Histórias positivas*. Rio de Janeiro and São Paulo: Editora Record.
Silva, Aguinaldo. 1975. *Primeira carta aos andróginos*. Rio de Janeiro: Pallas.
———. 1976. *A república dos assassinos*. Rio de Janeiro: Civilização Brasileira.
———. 1979. *No país das sombras*. Rio de Janeiro: Civilização Brasileira.
Sontag, Susan. 1988. *AIDS and Its Metaphors*. New York: Farrar, Straus and Giroux.
Station, Elizabeth. 1995. "Activists Take on AIDS." In *Fighting for the Soul of Brazil*, ed. Kevin Danaher and Michael Shellenberger. New York: Monthly Review Press. 197–203.
Telles, Lygia Fagundes. 1995. *A noite escura e mais eu*. Rio de Janeiro: Editora Nova Fronteira.
Todorov, Tzvetan. 1984. *Mikhail Bakhtin: The Dialogical Principle*. Trans. Wlad Godzich. Minneapolis: University of Minnesota Press.
Trevisan, João Silvério. 1986a. *Devassos no paraíso*. São Paulo: Editora Max Limonad.
———. 1986b. *Perverts in Paradise*. Trans. Martin Foreman. London: GMP Publishers.
Yúdice, George. 1992. "Postmodernity and Transnational Capitalism in Latin America." In *On Edge: The Crisis of Contemporary Latin American Culture*, ed. George Yúdice, Jean Franco, and Juan Flores. Minneapolis: University of Minnesota Press. 1–28.

CHAPTER THIRTEEN

The Impossible Body

Queering the Nation in Modern Portuguese Dance

André Torres Lepecki

> it may be that performance, understood as "acting out," is
> significantly related to the problem of unacknowledged loss.
> —Judith Butler

A Spectacular Absence

The body in public forms of representation in contemporary Portugal
has been described by art and cultural critic Alexandre Melo as invisible, absent, lacking. In a provocative essay for the weekly *Expresso* in
1993, Melo identified the image of the Portuguese body as pure negativity, as *the* absolute loss in the cultural national landscape. The absence
of a public discourse on the body in contemporary Portugal led Melo to
title his essay, ironically, "Do the Portuguese Have a Body?"[1]

In the 1990s, Melo's question echoes and relaunches important insights on Portuguese culture first brought forth by Eduardo Lourenço
in the late 1970s, in Lourenço's extraordinary readings on Portuguese
"imagology" collected under the evocative title *O labirinto da saudade*
(1978). The identification by Melo of this *lacking Portuguese body* is not
a nationalist call for a putative essential Portugueseness. Rather, it must
be read along the lines of Lourenço's suggestion that, since the nineteenth century, the Portuguese have been "absent from our own reality"
(1978: 65), and therefore immersed in a type of collective invisibility, an
unthinkable corporeality.[2] If Lourenço's observations were prompted
by the traumatic historical changes brought about by the revolution of
1974—the fall of the empire, the end of fascism, the incipient "Euro-

peanization" of an utterly isolated and underdeveloped country—what is significant in Melo's identification of a problematic corporeal *absence* in contemporary Portuguese cultural production is that his observations were prompted by two very explicit corporeal *presences:* the moving bodies of choreographers and performers Vera Mantero and Francisco Camacho.

Melo's essay was a response to a shared dance program held in the black-box stage of the National Theater Dona Maria II in Lisbon, where Mantero and Camacho presented two solos. Their work was perceived by Melo as a rare exception of publicly imagining, problematizing, and politicizing that which remains a ghostly lack in Portuguese cultural production: the bluntly physical body—desiring, sexualized, visceral. What in the *choreography* of those dancing bodies, in their disturbing presence and confined motions, so powerfully provoked in Melo the sudden illumination of a corporeal void in his society's cultural production?

This essay probes the ways in which particular choreographic work in Portugal is forcing the Portuguese spectator (perhaps for the first time in history) into a critical, sensorial, and semantic reproblematization of the country's surrounding culture, history, and self-image. Such probing is predicated on Eduardo Lourenço's proposal for an *imagologia* (imagology) of the Portuguese body, as "a critical discourse on the images that we [Portuguese] have been forging about ourselves" (Lourenço 12). The reader will find my interpretation of Portuguese choreography as cultural critique largely based on the Foucauldian insight that moments of historical and cultural change in the West are isomorphic to a reconfiguration of the body, and of the proprietary relations between self and body. I define choreography according to dance historian Susan Foster's proposition that choreography is a "theorization of embodiment," and therefore dance pieces constitute privileged sites for the cultural critic to scrutinize shifts in representations of the body that are also instrumental for my reading of choreographies.[3] Finally, a discussion of one of the main choreographic devices in question, the dancer's shutting of the eyes, will be interpreted according to rereadings of Lacanian theory of the gaze within performance and queer theories, by Peggy Phelan and Judith Butler.

For reasons of space, methodology, and argument, I will focus exclusively on the work of Francisco Camacho. Camacho's concern as a choreographer can be described as a consistent iconoclastic probing of national icons, Portuguese historical figures, and national obsessions. Camacho's iconoclastic work is grounded on a peculiar queer theatricality, lingering between a hyperbolic mimesis of national "truisms" and "tics" (what Camacho calls "depiction of behavior"), and a cruel sensuality, obsessed with the markers of gender and their operation in the formation of sexual desire. The work of Vera Mantero, despite its similar political concerns and dialogical proximity with Camacho's, proposes a very different choreographic universe, as well as a different imagology, more anthropological than national, therefore necessitating a separate approach and essay.[4]

Hovering on the abyss of this *spectacular corporeal absence,* Camacho organizes choreographies and performances where an image of a Portuguese corporeality can be portrayed, subverted, critiqued. The pieces by Camacho that so impressed Melo were two solos, both performed by Camacho himself: "Nossa Senhora das flores" (Our Lady of flowers, 1993), which Melo saw live, and the film version of "O rei no exílio" (The king in exile, 1991).[5] The former, Camacho emphasizes, is not an adaptation of Genet's homonymous masterpiece. In the latter, Camacho drew his inspiration from the figure of Dom Manuel II, the last king of Portugal. Between an exploration of desire and sexual identity in "Nossa Senhora" and an investigation on the fetishistic magic of political power in "O rei," both solos summarize Camacho's ongoing explorations of a (male) body whose identity is captured within the traps of history and representation. Although these two works summarize authorial obsessions, they also polarize them, and their reading conjointly poses some difficulties. These solos approach different thematics in two distinct moments in Camacho's career. Before discussing these works, a brief overview of Camacho's career is necessary, in order to familiarize the reader with his intricate, cruel, and overtly sensual universe.

Francisco Camacho's dance is centered, at least since his group piece "Quatro e o quarto" (Four and the room, 1990), on two main themes, allowing a queer reading of his work: the question of disciplinary regimes that thrust the body into a physical and symbolic space, both regulating and punishing it; and the question of the body as the magic center of power, as the primary concern of the law as well as of the pedagogical and fetishistic investment of the nation.[6] These thematics have been explored extensively in both group and solo works.

The first theme has been metaphorically treated by Camacho as an architectural problem. He choreographed two group pieces inspired by Le Corbusier's early modernism, the aforementioned "Quatro e o quarto" and the more recent "Primeiro nome: Le" (First name: Le, 1994).[7] Camacho's preoccupation with the impact of architecture on the body literally examines how "a new technology of power and a new political anatomy of the body start to be implemented" (Foucault 1979: 217). By addressing modernist models of the homogeneous and modular body, Camacho identifies how these models prescribe and produce not only "ways of living," but also a certain ideal anatomical model, based on a regimented masculine physicality, and utilized as the embodiment of the idealized universal subject.

The universal subject as modular and exemplary anatomical masculinity is marked by his disciplined conformity to a preprogrammed body. This programming involves both the anatomical and the physiological, gender and propriety, as it includes the body within the teleological temporalities of progress, reproduction, and economy. In his two pieces on Le Corbusier, Camacho shows how this corporeal project violently and inevitably brings forth no social liberation or individual fulfillment, but rather an unbearable normalization, an absolute schism between body and subject, pleasure and desire. This is a corporeality predicated on a fragmentary organization of the subject, and on a forceful evacuation of any verbal or corporeal self-articulation of a counternormative, free, and freeing desire. It is not without surprise, then— but certainly with a laughter too close to pain—that we encounter in Camacho's two pieces on Le Corbusier a choreographing of collapsing (sometimes crippled) bodies. The dancer's movements, sentences, and demeanor lie on the verge of a feverish, excessive, uncontrollable rage, sexual desire, and humor—nonexemplary, queer bodies who are highly sexualized, desiring and desirable, convulsing in autophagic empowerment.

What we find in those utterly fleshly characters in "Primeiro nome: Le," or in Camacho's ironic infantilization of the disciplined modular body in "Quatro e o quarto," is the revelation that any programmatic utopia of the body operates as disciplinary hegemony for the sake of a violently abstract identity. Just as Salvador Dalí once accused Le Corbusier of being "the inventor of the architecture of self-punishment" (Dalí 1996: 29), Camacho shows us how disciplinary regimes are introjected and organized as anatomies and subjectivities of self-repression. If Le Corbusier invented an architecture of self-punishment, Camacho seems to suggest that we are the only ones who are responsible for replicating such heritage.

The second theme in Camacho's work is his insistent invocation, rearticulation, and collapsing of the autobiographical with the historical. This theme emerges, obviously, in his explorations of Le Corbusier. But it is when addressing Portuguese historical figures that this collapse of history and presence achieves an uncanny lucidity regarding Camacho's surrounding culture. Camacho choreographed two pieces explicitly inspired by Portuguese royal figures. His group choreography "Dom São Sebastião" (King Saint Sebastian, 1995) collapses the figure of the saint with that of Dom Sebastião, the king whose early death in battle brought about the Spanish Phillipian domain of Portugal in the sixteenth century, and whose return is mythically attached to the restoration of the Portuguese empire. Also, Camacho's seminal solo "O rei no exílio" is exemplary of this ultimate blend of mask and self, of the historical, the biographical, and the autobiographical, of representation and presence. This solo leads us directly to the problem of a Portuguese national corporeality, and back to the evening Alexandre Melo was struck by this corporeality's absence.

The Exile from the Other

In "O rei no exílio" we have Camacho's voice, the voice of Dom Manuel II, and the voice of António Cabral, who chronicled the life of the exiled king. All three characters collapse into one single body whose status is ambiguous: neither self-performing nor performing an Other, neither totally autobiographical nor historical, this body lingers in representation, suggesting that "being" is but representation proper. Camacho uses three different voice registers for each persona. The voices are supplemented by the uncanny and decadent vocalizations of the late Portuguese lyrical singer Natália de Andrade, Nick Cave's cavernous tone, and the spectral utterances of the Slovenian industrial rock band Laibach. Shattered between the several voices that inhabit and surround this profoundly split character, this king-author contests the body's stability within the fields of representation, autobiography, and history from which he appears as forever exiled. History and autobiography merge in this solo as a device for cultural illumination. It is a historical fact that Dom Manuel II ended his life in exile, in London, after the republican revolution of 1910. However, because Camacho's character in this piece is also explicitly autobiographical, this being away, this exclusion, brings other implications to the question of exile.

In the sense that the king-author is marked as an outcast, that he chooses exile as his home, this self-exclusion launches a question: what is the space of exile given the king-author's shifting representation? The stage where "O rei" takes place (as well as in "Nossa Senhora das flores," the solo I will discuss shortly) is marked by sparsely displayed props, dim pools of light, a primordial, dark landscape already empty. In this "already empty" universe where this ambiguous national body (be it king or subject) claims its kingdom, in this traumatic isolation, the dancer's presence roams hesitantly, antihero engaged either in mesmerizing soliloquies or in soliloquy's physical counterpart. Both verbal and physical introspection hyperbolically mime a performative inscription of history upon the body. This inscription is that of primordial (and traumatic) national isolation mourning the death of the Other. Eduardo Lourenço writes: "All 'Histories of Portugal'...tell the celestial adventures of an isolated hero in a universe that was already empty. All happens as if we [the Portuguese] did not have an interlocutor" (17). In psychoanalytic terms, the function of the Other can be deemed as specular, in the sense that it secures the ego's stability as it confers upon a fragmented corporeal experience an ideal identity and coherent image. When lacking this structuring Other, that "interlocutor" (to use Lourenço's term), the I remains undefined. Lourenço openly problematizes this lack of the Other as a missing mirror, a "painful feeling each Portuguese endures because he or she does not have within reach those splendid and multiple mirrors in which more privileged cultures can revise themselves full-bodied and at once [de um só golpe de vista]" (71). Camacho's exile points precisely to this void that preempts the place of the Other.

By withdrawing himself from the field of the Other, by constituting himself as exiled, lost, lonely, beyond scopic reach, Camacho underlines the pathologies of the (Portuguese) representational field as inhabited by a constitutional blindness—a constitutional blindness that leads Lourenço to state that Portugal is both "*unthinkable* and *invisible* to itself" (49) because historically it has failed to constitute an alterity against which an ideal image and a corporeal identity might be erected. Similarly, Camacho's king-author appears always alone, trapped within a monomaniacal drive to constantly narrate himself, to describe himself endlessly, as if no other body existed, as if no exterior world existed beyond the boundaries of his skin.

No mirror image returns while the king-author narrates himself. He obsesses over private vices, fetishistic replacements for this forever lost Other from whom a dialogical self-image could be rendered. Cigarettes, liquor, and coffee are sensually and methodically used to give sacrament to the exiled bodies of both king and author—as if they were blessings, or caresses. While these are consumed, Camacho also manipulates them as probing devices, as if they were detached sensorial prostheses whose sole purpose is to validate the materiality of that body. Lacking the gaze of the Other, the king-author asserts his corporeality by the means of fetishes. In a scene in which Camacho sits on the off-centered golden throne of the king, he painfully enumerates all imperfections that constitute his own autobiographical body. Each imperfection is highlighted by the reddish glow of a lit cigarette he runs close to his skin, scanning his body. He blows cigarette smoke and pours liquor on his arms, then on his forehead, then on his lips, his chest, his sex. Earlier, using the chronicler's voice, Camacho had exalted the king's physical perfection. Now the author's voice takes over to describe a deformed body and a frightened psyche. This regally self-involved being is a body politic in crisis, turned toward the past, narcissistic, megalomaniac, small, dark. He sings, terribly off-key: "I believe in yesterday . . ." And this body rehearses for the first time an important gesture in Camacho's future work: this body shuts his eyes.

This literal denial of the gaze is important. In "O rei no exílio," blindness happens in a moment and it simply reinforces the idea of a lacking gaze implied in the notion of a body in radical exile. But this shutting of the eye as choreographic device will increasingly occupy center stage in Camacho's subsequent creations, most notably in his extraordinarily queer choreography "Nossa Senhora das flores," where absolute blindness is attached to a performance of gender. A reading of blindness and gender in this solo enhances and supplements the implications and signification of the exiled body.

Figure 1. "Camacho's blind body in tactile self-exploration displaces and problematizes the constitutive field of the gaze." Scene from "Nossa Senhora das flores." Dancer: Francisco Camacho. Reprinted with permission.

As Long as I Refuse to See You, You Can See Me

> Performed with eyes closed to both sacred and profane Spanish
> Medieval music, "Nossa Senhora das flores" is danced in clothes of both
> sexes and has been described as a "transvestite piece," according to
> Camacho. "For me it's not exactly right but I will leave it like that now,"
> he says. "It's a piece I don't like to talk about much—I haven't even
> written any text for it."

Camacho gave this surprising statement to a Scottish newspaper during
the presentation of "Nossa Senhora das flores" in Glasgow in 1994. If it
is unusual to find Camacho unable to articulate his own work, it is even
more extraordinary that he is unable to write "any text for it," thus un-
comfortably leaving the status of this solo in the "not exactlyness" of a
"transvestite piece." Such intriguing silence from the author regarding a
piece that is performed blindly presents the two required elements of
what psychoanalytic theory defines as foreclosure: (1) a primordial ex-
pulsion of the signifier (as in the inability to verbalize) in (2) the context of castration anxiety (as symbolized in the dancer's blindness). Even
before examining these elements (the silence of the author, the performance of blindness, and the public status of the piece as "transvestite
performance"), one affirmation is already possible: "Nossa Senhora das
flores" is profoundly marked and surrounded by indeterminacy.

The question is, how much of this indeterminacy derives from the
piece's explicit exploration of gender malleability, of sexual desire, and
of a polymorphous identity? What is the purpose of a blind dancing in
this performance of gender, in this ("not quite") "transvestite piece"?
What does it mean to choreograph a dance that diverts the eye from its
organic function, and plunges the dancer's gaze inwards, suggesting castration and foreclosure, in perhaps an all too Iberian gesture, as Dalí
and Buñuel had already done in *Un chien andalou?* Where is Camacho
pointing his and our gaze in his refusal to let his vision to step out?
What are we looking at, once we are confronted with this performance
of a body that, despite its presence, insists on thrusting forward its own
loss as its most marked identity?

To begin answering these questions is to limit the field of the piece's
indeterminacy. The first undetermined element that must be addressed
is the piece's status as a "transvestite performance." In her introduction
to the anthology *Crossing the Stage: Controversies on Cross-Dressing,* Lesley Ferris collapses "transvestite theater" with "drag performance" to say

that both are based on the impersonation of gender. The key word is *impersonation*—whether this impersonation appears as mimicry working to appropriate and contain heterosexual normativity "against the invasion of queerness" (Butler 126) or as mimicry working to subvert and explode the heterosexual norm.[8] However, in "Nossa Senhora" the question of impersonation and of a mimetic appropriation of gender is never addressed or performed. Camacho does not represent or mimic "woman"; nor does he represent or mimic "man."

I propose that "Nossa Senhora" cannot be classified as a transvestite or drag performance, for it lacks the crucial element that defines such performance: the desire to *impersonate* the (biological) opposite sex. Something else is taking place in Camacho's use of gender markers in the piece. What is happening in this mesmerizing solo is a highly complex *theatricalization of gender*. The distinction I make between a theater of gender and drag performance as defined by Ferris derives from a queer definition of *theatrical*. I use the term in the sense Butler defines it, as neither self-display nor self-creation, but as that which "mimes and renders hyperbolic the *discursive convention* that it also reverses" (Butler 232; emphasis added). Accordingly, I propose that the mimetic drive in "Nossa Senhora" is not invested in gender impersonation as it defines drag performance, but rather, this drive aims at a mimesis of heterosexual psychic anxieties and social dynamics; that is, what "Nossa Senhora das flores" mimics is heterosexual normativity itself.

Here lies the important queer turn in Camacho's use of drag as nonmimetic impersonation (drag as nondrag). Butler argues convincingly that "hegemonic heterosexuality is itself a constant and repeated effort to imitate its own idealizations" (125). That is to say, for Butler, heterosexuality is a mimetic apparatus. What Camacho performs in his mimesis of the norm's mimetic drive is precisely the blunt unveiling that the heterosexual hegemonic discursive convention *is in itself mimetic*. Although Camacho does not impersonate gender (as we will see shortly), I argue that his use of social markers of femininity and masculinity in "Nossa Senhora das flores" operates, in Butler's terms, to reflect "on the imitative *structure* by which hegemonic gender is itself produced and disputes heterosexuality's claim on naturalness and originality" (ibid.). This is why "Nossa Senhora," though not a "transvestite performance," still engages in the subversive queerness of a theatricalization of gender. It is important that Camacho's solo is structured around dressing and undressing. First he is dressed as "man," then he is naked "baby," then he is dressed as "woman." All these "identities" appear under quotation marks for, while passing through them, Camacho does not at all mimic what "man" or "woman" are supposed to "be" (or how they are supposed to behave). As each new skin-costume is used, Camacho's character, presence, and mannerisms remain the same. It is not that each set of social gender markers allows the performer a certain "being" exclusive of that marker, and therefore a certain "freedom" of choosing a gender to be. On the contrary, "Nossa Senhora" transverses the gender continuum, back and forth, without mimicry, without a longing for the "real," without any concern to portray (realistically or as caricature) the only two options heterosexual normativity has to offer ("man" or "woman").

What Camacho reveals is that these two options are themselves overdetermined. To impersonate one and the other is not to perform a liberating act but to step into a blind replication, a playing along with a certain closure of subjectivity, sexual identity, and pleasure that offers only a bipolar identification. This is what is so disturbingly queer about this performance's use of drag: at the end of it we do not even know if the man's suit was the proper "prop," the natural costume for that "man," for we are not even sure of what "man" might mean for Camacho's dancing body. Camacho suspends all proprietary relations between his body and what covers it, between his body and his gender, between gender and desire. It is because Camacho choreographs a polymorphous body that is always already in flux that "Nossa Senhora das flores" performs an ultimate subversion: while showing that sex and gender are permutable, it performs how "man" and "woman" are not exclusive and exclusionary polarities within the continuum of identity and desire. Or, again in Butler's words, "Nossa Senhora" performs the promise that "masculinity and femininity do not exhaust the terms for either eroticized identification or desire" (283 n. 17). The theatricalization of gender in "Nossa Senhora" creates a queer universe onstage, a universe where subversion is performed by hyperbolically mimicking not woman's body, not man's body, but the pedagogical, repressive, and normative hegemonic, heterosexual theorization of embodiment, performed as a disciplinary "discursive convention" that contains and validates our identity, sexual subjectivity, and desire.

How does one mimic a "norm"? It is with this question that the problem of the gaze, of blindness, and of foreclosure must be addressed as the piece's main rhetorical strategy. What can be the role of blindness in Camacho's contestation of the heterosexual norm, a blindness that is so hyperbolically used in "Nossa Senhora das flores"? The closing of the eyes (or, at other times, the refusal of the open eyes to meet the other's gaze, as if diseased, as if dead, eyes devoid of any motion) that first happens in "O rei no exílio," further developed in the 1993 duo "Auto-Retrato" and fully mastered in "Nossa Senhora das flores," can be interpreted as a mo(ve)ment of critical illumination. I have shown how Camacho's dance depicts the re-membering and the survival of the body in an ideological space that must be contested. It is in this sense that the function of the gaze in the ideological space of national imagology in contemporary Portugal becomes, for Camacho, an element in the circuitry of optical exchange between the performer and his Portuguese audience that must be deconstructed and subverted. It is within this economy of the gaze that Camacho's blindness in his performances on power and gender assumes its absolute force as a queer act.

The function of the gaze has been explored extensively by feminist theory, particularly in the identification and deconstruction of the "male gaze" in film. Despite the important contributions feminist film theory has brought to the discussion of gender representation in contemporary culture, it is necessary to note that the economy of the gaze in film operates in a very different manner than it does in live performance. In my reading of Camacho's blind dances, in analyzing his purposeful and forceful refusal to share the field of vision with his audience as a central queer act, I will operate with Peggy Phelan's proposal that the problem of the (male) gaze within a feminist analysis of gender in performance "must begin not with an analysis of the male gaze, but rather with a re-examination of the *economy of exchange* between the performer and the spectator in performance" (Phelan 1993b). It is this exchange in the economy of the scopic field in "Nossa Senhora"'s theater of gender that I find crucial for understanding Camacho's shutting of the eyes. In its struggle between gaze and blindness, between shadow and illumination, the dancing body in Camacho's work casts off the veil of the aesthetic and emerges, in his deliberate blindness, to suggest what Foucault had posited when discussing the problem of the apparition: "the eye was not always intended for contemplation" (1977: 148). Camacho's spectator must look for the causes of that blindness as the mechanism that withdraws the body's stability from the constitutive circuitry of the gaze.

Camacho's voluntary blindness puts the viewer's gaze askew: by deny-
ing the return of the spectator's gaze, the dancer escapes direct probing.
The audience cannot literally face the dance, even as it forcefully emerges
in front of them. Diverted from the face, the spectator's gaze is forced
into a metonymic slide along the dancer's body; attention is glued to
the skin of the dance. As the audience struggles to have its gaze returned,
it cannot but suddenly realize that, by dancing blindly, Camacho is giving himself to his audience in the most precious of ways: he is proposing the urgent imperative for a sensorial realignment in the dancer, in
the audience, and in the role of interpretation. The spectator must shift
his or her attention to the (exterior) space surrounding that blind body
in performance and to the (inner) space opened up by the shutting of
the eyes.

Zigzagging in the introspective circuitry of blindness and desire by
means of a theater of gender is the eternal return of the Portuguese
labyrinth of longing. Eduardo Lourenço notes that "the destiny of Portugal is to gaze toward its past" (77). For Lourenço, such a gaze, fixed on
the absence of what once was, returns in a specular way to organize the
national body as essentially diachronic, never synchronous, with itself.
Under this nostalgic fixation of the gaze, the national body emerges as
an apparition, a phantasmic body unable to match its desires and phobias
with any sort of reality principle. What is most disturbing in Lourenço's
extraordinary "mythical psychoanalysis of the Portuguese destiny" (the
subtitle of his book) is his observation that this looking back toward the
past is not a reflexive return to history, but a fictional blindness that
self-delusionally (re)produces and fixates what the Portuguese imagine
the past might have looked like. It is as if Portugal were not only lost in
a "labyrinth of longing," but that this maze were a house of mirrors,
eternally replicating the distorted image of a body whose original has
always been lost.

I would add to Lourenço's insight that not only the original cast for a
Portuguese corporeality has never existed; what Camacho's blindness
proposes is that the symbolic guarantor of the subject's presence is also
lacking in the Portuguese scopic field. Camacho's self-exile from the
field of the gaze by means of self-blindness dismantles the position of
power claimed by the gaze as that which sustains and controls subject
formation within the scopic. It is impossible to deny to that body its
agency; it is impossible to close our eyes to that body's materiality. This

materiality and agency operate by pointing to the audience's position as a blank space. It is as if, by eluding the return of the gaze, Camacho were forcing the materiality of his pleasurably and utterly transgressive body on our probing eyes. It is as if his project were to engage us too in stepping into blindness as a stepping into matter—into our bodies as matter.

Peggy Phelan notes that once the spectator is denied the possibility of meeting the eyes of the body in performance, that impossibility "defines the [performer's] body as lost" (1993a: 156). The body Camacho choreographs in "Nossa Senhora" doubles—or even triples—this loss. In its absolute indeterminacy, as it is lost in itself as it plunges into blindness, as it roams through an intricate path on the bare stage, as it perturbs the author in verbalizing on the piece's status, "Nossa Senhora" plunges into a labyrinth of referentiality while it avoids itself by literally refusing to look at itself. Its author, Camacho, cannot write or talk about it. While performing it, all he sees during the thirty minutes of the piece's duration is the back of his eyelid. He creates a character closed inside himself, profoundly invested in pleasure, probing his body as he probes the space that surrounds him, a space he forcefully avoids looking at.

This blind body in tactile self-exploration displaces and problematizes the constitutive field of the gaze as the place of the Other. There is a certain amount of discomfort in watching this solo, in occupying that place of (optical) Otherness: the overcharged sacredness of the music, the darkness of the set, the contained gestures of the dancer, the absolute frailty that emerges from Camacho's blind exposure all contribute to this discomfort. The refusal to achieve a level of explicit signification— the refusal to be a "drag piece," or a "piece on Genet," or a confessional piece on the choreographer's own sexuality—adds to the uncanny feeling. A certain sense of grief emerges as a psychic resonance to this continuous loss of references. A sense of mourning, the uncanniness one feels creeping in as the piece unfolds, highly contrasts with the absolute pleasure involved in parts of Camacho's sensual dance, and puts forth bluntly the question: What constitutes the absolute lost object of this performance?

Judith Butler proposes that "gender performance allegorizes a loss it cannot grieve" (235). For Phelan, the subversion of the economy of the gaze through blindness withdraws the performing body from optical exchange, thus constituting that body as lost. In a reversal of the trap of the gaze, and by the means of a theater of gender, I would argue that Camacho makes us realize that what we lose and mourn as we gaze at the dancer's movement is not only his presence, but also our own presence as constitutive of that body's subjectivity. We mourn our own erasure from the scopic field. We are there but we are the ones not being looked at. We are the ones being denied participation in the economy of the gaze. But if we surpass this dreadful revelation that we are participating in our own self-erasure as we watch a dancing body in undetermined gender identity, what we may find is the mimetic drive to plunge into introspection, to plunge into another space, to step into our own blind dancing.

As Camacho gets lost in his inner prospect, we can only wonder where he is plunging into when he closes his eyes, and here Camacho completes his excursions on exile and subversion. By subverting the gaze, he escapes the gaze's normative drive; by subverting the trope of cross-dressing, he subverts the heteronormative bipolar field of identity and representation. While shutting his eyes, he thrusts us into a queer intersubjective space.

Bring the Body Forth

What kind of political work or cultural critique can be efficacious under the sign of blindness, particularly if we consider that Camacho's work is bluntly sensual, sexual, and sometimes pornographic? Such is the theoretical question one must ask under the signifier *queer*. One must use it as signifier only, for it is not determined that such a term is at all operational in contemporary Portuguese sexual and cultural politics. I am thus tracing and identifying a physicality and a performance that might be beside the boundaries of "queer" proper. But *queer,* in its primary signification, and in its radical promise, is that which not only eludes, but also subverts the "proper." And it defies propriety by subverting property, namely, the appropriation and ownership of bodies and desires by heterosexual normativity.

Let us not forget the cultural and psychic context here. The context is Portugal, and Portugal has always created a discourse on its "essence" as being "exemplary, proper, clean," even in its utmost repulsive historical moments. For Eduardo Lourenço, Portugal's primary hallucination is that it was born without sin, miraculously. Its privilege and mission has been to enlighten the world. It is a country disembodied of its own vis-

ceral past, a country without entrails, a hollow body of sacrificial exem-
plarity. It is this hollow body whose violent contours Alexandre Melo
saw while watching Camacho's two solos discussed here, that made him
identify the lack of a visceral, living, desiring corporeality. "Only from
an exterior manner, when forced by brutal imperatives of catastrophic
order...do we consent to look at ourselves the way we really are," writes
Lourenço. In the context of a country that sees itself only through the
means of an enchanting narrativization of an incorporeal phantasmatic
self-image; in a country that still sees itself as unique and exemplary in
the world; in a nation without interlocutor, without the organizing
voice or mirror of the Other; in a country reveling in "aseptic national
image" (Lourenço 71) informing both its present and its incorporeal
mythical birth; in a country that holds no mirrors in which to behold
its self-image; in the midst of this collective hallucination where the
body plunges into invisibility in a manner so vivid one is led to wonder
in the pages of its most influential weekly whether there is such a thing
as a body in Portugal—in such a country, the act of bringing forth a
body, any body, bluntly, cruelly, fully, desiring, eschatological, fierce, visceral, sexual, is in itself an act both bombastic and extraordinarily
queer. Camacho forces a vision on Portugal from the inside. It is not
that he is portraying Portugueseness, or proposing a model for the Portuguese body, with his dance. He is not interested at all in proposing a
pedagogy of the national body through his dance. His choreographic
explorations of history are very distinct to those Futurist iconoclastic
Portuguese proposals from the 1910s, when Almada Negreiros saw in
the Ballets Russes the pedagogical ideal image for a modern Portuguese
body. What Camacho profoundly understands is that if we are to work
against this corporeal lack, it is not enough to present the body on a
stage. To disrupt the morbidity of this national predicament of never
being able to see itself in the eyes, this body on stage must emerge despite and beside any normative and pedagogical discourses on gender,
fatherland, nation, history, and tradition. It must emerge against those
discourses that refuse and refute the flesh.

   For Camacho it is crucial that the body in performance emerge as
that nervous system shattered by a fragmentary, violent past that is neither dead nor far away in time, but a past inscribed in our own bodies, a
past surviving its own absurdities within the living bodies on both sides
of the stage at the very moment of performance. In his choreographing

of convulsion, of obsession, of failing physiological systems, of the collapsing body, of the dance in absolute sensual pleasure, and in his invocation of ghosts, of ridicule and laughter, of sensuality and of obscenity, Camacho brings forth a dancing body that "fragments what was thought unified; it shows the heterogeneity of what was imagined consistent with itself" (Foucault 1977: 147). These are terms Foucault uses to describe the Nietzschean search for history. Similarly, Camacho shows how history is inscribed in our bodies, how it destroys our bodies, and how this inscription and destruction can never be read through the eyes of national pedagogy, of the nation's disciplining of bodies, of the reproduction of bodies under heteronormative law. Rather, for Camacho, the body emerges, performatively, "in the nervous system, in temperament, in the digestive apparatus; it appears in faulty respiration, in improper diets, in the debilitated and prostrate body of those whose ancestors committed errors" (ibid.).

In this essay, I have shown how Francisco Camacho's dance engages in a double deconstruction, a double iconoclastic drive, in a moment of national identity convulsion, that of the disciplined body of the dancer as a body in desire, and that of the disciplined national body as a body in imagological crisis. Such a double iconoclasm has as its main devices the reorganization of the scopic field by the means of blindness, the queering of identity markers by the means of a theater of gender, and a collusion of the autobiographical, the fictional, and the historic. With his cruel laughter and his sure step, with closed eyes and undetermined gender, Camacho brings forth a queer corporeality, lost mirror of a nation defaced by history.

Notes

I would like to express my gratitude to those who helped me during the writing of this essay. My wife, Annemarie Bean, with her sharp eye and judicial use of the English language, helped me revise the several drafts of the manuscript. Alexandre Melo in 1995 gave me the opportunity to write my first in-depth analysis of Francisco Camacho's work in the magazine he edits in Lisbon, *Belém*—a first rehearsal on the issues discussed in the present essay. Finally, my warmest thanks go to Francisco Camacho, whose infinite patience with my endless queries on his work is only matched by a friendship I dearly value.
    1. A reprint of Melos's essay appears in Melo (1995).
    2. All translations from Lourenço and other Portuguese texts cited are mine.

3. Susan Foster, oral communication, Department of Performance Studies, New York University, December 1997.

4. The work of Mantero is as important as Camacho's in its corporeal explorations. My doctoral dissertation examines how both Camacho and Mantero destroy normative discourses on the national body. Mantero's strategy, however, differs radically from Camacho's.

5. The film version of this piece was shot in 1992 in New York by Portuguese film director Bruno de Almeida.

6. I use the term *pedagogical* here in the sense Homi K. Bhabha gives to it in his classic essay "DissemiNation," in which he identifies a dynamic tension between "the people constructed as an a priori historical presence, a pedagogical object; and the people constructed in the performance of narrative, its enunciatory 'present,'" (1994: 147) which would constitute Bhabha's performative. I would add that the pedagogical construction of the people is the narrative work of the state, embedded in a historical past, a teleological time, and a redemptive future. Althusser and Foucault showed how this pedagogical work of the state is predicated on the production of (disciplined) bodies.

7. "Primeiro nome: Le" was awarded the prestigious Prémio ACARTE/Madalena Perdigão in 1995.

8. For a discussion of both functions of drag performance, see Butler (1993).

Works Cited

Bhabha, Homi K. 1994. "DissemiNation: Time, Narrative and the Margins of the Modern Nation." In *The Location of Culture*. London and New York: Routledge.

Butler, Judith. 1993. *Bodies That Matter: On the Discursive Limits of "Sex."* New York and London: Routledge.

Dalí, Salvador. 1996. *Dalí on Modern Art*. Trans. Haakon M. Chevalier. Mineola, N.Y.: Dover Publications.

Ferris, Lesley, ed. 1993. *Crossing the Stage: Controversies on Cross-Dressing*. London and New York: Routledge.

Foucault, Michel. 1977. "Nietzsche, Genealogy, History." In *Language, Counter-memory, Practice,* ed. Donald F. Bouchard. Ithaca, N.Y.: Cornell University Press.

———. 1979. *Discipline and Punish: The Birth of the Prison*. Trans. Alan Sheridan. New York: Pantheon.

Lourenço, Eduardo. 1978. *O labirinto da saudade: psicanálise mítica do destino português*. Lisbon: Publicações Dom Quixote.

Melo, Alexandre. 1995. *Velocidades Contemporâneas*. Lisbon: Assírio & Alvim.

Phelan, Peggy. 1993a. "Crisscrossing Cultures." In *Crossing the Stage: Controversies on Cross-Dressing,* ed. Lesley Ferris. London and New York: Routledge.

———. 1993b. *Unmarked: The Politics of Performance*. London and New York: Routledge.

CHAPTER FOURTEEN

Al Berto, In Memoriam

The Luso Queer Principle

Mário César Lugarinho
Translated by Fernando Arenas and Leonardo Mendes

For Jorge de Sá

a escrita é a minha primeira morada de silêncio
a segunda irrompe do corpo
movendo-se por trás das palavras
—Al Berto, O medo, 25

[writing is my first home of silence
the second bursts from the body,
moving behind the words]

Poet Al Berto (the pseudonym of Alberto Raposo Pidwell Tavares) is a foundational figure in the emergence of a "queer" literature in Portugal. Al Berto's poetic work is the product of a "literary series" in which a gay male subjectivity has traditionally appeared as a marginalized and invisible figure in its difference vis-à-vis mainstream culture.[1] However, the notion of "queer" implies not only a marginalized gay subjectivity, but also a way of being in the world, which, by virtue of its difference, is capable of adopting a critical stance in relationship to mainstream culture (see Jagose). Thus, my appropriation of the term *queer* will have political implications for the analysis of Portuguese literature, where canonical criticism has completely ignored the subject of homosexuality.

This essay aims to advance some theoretical hypotheses regarding the possibility of culturally translating the term *queer* for Portugal and Brazil, establish the place of Al Berto's poetry within the realm of Portuguese literature, and analyze various paradigmatic poems by Al Berto, as they reflect the passage from a "gay" to a "queer" sensibility and their implications for the understanding of Portuguese culture.

To Become: Gay Poetry in Portugal

It is necessary to use the labels *gay* and *queer* when discussing the contours of Portuguese poetry throughout the twentieth century. However, it is also necessary to establish the differentiating nuances between these two terms. Thus, we must distinguish between an earlier gay male poetry that thematizes the desire between a male subject and a male object and a more contemporary queer poetry based on the identity of a subject who politically revindicates his or her difference, as well as place, in history. Between these two discursive poles regarding homosexuality in the West, there is a path traversed by poets who developed a most singular craft of disguising and unveiling identity when encountering the other.

Fernando Pessoa and Mário de Sá-Carneiro, together with António Botto, are considered the first Portuguese poets in the twentieth century to discuss homosexuality.[2] In Pessoa and Sá-Carneiro we find the male subject's dislocation to unusual places within poetic discourse, in a free association of endless signifying possibilities as he attempts to linguistically define himself. In the case of Pessoa, this poetic practice results in the creation of "heteronyms" (or literary personalities), which entails a discursive dynamic where multiple meanings flourish and crisscross. Yet, within this complex ontological and semiotic web, we can still surmise a few governing principles for the purposes of interpretation. In the poetry of heteronym Álvaro de Campos, for instance, we find some of the most explicit examples of a nascent gay poetic discourse.[3] For example, in "Passagem das Horas" (Time's passage) we see:

Os braços de todos os atletas apertaram-me subitamente feminino
E só de pensar nisso desmaiei em músculos supostos
(Pessoa 1993: 224)

[The arms of every athlete have squeezed my suddenly female self,
And the mere thought made me faint in imagined muscles] (Pessoa 1998: 147)

Fui todos os ascetas, todos os posto-de-parte, todos os como que esquecidos.
E todos os pederastas—absolutamente todos (não faltou nenhum).

Rendez-vous a vermelho e negro no fundo-inferno da minha alma!
(Freddie eu chamava-te Baby, porque tu eras louro branco eu amava-te,
Quantas imperatrizes por reinar e princesas destronadas tu foste para
   mim!)

(Pessoa 1993: 224)

[I was every ascetic, every outcast, every forgotten man,
And every pederast—absolutely every last one of them.
Black and red rendezvous in the hell of my soul's depths!
(Freddie, whom I called Baby, because you were blond, fair, and I loved
   you,
How many future empresses and dethroned princesses you were to me!]
   (Pessoa 1998: 147–48)

In this poem, we observe a stream of consciousness that reflects the poet's dismemberment. In the process, the poet becomes multiple beings, thereby opening endless possibilities of interpretation. In the quoted fragment, the poetic self, adopting a male point of view, declares his love for a certain Freddie, after rendering explicit his condition of overflowing and inner fragmentation. Homosexuality is made explicit when, in order to be *everything,* the poet needs to become feminine or feminized. However, this does not necessarily mean a transsexualization from male to female, but rather a discursive assumption of femaleness (or of traits traditionally associated with "femaleness"), while not surrendering his male (biological) condition. The poet moves discursively between these states of being and does not relinquish them. The criticism of Pessoa's work has traditionally silenced these sex/sexuality/gender dynamics and looked elsewhere, most notably considering other important themes, such as the history of Portugal and the metaphysical reflections found in his work. What is obvious is that "heteronymity"—as a discursive strategy—is an efficient exercise of poetic otherness, at the same time as it transforms the representation of homosexuality into an avant-garde aesthetic practice. And yet, how can we explain, within the context of avant-garde practices, the poem "Antinous," originally written in English and signed by the poet? "Antinous" is certainly an example within Pessoa's poetic universe in which homosexual discourse manifests itself most clearly and directly. Inspired by the scene in which the Roman emperor Hadrian sees the dead body of his lover, who has committed suicide, the poem is a long narrative about love among equals, a lengthy amorous reflection on loss and grief:

Antinous is dead, is dead forever,
Is dead forever and all lovers lament.
Venus herself, that was Adonis's lover,
Seeing him, that newly lived, now dead again,
Lends her old grief's renewal to be blest
With Hadrian's pain!

(Pessoa 1974: 92)

The criticism focusing on the literary work of Mário de Sá-Carneiro suffers to a lesser degree from the same problem alluded to with regard to Pessoa. On the other hand, we can confidently state that Sá-Carneiro's work lies at the root of Pessoan heteronymy. Sá-Carneiro thematizes the existential anguish derived from the impossibility of a seamless, stable, and unified subjectivity, whereas Pessoa takes the issue of the "fragmented subject" to its ultimate consequence by creating dozens of other poets/authors. Sá-Carneiro's novel *A confissão de Lúcio* (1913) (*Lucio's Confession*, 1993), for instance, deals with the question of otherness, phantasmagoric identities, and masked homoerotic desire. Between Lúcio (the narrator) and Ricardo (his best friend), there is Marta, the lover of both of them. The narrative's denouement is astonishing indeed as the reader realizes that Marta's tenuous existence was the conduit through which both men expressed or lived their attraction and desire for each other. The following poetic fragment sheds light on this novel, as well as on Sá-Carneiro's narrative work in general, unveiling the meaning that remains hidden among successive critical (as well as canonical) readings of his work:

Eu queria ser mulher para me poder estender
Ao lado dos meus amigos, "banquettes" dos cafés.
Eu queria ser mulher para poder estender
Pó-de-arroz pelo meu rosto diante de todos, nos cafés.

Eu queria ser mulher para excitar quem me olhasse
Eu queria ser mulher para me poder recusar.
("Feminina," in Sá-Carneiro 1995: 148)

[I would like to be a woman
so that I could spread myself
next to my friends, over the "banquettes."

I would like to be a woman
so that I could spread powder on my face
in front of everyone at the cafés.

I would like to be a woman
so that I could arouse anyone who'd look at me
I would like to be a woman so that
I could say no.]

Homosexuality, as envisaged by Sá-Carneiro, does not follow (unlike Pessoa) an androgynous dynamic, but rather reflects the impossibility of being what one is in a society ruled by rigid, preestablished roles. Thus, as in the novel *A confissão de Lúcio,* to become a woman remains the only possible solution to the marginal status that is imposed on his erotic desire.

The *Orpheu* generation is the landmark for the rise of literary Modernism in Portugal, as well as for the appearance of "gay" poetry.[4] The continued thematization of homosexuality in Portuguese literature, however, became compromised after 1926, when censorship and strict control over cultural production was instituted by the Catholic-inspired Salazar dictatorship, which lasted until 1974. For many years, poetry became virtually the only means of expression for homosexuality in Portuguese literature. Since Abel Botelho (*O Barão de Lavos,* first published in 1891) and Sá-Carneiro (*A confissão de Lúcio,* first published in 1913), there has been a dearth of prose writing depicting the experience of gays and lesbians in Portugal.[5] Nevertheless, since *Orpheu,* poetry continues to be a most fertile ground for the discussion of male homoerotic desire (see, for instance, António Botto, Mário Cesariny, Gastão Cruz, Luís Miguel Nava, Joaquim Manuel Magalhães, Eugénio de Andrade, and, principally, Al Berto). The thematization of homosexuality, or better, the thematization of a desire that does not coincide with the dominant values of Portuguese conservative society, is represented by the emergence of Portuguese gay poetry. This type of poetry, however, flourished under the shadows of censorship, and therefore remained invisible within the Portuguese literary canon. Only at the end of the Salazar dictatorship, with the April revolution of 1974, were Portuguese gays able to reveal themselves and claim sociohistorical visibility.[6]

How to Translate *Queer* into Portuguese

In order to establish the contours of a queer poetry in Portugal and the importance of Al Berto's work within it, we must first devise an analytic model that is inclusive of Portuguese (as well as Brazilian) cultural particularities, at the same time as we explore the meanings and possible uses of the term *queer* for Portuguese-speaking cultures.

Sexual differences are paramount in Anglophone queer studies. However, if we are to consider the question of sexual difference in Portuguese-speaking cultures, we must also bear in mind historical and cultural particularities. These particularities prevent us from automatically translating key notions of Anglophone queer theory into Portuguese. For instance, the English-language construct of *queer* has no semantic equivalent in the Portuguese language. With this in mind, we must endeavor to translate this cultural construct in a more Derridian sense, that is, to reinterpret, reelaborate, and deconstruct.

The first question that we must consider, with regard to a language that does not possess a word with the semantic richness of *queer,* is the specific cultural field in which discourses about difference circulate. Indeed, the act of acknowledging difference in the Portuguese language also means recognizing the peripheral place occupied by this language and the cultures that speak it in a global context.

There are two critical paradigms that have dominated contemporary discussions regarding Portuguese culture and these are represented by Eduardo Lourenço and Boaventura de Sousa Santos. Both paradigms represent two distinct, though nonexclusive, views of Portuguese national identity. On the one hand, Lourenço—a philosopher and cultural critic—highlights the founding myths that were absorbed and interpreted by the intellectual elites during nine hundred years of Portuguese history. Sociologist Boaventura de Sousa Santos, on the other hand, believes that one of the central questions of Portuguese culture is the fact that throughout history Portugal has occupied a peripheral position in the context of European capitalism, at the same time as it was the center of a colonial empire. This simultaneously central and peripheral location from a geopolitical standpoint has given Portugal an ambiguous status in the context of world history. At the same time as it functioned as a cultural model for its colonies, Portugal was also significantly influenced by the cultures it colonized. Interestingly enough, Santos's insights were already hinted at in the writings of sociologist Gilberto Freyre and avant-garde poet Oswald de Andrade during the first half of the twentieth century in Brazil.

Freyre defines Brazil as a cultural hybrid resulting from three main influences: Portuguese, African, and Amerindian. However, he argues that the Portuguese influence ultimately left the deepest imprint in Brazilian culture, though this imprint was already different from metropolitan culture as it adapted to a new life in the tropics. Oswald de Andrade, for his part, has a different understanding of Brazilian culture. His work, and that of Brazilian Modernism in general, was shaped by the absorption and reworking of aesthetic and ideological influences stemming from the European avant-garde movements. Together with Mário de Andrade, the Brazilian Modernist poet, Oswald led a movement that had a profound impact on Brazilian high culture at the time, particularly in the realms of literature, painting, sociology, historiography, philosophy, and ethnomusicology. In essence, Oswald, along with his Modernist peers, took the idea of cannibalism that emerged from historiographical accounts of sixteenth-century Brazil, divested it from its negative connotations, and used it to explain Brazilian culture. The symbolic point of departure is the devouring of sixteenth-century Portuguese bishop Sardinha by Brazilian cannibalistic Indians. This event constitutes a "primal scene" from which to subsequently define Brazilian national identity. Thus, Brazilian culture is defined as having been historically shaped by a process of "cultural anthropophagy" by which foreign influences have been consumed, assimilated, and adapted to Brazilian realities. In this case, the Brazilian "cannibalistic savage" *devours* the other so as to become himself or herself an other. By absorbing and transforming foreign cultural influences, Brazil is not merely copying foreign cultural elements, but instead, through this process of cannibalization or "transculturation," is establishing its *difference* in the world.

In his musings on Brazilian culture in 1928, when "Manifesto antropófago" was published, Oswald de Andrade posited difference as the indelible hallmark of our unique and exoticized relationship with the other: "Nunca fomos catequizados. Fizemos foi Carnaval" (1978: 16) (We were never catechized. Instead, we organized a carnival ball). Among Brazilians, the cultural laws that have historically determined centers and peripheries were not quite absorbed.[7] They were carnivalized, becoming instead mere instruments of the cultural apparatus. Oswald de Andrade's aphorism, somewhat forgotten in these times of globalization, could well be rescued from the moment we understand the relative nature of the relationship between peripheral and core cultures. According to Andrade, there are no available centers within Brazilian culture. On the contrary, the "carnivalization" of culture in Brazil has produced a type of "non-sense" in the relationship between elites and working classes. Without clear centers, we are mediated through the act of "anthropophagy," that is, we devour the culture of the other, diluting our identity in an intense process of multiculturalization. Through such a perspective, we observe a certain "chaos" in Brazilian culture, where there seem to be no clear hierarchies regulating symbolic exchanges. Brazilian religious syncretism, for example, mixes Christian culture with African culture. As if in a permanent carnival, high and low, left and right, the sacred and the profane, the legal and illegal, all coexist in a seemingly harmonious fashion. Centers of power are dispersed throughout the culture, becoming even more diluted during the rituals of carnival. Citizenship and marginality emerge as fluctuating concepts that vary according to social and cultural circumstances.

The references to Oswald de Andrade are not gratuitous. Through Oswald's work together with that of Mário de Andrade, Caio Prado Jr., Sérgio Buarque de Hollanda, and Gilberto Freyre, a new and radical critical apparatus was developed in order to explain Brazilian culture, thus departing from dominant sociological and anthropological notions that were predominant in the 1920s and that were heavily influenced by nineteenth-century eugenics. In this context, Oswald de Andrade's idea of cultural anthropophagy in the early twentieth century celebrates the end of colonialism and cultural dependency in Brazil. Hence, anthropophagy would constitute a violent response to the way in which Brazilian culture had interacted with foreign models until then. Yet, according to Lúcia Helena (1985: 157), the "anthropophagous movement" did not intend to create obstacles in the cultural dialogue between the national and the foreign. Helena adds that Andradian anthropophagy is a metaphorically violent attempt to break away with tradition based on the memory of another violent event, that of colonialism, in order to posit a cultural utopia.

Renowned Portuguese sociologist Boaventura de Sousa Santos recognizes the peculiarities of Oswald de Andrade's ideas as he discusses peripheral cultures, particularly those of Portuguese-speaking peoples:

Andrade propõe-nos um começo que, em vez de excluir, devora canibalisticamente o tempo que o precede, seja ele o tempo falsamente primordial do nativismo, seja ele o tempo falsamente universal do eurocentrismo. Esta voracidade inicial e iniciática funda um novo e mais amplo horizonte de reflexividade, de diversidade e de diálogo donde é

possível ver a diferença abissal entre a macumba para turistas e a
tolerância racial. Acima de tudo, Oswald de Andrade sabe que a única
verdadeira descoberta é a autodescoberta e que esta implica presentificar
o outro e a conhecer a posição de poder a partir do qual é possível a
apropriação selectiva e transformadora dele. (1992: 120)

[Andrade proposes a beginning that, instead of excluding, cannibalistically devours the time that precedes it, be it the falsely primordial time
of nativism or the falsely universal time of eurocentrism. This initial and
initiated voracity founds a new and broader horizon of thought, of diver-
sity, and of dialogue from where it is possible to discern the enormous
difference between *macumba* ceremonies for tourists and racial tolerance.
Above all, Oswald de Andrade knows that the only real discovery is self-
discovery and that that implies making the other present and, at the
same time, knowing the position of power from which it is possible to
selectively appropriate the other and be transformed by it/him/her.]

Santos's words are extremely useful as they allow us to extend Oswald
de Andrade's analysis beyond Brazil and onto peripheral cultures in general. Andrade's thinking highlights a peculiar relationship with culture
(culture defined here as the realm of the symbolic), insofar as the can-
nibal annihilates the Other, putting himself in his place as someone
who occupies both the center and the margins, aware of his ubiquity.
Thus, in order to posit the emergence of a "queer" literature in Portuguese,
we must bear in mind the historically ambiguous status of homosexual
practices within these cultures.

In his essay "O pagode português," Luiz Mott reveals astonishing results.[8] Mott points to the ambivalent and fluid relations between Portuguese society and homosexuality, in which there were periods of heavy
repression, alternating with periods of tolerance, even as homosexuality
remained illegal and subject to persecution and prosecution. He claims
that in early modern Portugal, as well as in colonial Brazil, there existed
a "homosexual identity" that preceded the importation of twentieth-
century North American variants of "gay identity." Such early/nascent
"homosexual identity" was the product of the recognition of its difference vis-à-vis the repressive apparatus. Mott presents numerous cases
of individuals prosecuted by the Inquisition who did not relinquish their
"eccentric" condition, admitting to the pleasure they experienced in
their sexual practices. Such pleasure was not circumscribed to the sexual realm, but was also related to the practice of transvestism, the use of
cosmetics, and other "peculiar" habits. Such behavioral patterns and the

"identities" that were built on them are in consonance with the excentricity associated with peripheral cultures such as Portugal or Brazil, as pointed out by Santos. Beyond the economic and political excentricity of Portuguese-speaking cultures in colonial as well as postcolonial times, Mott, Santos, and Oswald de Andrade suggest an excentricity that is a "constitutive feature" of our cultures.[9] The excentric subject, even in a subaltern condition, from the sixteenth-century *fanchono* to the transvestite in the streets of Rio de Janeiro, may at times occupy center stage in Luso-Brazilian cultures.[10] For example, the drag queens who impersonated Portuguese *fado* diva Amália Rodrigues were famous during the Salazar regime, and transsexual Roberta Close became a mass-media phenomenon during the 1980s and 1990s in Brazil.[11]

Following Santos's analysis, it must be acknowledged that Brazilian and Portuguese cultures deal with difference in a peculiar manner. Portuguese and Brazilian cultural formations (the latter owing to its colonial heritage) have instilled an identity that is defined by a "frontier" or "border" condition in relationship to world cultural centers. Thus Brazilians and Portuguese experience the privileged as well as devalorized condition of being simultaneously Caliban and Prospero. They are frontier subjects at the borders between culture and barbarism, at the same time being the "cultivated European" and the "ignorant savage." If queer theory searches for a potential identity based on an overdetermined object of study, then, once queer theory is appropriated by Portuguese-speaking scholars, they must bear in mind a shady zone that extends between what is designated by the binary "straight" and "queer" within its Anglophone matrix and the less intense homophobia and greater tolerance for difference experienced in the practices of everyday life in Portuguese-speaking societies. As stated by Santos:

A zona fronteiriça é uma zona híbrida, babélica, onde os contactos se pulverizam e se ordenam segundo micro-hierarquias pouco susceptíveis de globalização. Em tal zona, são imensas as possibilidades de identificação e de criação cultural, todos igualmente superficiais e igualmente subvertíveis: a antropofagia que Oswald de Andrade atribuía à cultura brasileira e que eu penso caracterizar igualmente e por inteiro a cultura portuguesa. (1992: 134)

[The frontier is a hybrid and Babel-like zone where contacts are pulverized and ordered by means of micro-hierarchies that are less susceptible to globalization. In such a zone, the possibilities of identification and cultural creativity are enormous, all equally superficial and equally subvertible, such as the "cannibalistic" traits that Oswald de Andrade attributes to Brazilian culture, which I also consider very relevant to Portuguese culture.]

The importance attributed by Santos to Oswald de Andrade's thought is extremely valuable if we wish to appropriate the concept of *queer* for Portuguese-speaking cultures. Santos, in fact, inverts discursive hierarchies, based on Luso-Brazilian colonial dynamics, by privileging the point of view of the former colonized (or the margin), in this case Brazil, over that of the former colonizer (or the center), that is, Portugal. As a result, the act of inversion becomes subversion as the culture of the former colony suddenly explains that of the former metropole. Now, the act of unproblematically translating the concept of queer for a Portuguese-speaking periphery would constitute a betrayal of the cannibalistic traits that have forged Brazilian or Portuguese identities. Brazilian and Portuguese critics either reject the theoretical apparatus offered by Anglophone queer theory or we devour it cannibalistically with all the contradictions that such move may entail. Today, we already observe the emergence of a Lusophone "gay" identity molded on identities made in the United States, entailing sociopolitical activism, lobbies, and "coming out." On the other hand, we also observe specific socioeconomic and historical circumstances of countries such as Brazil and Portugal that produce other gay identities in working-class urban peripheries or among marginal beings located at the bottom of the social pyramid (transvestite prostitutes or male hustlers, for example). The latter have long been the most visible side of homosexuality in both Brazilian and Portuguese cultures. Therefore, to cannibalistically devour the term *queer* entails more than a mere translation or process of assimilation; it means adapting it to a Lusophone cultural sphere, radicalizing its "gay" component, as well as reinventing it. It also means including the politicized transvestite alongside the critical *bicha*.[12]

Anglophone queer theory does offer interpretive tools and useful insights for the analysis of homosexuality in Portuguese-speaking cultures. At the same time, its attempt at overcoming the binary heterosexuality/homosexuality in order to include other registers of sexuality, class, gender, race, nationality, and political ideologies, provides a valuable and more exhaustive framework for the analysis of peripheral societies such as Portugal and Brazil, at the same time as it links these societies to a much larger transnational framework of concerns uniting sexual and gender minorities throughout the world.

Al Berto: The Luso Queer Principle

Since the 1960s, various Portuguese poets—particularly Luís Miguel Nava, Gastão Cruz, Joaquim Manuel Magalhães, and Al Berto—have begun to systematically thematize sexual difference and homoerotic desire.[13] All of them are included in anthologies as some of the best examples of contemporary Portuguese poetry. However, once again, Portuguese academic criticism refuses to identify or discuss questions of sexual difference or homoerotic desire, and instead focuses on form and stylistic effects achieved by the mastery of language. Yet, alongside the poetic experimentation, typical of the 1960s avant-garde, we also find themes that insist on desacralization, marginality, and transgressive experiences. Hence, we witness the gradual emergence of a queer consciousness. Among all poets there is a profound tendency to use metaphors of difference as experienced in everyday life in a multiplicity of registers and tonalities. Gastão Cruz associates war images with an eroticism impregnated by violence in which pleasure and orgasm are expressed as historical guilt. Death, violence, and orgasm intersect in a powerful poetic discourse that points to transgression even though it cannot speak about the marginalized subjectivity that lies at its root. Luís Miguel Nava's poetry is constructed through an association between the conceptual and everyday life, that is to say, his poetry is born out of everyday life and one can never be separated from the other. In Nava's poetry, homosexuality becomes a metaphor that constructs everyday life, yet at the same time the subject is unable to achieve orgasm, because death as annihilation is the theme through which the promise of orgasm flows. In Joaquim Manuel Magalhães's poetry, everyday life appears as the structuring element. Poetry is based on the referentiality allowed by visual perception. The body appears as a place of fruition—and yet it is meaningless—that is to say, the body does not register anything beyond physical sensations. Language, almost devoid of metaphors, is not a supplement to orgasm.

With these three figures we witness a type of poetry imbued with a rhetoric connected to a group identity, rather than the reflections of an individual subject. The poetic discourse of Cruz, Nava, and Magalhães does not exhibit a preoccupation with the subject's place in history.

Portuguese culture, in fact, does not become an object of discussion from the point of view of a gay subject. In the work of these poets, homosexuality becomes a poetic metaphor, rather than a poetics. In contrast, it is only through the poetic work of Al Berto that one can detect a truly queer consciousness. Al Berto's poetry is, in fact, where gay identity and homoerotic desire are most evident in the context of Portuguese literature.

All of Al Berto's work produced between 1974 and 1997 (the year of his death) is collected in a massive volume, *O medo* (1998). The chronological sequence that shapes this volume allows the reader to note the gradual evolution of a poetic subject who moves from androgyny to homosexuality, from profound introspection to the emergence of a historical consciousness linked to sexual difference. Al Berto's poetry represents the journey from a first home of silence (that is, writing) to a second home (that of memory-skin and body), where a history of desire breaks the silence of writing. From "Equinócios de tangerina" (1974) to "Horto de incêndio" (1997), this journey is carried out step by step as a poetic project of experimentation and research. This project started in 1974, when Al Berto first wrote a small text titled "À procura do vento num jardim d'Agosto—*atrium*" (Searching for the wind in a garden of August—*atrium*):[14]

> na cal viva da memória dorme o corpo. vem lamber-lhe as pálpebras um cão ferido. acorda-o para a inútil deambulação da escrita.
> abandonado vou pelo caminho de sinuosas cidades. sozinho, procuro o fio de néon que me indica a saída.
> eis a deriva pela insónia de quem se mantém vivo num túnel da noite. os corpos de Alberto e Al Berto vergados à coincidência suicidária das cidades. (11)

> [the body sleeps in the quicklime of memory. a wounded dog licks its eyelids, it wakes him to the useless wandering of writing.
> abandoned, I walk on the path of sinuous cities. alone, I search for the neon sign that shows the exit.
> adrift with insomnia like one who is kept alive in the tunnel of the night. the bodies of Alberto and Al Berto bent toward the suicidal coincidence of cities.]

His poetic writing erupts somewhere in between Alberto and Al Berto. This is a fragmented discourse that emerges from the liminal space or borderline between the poet who writes himself and the body that transports him. Fragmentation is the only possible stratagem for the under-

standing of his world. From the social self, Alberto, to the poetic self, Al
Berto, one senses a degree of pleasure in the poet's writing at the margins, as his entryway into the world. What world? The world order that
is instituted by the poet's existence at the margins.

In "Equinócios de tangerina," Al Berto invests in writing procedures
that go beyond Portuguese poetic traditions. There are echoes of beat-
nik writing, with acid-induced landscapes and behaviors unusual in a
country that had only recently conquered democracy. The poetic subject expands itself through a project to be carried out by means of multiple sensorial experiences:

> um vapor lilás imenso e transparente
> as paisagens sucedem-se semelhantes às que já conheço desde a infância.
> o ácido voo é translúcido e mole, afia a memória, vai a lugares
> insuspeitos, atinge remotas camadas do corpo e do pensamento. no
> início Tangerina é uma flor branca, nasce do corpo e nele se alimenta e
> envenena. nele vive e cresce lentamente, transborda, sufoca e morre.
> morre. (15)

> [an immense and transparent lilac steam
> landscapes follow each other in succession, similar to those I've known
> since childhood. the acid flight is translucent and soft, it sharpens
> memory, it goes to unpredictable places, it reaches remote layers of the
> body and thought. at the beginning, Tangerine is a white flower, it grows
> from the body, feeding and poisoning itself from it. it lives within it and
> slowly grows, overflows, suffocates, and dies. it dies.]

From introspection, Al Berto's project opens itself to the expression of
desire. Tangerine used to follow the will of the wind in the gardens of
August, complying with the order of time and space, not fully exercising
the possibilities offered by desire. In fact, this first poetic moment oscil-
lates between the exercise of desire and its negation. But once again in
the poem "*atrium*," the flavor of the *project* should be noted, in which
the poet advances his unconsciousness to the spaces of memory within
his writing. In "*atrium*," the poet says:

> para sobreviver à noite decidimos perder a memória. cobríamo-nos com
> musgo seco e amanhecíamos num casulo de frio, perdidos no tempo.
> mas, antes que a memória fosse apenas uma ligeira sensação de dor,
> registámos inquietantes vozes, caminhámos invisíveis na repetição
> enigmática das máscaras, dos rostos, dos gestos desfazendo-se em cinza.
> escutámos o que há de inaudível em nossos corpos. (11)

[in order to survive the night we decided to lose our memory. we covered ourselves with dry moss and woke up in a cold cocoon, lost in time. but, before memory became a slightly painful sensation, we registered disturbing voices, we were invisible walking in the enigmatic repetition of masks, faces, and gestures breaking down into ashes. we listened to what is inaudible within our bodies.]

Here, Al Berto's writing practice reveals the body-memory, the skin-memory, the memory of the streets, of words, the memory that fragments itself in the unspoken and unrecognized practices of pleasure at Rua do Forte (Forte Street) that involve the playful gestures of the passing friend, and viscerally erotic poems. As he reminisces, the poet reconstructs through his writing the practices that only his everyday life registers. The act of remembering, of bringing to the present time what should be left in the past, what should not be mentioned, what should be silenced and hidden, is explicitly carried out, and often attributed to an other, or even, to an other and yet same poetic self. Illicit pleasure may appear as an external action on the part the poet, as an unauthorized attitude revealing what is repressed by the unconscious. In "Retrato de um amigo enquanto bebe" (Portrait of a friend while he drinks), Al Berto says:

o homem levantou-se
indiferente à revelação da alba titubeou tossiu
apoiado no magro ombro do rapaz
desapareceram pelas ruas estreitas do mar
entre redes cordas quilhas e remos

onde se embarca para o medo esquecido de mais um dia. (241)

[the man got up
indifferent to dawn's revelation he hesitated coughed
leaning on the boy's thin shoulder
they disappeared into the narrow streets of the sea
between nets ropes keels and oars

where one sails toward the forgotten fear of another day.

The memory loss mentioned in "*atrium*" is the result of a strategy that delegates the meaning of the day to "the other." This other becomes the basis for a series of nocturnal wanderings of desiring subjects who search for their object amid the city shadows. It is worth noticing that the city becomes the center stage for this drama. Yet, the meeting of subject and

object is filled with anguish and dissatisfaction because the object of desire (the "trick" or sexual partner) reveals the often tenuous and superficial nature of marginalized and furtive homoerotic encounters. Thus,
memory emerges as the instrument that may provide hope and a promise of fulfillment to the wandering and solitary subject. It is there that
the erotic utopia is founded and destroyed. This double possibility creates a dynamic that enables the gradual construction of an identity that
questions its place, time, and condition in the world:

> a memória está perfumada de violetas
> desprende-se dos pulsos escorre pela cal dos corredores
> persigo-me pela madrugada suja das palavras
> com o pressentimento de ter morrido longe de meu corpo
> encosto-me às esquinas disponíveis da cidade
> amachuco a vida debaixo dos sóis que te evocam
> oferecendo a espuma da boca a todos os desconhecidos.
> ("Persiana de água" 243)

> [memory has a violet perfume
> it loosens itself from the wrists flows down the walls of the chalked
>   corridors
> I follow myself in the dirty morning of words
> with the premonition of having died far away from my body
> I lean on the available corners of the city
> I crush the life under the suns that evoke you
> offering the foam of my mouth to all strangers.
> ("Water blinds")]

Oddly enough, contrary to traditional poetics, memory in Al Berto
promotes meaning as well as nonmeaning, suggesting the existence of a
subject who dwells within conflict at the borders between the center
and the margin, highly aware of his fluid identity that creates tension.
The poet thrives in this identity so as to build from it a subjectivity capable of fiercely critiquing the culture that relegates him to the margins
of the margins. Historical consciousness in Al Berto emanates from a
profound experience of multiplicity, though a multiplicity that is different from Fernando Pessoa's. The experience of multiplicity in Al Berto's
poetry is the result of the need to affirm sexual difference and the need
to establish an affirmative poetics of a marginalized sexual identity that
questions mainstream cultural conventions. Thus, within this context, Al
Berto is the queer subject who asserts himself within his discourse, speaking from margin to margin, favoring an interlocutor who can identify

himself or herself with the same practices silenced by writing, but which "skin-memory" unleashes. Far from offering a discourse directed at one specific type of interlocutor, however, the poet speaks to an unknown being, at this side of the margin where he is located, so as to allow his poetry to deconstruct hegemonic cultural formations. In "*atrium*" he says:

> Aqui está a imobilidade aquática de meu país,
> o oceânico abismo com cheiro a cidades por sonhar,
> invade-me a vontade de permanecer aqui, para sempre,
> à janela,
> ou partir com as marés e nunca mais voltar. (12)

> [Here's the aquatic immobility of my country,
> the oceanic abyss with smells of cities to be dreamed of,
> the desire to remain here forever by the window,
> or to leave with the tides and never return, overwhelms me.]

To deal with the myths of water that are so embedded in Portuguese culture to the point of also recognizing a historical stagnation of such mythical waters is a way of problematizing the very culture, as well as making visible within that culture unpredictable elements that have remained invisible until then. In "O mito da sereia em plástico português" (The myth of the mermaid in Portuguese plastic), Al Berto establishes a rare critical dialogue with the founding myths of Portuguese nationhood, most particularly with the ways through which fascism appropriated such myths:

> eu vi
> a sereia de plástico construir um país
> e um veleiro para se evadir na direcção doutras ilhas
> levando por bagagem os detritos dados-à-costa: garrafas brancas de gin
> nocturno sapatos inchados panos preservativos usados cacos de louça
> embalagens carcomidas cartões de caixas ao vento velas da imensa
> jangada vestígios de comida rápida pentes vidros filmes madeira
> fotografias que o tempo recusou morder
> . . . .
> eu vi a sereia em plástico português abrir um sulco de solidão
> o precipício
> e renegar o falso mel da terra debruçada sobre o esquecimento. (86)

> [i saw
> the plastic mermaid building a country
> and a sailboat to head off in the direction of other islands

carrying as luggage the remains of the sea: white bottles of nocturnal gin
swollen shoes pieces of cloth used condoms
fragments of china torn packages cardboard boxes to the wind sails of
    the enormous
raft traces of fast food combs glass film wood
photos that time refused to bite
. . . .
i saw the mermaid in Portuguese plastic open a furrow of solitude
the precipice
and reject the false honey of the land
perched over oblivion.]

Portugal's historical stagnation becomes submerged, disappearing in
the undercurrents of a national identity linked to the myths of the discovered maritime path and manifest destiny. In Al Berto's poetry, history is made of those images that impregnate his memory. His desire
emerges from the metaphors of the sea:

preciso encontrar o lugar certo para o nosso amor
queres vir comigo?
já avisto da gávea inquietantes iluminuras de rostos de afogados
mãos antigas como rochedos peixes fantásticos
bocas aflitas e tua boca mordendo
o cordame avariado pelo sal
ah meu amigo
eis o sofrimento de meus lábios gretados pelo sarro oceânico
eis as minhas unhas protegendo o sexo aberto
às monções aos ventos adversos às vagas rumorosas.
                                        ("Carta da flor do sol," 408)

[i must find the right place for our love
will you join me?
from the topsail i now see disturbing manuscript images
of drowned faces
ancient hands like rocks fantastic fish
distressed mouths and your mouth biting
the rope damaged by the salt
oh my friend
this is the suffering of my lips cracked by the ocean fur
these are the nails protecting the open sex
from monsoons adverse winds deafening waves.
                            ("Letter from the flower of the sun")]

And yet it is in "Luminoso afogado" that Al Berto's queer sensibility
flourishes. In his poetic trajectory since "*atrium*," Al Berto invokes mem-

ory in order to recognize the historical real. In the case of "Luminoso afogado," there is a monologue of a poetic subject who addresses the corpse of a drowned man. This dead-silent interlocutor incites a lengthy meditation on the possible relation between the margins and the center within a culture of imprecise internal borders. Al Berto circulates on the margins of the history and culture to which he belongs. The poem "Luminoso afogado" establishes a dialogue with Fernando Pessoa/Álvaro de Campos's poem "O marinheiro" (The sailor). This intertextual dialogue stresses the historical consciousness exercised by Al Berto as he brings the reality of desire to the poem's surface.

Thus, by means of literary artifice, Al Berto deconstructs not only the history of his country, but above all, his own personal history inscribed in his memory. Any meaning forged by memory creates new meanings, establishing the only possible dynamics as an alternative to the historical stagnation caused by the Portuguese myths related to water and the sea, that is, the implosion of the whole historical edifice, the return to the harbor "where we will no longer remember our bodies" ("o cais por fim, o cais onde desembarcamos e / de nossos corpos não nos lembraremos mais" ["Regresso ao cais," 244]). Hence, the history of Portugal is written through the poet's own personal history. Al Berto articulates both history and memory in such a way that the former will be read and understood by the latter. His memory creates a history at the same time as it demands a place in history for queer subjects. In "Luminoso afogado," memory moves toward an amnesiac condition, in an undefined time and space, where identity is built on the lack of referentiality that culture reserves for those who do not submit to its dictates. In Al Berto's poetry, an ahistorical queer subjectivity is constructed, assuming at once a liminal or border condition where it enunciates a poetry of silence and a body hidden behind words. His poetry interrogates and problematizes a history that elides and ignores the subjectivity that is posited therein. Within this context, the body plays a crucial as well as a paradoxical role in that its poetic representation constitutes an attempt to circumvent the limits imposed by the order of the real (in Lacanian terms), that is, to represent that which is nonrepresentable:

Existem Indias por descobrir, no segredo da noite de nossos desastres.
Caminhamos neste espaço de penumbras e de incertezas—onde a fala já
não cintila e as palavras são cinza....

O silêncio das viagens cumpridas.
E no meio deste silêncio uma ideia de voz, uma treva agarrada à
    memória.
Foi então que dei por mim a existir para lá da tua morte, como se
    asfixiasse. Mas o passado não é senão um sonho. Um brincadeira com
    clepsidras avariadas e algum sangue.
Não vale a pena estar triste.
Todas as histórias, todas mortes, acabam por se apagar.

Um barco tremeluz nas cortinas do quarto.
O horizonte é negro. A luz do dia extinguiu-se subitamente.
As mãos com que te toco, luminoso afogado, não são verdadeiras, nem
    reais—porque o tempo todo talvez esteja onde existimos. Embora
    saibamos que nesse lugar nunca houve tempo nenhum. (629)

[There are Indies yet to be discovered, in the secret of the night of our
    disasters.
We walk in this space of shadows and uncertainties—where speech no
    longer sparkles and words are ashes. . . .

The silence of the completed travels.
And in the middle of this silence a voice-idea, darkness clinging to
    memory.
That is when I noticed myself existing beyond your death, as if
    asphyxiating. But the past is only a dream. A game of damaged
    clepsydras and some blood.
It's not worth it to be sad.
All histories, all deaths are eventually erased.

A ship glimmers through the curtains of the room.
The horizon is black. Daylight suddenly extinguishes itself.
The hands with which I touch you, luminous drowned one, are not true
    nor real—maybe because time is only where we are. Even if we've
    known that in such place time has never been.]

Scott Bravmann points out in *Queer Fictions of the Past* (1997) that in
order to establish the parameters of a queer historiography reflecting
a community's active participation in the historical process there must
be an acknowledgment of discontinuities in the narratives offered by
the agents involved in the historical process. A queer historiography
would be the result of a confluence of these fragmented narratives. As
long as oral and written memory remain the province of official discourse, the history of Portuguese-speaking queers will necessarily be

the reconstruction of fragments in search of discursive gaps through which their identities may emerge. If queer identities in core cultures are born at the margins, on the periphery of capitalism, where the Portuguese language flourishes, the *luso* queer principle is born out of questioning the nonplace from which one speaks. The *luso* queer must not only deconstruct the culture in which she or he is located, but also problematize the geopolitical position of that culture where his or her marginalized identity emerges. Al Berto's poetry forces us to critically consider the location from which one speaks and the location one addresses, knowing full well that both locations overlap, pointing to the inherent contradictions within a cultural edifice that may implode or become shipwrecked. Ultimately, we are left with the piercing silent cry that stems from the impossibility of making a pact with the dominant discourses of history: the refusal of the silence of his writing.

Notes

1. The term *literary series* refers to a group of literary works that share common thematic, stylistic, or linguistic elements. This term may describe a national literature, a group of works that transcend national borders, or a group of works within a national literature that share common traits. See Tinianov (1979).

2. António Botto was a pioneer in the early twentieth century in that he produced the most unabashedly homoerotic poems ever in the history of Portuguese literature. His poems do not display the philosophical depth or existential angst that one witnesses in Pessoa or Sá-Carneiro, yet his texts exhibit a homosexual subjectivity that is much less troubled than almost any of the works by his better-known contemporaries. See the most recent edition of *As canções de António Botto* (1999)—Ed.

3. The term *discourse* is used here in a Foucauldian sense, that is, as a supra-grammatical instance in which a text is understood within the context of the historical, political, cultural, and ideological conditions of its production. In this sense we can argue for a gay discourse that is different from a queer discourse, where the conditions that produced the former are different from those of the latter.

4. *Orpheu* was the literary journal that launched Fernando Pessoa and Mário de Sá-Carneiro in 1915.

5. Abel Botelho is the author of the first novel in Portuguese to overtly thematize homoerotic desire and homosexual subjectivity *(O Barão de Lavos).* [Very few contemporary Portuguese prose writers have explored the thematics of male homoerotic desire. See Rui Nunes, *Grito* (1997) and *Cães* (1999); Alexandre Pinheiro Torres, *Amor, só amor, tudo amor* (1999); Guilherme de Melo, *A sombra dos dias* (1981) and *O que houver de morrer* (1989); and Inês Pedrosa, *Nas tuas mãos* (1997).—Ed.]

6. After numerous attempts at organizing themselves between 1974 and 1994, Portuguese gay men and lesbians finally attained political visibility in 1995 with the founding of ILGA-Portugal.

According to Portuguese legislation dating back to 1912, homosexuality (or "the practice of the vice against nature") was considered the equivalent of vagrancy. Between the 1930s and 1950s, men accused of homosexuality would be imprisoned for years in rehabilitation centers called *mitras*. Even those homosexuals of higher social status could not avoid humiliating interrogations by the police. Until the April revolution of 1974, the so-called morality police (polícia de costumes) would blackmail those perceived to be homosexual in exchange for silence. After the April revolution, there was a gradual liberalization of cultural habits and mentalities. In the 1970s and 1980s, homosexuality became more favorably viewed by certain sectors of the urban middle classes. For more information on the subject, see the ILGA-Portugal home page at http://www.ilga-portugal.org/homepage.html.

7. In anthropological terms, the elements that shape a culture, such as social memory, habits, and the symbolic universe, determine rigid boundaries between civilization and barbarism. According to Oswald de Andrade, Brazilian culture has made such boundaries more flexible, confusing the poles of civilization and barbarism. From a geocultural standpoint, we might add, based on Andrade's reflection on "anthropophagy," that Brazil has also relativized the dichotomy between center and periphery by "cannibalistically" absorbing cultural traits or expressions akin to Western Europe, and, more recently, North America, adapting them at the same time to specifically Brazilian circumstances.

8. Luiz Mott is a pioneering researcher of historical sources concerning homosexuality (or, to be more precise, sodomitic practices) in Portugal and Brazil since the Inquisition in 1534.

9. In his article "O pagode português," Mott points out that there was a flourishing "homosexual" subculture in the city of Lisbon between the sixteenth and eighteenth centuries in spite of an active and repressive Inquisition. [This observation is corroborated by historian David Higg's study on Lisbon in *Queer Sites.*—Ed.]

10. In early modern Portugal (as well as in colonial Brazil), the term *fanchono* had the connotation of "fairy," effeminate, or queer. The term seems to not have carried a negative connotation. *Fanchono* could also mean homosexual (or sodomite) and it suggested a group identity as well (see Mott [1988] and Higgs [1999]).

11. Throughout the 1980s and early 1990s, male-to-female transsexual Roberta Close became a major media sensation, and was popularly considered the most beautiful *woman* in Brazil.

12. The term *bicha* in Brazil means "faggot" or "queer." It has increasingly been appropriated by gays and divested of its negative connotations, although semantically the term refers specifically to homosexuals and/or transvestites/transsexuals. In Portugal, on the other hand, the word *bicha* is a neutral, everyday term to signify "line" or "queue" (as in "to stand in line"). In recent years, as a result of Brazilian influence, *bicha* has taken on a playful double meaning, particularly in Portuguese gay culture.

13. See Gastão Cruz, *Os nomes* (1974) and *Orgão de luzes: poesia reunida* (1990); Joaquim Manuel Magalhães, *Alguns livros reunidos* (1987) and *A poeira levada pelo vento* (1993); and Luís Miguel Nava, *O pão, a culpa, a escrita e outros textos* (1982) and *Vulcão* (1994).

14. This prose poem, which can be considered Al Berto's *ars poetica,* is the first poem in the collection *O medo.*

Works Cited

Amaral, Fernando Pinto. 1991. "Al Berto: um lirismo do excesso e da melancolia." In *O mosaico fluido: modernidade e pós-modernidade na poesia portuguesa mais recente,* ed. Fernando Pinto Amaral. Lisbon: Assírio & Alvim. 119–30.

Andrade, Eugénio de. 1980. *Obra poética (1940–1979).* Lisbon: Impresa Nacional-Casa da Moeda.

Andrade, Oswald de. 1978. "Manifesto antropófago." In *Do pau brasil à antropofagia e às utopias.* Rio de Janeiro: Civilização Brasileira.

Berto, Al. 1998. *O medo.* Lisbon: Assírio & Alvim.

Botelho, Abel. 1982. *O Barão de Lavos.* Porto: Lello.

Botto, António. 1999. *As canções de António Botto.* Lisbon: Presença.

Bravmann, Scott. 1997. *Queer Fictions of the Past: History, Culture and Difference.* New York: Cambridge University Press.

Cesariny, Mário, ed. 1998. *Antologia do cadáver esquisito.* Lisbon: Assírio & Alvim.

Cruz, Gastão. 1974. *Os nomes.* Lisbon: Assírio & Alvim.

———. 1990. *Orgão de luzes: poesia reunida.* Lisbon: Imprensa Nacional-Casa da Moeda.

Freyre, Gilberto. 2000. *Casa-grande e senzala.* 39th ed. Rio de Janeiro: Editora Record.

Guimarães, Fernando. 1989. "Uma outra poesia: de Joaquim Manuel Magalhães a Al Berto." In *A poesia contemporânea portuguesa e o fim da modernidade.* Lisbon: Caminho. 135–45.

Helena, Lúcia. 1985. *Totens e tabus da modernidade brasileira: símbolo e alegoria na obra de Oswald de Andrade.* Niterói/Rio de Janeiro: Eduff/Tempo Brasileiro.

Higgs, David. 1999. *Queer Sites.* London and New York: Routledge.

ILGA-Portugal. Oct 1999. http://www.ilga-portugal.org/homepage.html.

Jagose, Annamarie. 1996. *Queer Theory: An Introduction.* New York: New York University Press.

Lugarinho, Mário César. 1998. "A poesia portuguesa após o 25 de Abril: dos centros às margens." In *Poesia Hoje,* ed. Célia Pedrosa, Claudia Matos, and Evando Nascimento. Niterói: Eduff. 113–27.

Magalhães, Joaquim Manuel. 1981. "Alberto Pidwell Tavares: uma experiência editorial." In *Os dois crepúsculos: Sobre a poesia portuguesa actual e outros ensaios.* Lisbon: A regra do jogo. 81–83.

———. 1987. *Alguns livros reunidos.* Lisbon: Contexto.

———. 1993. *A poeira levada pelo vento.* Lisbon: Presença.

Melo, Guilherme de. 1981. *A sombra dos dias.* Lisbon: Livraria Bertrand.

———. 1989. *O que houver de morrer.* Lisbon: Editorial Notícias.

Mott, Luiz. 1988. "O pagode português: a subcultura gay em Portugal durante a Inquisição." *Ciência e Cultura (SBPC)* 40: 120–39.

Nava, Luís Miguel. 1982. *O pão, a culpa, a escrita e outros textos.* Lisbon: Imprensa Nacional-Casa da Moeda.

———. 1994. *Vulcão.* Lisbon: Quetzal.

Nunes, Rui. 1997. *Grito.* Lisbon: Relógio D'Agua Editores.

———. 1999. *Cães.* Lisbon: Relógio D'Agua Editores.

Pedrosa, Inês. 1997. *Nas tuas mãos.* Lisbon: D. Quixote.

Pessoa, Fernando. 1974. *Poemas ingleses.* Lisbon: Editora Ática.

————. 1993. *Poesias de Álvaro de Campos.* Lisbon: Editora Ática.

————. 1998. *Pessoa and Co.: Selected Poems.* Ed. and Trans. Richard Zenith. New York: Grove Press.

Santos, Boaventura de Sousa. 1992. *Pela mão de Alice: o social e o político na pós-modernidade.* Porto: Afrontamento.

Sá-Carneiro, Mário. 1989. *A confissão de Lúcio.* Mem Martins, Portugal: Edições Europa-América.

————. 1993. *Lucio's Confession.* Trans. Margaret Jull Costa. Cambs, England: Dedalus.

————. 1995. *Obra completa.* Rio de Janeiro: Nova Aguilar.

Tinianov, Yuri. 1979. "Da evolução literária." In *Teoria da literatura: formalistas russos*, ed. Boris Eikhenbaum. Porto Alegre: Globo.

Torres, Alexandre Pinheiro. 1999. *Amor, só amor, tudo amor.* Lisbon: Caminho.

Contributors

Severino João Albuquerque is professor of Portuguese at the University of Wisconsin–Madison. He is the author of *Violent Acts: A Study of Contemporary Latin American Theater* and *Tentative Transgressions: Homosexuality, AIDS, and the Theater in Brazil* (forthcoming); he has also contributed two long essays on the Brazilian theater to *The Cambridge History of Latin American Literature*. He is coeditor of the *Luso-Brazilian Review,* associate editor of *Hispania,* and a member of the editorial board of *Latin American Theater Review.* The main focus of his research is contemporary Brazilian theater; he has recently developed an interest in gender and queer issues in Brazilian literature and culture.

Fernando Arenas is associate professor of Portuguese, Brazilian, and Lusophone African literary and cultural studies in the Department of Spanish and Portuguese Studies at the University of Minnesota. He is developing research in Lusophone African literature, film, popular music, and media. His book *Utopias of Otherness: Nationhood and Subjectivity in Portugal and Brazil* is forthcoming from the University of Minnesota Press.

Jossianna Arroyo is assistant professor of Latin American and Caribbean literatures and cultures in the Department of Romance Languages at the University of Michigan, Ann Arbor. She specializes in Brazilian and Spanish Caribbean literatures and cultures, focusing on gender and queer studies, racial discourses, cultures of the African diaspora, and literary theory. She has published *Travestismos culturales: literatura y etnografía en Cuba y Brasil* and several articles in anthologies and journals such as *Revista Iberoamericana, Revista de Estudios Hispánicos,* and *Revista Canadiense de Estudios Hispánicos.* She is working on a project titled *Fin de siècle: Secrecy and Modernity in Caribbean Freemasonry,* an analysis of the diasporic connections between Freemasonry, spiritualism, and the languages of modernity in the Caribbean.

César Braga-Pinto is assistant professor of Portuguese, Latin American studies, and African studies at Rutgers, the State University of New Jersey, New Brunswick. He is currently working on a manuscript titled "Promises of History: Assimilation and Prophetic Discourses in Colonial Brazil, 1500–1700." He has published articles on issues of translation, colonial Brazilian literature, and twentieth-century literature and popular music.

Ana Paula Ferreira is associate professor of Luso-Brazilian literature, critical theory, and women's studies in the Department of Spanish and Portuguese at the University of California, Irvine. She is the author of *Alves Redol e o neo-realismo português* and several articles proposing poststructuralist readings of the Portuguese and Brazilian novel of social commitment. Recently she has published primarily in the area of contemporary Portuguese women writers, from feminist, gender, and postcolonial perspectives, and has recently completed the manuscript for a critical edition of collected short stories by women, *A urgência de contar: contos de mulheres dos anos quarenta.*

John Gledson is professor emeritus of Brazilian studies at the University of Liverpool. He is the author of *Poesia e poética de Carlos Drummond de Andrade* and of two books on Machado de Assis, *The Deceptive Realism of Machado de Assis* (on Dom Casmurro) and *Machado de Assis: ficção e história.* He has edited two volumes of Machado's newspaper columns *(crônicas)* and a recent anthology of his short stories *(Contos: uma antologia).* He also works as a translator and has published a translation of *Dom Casmurro* and of a book of selected articles by Roberto Schwarz, *Misplaced Ideas.*

Russell G. Hamilton is professor of Lusophone African, Brazilian, and Portuguese literature at Vanderbilt University. He is the author of *Voices* *from an Empire: A History of Afro-Portuguese Literature* and *Literatura africana, literatura necessária.* He serves on the advisory board of *Encarta Africana,* the African and African-American encyclopedia coedited by Kwame Anthony Appiah and Henry Louis Gates Jr., and contributed an essay on African literature in Portuguese, biographies of two Mozambican writers, and a biography of an Angolan novelist to the second CD-ROM version of *Encarta Africana.*

André Torres Lepecki is assistant professor in the Department of Performance Studies, New York University. His writing on dance and performance studies has appeared in numerous publications in Europe, the United States, and Brazil. His prior research focused on postcoloniality and representation in contemporary Portugal. He is editor of *Intensification: Contemporary Portuguese Performance* and cocreated, with designer Bruce Mau, the installation *STRESS,* a commission from the Wiener Festwochen 2000 for the Museum of Contemporary Art in Vienna. He is currently working on a book on still acts in contemporary European performance.

Mário César Lugarinho is professor of Portuguese and Lusophone African literature at the Universidade Federal Fluminense, Brazil. His current research focuses on the emergence of queer identities in literature written in Portuguese. His prior research centered on the reformulation of Portuguese and Angolan national identities through the poetry of Manuel Alegre (Portugal) and Agostinho Neto (Angola) during the liberation wars in Africa against Portuguese colonialism between 1961 and 1974.

Phyllis Peres is associate professor of Portuguese and Latin American studies and associate dean of undergraduate studies at the University of Maryland, College Park. She is the author of *Transculturation and Resistance in Lusophone African Narrative* and has published widely on Lusophone African, Portuguese, and African-Brazilian literature and cultures. She is currently writing a book on the Angolan literature of the 1950s.

Susan Canty Quinlan teaches Portuguese and women's studies at the University of Georgia. She has published *The Female Voice in Contemporary Brazilian Narrative, Visões do passado previsões do futuro: Ercília*

Nogueira Cobra e Adalzira Bittencourt, and a critical edition, *Lutas de coração/Inês Sabino.* She has published widely on contemporary Brazilian literature and feminist literary theory in the United States and Brazil, and is the editor of *ellipsis: Journal of the American Portuguese Studies Association.* She has held two research Fulbrights in Brazil and is former president of the Brazilian Studies Association.

Ronald W. Sousa is professor of Portuguese, Spanish, and comparative literature at the University of Illinois at Urbana-Champaign. He is author of *The Rediscoverers: Major Figures in the Portuguese Literature of National Regeneration* and coauthor of *Reading the Harper* and *The Humanities in Dispute.* He is also editor of *Enlightenment in Portugal* and contributor of numerous essays on Portuguese-language literature and culture and on literary theory to scholarly journals and collected volumes. He has translated several works of literature and literary theory into English, including *Control of the Imaginary,* by Luiz Costa Lima; *The Passion According to G.H.,* by Clarice Lispector; *Yes, Comrade,* by Manuel Rui; *Memoirs of a Militia Sergeant,* by Manuel António de Almeida, and (in collaboration) *The Murmuring Coast,* by Lídia Jorge.

João Silvério Trevisan is a writer, screenwriter, film director, playwright, and journalist who lives in São Paulo, Brazil. He has published several books of short stories and five novels, three of which have received the prestigious *Jabuti* award and one of which received the APCA prize. He has published three books of essays: *Devassos no paraíso,* published in English as *Perverts in Paradise* (1986), *Seis balas num buraco só: A crise do masculino* (Six bullets in only one hole: The crisis of masculinity), and *Pedaço de mim* (Piece of myself).

Richard Zenith lives in Lisbon, where he works as a freelance writer, researcher, and translator. As an editor, he is responsible for Pessoa's major prose work, *Livro do desassossego,* and for *A educação do estóico,* the first edition of the Baron of Teive, Pessoa's suicidal heteronym. His many translations include *113 Galician-Portuguese Troubadour Poems, Log Book: Selected Poems of Sophia de Mello Breyner,* and *Fernando Pessoa & Co.: Selected Poems,* which won the 1999 PEN award for poetry in translation. His own poetry has been published in a number of literary reviews.

Index